# Family Violence in India

# Family Violence in India

*Human Rights, Issues, Actions and International Comparisons*

Edited by

**Swati Shirwadkar**

**RAWAT PUBLICATIONS**

Jaipur • New Delhi • Bangalore • Guwahati • Kolkata

ISBN 978-81-316-0224-9


**Reprinted, 2016**



*Published by*
Prem Rawat for **Rawat Publications**
Satyam Apts, Sector 3, Jawahar Nagar, Jaipur 302 004 (India)
Phone: 0141 265 1748 / 7006 Fax: 0141 265 1748
E-mail: info@rawatbooks.com
Website: www.rawatbooks.com

*New Delhi Office*
4858/24, Ansari Road, Daryaganj, New Delhi 110 002
Phone: 011 2326 3290

Also at *Bangalore*, *Guwahati* and *Kolkata*

Typeset by Rawat Computers, Jaipur
Printed at Chaman Enterprises, New Delhi

# Contents

## Section Five
## Conclusion

# Acknowledgement

In the lengthy process from holding a series of seminars on the issue of family violence and human rights, to the compilation of the collection of papers for this volume, I was fortunate to have had help and the unstinting support from many people – friends, colleagues, office staff and my students. I would specially like to thank here my former colleague, Dr. K. Asha. Without her valuable help, the seminars would not have been possible. The theme of the seminar on the issue of family violence and human rights took a proper shape after discussions with friends and colleagues, Prof. Jaya Sagade and Dr. K. Asha.

When we started with the idea of the seminar, the major concern was to mobilize the finances. Prof. Sharmila Rege helped in organizing the funds. For both the seminars, we received financial help from the Department of Sociology, University of Pune, and other sources, viz., the I.L.S. Law College, Pune, Rawat Books, Mrs. Shubhada Kulkarni and an anonymous contributor, for the first seminar and the U.G.C., for the next one. I also wish to thank colleagues from other departments who offered help in different capacities for the success of both seminars.

Of the many papers contributed to the seminar, not all could be included. However, I sincerely wish to thank all the contributors.

The idea of publishing this collection of papers took shape because of constant support and discussions, with Prof. Edward

Gondolf. I would like to express my deep gratitude for his conceptual support, inspiration and patience. My family members and my parents always gave support and helped in spite of the inconveniences caused. Without all this the book would not have seen the light of day.

**Swati Shirwadkar**

# List of Contributors

**K. Asha**, Research Officer, Indian Council for Medical Research, Bangalore.

**Milind Bokil**, Field Representative, OXFAM International.

**V.S. Elizabeth**, Centre for Women and Law, National Law School of India, Bangalore.

**Meena Gokhale**, NGO and social activist, 5, Shivaranjani, Happy Colony L.1, Kothrud, Pune.

**Edward W. Gondolf**, Director of Research, Mid-Atlantic Addiction Training Institute, Professor, Indiana University of Pennsylvania, USA.

**R. Indira**, Chair and Professor, Department of Sociology and Women's Studies, University of Mysore, Mysore.

**Armine Ishkanian**, Associate Professor, London School of Economics, UK.

**Sanjay S. Jain**, Lecturer, Department of Law, University of Pune, Pune.

**Savita Kanade**, Social Scientist, K.E.M. Hospital Research Centre, Pune.

**Ranjana Kumari**, Director, Centre for Social Research, New Delhi.

**Helmut Kury**, Professor, Max Planc Institute, Germany.

**Hugues Lagrange**, Professor, CNRS and Sciences-Po, Paris.

**Justice Sujata Manohar**, Retd. Judge, Supreme Court of India.

**Kanchan Mathur**, Professor, Institute of Development Studies, Jaipur.

**Sanjeevanee Mulay**, Reader, Population Research Centre, Gokhale Institute of Politics and Economics, Pune.

**Durgambini Patel**, Reader, Department of Law, University of Pune, Pune.

**Shalini S. Phansalkar-Joshi**, District and Sessions Judge, Pune.

**Veena Poonacha**, Director and Professor, Research Centre on Women's Studies, SNDT University, Mumbai.

**Jaya Sagade**, Professor, ILS Law College, Pune.

**Swati Shirwadkar**, Professor and Head, Department of Sociology, University of Pune, Pune.

**Oishik Sircar**, Human Rights Lawyer and independent researcher, 2 Lake View Road, Kolkata.

**Ursula Smartt**, Professor, Max Planc Institute, Germany.

**U. Vindhya**, Professor, Department of Psychology, Andhra University, Visakhapatnam.

# Introduction

*Swati Shirwadkar*

In view of the current situation of society in India and the world over, the need to address the issue of family violence is arguably important and urgent. Unveiling the different aspects of family violence reveals that the issue needs to be understood in connection with the human rights discourse. International bodies and organizations are now actively taking interest in the issue of human rights.

Current research world over has brought out different types of abuse that take place within the family. A recent report of a multi-country study by World Health Organization (WHO) on profiling domestic violence shows that family violence cuts across all the countries of the world. Back home, for the first time, Indian National Family and Health Survey officially recorded the domestic violence (existence) data from different states in India. This brings out the necessity to address the issue of family violence. The new bill for prevention of domestic violence was passed in India after a lot of efforts. This recently passed prevention of domestic violence bill has the framework of human rights. Slowly, now, on international and national levels, there is recognition that family violence is a violation of human rights.

However, even today, at the societal level, we still face problems. Family matters are seen as a private area not to be intervened because of the 'culture of silence' regarding the issue of family violence. This has highlighted the importance of looking into the socio-cultural factors that are enmeshed with the problem. The traditional norms of Indian society condone violence and promote the patriarchal prerogatives. These factors are engraved in not only individual socialization but they also silently enter into our secular institutions in various ways. Legal machinery of the state can be just one example.

The context of globalization and the gendered dimension of the issue have raised new questions. At the global level, one finds other dimensions, such as race, immigrant status etc., added to this issue. Victims of family violence are found at different levels and hierarchies of age, gender, roles and relationships as well as in different situational contexts.

Another area that needs to be examined is the construction of myths and ideas around the family roles, gender hierarchies and their relation with the outside world and how manipulation of rights takes place through them. Certain forms of violence, such as female infanticide, violence related to fertility, torture, abuse and rape, are targeted against a particular gender. Some studies have also thrown light on how even the construction of the male is surrounded by myths that are propagated by different agencies. The issue of male sexuality, violence and human rights also needs to be addressed in the changing situation.

The very discussion of informed choice is still threatening to the society, particularly when we talk in terms of gender and sexuality. The violence promoted through various agents and their connections with the larger global processes also needs to be considered. In spite of the talk about educating our children about issues such as sexuality and violence, there is hardly any proper implementation of existing policies about generating awareness. Increasingly, young girls are being reported as being victims of sex-related crimes. Unfortunately, the basic shelter of family may not be a safe haven for all the girl children. Though the problem of battered women is acknowledged now, we do not want to talk about the intra-familial violence, particularly towards children. Cases of abuse against elderly and special groups are also coming up in India. This situation needs to be reviewed and the existing ways to counter the problem need to be discussed. Discussion of research that throws light on such issues becomes useful to understand the nuances of the problem.

While we need to strengthen the situation with legal reform, it has been increasingly realized that looking at the issue of family violence from human rights framework will help to understand the problem in a larger context.

When we think of violence and abuse that takes place within the family, it includes varied forms, such as, domestic violence or violence by intimate partner, honour killings, dowry deaths and torture, rape and sexual assaults, child sexual abuse, sexual harassment, to name just a few. The statistics of such crimes all over the world is overwhelming, notwithstanding the fact that it may be the tip of the iceberg. In most cases, it is gender-related. If the problem is of pervasive nature, it is imperative that the international community should take note of it for intervention. Though late, the United Nations has recognized the importance of rights of humans, and particularly girls, who are adversely affected in the private area of family.

The General Assembly of the United Nations adopted the Universal Declaration of Human Rights in 1948. It was declared as the common standard of achievement for all peoples and all nations, stating that the recognition of the inherent dignity and of the equal and inalienable rights of all members of the human family is the foundation of freedom, justice and peace in the world. Traditionally, the human rights discourse tended to revolve around the issues related to public life. Political and civil rights and the role of state dominated the human rights discourse. The 'third world' countries focused on the social and economic rights and the role of the state.

The debate and movement around human rights did not give much deserved attention to the issue of gender equality, which is one of the important issues in this context. However, the studies on the status of women all over the world brought out the slow progress in achieving gender equality.

Of late, the distinction between civil and political rights and social, economic and cultural rights has begun to break down. This is reflected in subsequent conventions adopted by the United Nations. Due to the consistent efforts of women's organizations, the international community had to take note of violence against women and children as a violation of human rights. However, there is also a realization that law reforms have their own limitations. For policy makers, activists, NGOs and academicians, the major challenge is how to evolve the human rights framework that is general, for the specific issue of victimization within the family.

For any policy measure, it is imperative to evolve a framework for defining the issue for measurement purpose. Theories that evolved through the study of violence, victimization and abuse have significantly contributed to this. Social, psychological and feminist theories looked at aggression, violence and abuse resulting from social, structural factors, learned behaviour, biological instinct, frustration, personality traits and also from mechanisms of power and control. Needless to say, there is no agreement among various perspectives to conceptualize the issue of family violence. Family violence has been described as a unique and fertile turf for violence between members of the same family. While it is sometimes broadened to include violence among the intimate relationships of partners (Straus, 1993), others have argued that it should be seen as violence against women (Yllo, 1993). There is no doubt that different conceptualizations have contributed a great deal in evolving the understanding and measurement of the problem. Rigorous efforts of activists and human rights movement, combined with extensive research substantiated by data, have helped in formulating policy measures.

International research has put in a lot of efforts in measuring different aspects such as the health consequences, economic setbacks and losses due to abuse and violence within the family. Women's organizations have consistently raised the issue of health and social cost of violence. In spite of these efforts, the situation in the 'third world' countries remains more complex. Recently, the rapid changes and opening up of the society for the market forces in India have thrown up many challenges to individual security. While we are making economic and technological progress and reforms in law to adopt international policies, new complexities and forms of victimization are coming up. In such a situation of social change, the role of social science is crucial.

How to address the issue more fruitfully as a social scientist? For this, we need to be more inclusive in our curriculum to study such issues. One of the ways to address the issue is to discuss and debate it, as well as to familiarize the students about the research, policy guidelines and interventions in this area, through our curriculum. Recently, the need to make the social sciences more applicable without loosing its rigour is felt strongly. Keeping these needs in view, the Department of Sociology, University of Pune, organized a series of seminars (on 12th and 13th January, 2006, jointly coordinated by Swati Shirwadkar and K. Asha, which was first in the series, and another by Swati Shirwadkar on 25th and 26th September, 2006) to discuss the work done by academicians, activists, practitioners, police personnel and legal experts working on the issue of family violence. (The first one was before and next one, after the latest bill for prevention of domestic violence was passed.) The need to include such issues in our curriculum was strongly felt by the student participants. This volume presents some of the papers presented in the seminars. We hope, it will be a step towards building up resource material for research as well as curriculum and also towards understanding of the issue of family violence.

Several questions crop up while having a broad overview of the issue of family violence. How to understand the different aspects of family violence from the human rights perspective? How is the Indian context different? What does the data say about it? What measures are taken to address the issue? Is it possible to learn from the international community or do we have to find out our own answers? Papers in this volume provide some answers to these questions. New research and curriculum, which translate the theories into developing the students' abilities of understanding the field reality, is the need of the hour. The papers in this volume will bring out some aspects of the issue of violence in different ways, such as legal and human rights issue, the challenges of globalization, technological development and the cross-cultural experiences. They also bring out the theoretical perspectives as well as micro studies supported by data.

In this volume, some papers discuss and trace the development of concepts and tools such as the rights language and the human rights machinery, including the international conventions and campaigns. The first section puts the issue of family violence in the broader context of human rights and related legal aspects. Veena Poonacha's paper examines the rights discourse to bring out the attempts to develop a more inclusive paradigm of rights. The paper gives an analysis of the responses to domestic violence to shift the narrow legal focus of the human rights and locates it within social action. However, the understandings of the issue of family violence as rights issue may not come easily even within the movement. U. Vindhya has demonstrated the complexities of this process in the case of movement within a state (Andhra Pradesh). This paper attempts to capture some defining moments in the engagement of the human rights movement with the issue of domestic violence with particular reference to Andhra Pradesh. The understanding of domestic violence, as a violation of the human rights of a woman, has not come easily. In the course of realizing that domestic violence has a rights dimension, there have been three major defining moments: conceptualization of the public/private dichotomy, engaging with the response of the criminal justice system, and the polarization between scholarship and advocacy.

Oishik Sircar raises some critical questions about the ideology and throws light on the crisis of human rights intervention. He draws attention to the danger of construction of Indian women as post-colonial victims and peripheral subjects. He critically examines the human rights law and the language of violence in context of integration of gender into the discourse. His argument identifies the hyper visibility of sexual violence caused duc to cultural sanctions. His analysis draws our attention to the construction of 'third world' women as captive subjects and making women's potential for resistance invisible.

It also becomes necessary to understand the legal framework of the issue as well as its limitations. There are some issues of critical importance, related to the institution of marriage and family, which we still fail to address properly. Issues such as age of marriage and dowry still haunt us.

With a long history of movements, we are not yet successful in eradicating some evil practices that deny the basic human rights. Right from the 19th century onwards efforts were made by social reformers to raise the age of marriage for girls. However, the problem still stands unresolved on a large scale. The paper by

Jaya Sagade explores socio-legal and human rights dimensions of an age-old problem of child marriages in India. It critically analyzes how the patriarchal social structure supports the practice of child marriage in the name of culture and tradition by suppressing women's life experiences and denying them some basic rights. The law regulating the age of marriage, though was enacted in 1929 in India, remains by and large unimplemented. There are substantive and procedural lacunae and contradictions in it. Based on the feminist theory "asking the woman question" the author argues that the young girls are discriminated by the law, culture and society against their counterparts on the basis of sex, gender and age when they are married off before they attain the legal age. It also asserts that child marriage is a form of slavery and it violates human rights of the young girls. It explores basic human right of equality and pleads that the Indian State is under obligation to protect, respect and fulfil the human rights of the young girls as it has ratified the relevant international human rights treaties.

In India, public awareness about the issue of family violence was largely generated because of the menace of dowry deaths. Physical torture, dowry deaths (and invisible 'kitchen' accidents) were viewed as a social evil since long time and yet in spite of the legal provisions, we are still far behind to get rid of the menace. Even with the long history of efforts of the reform movement onwards till present, we still fail to curb the greed for dowry and extended demands. Dowry is not only linked to the financial and other transactions but it is also considered a status and honour issue of the family. Sanjay Jain's paper examines the legal aspects, including an examination of constitutional provisions, regarding dowry. It points to the necessity to correct the legal loopholes to create a strong legal base to fight against the evil of dowry. That the limitations of law are evident when we look at the implementation is also highlighted.

Meena Gokhale presents a study conducted by a team of researchers from ILS Law College, Pune, on the efficacy of section 498A of IPC, prior to the provision of the new bill on prevention of domestic violence. The evidence shows the impact of section 498A as a preventive measure. However, the study also demonstrates that law is not a complete protection and relief. High acquittal rate and cases withdrawn or settled outside the court highlight the gap between books of law and ground realities.

V.S. Elizabeth points out that violence within the family is deeply rooted in gender-based power asymmetry and is reinforced by different social forces and agents, resulting in perpetuation of gender-based subordination. Cultural practices and religious beliefs hinder the enjoyment of human rights for women. In the light of both national and international law, she argues that violence against women is violation of human rights. The paper draws our attention to the fact that the states are satisfied that they have enacted laws in this context. However, as far as implementation and proper information is concerned, they plead helplessness.

While the issue of marriage and dowry-related violence is now acknowledged and there are efforts to address it, another area remains neglected, i.e., child abuse within the family. Child abuse is a serious social problem all over the world. Experts note that child abuse occurs broadly in three major forms, i.e., physical, emotional and sexual, which rarely occur in isolation. While physical abuse such as inflicting injury on child by various means or by use of objects sometimes is visible, emotional and sexual abuse largely goes unnoticed. In Indian situation, emotional abuse, such as psychological maltreatment, degrading, terrorizing, ridiculing, insulting, isolating and exploiting, is not only difficult to document but also difficult to be accepted as abuse due to cultural and structural issues. Recent cases and subsequent media reports show that it is difficult to mobilize the public opinion about this issue. This happens because it goes against the deeply held cultural beliefs about the private nature of the family sphere and the legitimacy of the power ascribed to certain roles.

While the Indian judiciary is increasingly responding to the pleas of NGOs to expand the definition of sexual abuse and exploitation of children, we pathetically lack public awareness and effort to curb the menace. Two papers, by Shalini Phansalkar-Joshi, on child sexual abuse and Durgambini Patel, on cruelty and physical torture of children, bring out the socio-legal aspects of the issue of violence against children. They also underscore the importance of recognizing the human rights of children rather than just making limited provisions to protect them. The legal provisions fail to recognize the child sexual abuse so as to give justice to children and this makes the situation more complicated. The experience from court cases shows that the victims are females in the stage of infancy to the stage of adulthood. Joshi also debunks the myth that only females become victims of child sexual abuse. Even male children are exposed to different types of abuses.

The second section focuses on the changing social context in India and efforts to counter the family violence. The issue of child abuse, for example, has to be seen in the Indian context to understand the complexities. This issue was first brought to the public attention by the pediatricians in their research and publications (Wiehe, 1998), and is still an extensively researched area throughout the world. Yet, threat of abuse and exploitation of children, far from reducing, is taking new forms with technological advancements. This is reflected in different areas, from alarming spread of porn sites on web to use of advance technology for female foeticide. Unfortunately, in India, violence within the family starts right from the stage of conception. Violence against female foetus resulting into skewed sex ratio still continues in spite of the laws against it. This trend continues in the young age group of children resulting into missing girls. Sanjeevanee Mulay's paper brings out the nuances of this issue supported by micro-level data obtained from Maharashtra. The study shows that with the spread of technological advances (sonography), level of training and the increasing paying capacity are leading us to the decimation of the girl-child. Unfortunately, technological developments may result into cruelty against particular gender and the denial of the right of being born.

Globalization and technological-economic progress, combined with faster communication system, have made the world a smaller place. Are these changes affecting women positively and empowering them? What are the costs? Ranjana Kumari's paper throws some light on the changing values, role pressures related to marriage and family in the context of globalization and the changing social situation. The paper brings out the discrepancies and uneven burden faced by women, including domestic violence. The most neglected area is the role of the perpetrators of violence, which needs to be understood for the purpose of intervention. Since focus of most of the research is on the victims, the perceptions of the perpetrators remain unexplored. Savita Kanade's paper brings out some facts, which can help to guide the intervention measures. The survey reveals that wife beating was justified by both men and women as a part of their normal life. The paper examines a less researched area, that is, men's attitudes towards wife beating and shows its correlation to actual practices. The work based on quantitative data suggests a need for evidence-based interpretation for intervention programmes for both men and women. Effective interventions may vary according to the local context and the situation. If the legal measures are not successful, one has to think of new innovations. Milind Bokil, in his paper, argues that the present situation with regard to domestic violence calls for innovative approaches and strategies for its resolution. It is further argued that since domestic violence is related to social institutions, such as marriage and family, mechanisms that can tackle these institutions would be helpful. His study explores whether the self-help groups are a useful medium to tackle the issue of domestic violence and suggests that these groups can act as watchdogs on institutions of marriage and family. While bringing out the unequal power relationship within the matrimonial family as a root cause of domestic violence, the qualitative data brings out other contributing factors for violence. The study presents the role of women's organizations in form of self-help groups and demonstrates that in particular situational contexts these groups can be an effective measure to curb family violence. R. Indira explores different aspects of the family violence. She argues that women's organizations have helped in giving a voice to the victims of family violence and have prompted the formal sector to respond to the needs of women who suffer in silence.

Forms of violence vary with cultural contexts. The third section presents some issues faced by special groups, such as different forms of violence and abuse, and exclusion from needed resources and policy development. With cultural variation and geographical differences, one finds different forms of violence within the family. Again, here too, gender bias becomes evident. From African continent to the immigrant groups in UK, cases of violence due to accusations of sorcery have surfaced. India and other south Asian countries are also not exceptions. In some pockets, cases of violence due to such accusations and blind beliefs still exist. The issue of social exclusion as a form of violence needs to be explored. Kanchan Mathur explores this in her paper. Through literature review, she brings out the pervasive nature of the problem of witch-hunt in India across the states. Her findings based on primary data focus on causes of labelling and forms of violence, including different forms of social exclusion that a woman is subjected to, when she is accused of being a witch or using witchcraft.

Deep impact of violence and abuse can be explored by epidemiological studies. Usually, physical abuse or economic exploitation can be seen and proved but the damage done by emotional and psychological abuse cannot be fathomed and is difficult to explore. The culture of silence has destroyed many lives in the name of preserving the prestige and honour of the family institution. K. Asha's study of the health costs borne by the victims and their silent suffering raises questions about the limitations of human rights approach. The paper debates on socio-biological theories related to sex differences over size and strength, reasons for psychological abuse and the need to understand the psychological dispositions of the abusers.

The multi-layered identity of culture, region, caste and class is ingrained in the process of socialization and any form of resistance or non-compliance to the expected role may invite further abuse, isolation and violence. Though the problem of portraying south Asian women as victimized is posed in an earlier paper, the field reality shows that it is difficult for Indian women to overcome the cultural barriers. Even for the Indian women immigrants to developed countries like Canada, accessing the policies and programme actions is not easy. The study of Indian immigrant women in Canada, by Swati Shirwadkar presents how South Asian sub-cultures of different regions, class, caste and religions, operating within a western cultural set-up, may create a complex web that prevents women to access the programme actions in a developed country.

The fourth section delineates the experiences of developed countries which have formed elaborate policies related to family violence. The international comparisons reveal the impact of policy, as well as challenges, in implementing it locally. There is a growing realization in the international community that we can build on sharing of each other's experiences to address this issue. While there cannot be any disagreement about the basic universal principles about equality and rights, the implementation may be a challenge due to cultural differences. For example, any impositions from above may not succeed and the primary aim may be lost. An understanding of local context, modifications for administering the measures may be necessary. For this, there is a need to understand the history and outcome of policies of other countries and then develop a comparative analysis. Some standardization of concepts and intervention principles may emerge from cross-cultural studies. While addressing the issue from human rights perspective, this will help in broadening our focus. Many countries are facing challenges due to new groups and their sub-culture. The papers in the section bring out the development and implementation of different measures, the challenges of local context and sub-cultural groups and they underscore the need of wider collaborations to foster change.

The development of the field of domestic violence has vastly grown in the United States but has received cursory examination, as stated in the paper on the sociological overview of the field of domestic violence in the United States by Edward Gondolf. The author brings out some useful and interesting facts that can contribute to social change, particularly related to the filed of domestic violence. It also underscores the importance of having alliances between different social forces. Social researchers and academicians can consider this potential from U.S. example, for a sustained effort for institutional reform and social change. While identifying major social forces that have converged and reinforced one another over the last thirty years, Gondolf brings out the expansion of services, reform practices and community responses. He also points out the limitations such as shortcomings of addressing the complexities or nuanced controversies within the field itself.

With an expansive review of literature, Helmut Kury and Ursula Smartt bring out different aspects of development in the field of domestic violence study in western society. With an overview of studies, risk factors, forms of reporting, and policy measures to address domestic violence in different countries, the existence of the issue of domestic violence in Germany is discussed in the context of legal measures. The study brings out the limitations of the legal as well as the policy measures and suggests exploration of new measures to address the issue more effectively.

In the wake of recent immigrant unrest in France, which made us take note of an entrenched society, Hugues Lagrange makes us aware about the intricacies of the issues in the French context. In his paper, the author presents a comparison of the legal aspects of the issue of family violence in France with India. The paper brings out the complexities of family situations among the migrants in France. It exposes the limitations of French efforts to address the issue of family violence in the context of cultural diversities of the French society. Armine Ishkanian, through her research, examines how domestic violence became an issue addressed by women's rights and human rights NGOs. She critically looked into the tensions between the foreign funding and the locally recognized issues and the means to address them. By examining the local reactions to the ways of addressing the domestic violence issue, she shows how NGO-donor relationships shape knowledge production and implementation strategies. The last section, which is in fact the valedictory address delivered by Justice Sujata Monohar at the seminar on 'Family Violence and Human Rights' organized by University of Pune, reviews the role of the state in responding to domestic violence. She also gives a broad overview of the issue of family violence and human rights.

In a nutshell, the volume will bring out the social complexities of family violence, putting it in a broader perspective of human rights. The cross-cultural research is discussed in order to balance global and local perspectives, and the need for both quantitative and qualitative research is demonstrated for arriving at universal principles for policy guidelines. The papers also trace legal and political developments on global and local levels and assess the impact of interventions and point out the new areas of research. They underscore the importance of addressing the different aspects of the issue of family violence and also bring out the limitations and dilemmas of ideologies, policies and interventions to address the socio-cultural complexities. Collectively, they also indicate some direction of social change and therefore, will be of help to those interested in the subject.

## References

Straus, M.A. 1993. Physical Assaults by Wives: A Major Social Problem. In Gelles, R.J. and Loseke, D.R. (ed.), *Current Controversies on Family Violence*. London: Sage Publications.

Wiehe, V.R. 1998. *Understanding Family Violence*. Thousand Oaks: Sage Publications.

Yllo, K.A. 1993. Through a Feminist Lens: Gender, Power, and Violence. In Gelles and Losoke (ed.), *Current Controversies on Family Violence*. London: Sage Publications.

SECTION ONE

# Human and Legal Rights

CHAPTER ONE

# On the fringes of human rights discourse

## Violence against women in intimate relationships

*Veena Poonacha*

Having grown out of the intellectual currents that swept across Europe in the 18th century, the human rights discourse represents some of humankind's noblest aspirations. Attempts to crystallize these aspirations in the aftermath of the two great wars of the 20th century has resulted in international documents, such as the Universal Declaration of Human Rights, the International Covenant of Civil and Political Rights and the International Covenant of Economic, Social and Cultural Rights as well as the Convention on the Elimination of All Forms of Discriminations Against Women. Articulating a global vision, these documents have sought to extend the realization of human rights both nationally and internationally. Cutting out narrow parochial boundaries of difference, these covenants have initiated several international agreements that spell out ideas of human rights. For instance, some states and regions like the Council established a European Court in 1960 for the protection of these rights, while the Amnesty International was established through private initiative to check the flagrant violation of human rights in different parts of the world. The various organs of the United Nations have also attempted to explicate these demands. Within the national boundaries, these rights are enshrined within national constitutions.[1]

### Power of the rights rhetoric

Apart from empowering individuals with knowledge of their rights, the language of human rights has fuelled socio-political movements.[2] It has enabled various marginalized groups (including women) to lay claim on their humanity and articulate their entitlements to the resources of the community. Consequently, claims for the recognition of new rights have proliferated dramatically in recent years. Emerging out of different ideological currents, the various categories of rights have created an extremely complex and problematic discourse.[3]

This paper is an attempt to examine the human rights discourse from the standpoint of women's experience. It is divided into three parts. While the first part examines the criticisms of the discourse that have emerged out of the various attempts to develop a broader and more inclusive paradigm of rights, the second part points out the ways in which the use of gender as an analytical category problematizes the discourse. The last part elaborates on some of the strategies that the various state and voluntary organizations have adopted over the past three decades to counter domestic violence. Locating these strategies within the broad framework of the rights discourse, the study hopes to take the human rights discourse out of its narrow legal focus and locate it within social action.[4]

## I

### Tensions in the human rights discourse

Undoubtedly, struggles to develop an inclusive vision of human rights have broadened the scope of the rights discourse. These attempts have also foregrounded the contradictions and tensions within the discourse. These tensions arise not only out of the inevitable conflict of interests between various sets of rights, but also from the continued resistance to new ideas. Additionally, they arise out of the theoretical underpinnings of various concepts as we try to express, define and extend the boundaries of these rights.[5]

The main criticism levelled against the human rights discourse refers to the fundamental question on who is the bearer of rights? Is it the individual (as articulated in the libertarian discourses of rights) or the community (as articulated in the communitarian notions of rights)? The underlying conceptualization of the individual in the libertarian discourse is that the individual is an independent entity capable of and in a position to make rational choices.[6] Such a conceptualization does not take into consideration the dynamic interrelationship between the individual and society. By defining the individual in opposition to society, it fails to acknowledge that individual choices are circumscribed by their lived experiences.

The discourse also presupposes a certain basic non-existent equality between people's conditions. It is difficult for those people on the fringes of society to realize their rights within a hierarchical social structure (based on class, race and gender differences), a problem that is exacerbated by an elitist and conservative legal system. In the communitarian discourse, rights are defined by the notion of the community as a homogenous unit; it fails to interrogate the existing power inequalities in the community or even within a family. These tensions become apparent while examining rights through a gendered lens.

Critical legal scholars also question the supposed neutrality of the law. They maintain that the law's alleged neutral principles are driven by the exclusionary politics of the affluent as well as their attempts to maintain the status quo. These create tensions between the four main pillars of the rights discourse, namely, liberty and freedom on one side and equality and justice on the other. For instance, the question of what sets the limits of individual freedom and liberty becomes important from the standpoint of protecting the rights of women and minorities. The question is what if person's right to free speech and expression creates conditions that have a negative impact on another individual's sense of self-worth? This obviously sets a limit to the freedom of speech held sacrosanct within the rights discourse. Civil libertarians believe that only acts, not beliefs or speech, should be punished and that the sentences should not be increased because the person perpetrating the act was motivated by or held unpopular beliefs including racist or sexist ones. The civil rights position maintains that the government can punish some criminal acts more severely than others, particularly if the motives are racist or sexist and therefore harmful to society.[7]

## II

### A gendered critique of the rights approach

A historical look at the struggles for women's rights makes it apparent that the language of human rights as articulated in the age of enlightenment fuelled women's claims for civil and political liberties. The feminist discourse of the 19th century recognized the prevailing socio-political impediments to women's rights; it did not however question either the class/race bias encoded in the libertarian discourse on rights, or the underling assumption that rationality was a necessary pre-condition for any claim for rights. These omissions tended to perpetrate a certain exclusionary worldview on rights: For it did not sufficiently acknowledge the ways in which the prevailing socio-economic inequalities prevented the realization of equality and liberty – the two foundational principles of the rights discourse.[8]

In India, because of certain historical specificities, the parameters of the debate were different. Deeply embedded within the language of rights articulated by the Indian feminist movement of the early 20th century were issues of nationalism and social transformation. Thus, influenced by the existing political philosophical discourses of nationalism and social justice, the first wave Indian women's movement sought to include in the rights discourse not only formal political rights, but also ideas about socio-economic justice. This becomes apparent in the Indian Women's Charter of Rights and Duties that was ratified by the Standing Committee of the All India Women's Conference (AIWC) at its meeting in Calcutta in 1946.[9]

The feminist movement that developed since the 1960s has pointed to the socio-political impediments to the realization of women's rights. It has critiqued the overwhelming misogyny in society that has denied women even their basic right to survival. Contradicting these arguments on the gendering of rights, it may be point out that the denial of rights is not necessarily gendered. Men (particularly from the marginalized sections of society) are also unable to access their rights. Therefore, it is argued that an analysis of rights from a gender perspective could well detract attention from issues that affect the whole community. Undoubtedly, the non-realization of even the basis rights to survival affects all sections of the community, particularly the more vulnerable. But, what cannot be overlooked is that as long as men and women play gender roles, the culturally constructed notions of entitlements which are embedded within them deny women even their claims to humanity and consequently they are seen as carriers of lesser rights.[10]

There is today clearly documented evidence to substantiate the claim that women are discriminated against and denied their fundamental right to survival, access to resources and control over their produce. In its final analysis, the process of gender socialization itself is a violation of basic human rights as it attempts to control women's autonomy and their dependence of thought and action. It makes them meek, plaint and subservient. When such a mindset is enmeshed within other blatant forms of denials, the stage is set whereby the realization of women's rights remain a remote possibility. The prevailing ideology disparages the woman and defines her as the "other". Such biases are often translated into violence. The effects of crimes against women are two-fold: (1) it enforces their subordination by creating a climate of fear that prevents women seeking out their entitlements to education and better employment opportunities; and (2) justifies their subordination through the portrayal of their victimhood. Crimes against women are not isolated aberrations, but geared towards defining the power relations between men and women.[11]

The feminist critique of the prevailing socio-political order has also led to a critique of theories as prejudicial to women. Research has enabled them to identify the gender blindness within dominant theories and shift the focus of enquiry from the vantage point of men to women. This has resulted in the abandoning of the overarching generalizations that characterized dominant discourses to emphasize on the experiential basis of knowledge.[12] The process has had specific implications for the rights discourse because the discourse (which, strictly speaking, straddles liberal political philosophy, ethics and legal theories) is premised on the assumption of the objectivity of knowledge – the "knower" is seen as existing outside the "knowable". Consequently, the rights discourse in its classical formulation did not necessarily take into account the socio-economic and political circumstances of people's lives; it assumed that individuals are able to actualize their rights through rational choice. Pointing to the constraints in women's lives, feminist theories have challenged the claims for neutrality within the epistemology of rights.[13]

The ensuing debates have thrown up several corollary questions on the assumed neutrality of the law and its ability to deliver justice to those who do not have equal access to the legal system. It has also (from women's social location) asked if gender equity could be achieved only if social policies recognize the special circumstances of women's lives and the ways in which the prevailing social order denies women their entitlements to education, economic independence, etc. Since, for instance, women's reproductive role as it is defined today is an obstacle to women's right to work and economic participation, it is asked if there is a need for special provisions in social policy to establish gender equity. Therefore, by stressing the differences in the conditions of men and women, feminists have asked for special concessions so as to make equality a reality. However, claims for special protections or even affirmative action through reservations, etc. also have their own limitations as they can inadvertently force women into clearly demarcated areas defined as feminine without changing the gender ideology.[14]

Feminists also critique the semantics of "rights talk" as enumerated within the Universal Declaration of Human Rights and the Indian Constitution. Pointing to the artificial dichotomy in the discourse between the public and the private spheres, it is argued that the documents define the relationship between the individual and the state within the public arena. Women's lives remain circumscribed within the private area of family and are therefore considered outside the purview of state protection. Violence within the home, for instance, gets ignored; attempts to intervene in cases of family violence is seen as an intrusion of the state apparatus in the private space of the home and a violation of individual rights (read "man"). Yet what fails to be accounted for is that by not interfering, the state fails to protect the rights of the more vulnerable members of society. To assume that the family and the right to privacy within it, is inviolate is a misconception as the same state intercedes in family matters when it formulates laws governing property and inheritance.[15] Additionally, there is a growing disillusionment on the capacity of the existing legal structure to promote gender justice. Insofar as the legal system operates on established precedents, it tends to uphold a conservative social order. The legal system is relatively powerless when compared to other ideological mechanisms in society to initiate social change.[16]

Feminist articulations have pointed to the politics of the human rights discourse and the ways in which the language of rights is used to justify control over women. The right to life, for example, is the most intrinsic to the entire discourse. A minimum definition of this right has, so far, been formulated within law as negative sanctions against murder and the unlawful deprivation of the life of the individual by the state. The attendant polemics have generally been concerned with the rationale for capital punishment as well as the right to life of the unborn. And yet as feminists have argued that in a society that glorifies war and sees capital punishment as legitimate, the sanctity of life cannot be seen as an absolute value. In the absence of safe contraceptives and women's control over their bodies, the denial of choices for women is merely an attempt to impinge on their reproductive rights.[17] In India, the parameters of the debate are coloured by the declining sex ratio as well as the absence of sexual/reproductive rights for women. Therefore, there is within the Indian women's movement a call for the better implementation of the PNDT Act in a way that does not further victimize women.

## III

### Responses to domestic violence

Feminist politics has pointed out that the aim of gender-specific violence is to enforce the existing inequalities between men and women. Often condoned in society, violence against women is seen as sustained by ideology and enforced by the material realities of women's lives. With fewer resources and entitlements in the family and community, women are forced to accept the reality of violence in their lives. The ways in which violence is culturally condoned becomes apparent while examining violence in intimate relationships. Such forms of violence may be minimally construed as the physical, emotional, sexual, psychological and financial abuse of a woman in her intimate relationships. In the Indian social context, this definition of intimate relationships would include all the intimidating acts by the members (both men and women) of her marital family. This is not to deny the vulnerability of women/girls in their parental homes; but rather to turn the spotlight on one aspect of the problem, increasingly foregrounded in international forum (such as the World Congress on Human Rights, Vienna, 1994 and the Fourth World Conference of Women, Beijing, 1995) as a human rights violation, requiring state intervention. The UN Platform for Action emerging out of the Beijing conference requires an explicit commitment from governments to check domestic violence (along with other gender crimes) in their respective countries. In keeping with this commitment, the Government of India has enacted the Domestic Violence against Women (Prevention and Protection) Bill.

Getting this bill passed in parliament has not been easy; it has required consistent effort by feminists to ensure its passage. Some of the difficulties that they faced were not merely because of conservative resistance to women's equality, but also because their epistemological location in women's lived experiences problematizes some of the bedrock assumptions within the discourse. This is because the human rights discourse, in its classical formulation, was largely construed as the relationship of the individual vis-à-vis the state and confined to the public space. Failing to acknowledge the hidden crime of domestic violence the human rights principle enjoined, the state shall not interfere in the private domain of the family and the legal system shall protect the individual from such intrusions. The introduction of the question of gender violence breaches the conceptual public-private divide in the discourse; it generates a fear of the erosion of individual rights by concomitantly increasing punitive state powers.

Furthermore, given the private nature of the violence, it is often difficult for a woman to provide evidence. It then becomes a question of her word against that of her husband's. The feminist requirement that a woman has a right to be believed (because of her socially enforced powerlessness) violates the presupposition of equality between individuals in the rights discourse. In such cases, to ensure justice to the woman, the onus of proof should be placed on the perpetrators of violence. Such a requirement violates the basic principle of the rights discourse that an accused has a right to be held innocent until proved guilty. To an extent, this explains the resistance to Section 498A of the Indian Penal Code criminalizing domestic violence.

## Strategies to deal with domestic violence

In an attempt to take the rights discourse outside the framework of law, this paper draws upon the findings of a study undertaken earlier to examine some of the innovative strategies to deal with domestic violence.[18] It makes it apparent that there are varied and multi-layered responses to domestic violence, which are subsumed in the overall struggle for gender justice. These strategies may be broadly categorized as those that seek to prevent/eradicate domestic violence and those that react/respond to such instances. Encoded in these broad categories are a variety of responses, which may be further delineated on the basis of their target groups and their expected outcomes.[19]

The preventive measures aimed at attacking the roots of violence can be broadly classified as three-fold, namely, research and documentation, social action and awareness generation. The first step to counter domestic violence requires research and documentation on the nature and extent of violence. It is from a clear social analysis of violence and an understanding of the use and limitations of the legal system that it would be possible to devise preventive strategies that are communicated to the field staff and social workers of the organizations. Secondly, social action to prevent violence requires neighbourhood vigilance and the creation of new socio-economic options (through employment opportunities and skill training) for women who are likely to face violence. It also requires the empowerment of women with the knowledge of their rights and enabling them to access information about the various government welfare schemes. Lastly, the awareness generation programme exposes the extent to which women's rights are violated through media campaigns and publicity programmes that seek to create gender-just laws and reform of the prevailing criminal justice system.

Reactive measures could also be classified as three-fold: (1) It requires research and documentation of cases and experiences to understand the lapses in investigation and the legal system. (2) It requires emotional, material and legal support to the survivor to enable her to rebuild her life as well as that of her children. (3) It also requires efforts to raise community/neighbourhood opinion against domestic violence and the mobilization of the entire community to oppose violence and support the woman. Additionally, there is need for shelter homes, short stay homes, legal aid counselling and child care facilities.

In India, these facilities are woefully inadequate. Therefore, many organizations (including the state-sponsored Mahila Samakya Programme) have experimented with innovative preventive and conciliatory measures. The organizations currently seek to form local women's collectives, through which the agenda for action is locally determined. Nonetheless, through effective networking between collectives, it is ensured that the individual local collectives are not isolated; they act on the confidence of support from the collectives of the neighbouring villages.

The Mahila Samakya Programme (like the now popular Self-Help Group movement) attempts to prevent violence through the empowerment of women. It is committed to ensuring that poor women have a say in development programmes. Seeking to reverse the prevailing "top down" approach to development, it establishes village level self-help groups. It aims at enabling the rural poor women to acquire the necessary knowledge and self-confidence to effect a change in their lives as women and as part of the rural community. It is through these collectives (which provide women with the necessary space to discuss and reflect) that women have tackled domestic violence and other social evils of child marriage, dowry and the *devadasi* system. These are no doubt cost-effective solutions that seek to change the existing power structures in the community. But, in the process of empowering the women to take charge of their lives, has the state abdicated its responsibility of providing referral services, shelter and protection to women?

It is in the context of the state responsibility to its citizens that this interrogation of the state/community responses to domestic violence takes place. For instance, various organizations make use of local village community/caste councils to effect conciliation. While these strategies do help to resolve conflict and bring about a measure of relief for the woman complainant, the question that remains is whether the support given by the caste/community power brokers is unconditional of requires certain compromises that may silence the woman complainant. Would a conservative power structure extend the same support to all women or only those who are seen to conform to their stereotypical notion of a good wife and mother? Furthermore, what kind of trade-offs the organization would have to make with the local power structures for the support it received in resolving the problems of the woman complainant? Would they in turn have to support the caste/community power elite in certain other instances of factional politics in the village community? By supporting the *status quo*, would they also not reinforce the prevailing conservative values in society, which may not allow social change?

To circumvent the costly and lengthy legal procedure, organizations have also experimented with non-formal legal mechanism. By utilizing the services of lawyers, retired judges, village elders and social activists, the organizations provide counselling, legal aid and support to women in violent homes. Seeking to bring about an amicable settlement, the legal aid committee calls both the parties for discussions. These committees work towards out-of-court settlements, which are often recorded (to maintain the appearance of legality) on stamp papers. The main clause included in such agreements is that the man or his family members will not use violence on the woman. Nonetheless, in the process of effecting conciliation, the agreement may also include clauses by which the woman admits that she had failed in her housewifely duties or was quarrelsome. She then promises that she would change her behaviour. The problem with such an agreement is that while conciliation has been effective and the organization is successful in sending the woman back to her marital home, it has also silenced the women. For the process may have inadvertently justified the violence and implied that the woman invited the violence on herself.

This limitation may also arise in the *Parivarik Mahila Lok Adalats* (family courts conducted by women) organized by the National Commission for Women. These courts organized even in remote areas with the help of the state legal aid and advisory bodies, state/district judicial machineries and the women's groups seek to resolve family conflicts. The point here is, can these ad hoc structures really deal with the complexities of the cases or in their hurry to resolve cases are they sending women back into the violent homes without adequate measures to ensure their safety? In case of a disputed verdict, would the man abide by the decisions of these ad hoc structures? If not, how will the family courts ensure the execution of their orders?

The various preventive and remedial strategies are also determined by the organizational ideology, which in this case would mean the construction they impute for the existence of domestic violence. To elaborate, an organization that believes that violence arises out of psychological aberrations in the family may approach it through psychological, vocational and family counselling services along with the medical treatment of the alcoholism.

This approach is also evident in the Family Counselling Cells (FCCs) established by the Central Social Welfare Board (CSWB), a semi-autonomous body that was constituted in 1953 by a parliamentary resolution. Since 1984, attributing the escalating violence against women directly to maladjusted families, the CSWB, through the State Social Welfare Advisory Boards (SSWABs), established FCCs attached to voluntary organizations. The venture was expanded in the 1990s to the establishment of FCCs attached to select police stations. Despite limitations of staff and infrastructure, the FCCs provide preventive, referral and rehabilitative services to women and children survivors of violence. Managed by trained social workers, some of the FCCs have effectively utilized the police to ensure that members of the complainant's marital family come for counselling. The FCCs attached to police stations, in particular, have been able to use police services effectively. Nonetheless, they have a conservative mandate to maintain the family unit in the interest of the children. This raises an important question: would the counselling process, from an anxiety to maintain the family, inadvertently silence women?

This silencing of women is also evident in the more conservative organizations that emphasize the welfare of the family (often to the detriment of women's interests), while the feminist organizations have developed what they term as "woman-centred" counselling practices. Feminist organizations do not see violence as aberrations in society but as intrinsic to patriarchal societies. Violence arises out of the existing power inequality between men and women. The woman-centred counselling practices that these organizations use recognizes that a woman's decision to stay in the marriage or leave it should be entirely her's. The function of the organization is to provide her with emotional support and guidance to rebuild her life. The idea is that the woman should be empowered to know what she wants, with the assurance that the organization will support her in her decision. Such organizations working in rural areas may constitute neighbourhood vigilance committees to prevent domestic violence. If the committee comes to know that a woman in their lane is beaten, they approach the woman (even if she is not a member of the organization) with an offer of help. But, unless the woman herself expresses a wish that the organization should interfere, they do not do so.

Due to the paucity of funds and infrastructure, some organizations (particularly in the rural areas) seek to provide counselling not through professional social workers, but by the women in the community who discuss the woman's problems and devise political action. There have been instances when the woman who requires temporary shelter has been taken into the homes of the women in the collective and subsequently, if required, helped to set up a separate residence.

The organizational ideology of community-based organizations may not include a direct focus on gender issues. These organizations also organize women's *sanghas* (collectives) and have devised innovative strategies to deal with domestic violence and the overall exploitation of women through interest aggregation. There are many instances when these organizations have with sensitivity and commitment tackled domestic violence. Nevertheless, based on our understanding of the ways in which women's rights seem to invariably conflict with that of a patriarchal community, one wonders how the organization will tackle the issue of domestic violence when confronted with the choice of upholding the cohesion of the community when it conflicts with the rights of the woman. Additionally, would they be able to tackle domestic violence issues if the perpetrator was an important member of their cadre and if their disciplinary action would in any way create fissures in their organization?

An important preventive measure adopted by the NGOs is through vocational training and income-generation programmes for rural women and teenage girls from the weaker sections of the population. This focus on teenage girls especially has long-term implications: It empowers them with a knowledge of their rights and also provides them with the economic means of being able to opt out of violent homes. As one of the young girls in a particular village said: "Many years ago, my mother wanted to withdraw me from school. The members of the organization advised her against it. They supported me through my school education and enabled me to become self-employed. The confidence that I have gained because of my association with them would enable me to resist any form of oppression or violence in the future."

Here, it is also necessary to focus on the All Women Police Stations (AWPSs) and the *Mahila Suraksha Samiti* (MSS), a statutory vigilance body in Gujarat, as examples of the vigilance, investigative and punitive state action. Established in the 1980s, in response to the demands made by the women's movement, the AWPS and the MSS indicate that the effectiveness of these measures is dependent on political will.

The AWPSs were established to make the right of police protection accessible to women and children; it was premised on the recognition that women hesitate to approach a predominantly male police force even in life-threatening situations. The current limitations of the AWPS should be contextualized within the overall deficiencies of the police force, which continues to function within the matrix of its colonial antecedents. The modern police force in the country was introduced during the British period as an instrument of repression. It continues to function within this framework because of political interference and the lack of political will to reform the system. Further, due to the poor service conditions, long hours of work and occupational stress, the police force is demoralized, particularly when it is confronted by the ineffectiveness of the criminal justice system. These overall problems are exacerbated for policewomen primarily because of the prevailing gender bias within the system, which sees them as peripheral. In addition, the predominantly male centric ethos neither takes into account the multiple roles of policewomen nor the special needs of the complainants. There are no proper referral services to provide immediate medical or legal assistance nor are the policewomen trained to handle such personal issues with sensitivity.

The ways in which to commitment of the political leadership influences state action is also apparent in the MSS programme in Gujarat. Although envisaged in 1987, it was only implemented in 1991. The committee (comprising women members of the Legislative Assembly, social workers, activists and researchers in Gujarat) was able to enforce meticulous police investigation in cases of atrocities against women as they had the backing of the state Chief Minister, its chairperson, and the Chief Police Officer, CID (Crime Branch) its member secretary. Through liaison with the police and a network of sub-units in the various districts and *talukas* (administrative sub-divisions in districts) the MSS was able to maintain vigilance against gender crimes and call to question criminal investigation procedures in such cases. It also sensitized the police regarding such crimes. Looking at the trajectory of the programme, it is apparent that it can be effective only so long as there is political backing for efforts to tackle crimes against women and non-interference by the state in the actions taken by the body.

This paper has sought to some of the contradictions that arise in attempts to introduce the gender question into the human rights discourse. Further, in an attempt to take the human rights discourse beyond the framework of the law, it has to look at some of the responses to domestic violence by the state and civil society. It has critically looked at some of the responses to domestic violence. It recognizes and appreciates the multiple strategies to counter domestic violence, despite shortfalls of funds and infrastructure (such as telephones, helplines, etc.) as well as support/referral services (such as shelter and child care facilities). There are also no crisis centres that offer protection for women and children (particularly in the night) against domestic violence. Studies have indicated that women often remain in violent relationships because of the lack of support services. They are unable to access state-run shelter homes without following lengthy procedures. These shelter homes are spartan and unwelcoming. They do not have medical aid or other facilities to make women and children feel cared for and protected. Many women cannot avail of the facilities, however minimal, because of the outdated rules. These shelter homes, for instance, do not take in women with children over a certain age limit; nor do they take in women with severe psychological problems, as they are ill-equipped to deal with them.

These inadequacies are particularly apparent while examining the effectiveness of state initiatives such as the All Women Police Stations and the Family Counselling Cells. The cases, which they have to deal with, are often serious enough to warrant immediate medical aid and protection for the women and children to recover from the trauma of their experiences. These cells however do not have provisions for immediate medical aid or child care and rest rooms. Despite these limitations, it is commendable that the counsellors of the FCCs, like their counterparts in the FCCs attached to voluntary organizations, work with sincerity and dedication. They have low salaries and lack job security. They are often burnt out because of the sheer volume of cases they are required to handle. The state must recognize the professional contributions of these social workers and counsellors and provide them suitable remuneration.

Despite these limitations, the study also makes it apparent that these organizations have (against overwhelming odds) created networks, support systems and structures that are cost-effective and efficient. These models need to be highlighted but unfortunately the rich experiences of the various organizations tend to be lost as there is very little documentation. But, it is also necessary to critically interrogate the practices within the human rights framework, to ensure that the struggle does not inadvertently silence the woman.

## Notes

1. Poonacha, Veena. *Gender in the Human Rights Discourse.* Mumbai: Research Centre for Women's Studies, SNDT Women's Studies. SNDT Women's University. (Contributions to Women's Studies, Gender and Politics, Book 1). 1995. pp. 17–24.
2. Schneider, Elizabeth M. 'The Dialectic of Rights and Politics: Perspectives from the Women's Movement' In Martha Fineman and Nancy S. Thomadsen (eds.) *At the Boundaries of Law: Feminism and Legal Theory.* New York: Routledge. 1991. pp. 301–319.
3. Alston, Philip. 'Making Space for New Human Rights: The Case of the Right to Development'. *Harvard Human Rights Year* Book. Vol. 1. (Spring) 1988. pp. 3–40.
4. Poonacha, Veena and Pandey, Divya. Responses to Domestic Violence in Karnataka and Gujarat (A Project funded by the International Center for Research on Women, Washington DC) Mumbai: Research Centre for Women's Studies, SNDT Women's University. 2000.
5. Berger, Iris. 'Categories and Context: Reflections on the Politics of Identity in South Africa'. *Feminist Studies.* Vol. 18. No. 2. (Summer) 1992. pp. 284–294.
6. Charvet, John. *Modern Ideologies: Feminism.* London. J.M. Dean and Sons. 1992. pp. 6–42
7. Hill, Steven. Liberty under Attack By Equality. *Z Magazine.* Vol. 7. No. 1. January 1994. pp. 11–14
8. Rosmarie, Tong. *Feminist Thought.* Oxford: Westview Press. 1998. pp. 1–10
9. Ibid.

10. Poonacha, Veena. *Understanding Women's Studies.* Mumbai: Research Centre for Women's Studies. SNDT Women's Studies. 1999. pp. 43
11. Desai, Neera and Krishanraj, Maithreyi. *Women and Society in India.* New Delhi: Ajanta.1987. pp. 254–291.
12. Gribich, Judith E. 'The Body in Legal Theory'. In Martha Fineman and Nancy Thomadsen. (eds.) *At the Boundaries of Law: Feminism and Legal Theory.* New York. Routledge. 1991. pp. 61–76
13. Cossman, Brenda and Kapur, Ratna. 'Trespass, Impasse, Collaboration: Doing Research on Women's Rights in India'. *The Journal of Human Justice.* 1991. Vol. 2. No. 2. pp. 99–118.
14. Kapur, Ratna and Cossman, Brenda. *Subversive Sites: Feminist Engagement With the Law in India.* New Delhi. Sage in association with the Book Review Literary Trust. 1996. pp. 286–290.
15. Eisler, Riane. Human Rights: Towards an Integrated Theory for Action. *Feminist Issues.* Vol. 7. No.1 (Spring) 1987. pp. 25–46.
16. Fineman, Martha A. 'Introduction'. In Fineman, Martha A. and Nancy S Thomadsen, *At the Boundaries of Law: Feminism and Legal Theory,* New York: Routledge. 1991. pp. XI–XVI.
17. Harrison, Beverly. 'A Theology of Pro-Choice: A Feminist Perspective on Abortion.' In Diana Eck and Jain, Devaki. *Speaking of Faith Cross Cultural Perspectives on Women Religion and Social Change.* New Delhi: Kali for Women. 1986. pp. 202–210.
18. Poonacha, Veena and Pandey Divya. *Responses to Domestic Violence in Karnataka and Gujarat* (A Project funded by the International Center for Research on Women, Washington DC) Mumbai: Research Centre for Women's Studies, SNDT Women's University. 2000
19. Poonacha, Veena. 'Responses to Domestic Violence: An Inquiry into Government and Non Government Action in Karnataka and Gujarat' (jointly with Divya Pandey). In Economic *and Political Weekly.* Vol. XXXV, No. 7. 12 February 2000.

    'Coping with Domestic Violence'. *One India, One People.* September 1999. Vol. 3/2. pp. 19–20.

CHAPTER TWO

# Human rights movement and domestic violence: an uneven terrain

## Reflections on the human rights movement in Andhra Pradesh

*U. Vindhya*

This paper attempts to capture some of the defining moments in the engagement of the human rights movement with the issue of domestic violence with particular reference to Andhra Pradesh and to the human rights organization, Andhra Pradesh Civil Liberties Committee (APCLC). In grappling with the rights dimension of domestic violence, the movement has had to traverse an uneven terrain engaging with the public-private dichotomy, the response of the criminal justice system, the prioritization of consciousness-raising over individual case work, and the polarization between scholarship and advocacy.

The sources for this paper are the very few reports and pamphlets published on domestic violence by the human rights movement in Andhra Pradesh and as an activist of APCLC, my own memory of the dynamics of activist meetings wherein these issues were discussed, debated and argued, combined often with bickering, gossip and back-biting!

Given the state of poor documentation of matters related to the human rights groups (or civil liberties organizations as these groups were then called) in the seventies and eighties, this attempt will hopefully help to recapture a slice of our social and political lives in the recent past, although embellished perhaps by the vantage point of historical hindsight.

## I

The year was 1989. APCLC, from its inception in 1973, had by then grown into a fairly large organization of fully functioning units in several districts all over the state of Andhra Pradesh. From the beginning, APCLC had viewed itself as a watchdog organization to highlight the suppression and systematic erosion of people's democratic rights and liberties, particularly political rights. In concrete terms, this meant that the APCLC was in the forefront of confrontation with the state over the issue of state violence to suppress the Naxalite movement.

By the late eighties, however, there was a sense of expansiveness as a correlate of the then Chief Minister, Channa Reddy's "liberal" policies towards the Naxalites. By then, the Karamchedu massacre that spurred the Dalit movement in the state had also taken place and APCLC was poised, as it were, to turn its attention to other forms of systematic oppression apart from state violence.

In July 1989, some of us had got involved with three incidents of deaths of young married women under suspicious circumstances in their husbands' homes. By some of us I mean some dozen odd members of a fledgling women's group called Stri Shakti, associated with a CPI (ML) party, and myself, the lone woman member of a 170-strong Visakhapatnam unit of the APCLC. We had got involved in organizing demonstrations and public meetings to highlight these crimes that had occurred in rapid succession in June-July 1989. In addition to publicizing these crimes, the protests were held to pressurize the rather reluctant police to register FIRs on the basis of the amendments to the law that had by then recently been introduced – Sections 498A and 304B.

It was perhaps for the first time that organized protests against what were popularly referred to as "dowry deaths" were held in the city. Till then, many of us had this notion, erroneous as it turned out, that such a form of violence was peculiar to

North India and that we in the south, particularly in Andhra Pradesh, were relatively safe.

This was at a time when the awareness that violence is an infringement of the rights of women encapsulated in the slogan "women's rights are human rights" had not permeated the consciousness of human rights activists at least in our state. Therefore, when I mooted the idea that we should do some research and find out first how many cases of such deaths were taking place and what was the response of the police and the courts, I met with two kinds of reactions from the group initially. Some members responded by saying that the APCLC was not part of the academia to begin doing research, implying in some sense that scholarship and advocacy were not mutually compatible activities and also that in the divide between theory and action, the supremacy of praxis has to be asserted rather unquestioningly. Others remarked that "dowry deaths" was a women's issue and perhaps best left to the purview of women's organizations.

Undeterred by these reactions, for the next two months, three of us, a colleague of mine in the university, a journalist who had been a member of APCLC earlier and myself went round the district courts for collecting data. We had no earlier literature to serve as guidelines as the research studies that were undertaken analyzing the response of the criminal justice system came only much later. After collecting information on the cases of deaths of women in their marital homes registered over a five-year period, we brought out a report *Dowry Deaths in Visakhapatnam District (1985–1989)* and updated the same the next year. The reports contained an analysis of the socio-economic profiles of the women and those accused of their murder or suicide, as well as of the outcomes of these cases in court.

By then, a conceptual shift in the human rights discourse had taken place. Reflected in the UN documents and illustrated by cases on the ground, the first defining moment in the engagement of the human rights movement with issues of domestic violence was the realization that women's rights are human rights. This was a significant conceptual shift and we should not lose sight of it. This shift was of course prompted by the feminist movement taking the lid off the glorified edifice of the family and showing it to be resting on a shaky foundation of inequality, domination and abuse.

The recognition of domestic violence as a human rights issue was also motivated by the feminists theorizing of the two spheres of social life – private and public – and how the human rights discourse was affected by the two-sphere theory of western liberalism. The focus of human rights on the public sphere meant that violation of rights in the private sphere associated with women and the family were not part of the human rights discourse almost till the 1970s. Thus, the public-private dichotomy that pervaded the human rights discourse revealed the male-centredness of the concept of human rights in its historical evolution of nearly four hundred years.

It was once again feminist analysis that had pointed out that the private sphere (the family) is not recognized as a site where violation of women's rights takes place. However, the public-private dichotomy on which feminist activism has thrived for years and which became central to the debate on domestic violence and the law was not really internalized at the level of the individual activist. I do feel that it is important to recognize this difference. Whatever may be the theoretical debates and conceptual shifts, prompted by international attention and domestic developments, the process of assimilating these developments and incorporating them in our thinking at the level of the individual is important because that is really what makes him or her take up the issue with enthusiasm and commitment.

Did this happen with the APCLC activist? The answer is that it did not. Two reasons for the lack of such an internalization immediately sprang to mind. One was the state-centric nature of the organization. In fact, I would say that we had not moved too far from the western liberalism-inspired notion of power as identifiable, quantifiable and predominantly employed by the state. This excessive focus on state power and violations of human rights by the state not only obfuscated the role of other actors but also prioritized state violence over everything else in the order of maximum importance.

I will illustrate this point with narration of an incident. In 1993, the few women activists of the APCLC all over the state had got together to organize a convention on domestic violence and issued a pamphlet with the heading, *"Let us oppose domestic violence along with state violence"*. The reaction to this title of the pamphlet was that of outraged incredulity among many activists. According to the majority of the (male) activists it was sacrilegious to place domestic violence on par with the violence committed by the state. This despite the fact that going by the sheer magnitude of the phenomenon, the number of deaths due to domestic violence listed by the pamphlet was in fact more than those killed by the state in "encounters" during that year. This attempt to what was termed as exaggerating the importance of domestic violence to the detriment of a much more pressing issue as that of state violence was viewed by a number of activists as part of an international conspiracy to bring in "soft" issues while glossing over the role of the state.

The second reason was the ambivalence attached to the privileged status of the family. On the one hand, the family was seen as a negative institution, a product of class society that will disappear in the socialist future. On the other hand, the family was considered as a negative effect of the operations of the laws of capital. It is not family life as such, but its particular capitalist form that was considered to be condemnable.

Parallel to this ambivalence about the family was the discussion of the role of the state with regard to the family. This discussion was situated at the crossroads of two discourses. One originates from the 19th century debate on fundamental rights as carving out a sphere of individual freedom, protected from the interventions of the state. In this context, the private, more specifically the domain of the family, is perceived as the ultimate refuge necessary for the development of an autonomous person.

The other discourse is linked to the feminist debates since the past two or three decades, which pointed out the interrelationship between the private and the public, and centred on the argument that this non-intervention of the state in the private domain served to preserve patriarchal domination within the family. However, as recent research has shown, neither has even the most liberal state ever renounced rulings on matters concerning the family nor has state legislation – the most radical form of opening up the private to the public – ever had the effect of rectifying gender inequality.

At ground reality and the level of the individual activist, this ambivalence associated with the family was best illustrated with the example of one of our activists who saw no contradiction between his public advocacy of civil liberties for people and his beating up of his wife at home. Though this is thankfully an atypical example, it serves to illustrate the ambiguity surrounding the private domain.

## II

The second defining moment was our actual involvement with the criminal justice system. It is of course now routine and commonplace to say that the handling of cases of domestic violence by the criminal justice system is ineffective but at that point of time the response of the judiciary in particular had not been examined and we had no earlier literature to go by. Our only impetus then was that as human rights activists we thought that it was only logically necessary to examine the working of the law in cases of domestic violence. What we found therefore from the dusty case record in the courts was therefore an eye-opener to us in several ways.

In addition to finding a high acquittal rate of 89 per cent and shocking interpretations of the law by the judiciary leading to a large number of the accused going free, we discovered a few other things as well, that shook some of our assumptions (Vindhya, 2002).

When we examined the socio-economic profile of the victims and the perpetrators, we found that a majority of the reported cases were from lower socio-economic sections. The pattern of these cases did not appear to substantiate the observations of some scholars who had then argued that domestic violence is more of a middle class behind-closed-doors phenomenon, bound by notions of privacy while women of lower classes and castes were subjected more often to rape and sexual assault and other forms of violence that were outside the domestic realm.

Reported cases (both the victims and perpetrators) in our investigation belonged to disenfranchised sections of society. At the risk of stating an overgeneralization, what seemed to be evident was that lower education, lower income resources and belonging to castes in transition were some of the factors associated with domestic violence. It can be said that these characteristics restrict men's opportunities to live up to the provider model of masculinity. Disenfranchised men then must rely on other social practices to construct a masculine image. Violence often becomes a social practice that enables men to express a masculine identity.

This brings us to another aspect of our relationship with the law. Women's groups in recent years have pointed out the ideological nature of rulings given in certain rape cases, such as that of Bhanwari Devi in Rajasthan and earlier of Mathura in Maharashtra. It has been argued that by acquitting the upper caste accused in these cases, the legal system, in effect, denied justice to the lower caste victims, implying that the system recognizes only chaste and virtuous upper class/caste women as those entitled to rights and justice. Going through the judicial pronouncements in our investigation however wherein there was scarcely any status differential between the victims and the perpetrators we felt as though the legal system does not recognize women per se as entitled to rights, regardless of caste and class.

In case after case, what was strikingly evident is a construction of womanhood by the judiciary that reflects stereotypical assumptions about women's rights in the family. Demands for gifts could not be proved and even if they were in certain cases, they were commonly regarded as customary payments that could not be construed as grounds for cruelty. If the woman was abused and harassed due to some other factor apart from economic demands, it was considered as an "integral aspect of our traditional culture" and thereby could be condoned. If the woman could not endure the abuse and committed suicide, then it was because the woman herself was emotionally overreactive and prone to suicide at the slightest provocation.

While the publication of the reports and the consequent publicity brought in its wake a large number of women and families approaching us for intervention, there was ambivalence here too. While it was relatively easier for human rights groups to take up the issue of sexual violence, there was a sense of unease surrounding the issue of intervention in domestic violence. Ever since the much-publicized crimes of rape of Mathura, Rameeza Bee and Maya Tyagi in the 1970s, the intervention was directed against the perpetrators who were in authority, particularly the police. Therefore, the focus of protest was against the excesses committed by the state, by its representatives in the police or army and by a further travesty of justice in the form of unjust and obnoxious judicial pronouncements.

Although APCLC did not directly take part in these agitations, these cases were cited approvingly and the interventions considered a legitimate area of human rights activity. Given the radical left affiliations of most human rights activists, it is not surprising that rape by the police was always quoted as one more example of the heinous nature of the state and also provided an illustration of the synthesizing of class and gender perspectives.[1]

Cases of domestic violence, on the other hand, did not present such a neatly defined picture. While it was true that it was the lower socio-income groups who were represented predominantly in the reported cases and that it was these sections who approached us for intervention, both the victims and perpetrators belonged to similar socio-economic status. The interrelations with class, caste and state were not as simple as they appeared in the cases of sexual crimes in which human rights groups had intervened. In fact, what became increasingly evident was that domestic violence appeared suspiciously like an essential aspect of a problematic masculinity.

This coincided also with the growing realization of women's groups that the focus on dowry violence had obfuscated the fact that violence could be callused by just about any reason. It was in fact the focus on dowry violence that had provided an opportunity to critique the consumerist greed and commercialization of marital transactions. I remember a favourite expression that was often heard in speeches at public meetings: *Behind every colour television set, is the tale of abuse and possibly death of a woman.*

This formulation received a jolt when the focus shifted from dowry violence to "just about any reason" for violence. In fact, when we examined the causes of violence, we found that it was not just dowry per se that was responsible for the violence but extended demands for gifts and alcohol addiction and extra-marital relationship of the husband that were primarily the triggering factors of the violence (Vindhya, 2000).

Although we do not have information on the incidence of alcoholism as a form of mental disorder in Andhra Pradesh, it is known that the state is one of the states with high rates of consumption of alcohol. It is also known that alcoholism is typically a male disorder in India. It remained for the women in the anti-arrack movement in Andhra Pradesh to make this connection between the political economy of alcoholism and domestic violence.

## III

As the demands for individual case work grew, it was this "domestic" nature of domestic violence that was seen to be linked to such dimensions such as exaggerated masculinity, socialization practices, incompatibility and the like that became rather difficult for human rights activists to make effective interventions. While advocacy in individual cases receded, paradoxically, more research on the nature and pattern of domestic violence, and on the working of the criminal justice system began to be generated.

The 1990s was therefore a period that witnessed a gulf between scholarship and activism. There has been a lot of discussion on the suspicion that activists have of theory-spouting academics and vice versa but when we look back over the past ten years or so, we do find that as more NGOs proliferated, more research studies began to be done by the NGOs as well as by independent feminist researchers. The political cutting edge of activism tended to decline. I am not suggesting that there is a cause-and-effect relationship between the two but there certainly seems to be a correlation. The protest actions of the 1980s seem to be a phenomenon of the past. While the research generated has helped us understand the complexities involved in violence, it is perhaps the iconic figures of Nisha Sharma and the like, who by saying "no" to dowry and preventing potential abuse, are the figures who are now able to capture public imagination.

## Note

1. It is of course another matter that by the 1990s research evidence indicated that a majority of sexual crimes were committed within the family and by perpetrators known to the victims.

## References

Vindhya, U. (2000). "Dowry deaths" in Andhra Pradesh, India: Response of the criminal justice system. *Violence against Women,* Vol. 6, No. 10, October, pp. 1085–1108.

— (2002). Private crimes and public sanction: Violence against women in the family. In M. Pernau, H. Reifeld, and I. Ahmad (Eds.), *Family and Gender: Changing Values in Germany and India.* New Delhi: Sage Publications.

CHAPTER THREE

# Captive subjects

## Gender, intimate violence and the crises of international human rights interventions

*Oishik Sircar*

The growth of the international women's rights movement and its emergence as a field of research and advocacy has led to a valuable but increasingly self-contained discourse, often cut off from developments in postcolonial conditionalities ('postcoloniality'), on the one hand, and conceptions of the different legal contexts in which international human rights operate, on the other. Such a trajectory of 'development' in human rights standards for women have no doubt had an enormous impact on women's lives worldwide, but simultaneously it is also culpable of creating the 'woman-as-victim' subject, 'geographically captive' in the 'barbaric' cultures of the 'third world'.

The nation-building projects of countries like India have an agenda of claiming ownership of this postcolonial subject to establish its 'authenticity'. And, the authentic, globally, then gets constructed as the 'other', sometimes the 'native'. The authentic subject has come to exist with a singular identity of the nation. And, the other multiple identities, especially of caste and class, have been appropriated to further authenticate the national identity, that remaining primary. Unfortunately, the creation of this hegemony of authentic national identities has also led to the creation of authentic postcolonial victims and peripheral subjects: the good woman as the culture bearer of the nation's identity and the 'sexual subaltern' threatening the very foundations of that same identity (Sircar, 2006a).

To keep the authenticity alive, postcolonial nations resist outside (read: Western) interventions to civilize the native. But, the very creation of the postcolonial identity allows the Western (now read: Imperialist) to further valorize the postcolonial native authentic identity through an essentializing project that targets identities as well as cultures. Gender, for one, gets a raw deal. The image that is produced is that of a truncated third world woman who is sexually constrained, tradition-bound, incarcerated in the home, illiterate, and poor, an image that is strikingly reminiscent of the colonial construction of the 'Eastern woman' (Kapur, 2005).

This image, however, is not contested through the postcolonial nation-building discourse. It only provides the victim subject a shared location from which women repudiate claims of being part of a Western culture, yet furnishing the creation of a unitary subject that enable them to make claims based on a commonality of experience (ibid.). The responsibility of the postcolonial nation then becomes to protect women and what they stand for, rather than protecting their rights.

Can this subjectivity of the Eastern woman be challenged through the language and practice of international human rights law, or is the discourse been oblivious, even responsible for its creation and continues to be so?

In this paper I will map the developments that led to the integration of gender into the international human rights law discourse and examine how the language of 'violence' and 'respectable victimhood' (from Vienna 1993 to Beijing 1995) has been privileged leading to the dislocation of 'discrimination' as envisaged by the Convention on the Elimination of All Forms of Discrimination Against Women (CEDAW), as the primary index for measuring women's human rights violations. What has been the consequence of this dislocation? With specific reference to the historic proceedings at the Vienna Tribunal and illustrations from the works of international organizations like Amnesty International and Human Rights Watch, the paper will attempt to identify the hyper-visibility of 'sexual violence' caused due to cultural/traditional sanctions in the 'third world', constructed by the international women's right movement to invisibilize the 'resistance potential' of women from the Global South.

After the formal integration of gender and sexuality in the international human rights discourse, these constituencies are increasingly being treated as subjects for human rights norm-setting. However, as the paper will argue, this 'achievement' has been resulting in regressive consequences for women's human rights in the 'third world'. To establish this contention, the paper will closely study the concept of 'worse the better' in international asylum jurisprudence, where the establishment of conditions of 'radical evil' (Baxi, 2006) are imperative to the guarantee of 'saving' the fleeing, 'disempowered' and 'vulnerable' Eastern woman from the clutches of barbaric postcolonial states.

A critique of the international asylum adjudication system is necessary to do a reality check with regard to what it can exactly offer when it comes to drawing the fundamentals of refugee rights guarantees from the basic principles of international human rights law. While human rights guarantees are understood to be universal and inherent across the world, when it comes to the determination of an asylum seeker as a refugee, to establish 'fell-founded fear' in an objective fashion, asylum adjudicating officers tend to generate simplistic, even derogatory, characteristics of asylum seekers' countries of origin, as areas of barbarism or lack of civility in order to present a clear-cut picture of persecution (Bhaba, 2002). The central guiding principle of this kind a construction of the asylum seeker as the 'native', who needs to be 'civilized' and rescued out of the clutches of a 'barbaric' state might be best described as "the worse the better" – the more oppressive the home state, the greater the chances of gaining asylum.

In the main, I will deal with the emerging debates and crises that the international human rights regime faces with regard to the postcolonial accusations of it being a 'civilizing-the-native' project and its creation of the third world 'woman-as-victim' subject, to establish how such an approach essentializes both gender and culture. In conclusion, the paper will suggest means through which a 'lens of marginalization' can be employed to bring the peripheral subjectivity of the 'woman-as-victim' to the centre – a move that will have the potential of busting the rhetoric of 'respectable victimhood' – to claim, through the apparatuses of the state, the rights to politico-cultural autonomy and 'plural' citizenship.

Among others, I specifically refer to the works of Alice Miller, Ratna Kapur and Jacqueline Bhaba. These feminist legal scholars and activists employ a discursive mix of human rights theory, postcolonial and subaltern studies and international relations theory to understand the politics behind the articulation of "women's rights as human rights" and decisively observe how such an articulation operates with regard to geo-political, social and cultural locations of women facing intimate and other forms of violence.

## Locating captive subjects

### *Intimate violence, private-public divide and state accountability*

The 'woman' within the international human rights law discourse is essentially constructed as a captive subject. She is 'stuck' at the precarious juncture of 'cultural captivity' – as the loyal, chaste wife – and political non-agency – as second class citizens, devoid of autonomy and bodily integrity. She is a subject who is perpetually vulnerable, due to the essentialized understanding of her 'weaknesses'. She is both hyper-visible in 'private' spaces as primary culture bearers of community and nation and invisible, because the enormity of her presence remains un-acknowledged if we see the nature of 'humanitarian' responses it attracts. Her vulnerability compounded with in/hyper-visibility further disenfranchises her of all agency to decide whether she wishes to claim humanitarian responses and what kind of responses is she willing to claim to break out of the situation where she is 'stuck'.

### *Making private violence public*

Traditionally, in human rights law, violation is understood as an act of the state or those acting in their capacity as state agents. This view only recognizes violations perpetrated by public authorities and fails to recognize the rights of women to be free from gender-based violence perpetrated in the so-called 'private' sphere. Notwithstanding the fact that women throughout the world are most often subjected to gender-related harms perpetrated in the 'private' sphere of intimate relationships, the state's refrain from intruding into that domain has allowed such violations of women's human rights to continue with impunity (Randall, 2002: 305, 306).

The feminist critique of international human rights law has primarily been an analysis of this public-private divide. The fact that the domestic arena is itself created by the political realm where the state reserves the right to intervention is a result of an imagined division between the public and private spheres (Romany, 1994: 94). Since what occurs in 'private' shapes their ability to participate in the public arena, when women are denied their human rights in private, their human rights in the public sphere also suffer (Bunch, 1995: 14).

As Johnstone points out:

> At the domestic level, the dichotomy of public and private may justify the state's failure to intervene in private relationships, a smokescreen behind which systematic violations of women's human rights have been rendered invisible. Law finds itself in the public realm, but if one cannot enter the public sphere, law and legal rights have nothing to offer. On one level, the classification of particular activities as public or private has been erroneous, because the classification depends on the gender of the actor, rather than the nature of the activity. On another level, the dichotomy itself is questionable, because all activities have both public and private natures. At both levels, political decisions to allocate certain activities to the private sphere have been used to justify the states' abdication of responsibility for that activity. (2006: 152)

As a consequence of the public-private dichotomy, intimate violence remains on the fringe: it is considered less severe and less deserving of international condemnation and sanction than officially/politically inflicted violence. But, when stripped of privatization, sexism and sentimentalism, gender-based violence is no less grave than other forms of inhumane and subordinating official/political violence, which have been prohibited by treaty and customary law and recognized by the international community as *jus cogens*, or pre-emptory norms that bind universally and can never be derogated from (Copelon, 1994: 117, in Lyth, 2001: 9).

Feminist scholars have stressed that the very jurisdiction of international human rights law is divided along these same public-private fault lines (Knop, 1993: 330). As international law evolved as a set of rules intended to regulate relations among states and as it remains centred on the state, women's experiences tend to get lost from the agenda (Lyth, 2001: 9). For instance:

- Many abuses against women have not been acknowledged as human rights violations because they are committed by private actors rather than by agents of the state.
- Civil and political rights hold a privileged position in human rights law despite formal recognition by the international community or their interdependence and indivisibility with economic, social and cultural rights.
- International norms concerning the life of the family call on states to protect the institution of the family and enshrine the right to privacy in the family (Sullivan, 1995: 126, 127, in ibid.: 9).

While the human rights doctrine in itself has led to greater scrutiny of state action, the engagements of women's rights activists and scholars at the international level have pushed the frontiers of state action to include even the failure of the state to prevent violence in the marital home. The process started with CEDAW, which places affirmative duties on the state to prevent discrimination, even by private actors. It is in this area of preventing violence against women that states become responsible for conduct of private actors even in what was considered the most sacred and distinct private space – the home/family (Coomaraswamy, 1996: 16).

In understanding the relation between the woman being violated and the state, it is important to point out that women suffer due to lack of infrastructure that protects them or enforcement of the existing laws providing them with effective redress (Bahl, 1997: 41). In other words, the state is responsible to the extent that it fails to provide or utilize the apparatus that could prevent or redress the wrongs. As already mentioned, the state has an affirmative obligation – understood as the concept of 'due diligence' in international law – to protect and prevent violence and its inability to do so amounts to persecution from non-feasance, that is, liability is conferred on the state for commission of those persecutory acts. The state would definitely be in breach of its obligations under international law, which requires it to punish those individuals – government agents or private actors – who commit human rights violations. The breach of such obligations and the inability or unwillingness in protecting a woman's human rights tantamount the state's connivance in the act of persecution (Sircar, 2006b: 264).

In spite of the recognition of 'due diligence' as a *jus cogens* norm in CEDAW and many other international human rights instruments, the family remains the valorized space for the woman – captive and incarcerated – in what even the UN believes to be the "natural and fundamental group unit of society" which is "entitled to protection by society and the state" (Article 16, UDHR). What this implies is that 'due diligence' will actually extend to making the state responsible for protecting the institution of the family, in turn insulating it from state intervention. Interestingly, this human right standard names the society and state as participants who are urged to take an active role in maintaining a social practice or institution and where the power of the state is invoked as a protective device (Rao, 1993: 74).

This raises concerns about the potential of international human rights law to deliver its promise of protecting women's human rights in the private sphere, especially when it is cloaked almost completely in the language of 'violence' and 'victimhood'. While the feminist critiques of the public-private divide allows for a critical re-look at the workings of statist human rights standards and agendas, by ensuring the application of 'due diligence', yet the same language of women's human rights as it is worded by the UN results in reifying women's subjectivities as agency-less and victims. What kind of a more critical lens can one use to then understand the underlying problematics and politics of "women's rights as human rights"?

It is at this juncture that it will be useful to quickly map the developments that led to the articulation of "women's rights as human rights" within the international human rights discourse to understand how self-contained this development has been, and more importantly, how this development has been effected relying on the construction of the 'woman-as-victim' subject, and bodily-harm as marker of violations.

### *Protecting women and not their rights?*

The recognition of violence against women as a human rights issue emerged almost four decades after the UDHR was adopted in 1948. This enormous lapse in time, in spite of the 'real space' within which gender-based violence operated, is in itself a glaring example of how much importance was given to women's issues in the UN. Issues of violence and gender were solely part of the bodies of International Humanitarian Law[1] (the 'Law of War') and Criminal Law[2] where it was only about political/state-effected forms of violence like rape in times of armed conflict, forced prostitution etc.

The first articulation that could have connections with issues of violence was the CEDAW, adopted in 1979. There was minimal recognition of violence against women in either the Mexico (1975) or Copenhagen (1980) World Conferences on Women. It was in 1985 at the Nairobi Conference that named violence as a concern and began a process of elaborating strategies to address the problem. With the 1986 UN expert group meeting on violence against women and a 1989 study on violence in the family, there began a shift from seeing women's experience of violence as simply a family/private problem to perceiving it as a larger problem and understanding such abuse as human rights concern (Sen, 2006: 55).

The articulation of violence against women, thus, came after the drawing up and adoption of CEDAW, which meant that violence was missing from this instrument. It is remarkable to note how for the framers of CEDAW, a causal connection between discrimination and violence was not evident. However, in 1992, the Convention's monitoring committee (which periodically adds explanatory, interpretive statements to the document) added General Recommendation 19 which states that violence against women is understood to be a form of gender-based discrimination and that states are to be held accountable for violence against women, including by private persons.

Many other developments followed in the 1990s, most importantly a Declaration on the Elimination of Violence against Women (DEVAW) in 1993 and the creation of the post of the special rapporteur on violence against women, its causes and consequences, who was appointed by the UN in 1994. The governmental Platform for Action, arising from the Beijing World Conference on Women in 1995, had a section on violence against women as one of twelve critical areas of concern (ibid.: 56).

The developments noted above have been very significant within the UN human rights system, where women's rights have been traditionally under-funded and under-valued, to finally elevate it to the status of 'mainstream' human rights. However, what began with the CEDAW in 1979 as a process of ending/challenging gender-based *discrimination*, claiming women's right to substantive equality, through the developments lost out to gender-based *violence* as the issue of primary and fundamental concern to the UN and the international women's movement (Miller, 2004: 20). Violence against women, or VAW, emerged as the 'only' issue that concerns women's human rights as is reflected through the developments stated above. What marked this shift from *discrimination* to *violence*? And, what effect did dislocating *discrimination* have on the larger question of women's rights in the global arena?

It was at the 1985 Nairobi World Conference on Women that violence received an unprecedented articulation. However, such articulation confined it to being understood only as a "women's issue" (ibid.). Starting with the 1990s, especially the global attention on rape as a war crime (with special regard to Rwanda and former Yugoslavia), VAW took centrestage in the theatre of women's human rights advocacy, and sexual violence was constructed as the most important element of VAW. The rallying call to states to end VAW received a resounding amplification at the 1993 Vienna World Conference on Human Rights (Vienna Conference). It was here that the adage "women's rights are human rights" was coined entirely in the language of 'violence'.

Here I refer to a seminal essay by Alice M. Miller, wherein she comments:

> The [...] move to make 'women's rights human rights' [...] succeeded primarily by following the form of the mainstream human rights paradigm of the time: a *focus on the body suffering from acts committed by the state* [...] VAW [...] was addressed either as a problem for development or as an issue of discriminatory denial of protection against crime [...] [The] attempt was to 'human rights-ify' violence against women (2004: 19) (author's emphasis).

This implies an understanding where bodily-harm becomes a marker of human rights violations and redress can be sought only when we take the state as the primary signifier of rights and the law as its primary legitimizing discourse. This is where we also understand how bodily-harm, which is sexual in nature, and has the potential to threaten/challenge/rupture the essentialized relationship between women and community/nation, creates a hyper-visibility of sexual violence that tends to invisibilize other forms of violations of women's human rights.

Within this discourse then, as soon as questions of violation of the 'body' arise, the law jumps in with forms of incarceration to protect the 'good body' from the 'bad body/ies'. These 'bad bodies' violate the 'good body' in very many ways: from rape to sexual assault. The important question to ask here is, when does the law consider a 'body' to be rapeable or assaultable? The law's responsibility springs to force on the basis of the creation of a construct of the 'good body', which can be raped and/or assaulted. Though 'rational' or 'reasonable' thought would make us assume that the law in its protective role applies impartially to all 'bodies', in reality, the law responds only when the act of 'violation' meets its own qualifying tests. Only when the legal construct of the 'good body' is 'under threat of violation', or has been 'violated', will the law be of any use. If the 'body' does not meet the legal standards of a 'violable body', there is no recourse. The 'good body' also remains violable forever and is in need of perpetual protection. The law further locates the 'good body' in constructed spaces. If 'violation' happens on a 'good body' in a space, which does not meet the notions of the legal construct, it is not considered a violation at all.

The operation of human rights law on women's bodies thus creates the protection vs. freedom quandary. What were the primary objectives of this entire body of law that was made to end VAW – was it to protect 'violable' bodies, or create enabling conditions for 'freedom from violence' for all bodies? The singular focus on sexual harm as the gravest form of VAW has resulted in the state exercising its responsibility – to protect women's bodies, but not their rights (ibid.: 17). And, what kind of 'body' qualifies for protection is constructed through the law, under influence from socio-political forces that are in a position to make it.

VAW and specifically sexual violence has been effective in forwarding the cause of women's rights advocates because it seemed to provide a means to make the gender-specific content of this violence visible to the key human rights bodies and actors. The result was where "women [made] demands and ladies [got] protection" (Miller, 2004).

It is important to understand how historic developments on women's human rights in the UN have worked both in progressive and regressive ways for women. Where on the one hand it embodied a horror that could no longer be ignored and had to be responded to by states, it also represented the woman purely as a victim subject and reaffirmed her image (especially of women from the South) as without power and in need of protection. If one recollects the victim testimonies presented at the "Women's Rights are Human Rights Tribunal" (Vienna Tribunal) at the 1993 Vienna Conference, we will realize how clearly they were focused on sexual violence. In a filmed documentation of the proceedings at the Tribunal, of the 15 or so testimonies shown, at least 10 deal with sexual assault in detention, incest, marital rape, forced prostitution or rape in armed conflict. This narrow frame of sexual harm has reduced women to suffering bodies in need of protection by the law and the state, than as bodies and minds in need not only of protection, but participation and equality (ibid.).

While the hapless suffering bodies of sexually victimized women gained visibility internationally as markers of the only kinds of violence women experienced, this push was also propelled through an understanding where the voices of victimized women had to be made respectable, to lend credibility to the work of women's and human rights advocates.

As Miller notes:

> A [singular] focus on harm makes the discussion on sexuality safe – which is to say, respectable. Some forms of anti-sexual violence advocacy dovetail with the interests of states and thereby gain 'respectability' as an element of 'credibility' to participate in making policy with a state [...] Focusing on the harm in sex rather than what good sex might be [puts advocates] beyond self interest and salaciousness, especially if her focus is on a powerless victim, someone who cannot conceivably be held responsible for [exercising any agency] [...]. (2004: 37)

Through the discussion so far I have attempted to both celebrate the strides made in international human rights law in articulating the need for responses to stop VAW, and at the same time, have cautioned about what those responses might entail for women's human rights in the long run. In spite of the historic developments on women's rights and state accountability in human rights law, we can still identify the location of the 'woman-as-victim' in the trajectory of rights-claims: she still remains captive within the constructs of family, home, community and nation. Her captivity is further valorized by human rights standards that invoke culture to create an imaginary geographical hierarchy of locations where the 'woman-as-victim' should and ought to be. In the next section I take ahead the discussion to understand what still continues to fuel the VAW approach to women's human rights, and how women victims from the postcolonial worlds are further victimized for their 'cultural captivity', invisibilizing all forms of resistance potential that they have.

## The 'postcoloniality' conundrum

### *Gender, culture and the crises of international human rights interventions*

My concern in this section is to deal with two issues: first, to develop an overview of what 'postcoloniality' means, and second, to establish a connection between postcolonial conditionalities and its interactions with international human rights law and how such interactions impact on gender and culture in the Global South.

The international human rights discourse has been fraught with the accusation of being 'Eurocentric' – meaning, that it has emerged out of the experiences of World War II, and was in essence a response to addressing conditions of rights-violations in the Euro-Americas. Though over time states have been able to reach a semblance of consensus, through the UN, on the 'universality' of 'inherent' and 'indivisible' human rights norms and standards. But, as many scholars have pointed out, the 'universality' thesis has its roots in the understanding of 'Enlightenment', and thus is deployed in a cruelly liberal fashion, where peoples in the Southern world are subjected to an 'othering' treatment if they refuse to conform with the Western 'universal' standards and their attempt of resistance is constructed as 'fundamentalist' (Kapur, 2005; Baxi, 2006; Bhaba, 2005; Mamdani, 2004). This is evident from the kind of 'invasions' that have taken place in recent times in the name of 'humanitarian intervention' in Afghanistan and Iraq, and continue in several African and South Asian countries – through governmental, non-governmental and evangelist missions.

Such an experience is not new for postcolonial nation-states who have had to face the accusation of being 'backward' and 'barbaric' since the time of their colonial occupation. Here, I will use the term 'postcoloniality', "not simply meaning as *after* colonialism but as the discourse of oppositionality that the encounter with colonialism brings into being – postcoloniality thus begins from the very first moment of colonial contact" (Menon, 2006: 207). Postcolonial conditionalities are thus the strategies used to create subjectivities – of the 'native' and the 'civilizer' – and the systems through which these identities are perpetuated much after the colonial withdrawal – the law being one such major system (Singha, 1998; Nair, 1996; Kapur and Cossman, 1996).

In the situation of being a 'post-colony', the 'cultural connection' is primarily invoked by Western 'interventionists' who continue to act upon the understanding that the 'natives' still need to be 'civilized' and women need to be 'rescued' from their 'geographic captivity' and 'barbaric' cultural practices.

The 'woman question' remains central to the colonial (simultaneously Imperial/Western) enterprise as gender continues to be an overdetermined subject at the heart of ideological and political struggles over the meaning of culture and nation. "This forms the rationale for colonial legal interventions in the interests of 'civilization' as well as the grounds of ['native'] resistance to colonial interference and impetus for reform [from] within [postcolonial] communities" (Basu, 2002: 111).

Postcoloniality continues to recreate, as Partha Chatterjee points out, the 'inner' and 'outer' zones that determine the mechanics of culture and its impact on women. 'Western' material resources and practices are seen as beneficial for the new nation undergoing 'modernization', but 'Eastern' spirituality and culture are understood as superior, and thus demand responses to protect its 'authenticity' from getting tarnished and contaminated by Western influences. The 'outer' forms of the colonizer's world are to be embraced but the 'inner' world of authentic culture and tradition is considered sacrosanct from external intervention. Reform for women, associated with the inner world, is, thus, supposed to come from within the community and not from outside (Basu, 2002: 111, 112; Chatterjee, 1997; Bannerji, 2001).

The fixed notions of 'Western' and 'Eastern' marked through imagined authentic symbols of women – as chaste, loyal wives and dutiful mothers – as ones that solely bear the burden of cultural authenticity – have resulted in essentialisms that conflate gender and culture along with the many subjectivities that might inform socio-politico-cultural identities of women, to invisibilize the plural identity that an intersectional experience of gender, class, caste, religion, nationality etc. can produce.

The distinction is then made clear – the 'Western' woman is independent, liberated and can exercise agency and thus does not require 'protection, whereas her 'Eastern' counterpart still remains a victim of degenerated orthodox cultures and must be rescued. The contested question is: who will rescue her? Her essentialized vulnerabilities and weaknesses are not issues under consideration between the dichotomies of east-west, first world-third world, west-'the rest', but who shall have the heroic claim of being the 'knight in shining amour' (apologies for the 'Victorian' adage), becomes the reason for all deliberation – will it be the 'civilized' white man or the 'barbaric' brown/black man?

Not surprisingly, most of the responses of international human rights law to protect women from violence have been directed towards the truncated 'third world' woman, who according to the 'Western' law-makers, is sexually constrained, tradition-bound, incarcerated in the home, illiterate and poor – an image that is strikingly reminiscent of the colonial construction of the 'Eastern woman' (Kapur, 2005). Expectedly, such a response has attracted the many self-proclaimed guardians of 'Eastern' culture to reject the entire body of international human rights law as 'Eurocentric', in turn using the argument of 'Relativism' to create a culture of impunity for themselves where violence against women can continue through state sanction.

It is this continuum that I will briefly explore by examining some human rights law interventions that allow the Enlightenment-induced liberal discourse of human rights law to cement both the assumed "moral superiority of the West over the rest and the existence of an intense eye upon the 'other' cultures that [are] deemed to be in need of changing their gender relations to become modern and enlightened" (Sen, 2005: 43).

### *Of crises, interventions and imagined victims*

It is an understood fact that only situations of crises invite interventions. Sometimes, the crises are real, sometimes constructed and imagined. If we look at the developments in international human rights law to accommodate the issue of VAW (as discussed earlier), we can deduce that the crises were indeed an outcome of the combination all the three factors. VAW was a *real* problem that necessitated a concerted response from the international community; the hyper-visibility of sexual harm as the gravest form of VAW was *constructed* through the language of 'respectable victimhood' and a singular focus on harm done too the gendered-body; and the women of the third world are *imagined* to be the victim subject, without any agency and in need for human rights protection from the violence inflicted upon them by their own cultures. How is this imagined cultural subjectivity of a third world woman's experience represented through human rights work and reporting? And, what kind of interventions does such representation attract?

In her influential essay, 'The Tragedy of Victimization Rhetoric', Ratna Kapur observes:

> [...] [R]eliance on the victim subject [...] in the context of [VAW] presents a position [...] [where] women in the postcolonial world are portrayed as victims of their culture, which reinforces stereotyped and racist representations of that culture and privileges the culture of the West. In the end, the focus on the victim subject reinforces the depiction of women in the postcolonial world as perpetually marginalized and underprivileged, and has serious implications for the strategies subsequently adopted to remedy the harms that women experience. It encourages some feminists [and women's human rights advocates] to propose strategies which are reminiscent of the imperial interventions in the in the lives of the native subject and which represent the 'Eastern' woman as a victim of a 'backward' and 'uncivilized culture. (2005: 99)

Kapur goes on to further point out the nature of state response a singular focus on the victim subject attracts:

> [The] victim subject and the focus on violence invite remedies and responses from states that have little to do with promoting women's rights. Thus, a related concern is that the victim subject position has invited protectionist, even conservative responses from states. The construction of women exclusively through the lens of violence has triggered a spate of domestic and international reforms focused on the criminal law, which are used to justify state restrictions on women's rights – for the protection of women. (ibid.: 100)

If one were to look at the numerous reports that international ('Western') organizations like Amnesty International (AI) and Human Rights Watch (HRW) have put together on VAW and have used them as campaign material, we would understand the trope that they follow. Consider some of the AI titles: *Women in Afghanistan: the Violations Continue; Bangladesh: Institutional Failures Protect Alleged Rapists; India: Amnesty International Campaigns against Rape and Sexual Abuse by Members of the Security Forces in Assam and Manipur; Pakistan: Honor Killings of Girls and Women* (cited in Visweswaran 2004: 484).

Using the crises-induced-intervention theory that I briefly talked about above, there is no denying the fact that the events of VAW being documented and reported are indeed real. But, the plight has been singularly focused on women from the South.

One of HRW's most well-known publications and one that is very popularly cited by researchers and advocates is the *HRW Global Report on Women's Human Rights*, published in 1995. The timing of its publication was indeed planned to coincide with the 1995 Beijing World Conference on Women and also immediately follows the historic developments of the 1990s on women's human rights. the 1992 CEDAW General Recommendation 19 on VAW, the 1993 Vienna Conference, and the 1994 DEVAW and appointment of the Special Rapporteur. At a time when VAW was receiving unprecedented global attention and demanded state responses to end VAW, the publication of the report of timed strategically. But if one looks through the 6-page contents section it will be hard to find reports on VAW in countries of the North. Barring two reports, one on 'Sexual Abuse of Women Prisoners in the U.S.' and another on 'Abortion and Women's Rights in Ireland and Poland', all the other reports are about the most egregious forms of VAW faced by women from Africa, South Asia and the Middle East. Even, the cover of the report shows the face of a woman who definitely looks distraught and South Asian!

Though the report does not specifically invoke culture and religion as variables for analyses, the overwhelming majority of cases from Southern countries automatically works as a process of constructing the imagination of barbaric and backward cultures and implicitly draws a stark distinction between the conditions of women in the East and West, and completely fails to arrest the phenomenon of VAW that cuts across cultures and nations. For instance, the report on 'Sexual Abuse of Women Prisoners in the U.S.' locates VAW in the US only inside police custody, invisibilizing all other structural forms of violence that women face both inside their homes and at work, and also comes across as naïve, ignoring racial issues that escalate VAW within custody – Black women being at the receiving end of such violence not only because of their gender, but also for their colour.

In 2003 AI started a 6-year-long Stop Violence against Women Campaign and published a report titled *"It's in Our Hands: Stop Violence against Women"*. Even if one cursorily flips through the publication, the images that stare at you from the pages, almost all of them are of women from the South. It is easier to make that out because all the photographs are in colour. This report, however, does provide some statistics that bust the myth of VAW, especially domestic/intimate violence being an exclusively Southern preserve. Chapter 1 of the study reports, among others:

- The Council of Europe has stated that domestic violence is the major cause of death and disability for women aged 16 to 44 and accounts for more death and ill-health than cancer or traffic accidents.
- In the USA, women accounted for 85 per cent of the victims of domestic violence in 1999 (6,71,110 compared to 1,20,000 men) according to the UN Special Rapporteur on VAW.

The question of representation of gendered-harm and its connection with culture was also evident through the testimonies presented at the 1993 Vienna Tribunal. In the run-up to the Tribunal hundreds of testimonies were gathered by the organizers, the Centre for Women's Global Leadership, but only a few were presented at the Tribunal. The testimonies were also considerably edited to highlight the goriest of details regarding the kind of violence the victim had faced.

One such testimony was by a Pakistani woman called Perveen Martha whose story focused on how she was set on fire by her husband in February 1984. In her analysis of this testimonial, Kapur notes:

> The listener was left with the impression that the 'burning of brides' is a feature of 'Asian' culture. The framing of Perveen's life through the lens of violence and the mechanism of personal testimonial did not disrupt the gender and cultural assumptions present in the audience's *imagination*. What was marginalized in the telling of the story was the fact that Perveen was a Christian who had been married for several years and had several children, who were not in her custody. Even in the transcript of her testimony, Perveen's broader story as a divorced Christian woman and parent is not in the foreground. The script focuses on the burning incident [...] though she had been subjected to physical abuse prior to [...] [that]. Constructing the story around the incident of burning is an exoticism move that plays into cultural essentialism and provides little insight into the *reality* of Perveen's life. Her husband had divorced her and she was struggling in court to secure maintenance and custody of her children [...]. It is important to understand her multiple subject positions and location as a divorced Christian woman, at a time when the military dictatorship of General Zia-ul-Haq in Pakistan was clamping down on women's rights generally (2005: 128) (author's emphasis).

Kapur refers to another testimonial in her essay:

> [...] Alpana Chandola [...] [was] described as a 'survivor of dowry violence'. However, her testimony revealed that she was also a survivor of domestic violence, beaten and abused from the first day of her marriage. Focusing on the dowry demand deflected attention from other reasons for the violence she experienced. Describing Chandola's experience of violence through the lens of dowry closed off a more complex socio-economic analysis of her experience and reinforced cultural stereotypes about how women in India experience domestic violence. (ibid.: 129, fn25)

The constant use of culture as a cause for VAW and the singular focus on bodily-harm has three regressive side-effects for women's human rights. First, it essentializes both gender and culture, invisibilizing plural practices that a culture might have and homogenizing the category of woman – completely disregarding intersectional experiences of existence and potential for resistance. Second, since VAW is constructed as visible bodily-harm, state responses are focused at only countering the visible violence and not the systems that fuel it. When the violence is not visible any longer, but continues in other insidious forms, the state can absolve itself of all responsibility, in turn subverting the principle of 'due diligence'. Third, focus on bodily violence is also a process of privileging civil and political rights over economic, social and cultural rights – denying women guarantees to enabling conditions and decision-making authority.

When it comes to talking about VAW in the third world, there is an almost purposeful attempt at establishing a connection between culture and violence, however, that never happens when VAW in the Western context is referred to. For instance, Uma Narayan has discussed how dowry murders are cast in the first world scholarship as an age-old Indian/Hindu practice, and she contrasts it with research on domestic violence murders in the US, which are not similarly cast as practices of 'American culture' through references to Christianity (Narayan, 1997: 82, in Kapur, 2005: 109).

Like the conflation of dowry murders with Indian/Hindu culture or practice the international activist and academic discourse on VAW is replete with works on female genital mutilation (FGM), honour killings, the imposition of the veil, and all such forms of VAW also have a captive location – the third world, especially Islamic countries that are touted to be on the other side of 'civilization', so much more after September 11. A political climate where the 'clash of civilizations' are primarily being fought on the grounds of cultural supremacy, it is evident why for the Bush Administration, the plight of women in Afghanistan was the justification for the illegal invasion. Even Western media propaganda represented unveiled women after the Taliban were defeated, as the marker of 'liberation' that the 'West' has finally achieved to effect.

In a film titled *"Women's Rights are Human Rights"*, made by AI, the cover states that "it is a well-focused and sometimes shocking denunciation of the violence that afflicts women in many countries of the world". The 'many countries' featured in the film are Egypt, Indonesia, Bosnia and Herzegovina, Kosovo, Gambia, Pakistan, Somalia and Turkey. And, the forms of VAW that the film documents are FGM, honour killings and as a slight digression rape as a war crime. Interestingly, the part on Honour killings (filmed in Pakistan) starts with images of veiled women on the street, with the sound of the *azaan* in the background and the voice-over saying that in Islamic law men are supposed to be protectors of women. Here again, culture is not explicitly invoked to draw a connection with honour crimes, but both the visualization and narrative clearly point towards that direction.

Such interventions and representations construct cultural practices to "occupy our imaginations in ways that are totalizing of a culture and its treatment of women, and are nearly always overly simplistic or a misrepresentation of the practice" (Kapur, 2005: 107). Be it veiling, honour crimes or FGM – none are universally practised in the Islamic world or in Africa and thus cannot be used as markers to put Islam into a homogenized bundle.

As Purna Sen succinctly remarks:

> Making culture the divisor [...] renders those who inhabit the culture under scrutiny problematic per se, and suggests that their salvation lies in abandoning this culture, and, by implication, adopting another. Almost invariably this Salvation is Western, Judeo-Christian culture. Is this really the answer? If the problem were [...] [Eastern or post-colonial cultures and religions], it might be – but then only if Western culture and religion had eliminated violence against women. And, as we know, this is far from the case. If violence against women exists in the cultures that criticize the 'other', as it clearly does, then existing cultural practices do not determine the safety of women, as in no culture are women assured freedom from violence. (2006: 62)

From here I take the discussion into the domain of international refugee and asylum law as another system of intervention. This body operates on the basis of establishing 'barbarity' as the qualification for gaining asylum – meaning, a guarantee for protection 'outside' of one's country when states fail to exercise 'due diligence' completely.

## "Worse the better?"

### *Gender-based persecution and the politics of asylum jurisprudence*

Although postcolonial feminist critiques of the liberal discourse of human rights law (Kapur, 2005; Visweswaran, 2004) have exposed the dangers of applying it unproblematicaly to questions of culture in the third world, international refugee and asylum law, which is a supplemental part of the body of human rights, has been playing a nobly truant role in continuing the imagined North-South divide of civility-barbarity. The situation gets complicated because of the fact that none of the South Asian countries are party to the 1951 UN Convention on the Status of Refugees (Refugees Convention) and its 1967 Protocol, thus being outside of any international obligation to protect the rights of those fleeing persecution in their own countries. Moreover, the 1951 Convention does not recognize 'gender' as a valid ground for being persecuted, expanding manifold the possibility of women's asylum applications being rejected.

One major way to escape gender-based violence, especially of the private nature, when the state is unable or unwilling to provide protection, is to flee – as a refugee seeking surrogate protection from the jurisdiction of another state. Such situations are regulated through the discourse of international refugee law, its standards premised primarily on the Refugees Convention. But, even within the refugee law discourse, protection of rights of women fleeing gender-based violence/persecution is measured only through their 'victim' status. Responses from states as well as agencies like the United Nations High Commissioner on Refugees (UNHCR) does not consider their special needs and requirements, nor are the responses framed in ways that privilege their 'voices'.

Though women's issues have become increasingly central to UNHCR's policies for close to two decades now, their conditions are always perceived as vulnerable victims of war or culturally sanctioned intimate violence. Evoking the picture of suffering and helplessness of refugee women, the UNHCR appeals to our humanitarian sympathy. Women are construed as more 'true' refugees, being the victims rather than perpetrators of violence.

This picture reduces a refugee woman to the level of an infant and leaves her without agency and responsibility (Malkki, 1995, quoted in Turner, 2000: 8).

It is well documented that the majority of the world's refugees are women (UNHCR, 2002), who bear the brunt of the most extreme forms of human rights abuse. In any civilian exodus, women and children normally make up an estimated 75 per cent of a refugee population. Yet, the Refugees Convention does not recognize 'gender' as a separate and independent ground for persecution. After all, the 1951 Convention – the Magna Carta of international refugee law – was crafted by an all-male panel and defined a refugee as someone with a well-founded fear of persecution based on *race, religion, nationality, membership of a particular social group* and *political opinion*. Not a single woman was present amongst the *plenipotentiaries* when the drafters of the Convention had met in Geneva. The founding 'fathers' did not deliberately omit persecution based on gender – it was not even considered (ibid.).

It was the dominant image of a political refugee – someone who is fleeing persecution resulting from his direct involvement in political activity – which informed the minds of the drafters. This understanding does not often correspond with the reality of women's experiences and the "law has developed within a male paradigm which reflects the factual circumstances of male applicants, but which does not respond to the particular protection needs of women" (Romany, 1994: 88).

Even, the existing bank of jurisprudence on the meaning of persecution is primarily based on experiences of male claimants where "[persecution] is [understood] by the criterion of what men fear will happen to them" (Charlesworth, 1994: 71). Female-specific experiences such as genital mutilation, bride burning, forced marriages, domestic violence, forced abortion or compulsory sterilization, have not been widely understood to qualify as persecution. Rape is the only exception (Macklin, 1995: 225).

In South Asia, where violence against women is endemic and human rights obligations of states are seldom met, they are indeed defenseless in their ability to seek protection from violence through the implementation of international law. State adjudication practices as well as the non-existence of a regional 'gender asylum law' regime do not afford them an opportunity to seek surrogate protection[3] under international refugee law. The result is a growing number of internally displaced women who are at greater risk because the government that should have protected them often commits the abuses they seek to escape. Moreover, because they have not crossed any international border to seek refuge or asylum, displaced persons can claim only minimal protection from international law (HRW, 1995: 101).

### *Gendered dimensions of persecution*

Article 1A(2) of the Refugees Convention, as amended by the 1967 Protocol relating to the Status of Refugees, defines a 'refugee' as:

> ...any person who... owing to a fell-founded fear of being persecuted for reasons of *race, religion, nationality, membership of a particular social group* or *political opinion*, is outside the country of his/her nationality and is unable or, owing to such fear, is unwilling to avail himself/herself of the protection of that country; or who, not having a nationality and being outside the country of his/her formal residence, is unable or owing to such fear, is unwilling to return to it. (author's emphasis)

However, there exists no comprehensive definition of concepts of 'persecution' and 'well-founded fear of persecution' in international law. The drafters of the Refugees Convention framed an open-ended and flexible approach to the concept of persecution in the form of a universal framework. The UNHCR's Handbook gives direction in this regard:

> ...it may be inferred that a threat to life or freedom on account of race, religion, nationality, political opinion or membership of a particular social group is always persecution. Other serious violations of human rights – for the same reasons – would also constitute persecution. (UNHCR Handbook on Procedures and Criteria for Determining Refugee Status, 1979: para 51)

The Handbook further states:

> The phrase 'well-founded fear of being persecuted' is the key phrase of the definition. It reflects the views of its authors to the

> main element of refugee character [...] Since fear is subjective, the definition involves a subjective element in the person applying for recognition as a refugee. Determination of refugee status will therefore primarily require an evaluation of the applicant's statements rather than a judgment on the situation prevailing in [her] country of origin. (UNHCR Handbook o· Procedures and Criteria for Determining Refugee Status, 1979: para 37)

Women face special difficulties in obtaining refugee status. Two issues arise here: the ground upon which someone is granted refugee status, and the process of establishing these grounds. To identify the 'ground' one has to go with the understanding of 'persecution' and to 'establish the process' of arriving at the ground; one will have to understand 'well-founded fear'.

Thus, to gain recognition as a refugee, the asylum applicants must demonstrate that (1) the level of harm they have experience rises to persecution, (2) their own government cannot or will not protect them from the harm, and (3) the persecution is based on one of the protected grounds included in the definition (Martin, 2004: 28).

Why is the definition of persecution is necessarily linked to the five specified grounds only? In an attempt to redefine 'persecution', Alexander Aleinikoff points out:

> My sense is that this gets at something other than simply the level of harm; call it a 'qualitative' or 'normative' aspect of the definition of persecution. That is, persecution connotes unacceptable, unjustified, abhorrent infliction of harm, not just simply a particular degree of harm. (1991: 298)

One can draw from this understanding to state that the non-inclusion of 'gender' as a ground does carry a notion that calibrates pain and suffering on a scale where 'gender' cannot match up to the kind of *unacceptable, unjustified* and *abhorrent* infliction of harm that the existing grounds of *race, religion, nationality, political opinion* or *particular social group* attract.

The claim to refugee status by women facing gender-based persecution also presents special difficulties. There are cases which involve women who are victims of domestic violence or who fear harsh or inhuman treatment because of having transgressed social mores that confine them specific spaces, tasks and responsibilities. Even, when they are able to demonstrate that the harm is so great that it constitutes persecution and they have exhausted all efforts to receive protection from their governments, they are still faced with showing that the persecution is based on one of the protected grounds. As is known to us, gender is not one of the bases for persecution in the Refugees Convention definition (Martin, 2004: 31).

As already discussed, the definition of persecution in refugee law contains two elements: first, persecution not only requires that a claimant be at risk of sustaining serious harm, and second, that she cannot expect meaningful protection from that harm in her home country. Thus, recognizing that gender-related harm which threatens basic human rights of women constitutes serious harm alone is not sufficient to warrant the label of 'persecution', the harm feared must be directly or indirectly attributable to the state and that the individual cannot expect meaningful protection from these state authorities in the country of origin (Adjin-Tettey, 1997: 54).

According to Susan Forbes Martin, "Even more [problematic] are situations in which women flee their country because of severe sexual discrimination [...] While the universal right to freedom from discrimination on the ground of sex is recognized [...] the dividing line between discrimination and persecution is not a clean one" (2004: 31). Thus, eventually the criterion that is particularly significant in cases dealing with gender-persecution and that differ from other asylum application, is which acts amount to persecution.

The term 'gender-based persecution' refers to asylum applications of women premised on issues pertaining specifically to their gender. These claims can be separated into two general categories. The first focuses on persecution commonly faced by women such as – rape, genital mutilation, domestic violence and bride burning, among others. The second category includes claims that constitute persecution because of the applicants' gender, that is, persecution for disobeying repressive gender discriminatory laws or for not conforming with social mores that are offensive to women. This category also includes situations that discriminate against women and strictly prohibit them from engaging in certain activities (Bahl, 1997: 34).

In other words, gender-based persecution would include:

- When a woman is persecuted *because* of her gender, it addresses the causal relation between gender and persecution, her gender is the reason for why she is persecuted.
- When a woman is being persecuted *as* a woman, it is the *form* of persecution that is sex/gender-specific. Understanding the ways a woman is persecuted *as* a woman is critical to naming as persecution things that are done to women and not to men.
- When gender can be considered to be a risk factor that makes a woman's fear of persecution more well-founded than that of a man in similar circumstances (Lyth, 2001: 16).

The definition of refugee in the Refugees Convention is one that is not simply silent on the category of 'gender', but behind it lies narrow interpretations and assumptions of the conventional refugee that rarely fit the experiences of women. In practice, women have greater difficulty in satisfying the legal requirements for refugee status because of certain inherent male biases in the law. Women are less likely to meet the eligibility criteria for refugee status because of non-recognition of gender-based persecution, as well as the social and political context in which their claims are adjudicated. According to Nancy Kelly (1993: 265) the problem is two-fold: first, the Refugees Convention definition of 'refugee' does not specifically identify gender as a base for protection; and second, in applying the refugee definition, adjudicators have traditionally neglected to incorporate gender in their interpretation of the grounds of persecution enumerated in the Refugees Convention. This is especially true of male adjudicators who tend to regard gender-based persecution as a private and personal matter rather than as a socially significant phenomenon. Applications are continuously considered as falling outside the requirements of the Refugees Convention and rejected on the basis that the perpetrator is a private actor for whom the state cannot be made accountable. At times, fear of treading on state sovereignty has led advocates for cultural relativism to warn against interpreting traditional and historically sanctioned practices as persecution.

This is also due to the general failure of the international refugee and asylum law regime in not recognizing systemic denial of social and economic rights while emphasizing individual targeting and specific deprivation of civil and political rights. Besides, as already discussed, human rights law and discourse tend to privilege male-dominated public activities over the activities of women, which take place largely in the private sphere (Crawley, 2000: 17).

The key criteria for being a refugee are drawn from the public realm dominated by men. With regard to women's activities in the private sphere, there is primarily silence, which assigns the critical quality 'political' to mostly public activities. Thus, state oppression of a political minority is likely to be considered political unlike gender oppression at home (Indra, 1987: 3). Moreover, in rejecting gender as a legitimate ground for persecution, state authorities may easily dismiss people, especially women, whose economic, cultural and social rights have been violated as 'economic migrants' (Raj, 2001: 170).

### *'Gender' as a sixth ground?*

This omission of gender as a separate ground for persecution has had severe implications for many female asylum seekers across the world. As a consequence, debates have focussed on whether women's experiences can and should be interpreted so that they may be included into the already existing grounds or whether it is instead necessary to introduce gender as a sixth ground. Another consequence of the Convention's non-recognition of 'gender' is that it becomes difficult to understand which convention 'ground' is the most appropriate for raising claims for gender-based persecution.

The question is whether the addition of gender as a sixth ground can bring about a reconceptualization that would reveal, instead of conceal, the persecution that has its origin in women's distinctive existential and material state of being? (Lyth, 2001: 28).

In an authoritative paper by Roger Haines for the Global Consultations on International protection of the UNHCR, it is pointed out that adding 'gender' as a sixth ground to the Refugees Convention runs the risk of implying that gender need not be treated as intrinsic to all of the five grounds that are named in the convention. Haines writes:

> The failure of decision-makers to recognize and respond appropriately to the experiences of women stems not from the fact that the 1951 Convention does not refer specifically to persecution on the basis of [...] gender, but rather it has often been approached from a partial perspective and interpreted through a framework of male experiences. The main problem facing women as asylum seekers is the failure of decision makers to incorporate the gender-related claims of women into their interpretation of existing enumerated grounds and their failure to recognize the political nature of seemingly private acts of harm to women. (2003, quoted in Newland, 2003: 2)

Heaven Crawley seconds Haines' contention by stating: "Simply adding gender or sex to the enumerated grounds of persecution would not solve the problem. The bars to women's eligibility for refugee status lie not in the legal categories per se, but in the incomplete and gendered interpretation of refugee law, the failure of decision-makers to acknowledge and respond to the gendering of politics and of women's relationship to the state" (2000: 17). Still how refugee law could be more effective in strengthening other forms of protection is that refugee law, in part, takes an integrative perspective on women's rights. "By interpreting forms of violence against women within mainstream human rights norms and definitions of persecution, refugee law avoids some of the problems of marginalizing women's rights in international law" (Anker, 2002: 133).

However, there is a need for scholars, activists and policy makers working on refugee rights to be skeptic of the kind of repercussions inclusion of 'gender' as a separate ground for persecution might have. Such an inclusion would definitely be a very significant development, but it would also tend to homogenize the 'woman' category by assuming that women's experiences of persecution everywhere follow the same patterns and trends irrespective of their cultural and geopolitical locations.

To avoid essentializing both gender and culture, the framework for asylum determination needs to be transformed to accommodate the inclusion of women not as a special case, but one as many different categories where women's experiences are contextualized not just with regard to their sex or gender, but one which takes into consideration the linkages and interactions of their gender identity with that of their caste/colour/race/national/political identities. This approach suggests that the problem is not so much the invisibility of women but rather how their experiences have been represented and analytically characterized (Crawley, 2000: 19).

### *Politics of seeking asylum*

In the process of determining asylum claims questions of human rights abuse arise, generally, in three circumstances: persecution in the state of origin (the basis of the claim to asylum); rights violations in the course of migration (which may impinge on the substance of the claim); and abusive host state practices at the point of reception (which may relate to procedural questions about where a claim should be lodged or whether the applicant is credible).

In one of her influential essays titled "Internationalist Gatekeepers?: The Tension Between Asylum Advocacy and Human Rights", Jacqueline Bhaba (2002: 156–57) points out that refugee movements today are increasingly becoming more torturous and facilitated by commercial intermediaries and false documents. According to her, in a situation like this, the bona fide of the asylum seeker raises some critical questions: What is the nationality of the applicant? Which state should be responsible for providing protection in cases where the applicant's flight itinerary has involved various safe 'third' states en route to the state where asylum is being sought? Why did the applicant not present her asylum claim at the first opportunity?

Bhaba goes on to further point out that in a climate where escalating concerns about terrorism, economic recession, and state security heighten exclusionary and xenophobic impulses in developed states considering asylum applications, the challenge of establishing a particular host state's obligation to protect is particularly great (ibid.).

A critique of the international asylum adjudication system is therefore necessary to do a reality check with regard to what it can exactly offer when it comes to drawing the fundamentals of refugee rights guarantees from the basic principles of international human rights law. While human rights guarantees are understood to be universal and inherent across the world, when it comes to the determination of an asylum seeker as a refugee, to establish 'fell-founded fear' in an objective fashion, asylum adjudicating officers tend to "generate simplistic, even derogatory characteristics of asylum seekers' countries of origin, as areas of barbarism or lack of civility in order to present a clear cut picture of persecution" (ibid.: 162). The central guiding principle of this kind a construction of the asylum seeker as the 'native', who needs to be 'civilized' and rescued out of the clutches of a 'barbaric' state might be best described as "the worse the better" – the more oppressive the home state, the greater the chances of gaining asylum (ibid.).

With specific reference to violence against women, absence of regional or national laws have also meant that women facing persecution on grounds of gender can only avail of the recourse of applying for asylum to a Northern country. This, beyond being a practical constraint, is culpable of creating the stereotypical image of the third world woman-as-victim subject. An examination of case law in various Northern countries will make it evident that most cases of gender-based persecution concern women from the South who face culturally sanctioned forms of violence. Similar to the problems of addressing 'gender' as a special ground for persecution, the present politics of asylum jurisprudence considers the third world 'native' woman to be tradition-bound, incarcerated in the home, illiterate and poor and most importantly in need of Western intervention for 'protecting' and 'saving' her from violence (Kapur, 2002: 18). Moreover, her attempt to flee persecution is constructed as her desire to live in a 'liberal' and 'equal' society – epitomized by cultures in the West – and renouncing her 'own' barbaric culture. The need for a 'gender asylum regime' in South Asia is thus necessary for not only advancing asylum jurisprudence in the region, but also challenging and countering the existing constructs of the Eastern-native-disempowered-woman, which at best victimizes and at worst infantilizes them.

## Not a conclusion: towards a more rigorous interrogation

Having raised more questions than providing answers, requires that I propose directions in which we can take ahead this debate, not to 'liberate' the 'captive subjects', but to employ lenses that will enable us to look at them differently, not only gaze at them, but also create conditions for us to welcome their gaze back. What I suggest here are not original or ingenious ideas, but ones that have been informed by the works of the scholars I have been referring to. They are not meant to sound prescriptive, merely suggestive. They remain open to challenge as more consistent interrogation of imagined ideas must remain the *leit motif* of all human rights work in times where hegemonic appropriation of knowledge and practice threatens subaltern existence at every step.

There is a need to bust the mechanics of 'binary logic' on the basis of which most of our human rights work is premised: East-West, Civility-Barbarity, Right-Wrong, Agency-Victimhood, War-Peace, State-Non-State, Private-Public etc. Breaking out of the binaries can allow possibilities that can better capture the existential complexities of the violated subject and create spaces for their participation in determining justice-seeking responses.

Our work should not outright reject essentialism, but recognize its deployment as a strategy and understand the limitations and dangers of using it as a campaign tool for claiming rights. Essentialism is helpful, but an over-reliance on it can subvert the very objective with which it was deployed.

We have to move beyond identifying women merely as victims, and recognize the resistance potential that she as a peripheral subject possesses. For instance, a woman in Iran might wear the veil to offer resistance in more than one way: she wears it to access public spaces which would otherwise be inaccessible to her, and at the same time she wears the veil as a Muslim holding up a symbol to resist the 'imperial' gaze that wants to imagine liberation *for* her.

The concept of state accountability must be understood not merely with regard to compensating the violated, constructing her identity as a victim-survivor – but should be extended to 'due diligence' that will recognize her as a citizen, to expand its base to not pit freedom against protection and ensure enabling conditions to exercise civil citizenship and guarantee reparation.

Captivity can be one of the many experiences that mark the existence of women in the South. However, for those of us who deduce that through looking at them from afar, it is simply a perceived experience. Even if we work to establish its reality, it would still never qualify to be the only one. It is this recognition of a multiple and layered existence, one that does not calibrate pain, but looks at disadvantage through the lenses of intersectionality – which will allow us to resurrect a more emancipatory politics for claiming women's human rights.

## Notes

1. International Humanitarian Law is governed by the Geneva Conventions of 1948 and its accompanying protocols.
2. International Criminal Law was applied for adjudication at the International Criminal Tribunals in Rwanda and the former Yugoslavia and is presently enshrined on the Rome Statute of the International Criminal Court. The demand for reparation by former Japanese 'Comfort Women' was made on the basis of International Criminal Law principles.
3. Refugee law provides surrogate national protection to individuals when their states have failed to fulfil fundamental obligations, and when that failure has a specified discriminatory impact. Under the Refugees Convention, the responsibility to provide international protection – a surrogate to the ruptured, national protection – is placed in states that are parties to the Convention.

## References

### Books

Bannerji, H. (2001). *Inventing Subjects: Studies in Hegemony, Patriarchy and Colonialism*. New Delhi: Tulika.

Baxi, U. (2006). *The Future of Human Rights*. New Delhi: Oxford.

Crawley, H. (2000). *Refugee and Gender: Law and Process*. Bristol: Jordan.

Kapur, R. and Cossman, B. (1996). *Subversive Sites: Feminist Engagements with Law in India*. New Delhi: Sage.

Kapur, R. (2005). *Erotic Justice: Law and the New Politics of Postcolonialism*. New Delhi: Permanent Black.

Malkki, L. (1995). *Purity and Exile: Violence, Memory and National Cosmology among Hutu Refugees in Tanzania*. Chicago and London: Chicago University Press.

Mamdani, M. (2004). *Good Muslim, Bad Muslim: Islam, the USA and the Global War Against Terror*, New Delhi: Permanent Black.

Martin, S.F. (2004). *Refugee Women*. Oxford: Lexington Books.

Nair, J. (1996). *Women and Law in Colonial India: A Social History*. New Delhi: Kali for Women.

Singha, R. (1998). *A Despotism of Law: Crime and Justice in Early Colonial India*. New Delhi: Oxford.

### Articles

Adjin-Tettey, E. (1997). Failure of State Protection within the Context of the Convention Refugee Regime with Particular Reference to Gender-related Persecution, *Journal of International Legal Studies* 54.

Aleinikoff, T.A. (1991). The Meaning of 'Persecution' in U.S. Asylum Law. In H. Adelman (ed.), *Refugee Policy: Canada and the United States*, pp. 296. Toronto: York Lanes Press.

Anker, D.E. (2002). Refugee Law, Gender, and the Human Rights Paradigm, *Harvard Human Rights Journal* (15) 133.

Bahl, A. (1997). Home is Where the Brute Lives: Asylum Law and Gender-based Claims of Persecution. *4 Cardozo Women's Law Journal:* 34.

Basu, S. (2002). Claiming Transgression: The Bengali 'Feminist' Magazine Sananda and the Discourse of Sexuality, in Brinda Bose (ed.) *Translating Desire: The Politics of Gender and Culture in India*, New Delhi: Katha, pp. 106–131.

Bhaba, J. (2005). Embodied Rights: Gender Persecution, State Sovereignty and Refugees, in Nira Yuval-Davis and Pnina Werbner (eds.), *Women, Citizenship and Difference*, New Delhi: Zubaan, pp. 178–190.

——. (2002). Internationalist Gatekeepers?: The Tension between Asylum Advocacy and Human Rights. *15 Harvard Human Rights Journal:* 155.

Bunch, C. (1995). Transforming Human Rights from a Feminist Perspective. In Julie Peters and Andrea Wolper (eds.), *Women's Rights, Human Rights.* Great Britain: Routledge.

Charlesworth, H. (1994). What are Women's International Human Rights. In Rebecca J. Cook, (ed.), *Human Rights of Women: National and International Perspectives,* Philadelphia: University of Pennsylvania Press. p. 71.

Chatterjee, P. (1997). The Nation and its Women, in Ranajit Guha (ed.), *A Subaltern Studies Reader: 1986–1995,* New Delhi: Oxford, pp. 240–262.

Coomaraswamy, R. (1996). Reinventing International Law: Women's Rights as Human Rights in the International Community. *Bulletin of Concerned Asian Scholars.* Vol. 28. Issue 2, p. 16.

Copelon, R. (1994). Intimate Terror: Understanding Domestic Violence as Torture. In Rebecca J. Cook (ed.), *Human Rights of Women: National and International Perspectives.* Philadelphia: University of Pennsylvania Press, pp. 116–152.

Haines, R. (2003). *Gender-related Persecution.* In Erika Feller et al. (eds.), Refugee Protection in International Law: UNHCR's Global Consultation on International Protection, p. 319. Cambridge: Cambridge University Press.

Indra, D. (1987). A Key Dimension of the Refugee Experience. *Refuge 3.*

Johnstone, R.L. (2006). Feminist Influences on the United Nations Human Rights Treaty Bodies. 28 *Human Rights Quarterly:* 148.

Kapur, R. (2002). The Tragedy of Victimization Rhetoric: Resurrecting the 'Native' Subject in International/ Post-Colonial Feminist Legal Politics. *15 Harvard Human Rights Journal: 1.*

Kelly, N. (1993). Gender Related Persecution: Assessing the Asylum Claims of Women, *Cornell International Law Journal,* 26: 625–71.

——. Gender-Related Persecution: Assessing the Asylum Claims of Women. *Cornell International Law Journal* (26) 625.

Knop, K. (1993). Re/Statements: Feminism and State Sovereignty in International Law. *Transnational Law and Contemporary Problems.* pp. 293–344.

Macklin, A. (1995). Refugee Women and the Imperative of Categories. *Human Rights Quarterly* (17) 225.

Miller, A. (2004). Sexuality, Violence against Women and Human Rights: Women Make Demands and Ladies Get Protection, *Health and Human Rights* 7(2): p. 17.

Newland, K. (2003). Seeking Protection: Women in Asylum and Refugee Resettlement Processes. Issue Paper for the United Nations Division for the Advancement of Women, Expert Consultation on Migration and Mobility and How this Movement Affects Women. Malmo, Sweden.

Raj, S. (2001). The Gender Element in International Refugee Law: Its Impact on Agency Programming and the North-South Debate. Indian Society of International Law. *Yearbook on Humanitarian and Refugee Law 170.*

Randall, M. (2002). Refugee Law and State Accountability for Violence Against Women: A Comparative Analysis of Legal Approaches to Recognizing Asylum Claims Based on Gender Persecution. 25 *Harvard Women's Law Journal: 305.*

Rao, A. (1993). Right in the Home: Feminist Theoretical Perspective on International Human Rights. In Ratna Kapur (ed.) 1 *National Law School Journal* (62).

Romany, C. (1994). State Responsibility Goes Private. In Rebecca J. Cook, (ed.), *Human Rights of Women: National and International Perspectives*, p. 88. Philadelphia: University of Pennsylvania Press.

Sen, P. (2006). Crimes of Honor: Value and Meaning. In Lynn Welchman and Sara Hossain (eds.) *Honour: Crimes, Paradigms and Violence against Women*. New Delhi: Zubaan, pp. 42–63

Sircar, O. (2006a). Good Body, Bad Body and No Body: Interrogating Feminist engagements with Sexual Autonomy and Law, Paper presented at Cultures of the Body: 11th International Cultural Studies Workshop, Centre for Studies in Social Sciences (CSSS), Kolkata, in Goa.

—. (2006b). Can the Women Flee? Gender-based Persecution, Forced Migration and Asylum Law in South Asia, in Navnita Chadha Behera (ed.) *Gender, Conflict and Migration: Women and Migration in Asia* Vol. 3. New Delhi: Sage.

Sullivan, D. (1995). The Public/ Private Distinction in International Human Rights Law. In Julie Peters and Andrea Wolper (eds.) *Women's Rights, Human Rights*. Great Britain: Routledge.

Turner, S. (2000). Vindicating Masculinity: The Fate of Promoting Gender Equality. *Forced Migration Review* 9: 9.

Visweshwaran, K. (2004). Gendered States: Rethinking Culture as a Site of South Asian Human Rights Women, 26.2 *Human Rights Quarterly*, pp. 483–511.

**Unpublished Thesis**

Lyth, A. (2001). Where are the Women? A Gender Approach to Refugee Law. LLM Thesis, Lund University.

**Reports**

Amnesty International. (2004). It's in Our Hands: Stop Violence Against Women. London: Amnesty International.

Human Rights Watch. (1995). The Human Rights Watch Global Report on Women' Human Rights. New Delhi: Oxford University Press.

**Films**

*The Vienna Tribunal*. 1994. Dir. Gerry Rogers. Produced by the Centre for Women's Global Leadership: Rutgers University, 48 mins. Color. VHS.

*Women's Rights are Human Rights*. 2001. Dir. Ayfer Ergun, Produced by Amnesty International Netherlands, 30 mins. Color, VHS.

**Documents from United Nations**

The UN Convention Relating to the Status of Refugees, 28th July 1951: 189 UNTS 137.

UN Declaration on the Elimination of Violence Against Women, A/C.3/48/1.5.23 February 1994.

UNHCR EXCOM. "Note on Refugee Women and International Protection". EC/SCP/59 (28 August 1990).

—. 44th Session, Refugee Protection and Sexual Violence, Conclusion 2, A/AC.96/XLVI/CRP.3 (1993).

—. Conclusion no. 39 (XXXVI), Refugee Women and International Protection, UN Doc. HRC/IP/2/Rev. 1986.

UNHCR. "Handbook on the Procedures and Criteria for Determining Refugee Status". Geneva, 1979.

—. "The State of the World's Refugees: A Humanitarian Agenda". 1997.

CHAPTER FOUR

# Age of marriage and the debate on human rights

*Jaya Sagade*

Child marriages in India are supported by the age-old socio-cultural and religious practices despite the legislation restraining it. It has physical, social, economic and developmental consequences that a girl child is forced to face due to her marriage at an early age. Child marriage is a form of physical as well as mental violence against a girl child committed by members of her own family including her own parents. The Indian legal framework has addressed the issue of child marriage. However, the problem of child marriage is not addressed from the human rights perspective of the young girls.

Human rights established in international human rights treaties and the Constitution of India can be applied to prevent child marriages in India. The language and the concept of human rights have been developed through the struggle of individuals and groups. Many individuals find human rights empowering because they provide means by which individuals can legitimately assert their interests.[1] Human rights that are backed by the Indian Constitution have become the source of realization of the rights of the disadvantaged and have not merely remained aspirations. This essay analyzes not only those human rights that are obviously violated by child marriage but also covers more comprehensive wrongs implicating a broad spectrum of human rights to address both causes and consequences of child marriages.

The challenge here is not only to identify those rights that might be infringed but also to suggest possible remedies. States parties to these conventions are under legal obligation to ensure that domestic legislation conforms to international human rights. They are also obliged to investigate and remedy the conduct of individuals in violation of these human rights. The paper attempts to suggest ways by which the government might be held accountable for its failure to prevent child marriages and suggest strategies for remedying violation of human rights of those young girls.

A number of international human rights treaties that have addressed the issue of age at marriage are based on the Universal Declaration of Human Rights (UDHR) adopted in 1948. The primary international human rights conventions[2] concerning the young girls' human rights are the Convention on the Elimination of All Forms of Discrimination against Women, 1979 (Women's Convention)[3] and the Convention on the Rights of the Child, 1989 (Children's Convention).[4] These conventions manifest the fundamentals of UDHR and reassert UDHR's two legally binding covenants, viz., the International Covenant on Civil and Political Rights, 1966 (ICCPR)[5] and the International Covenant on Economic, Social and Cultural Rights, 1966 (ICESCR).[6] Besides, other international treaties that are significant in the discussion are the Convention on Consent to Marriage, Minimum Age for Marriage and Registration of Marriages, 1962 (Marriage Convention)[7] and the Supplementary Convention on the Abolition of Slavery, the Slave Trade, and Institutions and Practices Similar to Slavery, 1956 (Slavery Convention).[8]

The major international human rights conventions have established committees to monitor the compliance of states parties with the treaty obligations. Under the Women's Convention, there is a Committee on the Elimination of Discrimination against Women (CEDAW) and under the Children's Convention, there is a Committee on the Rights of the Child (CRC); Human Rights Committee (HRC) under ICCPR, and Committee on Economic, Social and Cultural Rights (CESCR) under ICESCR. These committees receive the periodic reports that states parties are required to submit to show how they have responded through their laws, policies and practices to comply with the respective conventions. To assist countries in their reporting obligations, CEDAW, HRC, and CESCR have developed a series of General Recommendations/Comments.[9] These recommendations/comments develop the standards of performance applicable to measure the compliance with human rights norms.

Another important international mechanism that has evolved for raising human rights grievances is a complaint procedure.[10] For instance, the individual complaint procedure is established under the First Optional Protocol to ICCPR. Recently, an Optional Protocol has been adopted to the Women's Convention by the General Assembly.[11] A provision is made for the receipt of individual complaints by the monitoring body concerned. However, an individual cannot lodge such complaint unless she has exhausted domestic remedies. The views or recommendations of the UN treaty bodies are not formally binding on the states parties as a matter of international law.[12]

Apart from these mechanisms,[13] the UN has evolved another mechanism to arrive at consensus for the advancement of human rights of individuals. It has sponsored a number of international conferences to address the issue of human rights. The World Conference on Human Rights, held in Vienna (the Vienna Conference) in 1993, focused on human rights of women among other matters. The International Conference on Population and Development (ICPD), held in Cairo in 1994 and the Fourth World Conference on Women (FWCW) held in Beijing in 1995, are the two major conferences, which focused on women's right to sexual and reproductive health. These conferences specifically developed the standards for the promotion of the human rights of the adolescent girls.

More than ten years have passed since the Cairo and Beijing conferences took place. International agencies have taken account of what has been achieved by these international conferences for realizing women's human rights. The United Nations General Assembly has passed the resolutions, for the future actions that needs to be undertaken by governments, non-governmental organizations (NGOs), civil society and international agencies.

### Obligations of government to implement human rights

Individuals expect protection from the state. They count on state for their safety and well-being.[14] The human rights violations by the state therefore add an element of insult and indignity to the sufferings of individuals. The primary object of international human rights law is not to punish states, but to see that states do comply with their obligations, which they have accepted by ratifying the international human rights treaties, and thus prevent future violation of human rights. International human rights law compliance mechanisms respect the unique character of human rights treaties and ensure that the remedies afforded serve to deter future violations and uphold the legal order that the treaties create.

The international law of state responsibility for human rights violation has evolved significantly in recent times.[15] By ratifying or acceding to the international conventions, states parties accept the legal duties to abide by the conventions and thereby are required to take steps to protect the exercise and enjoyment of human rights, to investigate violations, to provide effective remedies to victims. It is worth exploring which acts of violations of women's human rights are imputable to states parties.

For instance, child marriage performed by private individuals does not necessarily implicate the responsibility of the state. However, when the state tolerates or excuses child marriages by not prosecuting those who are responsible for contracting child marriages, the state bears the responsibility, as marriage is a state-sanctioned institution. The state is responsible not directly for contracting child marriages, but for its own lack of diligence to prevent the private act of contracting child marriage through its executive, legislative or judicial organs. The state is also responsible because child marriage violates specific human rights that are binding on the state as a matter of international law. The responsibility of states is not simply not to engage in human rights violations themselves, but to meet international obligations to deter and condemn such violations anticipated by private persons.[16]

All human rights impose three types or levels of obligations or duties on states parties – the obligation to respect, protect and fulfil human rights:[17]

- Obligation to *respect* rights by which states are prohibited from interfering with the protection, promotion and enjoyment of the human rights. These are the negative obligations.
- Obligation to *protect* rights by which states are required to prevent harm to individuals from all including private parties. These are the positive obligations.
- Obligation to *fulfil* rights by which states are required to take affirmative measures for realization of human rights including appropriate legislative, administrative, budgetary, judicial, promotional and other measures. These are again the positive obligations.

India has ratified all of the above mentioned conventions[18] and is, therefore, under an obligation as a matter of international law to respect, protect and fulfil human rights of the girls referred to in it. Such ratification puts an obligation on the Indian State to bring its legislation and policies into line with the standards of the treaty concerned. Moreover, effective implementation of these laws and policies is essential to ensure compliance with these treaties. The standards laid down in these conventions do not automatically become the part of Indian domestic law so as to create rights in favour of individual citizen. The Indian Parliament is required to enact legislation to give effect to the rights incorporated in these conventions. This is implicit from Article 51 (c) and Article 253 of the Constitution. Article 51(c) reads as:

> The State shall endeavour to foster respect for international law and treaty obligations in the dealings of organised peoples with one another.

Article 253 of the Constitution gives "power to Parliament to make any law for implementing any treaty, agreement or convention with any other country or countries or any decision made at any international conference, association or other body". By referring to these provisions, it would be worth analyzing India's efforts to comply with the international treaty.

## Child marriage and international human rights[19]

Human rights are the rights of individuals in society. To call them as 'human' implies that all human beings have them, equally and in equal measure, by virtue of their human dignity, regardless of sex, race, age, social class, economic position, religion, culture or other parameters. Implied in one's human dignity, human rights are inalienable and imprescriptible. Human rights are the rights, not just the aspirations, and are not dependent on privilege. As 'rights', they imply that they are claims 'as of right' and 'entitlements'.[20] Thus, they are the instruments through which particularly powerless individuals and groups can claim human dignity.

Marriage is a state sanctioned institution. Therefore, failure on part of a state to address the prevention of child marriages of the young girls is an indication of social injustice. It is a result of exclusion of injustices that women experience. In the following pages, we will try to establish that with the human rights approach such injustice could be remedied. Our argument is that human rights are denied to the young girls when they are given in marriage by their parents under the guise of social, cultural, religious and economic reasons as child marriage causes multiple harms to young girls. Child marriage:

1. takes away their autonomy as they do not have choice of life partner, and right to decide the timing of the marriage;
2. exposes them to violence and abuse which may result in emotional and psychological problems and sometimes even in desertion and divorce;
3. creates problems for their reproductive health in terms of maternal mortality and morbidity;
4. does not give them opportunity to decide freely and responsibly the number and spacing of their children;
5. reaffirms stereotypes of women to child bearing roles;
6. takes away their right to education which in turn;

7. denies them opportunity to become economically independent;
8. undermines their self-confidence;
9. hampers their decision-making power;
10. affects their overall well-being;
11. hinders their ability to participate to the fullest extent in the life activities.

These harms resulting from the child marriage could be classified into two broad categories:

- harms resulting from the fact of the child marriage itself, and
- harms resulting as a consequence of the child marriage.

Consequences of the child marriage could be further classified into:

- consequences of the child marriage on the health particularly the reproductive health, and
- consequences of the child marriage on the development of young girls.

Each of these harms takes away one or the other human right of the young girls. These human rights can be analyzed in a variety of ways. Human rights originating in the various international human rights instruments, including women's and children's conventions, are clustered around these categories of harms.

### Rights affected due to child marriage

Child marriage violates a number of human rights of young girls that can be separately identified in various human rights conventions. These rights include the right to equality, right to marry and found a family, right to liberty and security, and right to be free from slavery. Right to equality could be discussed under the two sub-headings: right to sexual and gender non-discrimination and right to non-discrimination on the ground of age, and lastly how the intersectionality of sex, gender and age are compound by the cultural and traditional customs. For the want of space, we are limiting the scope of this essay and only focusing on how child marriage violates right to equality of the young girls.

### *Right to equality*

The prohibition of discrimination is among the most fundamental principles of international human rights law. As stated in the UN Charter, one of the four overarching purposes of the UN is "to achieve international co-operation in promoting and encouraging respect for human rights and for fundamental freedoms for all without distinction as to sex, race, language or religion."[21]

The Universal Declaration and the two UN Human Rights Covenants – ICCPR and ICESCR – require governments to prohibit discrimination of any kind in the exercise of protected rights, such as on grounds of sex, race, colour, language, religion, political or other opinion, national or social origin, property, birth or other status.[22] The right of women to equality with men (as distinct from the right to non-discrimination) has received attention since the advent of the United Nations. In its first preambular paragraph, the UN Charter "reaffirms faith" in a number of fundamental principles, including the "equal rights of men and women."[23] Article 3 of both ICCPR and ICESCR obliges states parties "to undertake to ensure the equal rights of men and women to the enjoyment" of all the rights set forth in each Covenant. The Women's Convention in its title itself focuses on the elimination of "all forms" of discrimination against women. It recognises the right to protection against discrimination on the ground of sex and gender.[24] The Children's Convention endorses the right to non-discrimination on the ground of sex[25] as well as on the ground of age.[26]

### *Right to non-discrimination on grounds of sex and gender*

Sex is a prohibited ground of discrimination under all the international human rights conventions.[27] In fact, it has been argued that the prohibition of sexual discrimination is now part of customary international law, which binds all the states even without their express ratification of a treaty.[28] The main treaty stating various rights included within the overarching right of women to the enjoyment of human rights on the basis of equality with men is the Women's Convention. It obliges states parties "to pursue by all appropriate means and without delay a policy of eliminating discrimination against women" and to "take in all fields... all appropriate measures ... to ensure the full development and advancement of women, for the purpose of guaranteeing them the exercise of the enjoyment of human rights and fundamental freedoms on a basis of equality with the men."[29] Discrimination against women is defined in Article 1 as:

> [A]ny distinction, exclusion or restriction made on the basis of sex which has the effect or purpose of impairing or nullifying the recognition, enjoyment or exercise by women, irrespective of their marital status, on a basis of equality of men and women, of human rights and fundamental freedoms in the political, economic, social, cultural, civil or any other field.

The definition has several distinctive features. First, it states that women are entitled to enjoy human rights on the basis of equality with the men, and not merely free from discrimination on the ground of sex.[30] Second, the right to equal enjoyment extends to rights in any field including economic and social.[31] Third, it extends to the protection against measures that have the effect of improving women's equal enjoyment of rights.[32,33]

Thus, the Women's Convention addresses discrimination on the grounds of biological as well as political, social, economic and cultural constructs, and thereby accounts for disadvantage that woman suffers. Article 3 of the Women's Convention reads as:

> States parties shall take in all fields, in particular in the political, social, economic and cultural fields, all appropriate measures, including legislation to ensure the full development of and advancement of women...

It characterizes women's inferior status and oppression not just as a problem of inequality between men and women but rather as a function of sex and gender discrimination against women.[34] It moves from a sex-neutral norm to the recognition of the fact that the law must respond to the special needs of women by understanding the pervasive and systemic nature of discrimination against them. Article 5 of the Women's Convention states:

States parties shall take all appropriate measures to modify social and cultural patterns of conduct of men and women with a view to achieving the elimination of prejudices and customary and all other practices, which are based on the idea of inferiority of the superiority of either of the sexes or on stereotyped roles for men and women.

Thus, it goes beyond the UN Charter, UDHR, ICCPR and ICESCR to address the disadvantaged position of women in all areas of their lives. The Women's Convention identifies the need to confront the social causes of women's inequality by addressing "all forms" of discrimination that women suffer.[35] It thereby accounts for women's life experiences. It requires "states parties to eliminate even the private discrimination against women by any person."[36]

The practice of child marriage of girls violates the right to equality on the ground of sex as well as gender. It violates the right in both forms of equality – formal as well as substantive equality. The prohibition against sex discrimination has largely been interpreted to require that likes be treated alike or those who are similarly situated are to be treated equally.[37] Within this prevailing conception, equality is equated with sameness. When the two are same, they are to be treated equally. Any difference in treatment to individuals or groups constitutes discrimination. This is a formal equality. The practice of child marriages of girls when looked at from this narrow perspective of formal equality treats them differently than boys of their age and thus thereby discriminates against them on the ground of sex and violates their right to formal equality.

It is not only on the basis of formal equality that the practice of child marriage of girls could be challenged. It violates substantive equality too. The focus of substantive equality is not simply on equal treatment but rather on the actual impact of the practice on individuals or groups. The focus is not on sexual discrimination but on gender discrimination. The focus is not on the sameness or difference, but rather on disadvantage. The central inquiry of substantive equality approach is whether the practice in question contributes to the disadvantage. Accordingly, discrimination consists of treatment that further disadvantages a group that has historically and socially experienced systemic oppression.[38] The object of the substantive equality approach is to eliminate the existing inequality in day-to-day life suffered by the disadvantaged and seeks to eliminate it by positive measures. The Women's Convention, as pointed out above, addresses the formal as well as substantive equality and discrimination based on sex and gender.

The concept of gender is constructed by social, economic and cultural considerations. The girl child is discriminated against from the earliest stage of life through her childhood and into adulthood.[39] The first lesson that a female child is made to learn is that the differential treatment between her and her brothers is a fact of life.[40] The practice of son preference is a deeper form of discrimination perpetrated against the girl child. Lineage continuity and succession to the property are some of the considerations underlying the desire to have sons. Another reason for the girls child's inferior status in her family is that since by custom a daughter, on her marriage, is expected to leave the parents' home to join her husband's home, parents depend on their sons for material support during their old age.

The practice of child marriage usually victimizes girl children. Girls are perceived as burdens by their parents. The child marriage of their daughter relieves them of the responsibilities attached to raising a girl. At the same time, as the girl's parents are relieved of their burden, the groom's parents also benefit because they gain an unpaid slave and often dowry. The purpose of the marriage in the Indian context is the transference of father's dominion over a woman in favour of her husband. This transfer is then expected to take place at an early age so as to allow her to adapt to her socially determined position.[41] Another reason for chiid marriage of young girls is to control her sexuality[42] and reproduction, which is at the heart of unequal gender relationships. Through culturally embedded concepts of virginity and chastity, women's sexuality is not only controlled by men but is often a symbol of the honour and status of a family.[43] The society has undue concern about female virginity, and awareness of its absence severely hampers the marriage prospects of the young girls. The practice of child marriage reduces the possibility of any suspicion arising regarding the virginity of a young girl. Marriages are arranged therefore either immediately after or sometimes even before she attains puberty.

These social, economic and cultural justifications for child marriage adversely affect the girl children's health, education and development. It contributes to their already low position in the family and society, subordinates them further, and thereby results in the denial of substantive equality to them, discriminates against them, and aggravates their systemic oppression.

Article 2(f) of the Women's Convention calls upon states parties to:

> [T]ake all appropriate measures, including legislation, to modify or abolish existing laws, regulations, customs and practices which constitute discrimination against women.[44]

The Women's Convention further calls upon, through Article 5, the elimination of all cultural practices, which are based on the inferiority or stereotype roles of men and women. As stated earlier, it calls upon states parties to take all appropriate measures to modify the social and cultural patterns of conduct of men and women, with a view to achieving the elimination of prejudices and customary and all other practices, which are based on the idea of the *inferiority or the superiority* of either of the sexes or on *stereotyped roles* for men and women.[45]

Articles 2(f) and 5(a) of the Women's Convention, when read together, put an obligation on states parties to take appropriate measures to modify cultural practices, such as child marriage, by passing or reforming legislation, taking steps for effective enforcement of such legislation, and making efforts to change the attitudes of people to those cultural practices. These provisions of the Women's Convention therefore reiterate a feminist viewpoint and require states parties to take appropriate measures to remedy a situation where women's experiences have so far been excluded.

Apart from this, the young girls are denied the same degree of choice as the men in countries where marriages are arranged by the parents. They have little say in deciding the timing of their marriage or selecting their spouse. Conditioning of their mind and psychological framework is built up in such a way that they feel duty bound to respect the decision of their parents. In case of arranged marriages of young girls the question of their choice therefore becomes irrelevant. When the parents find a groom for their young daughter, they do not ask for her consent. Even if they ask, it does not mean much in reality, as culturally daughters are groomed to believe that parents always act in their "best interest".

At the same time, it is equally true that selection of a groom largely depends upon the class and caste to which the parents belong. Economic, social and educational positions are inevitable factors that restrict the choice by the parents of a groom for their daughter. Woman's lack of independent status by any of these considerations further reduces her chance of having any say in the matter of her marriage. As a consequence, when child marriage takes place, the right to choose the husband is denied to a girl and thereby her autonomy is not respected. As a result, she is discriminated against on the grounds of sex at the point of entering into marriage. It violates her right to equality at the point of entering into marriage stipulated in Article 16(1) of the Women's Convention. Article 16(1) calls upon states parties:

> [T]o take all appropriate measures to eliminate discrimination against women in all matters relating to marriage and family relations and in particular to ensure, on a basis of equality of men and women:
> 1. The same right to enter into marriage.
> 2. The same right to freely choose a spouse and to enter into marriage only with their free and full consent.

In this connection, CEDAW's General Recommendation 21 on "Equality in Marriage and Family Relations" on Article 16(1)(a) and (b) of the Women's Convention is very significant. It observes:

> A woman's right to choose a spouse and enter freely into marriage is central to life and to her dignity and equality as a human being. An examination of States Parties' reports discloses that there are countries which, on the basis of custom, religious beliefs or the ethnic origins of particular groups of people, permit forced marriages or remarriages. ... Subject to reasonable restrictions based for example on a woman's youth or consanguinity with her partner, a woman's right to choose when, if, and whom she will marry must be protected and enforced at law.[46]

Even before the Women's Convention, ICCPR and ICESCR emphasized the free consent of the parties to a marriage. Article 23 of ICCPR states:

3. No marriage shall be entered without the free and full consent of the intending spouses.

4. States parties to the present Covenant shall take appropriate steps to ensure equality of rights and responsibilities of spouses as to marriage, during marriage.

Article 10(1) of ICESCR also reiterates that marriage must be entered into with free consent of the intending spouses.

Thus, all three conventions specifically guarantee to men and women the equal right to enter into marriage with free and full consent. Child marriage violates this right. Free consent is not only the one that is without force or coercion. But it has a positive element in it. It has to be an informed consent exercised with free will and determinism. To exercise the free, full and informed consent for entering into a marriage, a person needs to have physical and mental capability to understand the meaning and responsibility of marriage. A person has to have proper information about the other spouse, the pros and cons of proposed marriage and its repercussions on the future life. A person needs to be in an open environment with proper opportunity to express her will. Obviously, as a 'child', she lacks such understanding due to her underdeveloped physical and mental capacity. And, even if she has such understanding, the parents do not assign importance to it and ignore her evolving capacities.[47]

HRC, in its General Comment 28 on the Equality of Rights between Men and Women, mentioned that:

> States are required to treat men and women equally in regard to marriage in accordance with Article 23... Men and women have the right to enter into marriage only with their free and full consent, and States have an obligation to protect the enjoyment of this right on equal basis. *Many factors may prevent women from being able to take the decision to marry freely.* One factor relates to the minimum age for marriage. That age should be set by the State on the basis of equal criteria for men and women. These criteria should ensure women's capacity to make an informed and uncoerced decision. A second factor is in some States may be that either by statutory or customary law a guardian, who is generally male, consents to the marriage instead of the woman herself, thereby preventing women from exercising a free choice.[48]

HRC though this comment has responded to the realities of life that prevent women from taking freely the decision about their marriage. There are many factors, such as young age, economic dependence and powerlessness, which do not allow women to exercise the decision about marrying freely. Elder men in the family many a time do take the decision about their marriage on their behalf. Marriage being a state sanctioned institution, there is an obligation on states parties to ensure that men and women are treated equally in regard to marriage by taking appropriate measures. HRC has reiterated this obligation of states parties by taking cognizance of women's experiences.

One of the legal ways to assure a bride's free and full consent to the marriage against her is to make the registration of marriage compulsory. Registration of marriage is certainly a critical issue because it offers a point at which states can be involved in preventing discrimination in marriage against women. States can pass a law by which a marriage should be allowed to register only when the condition regarding the age and consent of the parties is fulfilled. Otherwise, such marriage should have no legal effect.

### *Right to non-discrimination on ground of age*

There are adverse consequences on the health, education, development and status of young girls because of child marriage. Girls are far more likely than boys to be married early and to much older men than of their age. Culturally, it is expected that man should be older than his wife, and in many countries this practice is supported by the law. Not only are that the young girls affected disproportionately but the practice of child marriage also has consequences for them that it does not have for boys when they are married at much younger age as compared to boys.

There is no provision in CRC, which specifically bans the practice of child marriage. However, Article 2.2 of the Children's Convention places a duty upon states parties:

> [T]o take all appropriate measures to ensure that child is protected against *all forms of discrimination* or punishment on the basis of the status, activities, expressed opinions, or beliefs of the child's parents against, legal guardians or family members. (emphasis added)

All forms of discrimination would mean discrimination on the basis of age also. When young girls are given in marriage, they are discriminated on the basis of age against the older boys in which case the discrimination is compounded by sex. States parties are required to take legal as well as extra-legal steps to protect young girls from such discrimination.

One of the legal ways to assure non-discrimination on the ground of age is to pass legislation that prescribes the same minimum age of marriage for both the parties and for the compulsory registration of marriage. Unless the condition regarding the age is complied with a marriage should not be registered, and in the absence of the registration the marriage should have no legal effect.

## Intersectionality of sex, age and gender discrimination

The above discussion points out that young girls are discriminated on the basis of age, sex, as well as gender. Women are discriminated on the basis of sex and gender in marital relations, but the young girls are further discriminated on the basis of their age. Intersectionality of these three grounds discriminates against girl children qualitatively as well as quantitatively.[49] Such discrimination is additionally compounded by cultural and traditional justifications and is supported by the patriarchal social system.[50] That is the reason behind its securing legitimacy and continuation in spite of international efforts to denounce it. As emphasized by Crenshaw, there is a need to demarginalize the intersection of age, sex and gender that will help preclude child marriage of young girls.[51]

No social group has suffered greater violation of its human rights in the name of culture than women. A cultural explanation of the gendered social practice of child marriage has to be challenged by asking the woman question. Only when women are kept at the centre of the discussion can the gender complexity of the cultural argument be exposed.[52] Articles 2(f) and 5(a) of the Women's Convention are premised on the notion that, where cultural constructs of gender are an obstacle to the achievement of woman's equality, it is the cultural practice that has to give way. Woman's rights are not to be sacrificed in situations where their realization requires modifying social and cultural patterns of behaviour.[53] Women's experiences in fact need to be reflected while defining the cultural norms.

In 1993 the Vienna Conference declared that the human rights of women should form an integral part of the United Nations human rights activities.[54] In 1995, the Fourth World Conference on Women succeeded in bringing about a new international commitment to the goals of equality and development for all women everywhere, and moved the global agenda for the advancement of women into the 21st century. The Beijing Declaration and the Platform for Action adopted unanimously by representatives from 189 states, a powerful agenda for women's empowerment and gender equality. It spelt out twelve critical areas of concern.[55] The Beijing Platform for Action defined a set of strategic objectives and spelled out actions to be taken by governments, the international community, non-governmental organizations and the private sector for the removal of the existing obstacles to women's advancement. The girl child was one of the special categories to which the Beijing Platform for Action paid attention. Governments, through their commitments, recognized at Beijing that the human rights of the girl child are an inalienable, integral and indivisible part of universal human rights, must be promoted, protected and recognized at all stages of the life cycle.

The need to eliminate all forms of sex and gender discrimination against women was an integrative and universal theme in POA[56] and PLA.[57] Both the documents urged the states "to eliminate all forms of discrimination against the girl child and the root causes of son preference, which result in harmful and unethical practices." The countries which have endorsed POA and PLA and the states parties that have ratified the Women's and Children's Convention are thus duty bound to address these issues for the protection of the young girls' rights. Governments committed themselves to take the effective steps for mainstreaming of gender that called for the re-examination of society in its entirety and its basic structure of inequality. The focus was, therefore, no longer limited to women and their status in society but was committed to restructuring institutions and political and economic decision-making in society as a whole.

As a follow-up to the Beijing Conference, ECOSOC[58] and the General Assembly[59] requested the Commission on the Status of Women to identify, emerging issues, trends and new approaches to issues affecting the situation of women or the equality between women and men that required urgent consideration. The UN General Assembly then called for a special session to review the progress made during the five years since the Beijing Platform of Action was adopted. The special session was convened under the theme "Women 2000: Gender Equality, Development and Peace for the 21st Century".[60] It provided the opportunity for governments and civil society to share good practices and examine current challenges and obstacles encountered in the implementation of the Beijing Platform for Action.

Governments and the international community once again reaffirmed their commitment to the Platform for Action and a common development agenda with gender equality as an underlying principle. They recognized that the efforts towards ensuring women's advancement needed to combine a focus on women's conditions and basic needs with a holistic approach based on equal rights and partnerships, promotion and protection of all human rights and fundamental freedoms. There is a clear endorsement to women's experience. Certain areas, such as education, social services and health, including sexual and reproductive health, and violence against women and girls, were identified as requiring the focused attention. Thus, in pursuance of the Beijing +5, a binding commitment has been taken up by the countries. Considering the major focus areas that were identified by Beijing +5, one could see that child marriage is certainly a priority issue. One needs to see how the governments are going to respond in practice.

Therefore, at the cost of repetition, it is necessary to mention that compulsory registration of marriage is the best solution to reduce the severity of intersectionality of various grounds of discrimination against the girl child that is caused due to child marriage. The countries, which have ratified the above-mentioned international human rights conventions, particularly the Women's Convention, are duty-bound to enact legislation that stipulates the minimum age of marriage, free consent of girls, and compulsory registration of marriage. Such legislation has to declare that non-compliance with any one of the three conditions would make the marriage void.

### Right to equality: India's obligation

The Indian Constitution provides the right to equality as a fundamental right to all citizens. Article 14 of the Constitution states:

> The State shall not deny to any person equality before law or the equal protection of the laws within the territory of India.

Article 15 speaks about prohibition of discrimination. It reads as:

The state shall not discriminate against any citizen on grounds only of religion, race, caste, sex, place of birth, or any of them.... Nothing in this Article shall prevent the state from making any special provision for women and children.

However, it is one thing to guarantee equality in the Constitution and another thing to make it a social reality. Indian tradition and culture are so male-dominated that even after 60 years of the Constitution, women generally experience inequality throughout their lives. Child marriage is one such example where girl children face discrimination through the legislation as well as cultural and traditional practices. Once the girl is given in child marriage, she is denied an equal opportunity, like her counterpart, to education and further development. Additionally, she is likely to face problems regarding her mental and physical well-being, including her reproductive health. Thus, her marriage at young age discriminates against her in all possible ways and takes away her right to equality. Legitimacy to the practice of child marriage is the clear indication of denial of recognition of her experiences. Therefore, a cultural explanation of gendered social practice of child marriage has to be challenged by applying the woman's question. Only when women are kept at the centre of the discussion that the gender complexity of the cultural argument could be exposed.

India has a legislation – Child Marriage Restraint Act (CMRA) – that specifies the different minimum age for marriage – 18 years for a girl and 21 years for a boy, which in itself is discriminatory on the basis of sex. Thereby it violates the young girls' right to formal equality assured by Article 14 of the

Indian Constitution and discriminates on the ground of sex. CMRA does not provide for the registration of marriages nor does it require the free consent of the parties to a marriage. In the absence of such provisions, it is difficult to ascertain whether the girls are able to take freely the decision about their marriage. Apart from CMRA, the other existing marriage laws, based on religion, do not mention about the consent of the parties to a marriage and do not provide for the compulsory registration of marriages.[61] In the absence of such provisions in CMRA or in personal laws, it is difficult to ascertain the exact percentage of child marriages and further difficult to control such marriages.

Apart from the constitutional provisions and domestic legislation on the minimum age of marriage, India has ratified ICCPR and ICESCR and particularly the Women's Convention and Children's Convention and is, therefore, duty-bound to protect the right of girl children to non-discrimination on the grounds of sex, gender and age. Marriage is the matter that falls within the purview of religion-based personal laws in India and all these personal laws discriminate against women on the basis of sex as well as religion. India has filed a declaration to Article 16 of the Women's Convention.[62] The declaration reads as:

> With regard to Articles 5 (a) and 16 (1) of the Convention on the Elimination of All Forms of Discrimination against Women, the Government of the Republic of India declares that it shall abide by and ensure these provisions in conformity with its policy of non-interference in the personal affairs of any community without its initiative and consent.[63]

India has thereby excused herself from not eliminating the discrimination based on sex, gender and religion in the field of personal laws.

Analysis from the feminist perspective of CMRA, personal laws of marriage, and Indian government's position vis-à-vis the international human rights instruments substantiate an argument that the government is not prepared to review its laws and the practices that are derogatory to women in the name of culture and religion. The practice of son preference, differential treatment between her and her brother, neglect of her health, education, overall inferior status in the family, and undue concern about her sexuality are some of the important reasons for child marriage. The state has not valued these experiences of women and hence has not initiated effective measures, including legal, to change the attitude of people, though child marriages of the young girls are taking place on large scale and are adversely affecting their future lives.

India filed an initial report before CEDAW,[64] which was considered in January 2000.[65] The Government of India did not make any direct reference in its report to the issue of child marriage. CEDAW also did not raise the issue of child marriage directly, however, it commented in its concluding observations on the religion-based personal laws and sexual discrimination. However, CEDAW raised a question in this context and enquired about the steps taken by the Indian government to adopt a gender-just uniform civil code.[66] The reply was given by the government that the policy of the government was of non-interference in the matters of personal laws and would continue the same unless the initiative for changes comes from the respective communities to change the laws.[67] CEDAW commented:

> The Committee notes that steps have not been taken to reform the personal laws of different religious and ethnic groups in consultation with them so as to conform with the Convention. The Committee is concerned that the Government's policy of non-intervention perpetuates sexual stereotypes, son preferences and discrimination against women.[68]

CEDAW also expressed its concern about the declaration entered to Article 16 (1) of the Women's Convention by India. CEDAW commented:

> The Committee urges the Government to withdraw its declaration to Article 16(1) of the Convention and to work with and support of women's groups as members of the Community in reviewing and reforming these personal laws. The committee also calls upon the Government to follow the directive principles in the Constitution and Supreme Court decisions and enact a uniform civil code.[69]

India has also filed a declaration regarding registration of marriage provided in Article 16(2) that provides for the compulsory registration of marriages.[70] The declaration states:

> With regard to Article 16 (2) of the Convention on the Elimination of All Forms of Discrimination against Women, the Government of the Republic of India declares that though in principle it fully supports the principle of compulsory registration of marriages, it is not practical in a vast country like India with its variety of customs, religions and level of literacy.[71]

The declaration is worded in such a way that there is no commitment to change the situation in future.

The National Commission for Women, in its 1994 Marriage Bill, recommended to the government that registration of marriages should be made compulsory to prevent child marriages. CEDAW expressed its concern about the registration of marriages in the following words:

> India has not yet established a comprehensive and compulsory system of registration of births and marriages. The Committee notes that inability to prove those important events by documentation on trafficking, child labour and *forced or early marriage*.[72] The Committee calls upon the Government to provide adequate resources and establish a system of compulsory registration of births and monitor implementation in co-operation with women's groups and local bodies. It urges the Government to withdraw the reservation to Article 16(2) of the Convention.[73]

CEDAW also referred to the Marriage Bill drafted by the National, Commission for Women in 1994 and called upon the government to strengthen law enforcement and introduce reforms proposed by the National Commission for Women.[74] The Marriage Bill has declared child marriage void. In the light of these comments, India is obligated as a matter of international human rights law to make the registration of marriages compulsory. Reservations or declarations to any of the international treaties are not supposed to be incompatible with the object and purpose of the Conventions.[75] The declaration filed by India to Article 16(1) is the best illustration of such incompatibility.

HRC in its General Comment 24 on issues relating to reservations or declarations made upon ratification has mentioned in clear terms that:

> The Covenant consists not just of the specified rights, but of important supportive guarantees. These guarantees provide the necessary framework for securing the rights in the Covenant and are thus essential to its object and purpose. Reservations designed to remove these guarantees are thus *not acceptable*.[76]

It further stated that:

> Domestic laws may need to be altered properly to reflect the requirements of the Covenant; and mechanisms at the domestic level will be needed to allow the Covenant rights to be enforceable at the local level.[77]

Regarding the effect of unacceptability of the reservation, it mentioned that the reservation would generally be severable, in the sense that the Covenant would be operative for the reserving party without the benefit of the reservation.[78] At the end HRC mentioned that states should also ensure that the necessity of maintaining reservations be periodically reviewed and that they be withdrawn at the earliest possible moment.[79]

By implication CEDAW should also judge an incompatibility of any of the reservation or declaration filed by India. India's Declaration is incompatible with the object of Article 16 of the convention, as the religion based personal laws in India do discriminate against women. Further, non-declaration of child marriage as void by not amending the existing laws is against Article 16(2) of the Women's Convention. And, by not providing for the compulsory registration of marriages and excusing from making it so in future by filing the declaration to Article 16 is defeating the object of this article. Even, the language of the declaration is such that there is no possibility of changing the situation in future. India's declaration to Article 16 therefore should be declared as not acceptable by CEDAW. As mentioned by HRC, its effect would be that India would not be able to claim benefit of the declaration and would be responsible to answer to CEDAW.

CEDAW therefore though has touched upon in an indirect manner the issue of child marriages in India, in future it should address the issue more directly to the government. It should declare child marriage as discriminatory harmful cultural practice, should recommend the desired changes in the existing laws, and ask more forcefully to withdraw the reservations by communicating that these are incompatible with the convention and hence unacceptable.

CRC noted in its concluding observations on India's report the persistence of discriminatory social attitudes and harmful traditional practices towards girls, including female infanticide, selective abortions, low school enrolment and high drop-out rates, and early and forced marriages.[80] It expressed its concern about the religion-based personal laws, which perpetuate gender inequality in areas such as marriage, divorce, custody and guardianship of infants, and inheritance prevalent in India.[81] CRC recommended that:

> In accordance with Article 2 of the Convention, the Committee encourages the State party to ensure the enforcement of protective laws. The Committee encourages the State party to continue its efforts to carry out comprehensive public education campaigns to prevent and combat gender discrimination, particularly within the family. To assist in these efforts, political, religious and community leaders should be mobilised to support efforts to eradicate traditional practices and attitudes, which discriminate against girls.[82]

CRC, while expressing its concern about the health of adolescents, commented that:

> The Committee is concerned that the health of adolescents, particularly girls, is neglected, given, for instance, a very high percentage of early marriages, which can have a negative impact on their health. Adolescent suicides, especially among girls ...are serious concerns for the Committee.[83]

It recommended that:

> [T]he State party strengthens the existing National Reproductive and Child Health programme, targeting the most vulnerable groups of the population... The Committee recommends continued allocation of resources to the poorest sections

> of society and continued co-operation with and technical assistance from, *inter alia,* WHO, UNICEF, UNAIDS and civil society.[84]

CRC recommended that India should continue its efforts to carry out extensive campaigns to combat harmful traditional practices, such as *child marriages,* and to inform, sensitize and mobilize the general public opinion on the child's right to physical and mental integrity, and safety from sexual exploitation.[85]

CRC has expressed in its concluding observations its serious concern regarding the high percentage of child marriages of girls prevalent in the country. CRC has clearly mentioned that the practice of child marriage is discriminatory and violates human rights of girl children guaranteed under the Children's Convention. Its recommendations need to be pursued by NGOs, and civil society.

India also participated in the FWCW at Beijing in 1995 and its follow up done in the year 2000 through prepcom and special session – Beijing +5. As mentioned before, the protection of the human rights of girls was approved as one of the twelve critical areas by Beijing and Beijing +5 to be focused on in coming five years. Eradication of child marriage in India therefore certainly needs attention of the government.

International treaty monitoring bodies, particularly CEDAW, CRC and HRC, have taken the cognizance of the gendered conditions that facilitate or enable child marriage from the feminist perspective through the concluding observations and General Recommendations/Comments. India is under obligation to respond to these recommendations. The state needs to prevent child marriages by taking all efforts including the legislative changes. It needs to bring in more flexibility in its policies so as to adopt the feminist thoughts that demand enough space for women's considerations, their interests, experiences and values. Only if such an attitude is adopted by the state, there is a possibility of fulfilment of human rights of the young girls.

## Conclusions

There is a long road from the ideal set forth in international human rights documents to pragmatic reality for realizing the young girls' human rights especially in the context of child marriage. This would require fundamental changes in ideas and patterns of behaviour, as well as the establishment of mechanisms to monitor and enforce the relevant laws. International Conference on Human Rights at Vienna, 1993; on Population and Development at Cairo, 1994; and Fourth World Conference on Women at Beijing, 1995 stand as milestones on the road to women's empowerment and enjoyment of their human rights. Cairo +5 and Beijing +5 meetings have given further momentum to women's empowerment. The goals hereinafter are to develop and refine monitoring and follow-up mechanisms in order to facilitate the long and tedious process of ensuring implementation of women's human rights. Civil society has a critical role to play in the process. The partnership between the government and NGOs is essential for formulation, implementation and evaluation of policies and development objectives and activities. NGOs are important voices of people. Their association and networks provide an effective means of focusing local and national initiatives and addressing social, legal, political and economic developmental concerns. People's participation in the whole process is also extremely significant.

The conclusion is that the legal protection is extremely important for the promotion of rights of any powerless, non-vocal, vulnerable group of society. In case of the adolescents, it is the responsibility of the national and international community to see that the rights of the adolescents are protected, promoted and fulfilled through proper legislation. However, it is equally important to keep in mind that mere passing of any law would not achieve its objectives unless it is meaningfully strengthened by other support mechanisms. Finally, one cannot forget that a strong political will is a condition precedent to succeed in any mission whether at a national level or the global level. And, a meaningful political will could be created only through democratic process and pressures. For which we all need to work relentlessly.

## Notes

1. Rebecca Cook, *et al., Advancing Safe Motherhood Through Human Rights* (Geneva: World Health Organization, 2001), p. 4.
2. Treaties, conventions, covenants are the different term which are used interchangeably.
3. Convention on the Elimination of All Forms of Discrimination against Women, G.A. Res. 34/180, UN GAOR, 34th Session., No. 46 at 193, UN Doc.A/39/45 (1979) (entered into force, September 3 1981) entered into force for India on August 8, 1993.
4. Convention on the Rights of the Child, G.A. Res. 44/25 (XLIV), UN GAOR, 44th Session, Supp. No. 49 at 167, UN Doc. A/44/49 (1989) (entered into force September 1990) entered into force for India on January 11, 1993.
5. International Covenant on Civil and Political Rights, G.A. Res. 2200A (XXI), UN Doc. A/6316 (1966) (entered into force, March 23, 1976) Entered into force for India July 10, 197
6. International Covenant on Economic, Social and Cultural Rights, G.A. Res. 2200A (XXI), (entered into force, March 23, 1976) entered into force for India July 10, 1979. There are also other regional Conventions, viz., The European Convention on Human Rights, The American Convention on Human Rights and The African Charter on Human and People's Rights. These are not discussed in the thesis as the focus of the thesis is on India.
7. Convention on Consent to Marriage, Minimum Age for Marriage and Registration of Marriages, G.A. Res. 1763 A (XVII), (1956) (entered into force, December 9, 1964). India has not ratified it.
8. Supplementary Convention on the Abolition of Slavery, the Slave Trade, and Institutions and Practices, Similar to Slavery, G.A. Res. 608 (XXI) (1956) (entered into force April 30, 1957) India has ratified it on June 23, 1960.
9. United Nations, International Human Rights Instruments, Compilation of General Comments and General Recommendations Adopted by Human Rights Treaty Bodies, HRI/Gen/1/Rev. 2, 29 March 1996.
10. Andrew Byrnes, "Enforcement Through International Law and Procedure" in Rebecca Cook (ed.), *Human Rights of Women* (Philadelphia: University of Pennsylvania, 1994), p. 195.
11. The UN General Assembly Resolution A/54/4 on 6th October 1999, has entered into force on 22nd December 2000.

12. For instance, under Article 8 of the Optional Protocol to the Women's Convention States Parties are required to submit their observations to CEDAW. However, normally it is expected that States Parties will be inclined to follow the recommendations, comments, of the Committee. See Torkel Opsahl, "The Human Rights Committee" in Philip Alston (ed.), *The United Nations and Human Rights: A Critical Appraisal* (Oxford: Clarendon Press, 1992), p. 431.
13. There are other mechanisms such as the Communication procedure of the Commission on the Status of Women and ECOSOC Resolution 1503 intended to receive information on the human rights situation in individual countries. However, both are little known and therefore little used. See Byrnes, supra note at p. 205. The third important mechanism adopted is of the thematic Special Rapporteur who is appointed by the Commission on Human Rights.
14. R. Pound, *Social Control Through Law* (London: Oxford University Press, 1942), p. 25.
15. Kamminga, *Inter-State Accountability for Violations of Human Rights* (Philadelphia: University of Pennsylvania Press, 1992), p. 486.
16. Rebecca Cook, "State Accountability under the Convention on the Elimination of Discrimination against Women" in Cook (ed.), *supra note*, p. 228 (238).
17. Maastrict Guidelines on Violation of Economic, Social and Cultural Rights. See also Rebecca Cook and Fathalla, M.F., "Duties to Implement Reproductive Rights" (1998) 67, *Nordic Journal of International Law*, p. 1.
18. Except the Marriage Convention.
19. See generally, International Planned Parenthood Federation, *Charter on Sexual and Reproductive Rights* (1995).
20. Louis Henkin, "Where are we going from here?" in Martin (ed.), *International Human Rights Law and Practice: Cases, Treaties and Materials*, pp. 21–23 (Cambridge: Kluwer Law International, 1997).
21. UN Charter, Article 1, see also Article 55(c).
22. Article 2 of the Universal Declaration, Article 2.2 of ICESCR, Article 2.1 of ICCPR.
23. We the peoples of the United Nations determined to save succeeding generations from the scourge of war..., and to reaffirm faith in the fundamental human rights, in the dignity and worth of the human person, in the equal rights of men and women and of nations of large and small ... have resolved to combine our efforts to accomplish these aims ...
24. Articles 1 to 5 of the Women's Convention.

25. Article 2.1.
26. Article 2.2 right to non-discrimination on the ground of other status such as age.
27. See generally, Anne Bayefsky, "The Principle of Equality or Non-discrimination in International Law" (1990) 11, *Human Rights Law Journal*, p. 1.
28. See, Ian Brownlie, *System of Nations: State Responsibility* (Oxford: Clarendon Press, 1983), p. 81.
29. Articles 2 and 3 of the Women's Convention.
30. Rebecca Cook, "International Protection of Women's Reproductive Rights" (1992) 24 *New York University Journal of International Law and Politics* 645, pp. 678–79.
31. Ibid.
32. Ibid.
33. The Human Rights Committee has explained the prohibition of discrimination in ICCPR to have essentially the same meaning. Human Rights Committee, General Comment 28 para 2, 5, 7 – HRC, General Comment 28, UN GAOR 2000, UN Doc. A/55/40, Annex. VI, p. 133.
34. T. K. Sundari Ravindran, "Engendering Health" (2000) 489, *Seminar*, p. 34.
35. See Rebecca Cook, *Women's Health and Human Rights*, (Geneva: WHO, 1994), pp. 19–20.
36. Article 2(e).
37. See Kathleen Mahony, "Canadian Approaches to Equality Rights and Gender Equality in the Courts" in Cook, supra note at p. 437 (442).
38. Ratna Kapur and Brenda Cossman, "Women, Familial Ideology and the Constitution" in Ratna Kapur (ed.), *Feminist Terrains in Legal Domains* (New Delhi: Kali for Women, 1996), pp. 61–64.
39. Beijing Platform for Action, Report of the Fourth World Conference on Women, Beijing, September 1995, UN Doc A/CONF.177/20 (1995) at 112, para 259; M. Mukhopadhyay and Sliver Shackles, *Women and Development in India* (Oxford: Oxfam, 1984), p. 11.
40. Ibid., Mukhopadhyay, pp. 11–12.
41. Malini Karkal and Irudaya Rajan, "Age at Marriage: How Much Change" (1989) 24, *Economic and Political Weekly*, p. 505.
42. Michael Koeing, "Patriarchy, Women's Status and Reproductive Behaviour in Rural North India" (1992) 21 *Demography India* 145, See

Report of the Special Rapporteur on Violence against Women submitted in January 2002, E/CN.4/2002/83, para 103.

43. See Purnima Mane, "Socialisation of Indian Women in their Childhood: An Analysis of Literature" (1991) 52 *Indian Journal of Social Work* 81.
44. Article 2 (f).
45. Article 5(a), (emphasis added).
46. CEDAW, *General Recommendation 21*, UN GAOR, 1994, Doc. No. A/47/38 para 16.
47. See Article 5 of the Children's Convention.
48. HRC, General Comment 28, UN GAOR 2000, UN Doc. A/55/40, Annex VI, 133, para 23, (emphasis added).
49. See Kimberlé Crenshaw, "Demarginalizing the Intersection of Race and Sex: A Black Feminist Critique of Antidiscrimination Doctrine, Feminist Theory and Antiracist Politics" (1989) *University of Chicago Legal Forum* 139 and also Kimberlé Crenshaw, "Mapping the Margins: Intersectionality, Identity Politics and Violence against Women of Colour" (1991) 43 *Stanford Law Review* 1241; Colleen Sheppard, "Grounds of Discrimination: Towards an Inclusive and Contextual Approach" (2001) 80 *The Canadian Bar* 893.
50. M. Eaton, "Patently Confused: Complex Inequality and Canada v. A.G. Canada" (1994) 1 *Rev. of Constitutional Studies* 203 at 231.
51. Crenshaw, supra note at 151.
52. Arati Rao, "Politics of Gender and Culture in International Human Rights" in Peters, supra note at 169.
53. Ann Elizabeth Mayer, "Cultural Particularism as a bar to Women's Rights: Reflections on the Middle Eastern Experience" in Peters, supra note at 176 (179).
54. GENERAL A/CONF.157/23 at I–1.
55. Some of the most relevant areas were: education; social services and health; including sexual and reproductive health; the HIV/AIDS pandemic; violence against women and girls; the persistent and increasing burden of poverty on women; vulnerability of migrant women including exploitation and trafficking; the development of strong, effective and accessible national machineries for the advancement of women; and the formulation of strategies to enable women and men to reconcile and share equally work and family responsibilities.
56. Para 4.16, 4.25.
57. Para 97, 277.

58. E/1996/6.
59. A/Res/52/231.
60. A/55/341 It was held in New York, 5–9 June 2000.
61. Except the Muslim personal law.
62. *UN Treaty Collection: Treaty Reference Guide.* It gives Definitions of Terms used in the UN treaty Collection. (www.untreaty.un.org/English/guide.asp). The term "declaration" is used for various international instruments. However, declarations are not always legally binding. The term is often deliberately chosen to indicate that the parties do not intend to create binding obligations but merely want to declare certain aspirations.
63. Declaration of India to the Women's Convention.
64. CEDAW/C/IND/1.
65. CEDAW/C/SR/452, 453 and 462.
66. CEDAW, 22nd Session, Jan 2000, *Response to Questions on India's First Report on CEDAW,* (Permanent Mission of India to the UN, New York, 2000) (Hereinafter Response GOI) Question No. 68, at 34.
67. Ibid., at 36.
68. CEDAW/C/2000/1/CRP.3/Add.4/Rev.1, 1 February 2000, para 31.
69. Ibid., para 32.
70. It is interesting to note that at the drafting stage on the Women's Convention India supported the principle of the registration of marriages. Lars Adam Rehof, *Guide to the Travaux Préparatoires of the United Nations Convention on the Elimination of All Forms of Discrimination against Women* (The Netherlands: Martinus Nijhoff Publisher, 1993) at 184.
71. Declaration of India to Article 16.
72. CEDAW/C/2000/1/CRP.3/Add.4/Rev.1, 1 Feb 2000, para 33; emphasis added.
73. Ibid., para 34; emphasis added.
74. CEDAW/C/2000/1/CRP.3/Add.4/Rev.1, 1 February 2000, para 30.
75. Article 19(3) of the Vienna Convention on the Law of Treaties. It stipulates that where a reservation is not prohibited by the treaty or falls within the specified permitted categories. A state may make a reservation provided it is not incompatible with the object and purpose of the treaty.
76. HRI/GEN/1/Rev.2, November 4, 1994, para 11; Emphasis added.
77. Ibid., page 45, para 12.
78. Ibid., page 47, para 18.

89. Ibid., page 48, para 20.
80. Concluding Observations of the Committee on the Rights of the Child: India, 23/02/2000, CRC/C/15/Add.115, para 32; emphasis added.
81. Ibid.
82. Ibid., para 33.
83. Ibid., para 50.
84. Ibid., para 51.
85. Ibid., para 77.

CHAPTER FIVE

# Taking women seriously

## An introspection on law's engagement with the evil of dowry

*Sanjay S. Jain*

I would like to begin my analysis by making a reference to one of the most provocative and yet original works dealing with dowry by Veena Talwar Oldenburg.[1] This book argues that contemporary notion of dowry, which is perceived to be a threat to the dignity of women both by feminists and law makers, was not originally the same. By exploring the historical details she comprehensively negates the charge of the imperialists that dowry is linked with violence against women and owes its origin as understood at present to Indian culture. By making a detailed study of archival documents, she claims to uncover a colonial conspiracy by imperialists, which they effectively hatched to suppress their own economic interests and deliberately linked dowry with female infanticide. As a matter of fact, certain land reforms, ruthless taxing policy to collect revenue, transformation of property rights to provide hegemony to the males and so on, provided an ugly shape to the ancient custom of dowry, which was in good old days perceived to be providing a sort of support to women after their marriage by giving them control over certain portion of property, which is even today as it was in the past recognized by law as 'stridhan'.

In this connection, an observation of Manu is worth citing:"What was given before the nuptial fire, what was given on the bridal procession, what was given in token of love, and what was received from her brother, mother or father, that is called the six-fold property of a woman. Such property, as well as a gift subsequent and what was given to her by her affectionate husband, shall go to her offspring even if she dies in the lifetime of her husband."[2] Thus, Oldenburg has convincingly established beyond all doubts that as a prevalent ancient custom, dowry was never associated with coercive demands on part of the bride-groom or his relatives. It is only after the colonial invasion that our communities at large began to suffer economically bringing under fire all our good old customs including that of dowry.

Many social reformers like Raja Ram Mohan Rai, Ranade, Ishwar Chandar Vidya Sagar and Mahatma Gandhi dedicated their lives to eradication of various social evils, including the evil of dowry.

The result of the social reformers bore fruits to some extent when first of all Sind Leti-Deti Act was passed in the year 1939. This Act prohibited payments in excess of limits specified in the list applicable to the girl's family, which were made either by the respective panchayat or in case of their failure by the provincial governments. When these lists were registered and published, these were binding upon every member of the respective panchayats and violation of which was made punishable.[3] After the independence there were two states, Bihar[4] and Andhra Pradesh[5] which passed Dowry Prohibition Act in their respective states and ultimately the present Act was passed in 1961 and was made applicable throughout India except the state of Jammu & Kashmir.

On this background, we now turn to discuss and critically analyze anti-dowry legislation.

## I

### Brief outline of anti-dowry legislation

In order to critically examine and analyze anti-dowry legislation, we would first outline in condensed form the legal norms instituted to combat the taking, giving, demanding dowry.

To tackle the social evil of dowry, legislature has responded in two distinct ways. It first enacted Dowry Prohibition Act, 1961 and then during the later 80s promptly responded to the anti-dowry campaign launched by women's movement, by incorporating a number of provisions in IPC,[6] CrPC[7] and Indian Evidence Act.[8]

Being the welfare legislation, it is applicable to all the citizens of India baring the state of J&K. While section 2 of the Act defines the term "dowry" as any property or valuable security given in connection with a marriage, section 3 thereof makes giving or taking of dowry and the abetment of the same as a punishable offence. Section 4 provides penalty for demanding dowry and section 4–A bans advertisements on matrimonial, based on the ground of dowry. Section 5 makes void an agreement for giving and taking the dowry, and section 6 contemplates a legal obligation on the person who actually receives the dowry to transfer the same to the women in whose marriage it is given or to her children, heirs or parents as the case may be, in the event of her death. Sections 7 and 8 provide provision as to the cognizance of offence. Section 8–A provides provision as to the burden of proof in certain cases and section 8–B provides for the appointment and powers and functions of the Dowry Prohibition Officers. Sections 9 and 10 empower respectively the central as well as the state governments to make rules.

Having outlined the basic provisions, we will now critically analyze some of the important aspects of this law.

### *Problematic definition of dowry*

As per the Dowry Prohibition Act (originally passed in 1961 and amended three times in the 1980s), dowry is defined as "any property or valuable security given or agreed to be given either directly or indirectly by one party to a marriage to the other party to the marriage or by the parents of either party to a marriage or by any other person, to either party to the marriage or to any other person at or before [or any other time after the marriage] in connection with the marriage of the said parties."[9]

As per section 3 (2) sub-clauses a and b of the Act, dowry is forbidden but gifts are allowed. The Act cannot be invoked against the giving and taking of presents at the time of marriage by the bride and bridegroom without any demand having been made, provided that such presents are entered in a list maintained in accordance with the rules, made under this Act.

The gifts made to the bridegrooms by or on behalf of the bride or any person related to the bride are also legal provided that, such presents are of a customary nature and the value thereof is not excessive, in relation to the financial status of the person by whom, or on whose behalf, such presents are given.[10]

A close look at these provisions would make it clear that language employed in these sections is a sort of cog wave of confusions and contradictions.

The interrelationship between section 2 and section 3 (2) is deeply problematic. The relationship gives rise to a number of troubling and poignant questions, viz., who decides what a voluntary gift is and what is given under pressure of a demand? How do we decide what is excessive in relation to income by way of gifts when in India no more than 1 to 2 per cent people declare their incomes and those too are grossly under reported? How do we judge the paying status of a family if most of their wealth is in black money and property holdings held in bogus names to escape taxes?[11]

Moreover, definition of dowry as contained in section 2 of the Act is extremely deterministic and if read in the light of section 3(2) runs like a straight-jacket formula, and completely overlooks the flipside of the issue.

In most cases, at the time of marriage, a girl's parents will say or at least put up the show that whatever they are giving is out of love for their daughter and, therefore, voluntary. However, as soon as strains develop in the marriage and it reaches a breaking point and the girl's family decides to take legal recourse, the very same gifts of love are termed as dowry items given under pressure or demands from the groom's family.[12] Thus, section 3(2) has the potential to backfire and completely subvert the definition as contained in section 2 of the Act. In our humble opinion, section 2 in its present form has evidently more problems than solutions. It is also to be stated that the definition of dowry as contained in section 2 of the Act in its present form has rather unnecessarily lumped together dowry and bride price.[13] Therefore, it should be replaced by a more functional definition.[14]

### *Constitutionality of section 3(1)*

It may be argued that culpability of bridegroom is justified for taking and demanding dowry on the assumption that he has some role in the marriage negotiations,[15] but what about the culpability of the bride for giving dowry as becomes evident from the language of section 3(1). Whether the proposed bride is legally capable of playing any significant role in the fixing of her own marriage? The answer is of course no.

In our opinion, to the extent of implicating the bride for giving dowry, section 3(1) is arbitrary and is violative of Article 14 of our Constitution. Equally, it is also violative of Article 21 in the sense that punishment meted out to the bride for giving dowry clearly suffers from the voice of being cruel, inhuman and degrading.[16]

Moreover, with respect to other dowry givers also, the law has never been invoked. Where are the dowry givers gone? At least we are not aware of a single reported case, in which section 3(1) has been invoked against the dowry givers. Of course, "dowry can be taken only if it is given and therefore to this extent prosecution agencies are seriously guilty of having grossly underused section 3(1). And, as a matter of fact, their inaction is at odds with section 7(1)".[17]

### *Rules under section 9(2)(a) unefficacious*

Section 3(2) specifically refers to the maintenance of lists of presents by bride and bridegroom and in accordance with section 9 (2) (a) and central government has framed certain rules[18] to the same effect. However, when we look at these rules, we are completely bewildered. The rules even do not go so far as to provide that these lists shall be treated as a piece of evidence before a competent court. How perfunctory the rules are would become crystal clear from the fact that there is utter absence of any attempt to provide any kind of legal sanctity to these lists. Should not there be a provision to provide for attestation on these lists by the competent witnesses? Should not there be a provision for getting these lists registered with the competent authority or the Dowry Prohibition Officer as the case may be? Moreover, there is hardly any mention neither under section 3(2) nor section

9 about the consequences of failure to prepare such lists.[19] In our view, these rules in their present form are merely ornamental in nature and should be suitably amended to incorporate aforementioned suggestions.[20] As a matter of fact, non-maintenance of lists is bound to rob section 3(1) and section 6 off their rigour. How can it be possible to prove dowry taking without their being any lists? Therefore, incorporation of a rebutable presumption under Indian Evidence Act to the effect that "when the question is whether the person has committed the offence of taking dowry under section 3, then, on the basis of lists of presents and gifts as maintained in accordance with rules or in absence of such lists on the basis of the allegation of dowry harassment on the part of the wife or her relatives within seven years of the marriage, if it appears prima facie to be true, then the court shall presume that a person had committed offence under section 3" is the need of the hour.[21]

### *Strengthening of section 4*

Section 4 of the Act, which makes the demand of dowry an offence, must be interpreted broadly and independently of the technical definition of dowry under section 2. Moreover, the section may be suitably amended to clarify that each demand of dowry constitutes a separate offence. In other words, persistent demands must attract the doctrine of continuous offence and the same must be visited with much more stringent punishment. At present, in sharp contrasts to other offences under the Act, offence under section 4 attracts relatively milder punishment.[22]

### *Futility of section 5*

According to section 5 of the Act, any agreement for the giving or taking of dowry shall be void. That is to say, agreement to pay dowry is not a valid consideration so as to affect an otherwise valid marriage. However, the law is not as clear as it should have been and fails to resolve a most pertinent question, as to whether in such a case, the marriage solemnized and consummated upon an agreement, shall also become void under this section?[23] Moreover, it is far from easy or for that matter almost impossible to prove such an agreement. As a result, section 5 becomes inconsequential.

### *Strange features of section 6*

At the top of it all there is section 6, which is yet another interesting and peculiar section,[24] a look at its marginal note says it all, viz., "dowry to be for the benefit of the wife or her heirs."

Before unravelling the inherent contradictions and complications with which it is fraught, we will highlight the wife empowering aspect of this section, i.e., the dowry paid under the Act is construed to be the sole property of the woman in whose marriage it is given whether or not it is given by her parents, husband or parents-in-law or any other person. Thus, according to Paras Diwan, this section has made even extorted dowry into stridhana thereby changing the nature of stridhana which customarily consisted only of voluntarily given gifts.[25]

Moreover, for the purposes of this section, the definition of dowry has specifically been confined to cover only dowry paid on behalf of the wife and in connection with her marriage.[26] Thus, husbands cannot have resorts to this section to seek transfer of bride price to them. By providing so, the section has prevented victimization of wife by way of criminal prosecution.

The section suffers from a number of inherent contradictions:

1. where any dowry is received by any person other than the woman in connection with whose marriage it is given, such a person is simultaneously saddled with two distinct liabilities:[27]
   (i) He is deemed to be the trustee of such a property of the woman till he transfers it back to her (within period of three months from the receipt of it if she is above 18 years and if she is a minor[28] then within three months of her attaining majority).
   (ii) He is also an accused for taking or demanding dowry under sections 3 and 4 of the Act.
2. The only way out for such a person therefore is to deny having ever received any dowry on behalf of any such woman in order to escape the wrath of sections 3 and 4. In our humble opinion, in order to materialize the objective of this section, it becomes imperative that charges under sections 3 and 4 must be dropped against such person[29] and

on the other hand a mechanism must be evolved to ensure that property is transferred to the wife or in case of her death to her children, and in absence of them to the state. The aforesaid suggestion would necessitate fine-tuning and dissecting of section 6.

3. Since under sections 3 and 4, taking, giving and demanding dowry and abetment thereof amount to offences, the proposal of transferring dowry back either to her heirs (which also includes her husband) or to her parents in case she dies within seven years of marriage other than in normal circumstances is against public policy and common sense. On the other hand, if the property is transferred to her children, the dowry would automatically transform into a gift and in absence of them if it is transferred to the state, the state may utilize the same for the welfare of dowry harassed women.
4. Last but not the least, the assumption that state is capable of enforcing the obligations under this section is unrealistic and therefore this section is bound to remain a dead letter in law,[30] till it is suitably amended to incorporate the aforesaid suggestions.

Before concluding the discussion on the Act, it would be most relevant to briefly examine the important question why the Act has not produced desired results.

II

## Basic flaws

Clearly, what was desired by the legislature is prohibition of payment of dowry in certain circumstances and not its complete abolition. Thus, the legislature was not in favour of completely doing away with the practice of offering gifts and presents before, at the time of or even after the marriage by relatives of either party to the marriage so long as such offerings are of voluntary character and of customary nature.[31] To obtain this result, it seriously compromised the definition of dowry by carving out exceptions to it under section 3(2). In our opinion, section 3(2) almost completely destroys the conceptual clarity of the term 'dowry' by making it extremely open-textured and content-independent. Moreover, gender-neutral character of the definition of dowry completely shifts the focus away from the obvious fact that dowry leads to the subordination of women.

Another noteworthy feature of this legislation is its overemphasis on sanctions. Most of the provisions in this Act are framed in the form of what Prof. Joseph Raz[32] terms as "consequentialist rules", i.e., to say non-observance of rules would attract sanction.[33] The Act does not give much importance to other forms of redressal like spreading awareness, mobilizing public opinion, consciousness raising, sensitizing government officials and civil society, etc. As a matter of fact, the legislature appears to be interested in providing earnest legal redressal only in cases of the most aggravated forms of dowry harassment, i.e., dowry deaths.[34] Section 304–B, which is a forerunner of the anti-dowry campaign[35] of late 80s, is said to have reformed dowry law. However, in our opinion, this section does not reflect in any sense the "lived experiences of women during most horrifying circumstances". On the other hand, it certainly reinforces crude technicalities of law, thus, no sooner is it established that diseased wife was not subjected to dowry harassment "soon before her death" than the culprits are out of the purview of this section, and easily get away with less severe penalty under section 498–A. However, story does not end here; defence lawyers do not hesitate to attribute the act of suicide to a diseased wife on the ground of lack of evidence against their clients. Can it not be argued that, by attributing act of suicide to the diseased wife merely because there is no evidence against their clients, they are attributing to her waiver of fundamental right to life and personal liberty guaranteed by Article 21 of our Constitution.[36]

There is yet another crucial point. Often distinction between dowry harassment and domestic violence is played down and it is collapsed into a deterministic doctrine,[37] "dowry harassment alone amounts to domestic violence."[38] Whether dowry harassment is the only reason for domestic violence? What about the less serious forms of dowry harassment? Why the legislature is not interested to address this issue in its lesser proportions? If the effective interventions are made at the initial stage itself (during the lifetime of the dowry harassed wife), situations would not turn from bad to worse. Is there not a need to educate the parents to throw their support around their daughters during their lifetime (i.e., to say when they complain of dowry harassment of less serious form) rather than giving more importance to prosecution of bride-burners or dowry-murderers? The Act does not have any mechanism to enable or empower dowry-harassed wives to take effective action against their in-laws and husbands. Obviously, by sending their husbands or in-laws to jails, they would only attract wrath and anger of the community and would further isolate themselves even from their own family members and thereby, would be vulnerable to more abuse. There should be a provision to ensure protection to dowry-harassed wives during the pendency of the cases.[39]

In our opinion, ward members or corporators[40] must be identified as important players to monitor earnest implementation of this law. Being placed on the bottom of the decision-making process, they may coordinate with police and the prosecution machinery to take cognizance of unreported cases of dowry harassment. For this purpose, an obligation may be cast upon them to carry out surveys of their respective wards from time to time so as to collect information about:

1. number of marriages taken place in a particular period;
2. whether the gifts and presents offered during the marriages are properly listed in accordance with Dowry Prohibition (Maintenance of List of Presents to Bride and Bridegroom) Rules, 1985;
3. whether any bride returned from the "mandap"[41] of marriage under protest owing to demand of dowry; and
4. whether newly married women are suffering from dowry harassment.

It is equally important to impose mandatory obligations on every member of civil society to give information about the commission or the likelihood of the commission of dowry-related offences to the nearest magistrate or police officer.[42]

In short, what is required is a comprehensive and multidimensional dowry prohibition programme,[43] and in order to make this programme result-oriented in every district dowry prohibition authority must be established and it should be assigned the tasks of evolving institutional mechanisms and personnel development to combat this deeply rooted evil. At the same time, economic empowerment of women by way of improving their inheritance rights must also be viewed as first and foremost urgency.[44] It would go a long way in improving the record of Dowry Prohibition Act, if we shift our focus away from sanctions to awareness, agitation, empowerment and education.

III

## Role of judiciary

Having briefly analyzed the provisions of the Dowry Prohibition Act, 1961, and pointed out some of the basic flaws in the existing legal regime and having provided some constructive suggestions, we will now briefly examine the role of judiciary in combating dowry harassment. It is beyond the scope of this paper to provide a detailed narrative[45] and hence, the discussion is confined to a recent judgment of the Supreme Court on this issue.

Recently, the Supreme Court has responded to a PIL[46] for the effective implementation of the Dowry Prohibition Act, 1961. The writ petition was filed on 31 July 1997. The main prayers were for the issue of writs of mandamus directing the Central Government to frame rules under section 9 of the Act, directing the State Governments to frame rules under section 10 of the Act and providing for additional functions to be performed by the concerned officers under section 8–B of the Act, for appointment of Dowry Prohibition Officers by states as required under section 8–B; to furnish details regarding the working of Dowry Prohibition Officers wherever they have been appointed; for setting up of Advisory Boards as mandated by section 8–B of the Act; and to furnish details of the composition of the Boards and their working, if the Boards have already been established in any particular state and for other incidental reliefs to make the working of the Act more effective.[47]

In response to the aforesaid, various interim directions were issued from time to time by the apex court.

In the context of the developments that have taken place, it is submitted by the amicus curiae appointed by this court during the final hearing of the petition that no serious effort has been made to implement the provisions of the Act and the rules and unless directions are issued by this court it is highly unlikely that the provisions of the Act and the rules will be effectively implemented. It is, therefore, submitted that this court may direct the Central Government and the State Governments to give wide publicity to the relevant provisions of the Dowry Prohibition Act, 1961 and Rules 2 and 3 of the Dowry Prohibition (Maintenance of Lists of Presents to the Bride and Bridegroom) Rules, 1985 by appropriate means including educating the student community about the relevant provisions and the mandatory requirements of the Act and the rules. It is further submitted that the State Governments may be directed to appoint sufficient number of Dowry Prohibition Officers with independent charge in each district of the concerned state, commensurate with the population of the district and to ensure that only dedicated and sincere officers are so appointed. It is submitted that directions may be issued to the Dowry Prohibition Officers to take immediate steps for strict enforcement and implementation of the provisions of Sections 3, 4, 4A and 6 of the Dowry Prohibition Act, 1961 and Rules 2 and 3 of the Dowry Prohibition (Maintenance of Lists of Presents to the Bride and Bridegroom) Rules, 1985.

Learned counsel also submits that the Central and State Governments may be directed to file compliance reports in this court. One of the serious aspects pointed out is that the Central Government has not yet framed the rules under Section 9(2)(b) of the Dowry Prohibition Act, 1961 and a direction may be issued to the Central Government to frame the necessary rules. It is also submitted that a direction may be issued to the government to consider bringing in legislation irrespective of caste or creed making it compulsory to register marriages and furnish the list of gifts as contemplated by the Act and the rules. Learned counsel also submits that regarding seekers of government employment information may be sought for from them whether one had taken any dowry at the time of his marriage and whether he had filed a declaration as contemplated by the Act, and if he has taken dowry, whether he has transferred it to its wife or her heirs as required by Section 6 of the Act. Such declarations should be sought for even from those who are already employed. Learned amicus curiae submits that unless time-bound directions are issued by this court, the implementation of the Act and the rules, and the consequent rooting out of the evil, will remain as tardy as it has been for more than 46 years. The legislation will remain a mirage.

On the other hand, learned counsel for Union and the State Governments assures that every step will be taken by the governments for implementation of the Act and the rules and further steps will be devised for making the Act more effective and the Dowry Prohibition Officers more active with a view to eradicate the evil.

Taking note of the compliance of the various directions, the Supreme Court observes: "In view of the directions thus issued, almost all the States have framed rules under the Act. Most of them have adopted the model rules. The Dowry Prohibition Officers have been appointed by almost all the States."

However, taking a very strong exception to the promising attitude of the state, the Supreme Court observes: "In view of the fact that even today, none of the respondents is in a position to tell us that the evil has been eradicated or brought down in any part of the country. It is also seen that directions have to be issued even to frame rules and even today rules as contemplated by Section 9(2)(b) of the Act have not been framed."[48]

According to the Supreme Court, mere assurances without zeal would not help to effectively implement the Dowry Prohibition Act. It also takes judicial notice of alarming rights in the dowry death cases and having expressed its utter disappointment about the performance of the government in the implementation of the Dowry Prohibition Act, it assumes the role of an activist and observes: "When there is failure on the part of the Executive to strictly implement a law like the one in question, enacted to tackle a social problem which has assumed menacing proportions, the Court has a duty to step in with a mandamus to direct its implementation rigorously and effectively."[49]

Accordingly, the Supreme Court finds it mandatory "to step in and issue some more directions to the respondents in addition to incorporating the directions already issued by this Court by way of interim measure as part of this final judgment."[50]

Thus, the Union of India and the states are directed to:

1. take more effective steps to implement the provisions of the Dowry Prohibition Act, 1961 with particular reference to Sections 3 and 4 thereof and the various rules framed thereunder.
2. activate the Dowry Prohibition Officers;
3. take steps to ensure that submitting of the list as contemplated by the Act and the rules is strictly implemented;
4. consider whether appropriate rules cannot be framed for compelling males, seeking government employment, to furnish information on whether they had taken dowry and if taken, whether the same has been made over to the wife as contemplated by Section 6 of the Act, calling for such information also from those already in employment;[51]
5. take steps for the effective stepping up of anti-dowry literacy among the people through Lok Adalats, radio broadcasts, television and newspapers so as to arouse the conscience of the people against the demand and acceptance of dowry; and
6. devise means to create honest, efficient and committed machinery for the purpose of implementation of the Dowry Prohibition Act, 1961 and the various rules framed there under.[52]

Besides, the Central Government has been directed to frame rules under Section 9(2)(b) of the Act if it has not done so.

In the course of this judgment, the Supreme Court also recognizes the limitations of legal strategies and emphasizes the complementary role of the civil society in bringing social transformation. The court observes: "Possibly, a social revolution is needed to put an end to the menace. Refusal by the bride's father to pay dowry, refusal of the girls to get married if dowry is insisted upon and the attaching of a social stigma to those who demand dowry, can alone ultimately put an end to this system or at least reduce its prevalence."[53]

Clearly, the Supreme Court is emphasizing upon the method of consciousness rising as an effective instrument along with the institution of law to eradicate the "social evil of dowry". The apex court also emphasizes on the proactive role of young women and men in this context. It observes: "We have no doubt that our young and enlightened women would rise to the occasion to fight the evil which tends to make them articles of commerce. We also hope that our educated young males would refuse to be sold in the marriage market and come forward to choose their partners in life in a fair manner."[54]

Having noted this judgment in some detail, we will now attempt to provide a bird's eye view of overall judicial attitude towards the problem of dowry harassment.

A careful analysis of the judgment would make it clear that to eradicate social evils like dowry with the institution of law, civil society also has a very important role to play. The Supreme Court has very rightly emphasized on the employment of tool of consciousness-raising along with law to bring social transformation. It is rejoicing to see the court perceiving an empowering role for women as well. However, it is far from easy to seek implementation of direction 4 above. It would have been appropriate to establish a monitoring committee to oversee the implementation of these rather extensive and far-reaching directions. The apex court could have identified a constructive role for National Commission of Women (NCW) in this matter.

### *Bird's eye view of judicial approaches*

Clearly, the Supreme Court and the High Courts have shown sensitivity to the issue by ingenuously interpreting the legal provisions and by way of transforming principles like benefit of doubt, circumstantial evidence, etc.[55]

By interpreting the term 'dowry' in the light of socially prevailing facts, the Supreme Court has also tried to rescue women from dowry harassment in ongoing marriage-like relationships[56] as well. Recognizing the socio-criminal nature of the offence courts have also sought to rely upon a number of provisions of the IPC like sections 201,[57] 405 and 406,[58] and sections 173(8) and 174(3)[59] of the CrPC to enlarge their jurisdiction to arrest the problem of dowry harassment.

Significantly, the Supreme Court has also employed writ jurisdiction under Article 32 to oversee and monitor the implementation of the Dowry Prohibition Act.[60] It has also entertained writ petitions linking dowry harassment with violation of right to human dignity and right to life guaranteed by Article 21.[61] Similarly, the courts have enlarged the rule of *locus standi* to provide adequate leeway to the public-spirited individuals and NGOs to take up this issue by way of PILs. Thus, in these respects, this author would identify new parameters being evolved by the judiciary to tackle the issue.

However, we also have few concerns. Firstly, it appears that even the higher judiciary does not perceive the impact of dowry harassment as vulnerable on the lives of women as that of sexual harassment; whereas the fact remains that the menace of dowry harassment has assumed far more alarming proportions and has left women virtually susceptible to their deaths.

Secondly, the judiciary has also been unable to involve either the Law Commission of India or the National Commission of Women and other related NGOs to institute the process of constant critique and reforms. In this sense, its response is markedly different with regard to the handling of sexual offences against women.[62] Can it be argued that the social nature of the offence of dowry has deprived it of the attention it should have received from the court? Whether sexual offences deserve more attention than the social offences like dowry?

Thirdly, courts have not shown any willingness to identify dowry harassment as a human rights issue and, thereby, have not employed human rights discourse instituted mainly by the CEDAW (Convention on the Elimination of All Forms of Discrimination Against Women) to problematize the social practice of dowry.[63] Can it not be argued that dowry harassment should be perceived as discrimination[64] because it amounts to subordination of women and, thereby, squarely attracts the provisions of CEDAW? – Fourthly, the courts have largely remained skeptical of providing constitutional foundation to the rights of victims of dowry harassment. Can it not be argued inter alia that dowry is a "practice derogatory to the dignity of women" and as such should be renounced?[65]

Fifthly, whether the gender-neutral nature of the offence of dowry is justified? Can it be claimed that women and men are equally vulnerable to dowry harassment? In our opinion, these questions have never been taken up for discussion by the courts. It is the surmise of the author that had this offence been couched in gendered form, it would have been tackled by the courts with far more activism than at present. Its gender-neutral character has clearly shifted the focus away from the crucial fact that dowry subordinates and commoditizes the women. What alone has received focus is the fact that dowry harassment leads to dowry murders, thereby confining the attention to the most aggravated form of the offence and as a result issues like "why dowry is paid or taken or how a woman should combat dowry harassment during her lifetime and whether the state has any role to play in her ongoing struggle, etc.?" have gone unnoticed and undeliberated.

Sixthly, by confining the redressal against dowry harassment to criminal law alone, the courts have not explored the potential of other forms of redressal like civil law, constitutional law, law of torts and human rights law, etc., as transformative tools for women. Thus, the courts have not explored the possibilities of framing remedies so as to rehabilitate the dowry-harassed women. Undue focus on criminal law as a remedy has clearly resulted in extraordinary dependence on the police, which in the absence of effective sensitization training, has been unable to produce desired results.[66]

## Summing up

In spite of having instituted a legal regime to redress and combat the social evil of dowry, the state has not been able to obtain desired results. In our opinion, the law has been found wanting to tackle this issue in a number of respects. Firstly, the law has failed because it has lacked the required complexity to arrest subtleties of a deeply entrenched and socialized practice of dowry. Secondly, by focussing unduly on punitive dimensions and by failing to provide effective and positive empowering strategies for women, the law converted itself into a paradise of conning lawyers.[67] Thirdly, the anti-dowry campaign, which was launched in early 1980s against the backdrop of dowry deaths and suicides of young married women in suspicious circumstances, indeed was able to mobilize the legislature and got enacted regime of criminal law, but its undue focus on the most aggravated form of dowry harassment, i.e., dowry deaths and lack of any systematic agenda in linking issue of dowry with other vital human rights of women., viz., right to education, right to nutritious food, right to choose one own partner in marriage, right to reside in matrimonial home, right to matrimonial property, etc., ultimately failed it.

In our humble opinion dowry being a highly socialized practice cannot be curbed only by enacting laws; in fact, state and civil society must join forces: state must continue to pay attention to the effective implementation of the law and civil society must launch a comprehensive programme of mass mobilization to generate the public opinion against this social evil. In this programme contribution of young women and men has vital role to play.

## Notes

1. *Dowry Murder: The Imperial Origins of a Cultural Crime*, OUP, 2002.
2. *The Political Economy of Dowry: Institutionalisation and Expansion in North India* by Ranjana Sheel, Manohar Publication, 1999, p. 49.
3. Ibid., pp. 161–162, supra note 2.
4. See Bihar Dowry Restraint Act, 1950.
5. See Andhra Pradesh Dowry Prohibition Act, 1958.
6. See sections 498–A and 304–B of IPC.
7. See sections 173(8),174 (3) and 198A CrPC.
8. See 113A and 113B of Indian Evidence Act.
9. See section 2 of Dowry Prohibition Act 1961.
10. See section 3, sub-clause 2.
11. Madhu P. Kishwar, "Strategies for combating the culture of dowry and domestic violence in India", May 2005, available at www.un.org/.
12. Ibid., supra note 8.

13. Author is unaware of even a single reported case in which the bride or her relatives have been booked for taking or demanding dowry from the bridegroom under section 3(1) of the Act. Obviously, the concept of bride price has no relevance at present and even a look at the parliamentary debates which preceded the enactment of DPA does not provide any justification for inclusion of bride price in the definition of dowry. For parliamentary debates, see p. 165, supra note 2.
14. Law Commission of India while acting suo moto has suggested in its 91st report following definition of dowry "dowry means money, or other things estimable in terms of money, demanded from the wife or her parents or other relatives by the husband or his parents or other relatives, where such a demand is not properly referable to any legally recognized claim and relatable only to the wife's having married into the husband's family."
15. In a recent case State of A.P. versus Rajgopal AIR 2004 SC 1933; Supreme Court, while finding some of the family members guilty of dowry harassment exonerated husband.
16. In its obsession to make the practice of dowry punishable, the legislature choose to deviate from its general policy of not to victimize women through the criminal prosecution rather unjustifiably. See, for example, section 497 of IPC which makes adultery as an offence, specifically exonerate wife from its purview.
17. I wonder whether the police officials can be booked under section 166 of IPC, viz., public servant disobeying law, with intent to cause injury to any person.
18. See 1985 rules (1) The bride shall maintain the list of presents given to the bride. (2) The bridegroom shall maintain the list of presents given to the bridegroom. (3) The lists shall be prepared at the time of marriage and shall be in writing. (4) The list shall contain a brief description of each present, approximate value, the name of the person who presented it, relationship of the presenter to the bride or the groom. (5) The list shall be signed (or thumb impression) by both the bride and the groom.
19. Section 3(2) is a non obstenti clause and as a result has to be interpreted strictly in accordance with the provisos, i.e., proviso a and b logically. Therefore, there is a strong case for the argument that in the absence of lists of the presents and gifts having been made at the time of marriage to the bride and bridegroom without there being any demand, may also be covered by the definition of the dowry. At the first blush this view may appear to be technical but then courts have interpreted this Act extremely technically in many cases.

20. The rules in their present form clearly suffer from the voice of "non-application of mind" and fail to appreciate the mechanism adopted in the Leti Deti Act of 1939.
21. May be added as section 113 C to the Indian Evidence Act.
22. In the light of the amendment to section 2, demands of dowry even after the marriage are clearly implicated by section 4 and when it is read with section 3(1), the accused could be booked under both the sections, for taking and demanding dowry as well. See L.V. Jadahv versus Babasaheb Pawar, AIR SC 1983 1219.
23. Application of principles of law of contract to cover the social problem like dowry has no justification. The same appears to have been done by way of sheer analogical extension.
24. The section has its roots in the statement and objects of the Act, which inter alia provides "It is, however, felt that a law which makes the practice punishable and at the same time ensures that any dowry, if given does ensure for the benefit of the wife will go a long way to educating public opinion and to the eradication of this evil … ."
25. *Dowry and Protection to Married Women*, 1987, Deep and Deep, New Delhi, p. 171.
26. For the purposes of this section, the otherwise gender neutral definition of dowry becomes gendered and it is possible to argue that once the marriage is consummated, section 3(1) cannot be invoked against wife for giving dowry.
27. It is not easy to appreciate marriage of equity and criminal liability as appears to be at the foundation of this section.
28. The section explicitly recognizes the violation of Child Marriage Restraint Act.
29. If the persons would go to jail for committing the offences under sections 3 and 4, how can they act as trustees and take care of the property on behalf of the women? Moreover, can a marriage be continued if the state intervenes and prosecutes such persons under sections 3 and 4?
30. There is a proposal by the Supreme Court to the government according to which taking or demanding dowry on part of government servants must be treated as misconduct through an amendment of the Indian Services (Conduct) Rules, 1968.
31. See Article 17 of Indian Constitution. It has been incorporated to abolish untouchability altogether. Can it not be argued that just as untouchability, leads to subordination and discrimination of dalits, dowry also leads to subordination and discrimination of women? Does it not derogate the dignity of women? Thus under patriarchal

lens, legislature appears to have viewed the impact of dowry on women, rather insensitively.

32. See generally " concept of legal system" 1980, by Joseph Raz.
33. At present, Sanction Theory does not enjoy much support either from the criminologists or the philosophers. See generally "Law and Obligations" by Leslie Green at pp. 514–547 in The Oxford Handbook of Jurisprudence and Philosophy of Law, edited by Jules Coleman and Scott Shapiro, 2002.
34. Researcher believes that the term 'dowry death' is misleading. It contributes towards making domestic violence in India appear as uniqueand exotic phenomenon. What a man states as his reason for beating a wife cannot be treated as the cause of that violence. For example, if a violent incident is triggered off in a home in Germany by a man flying into a rage and battering a woman to death saying, you are a lousy cook. Or that you are fat and ugly, we don't call such crimes as lousy cooking murders. Or ugly looks murder. As a matter of fact classification of homicides as dowry murders and non-dowry murders made in section 304(B) [minimum imprisonment of seven years, and can be reduced by giving special reasons in writing, maximum punishment of life imprisonment] and 302 [minimum imprisonment life imprisonment and maximum is death penalty] of IPC respectively is not merely deeply problematic from the stand point of morality but in terms of constitutional law (article 14) also, it is untenable.
35. See for excellent critique, "Campaign Against Dowry: Implications and Limitations', pp. 19 in Flavia Agnes (ed.), *Feminist Jurisprudence-Contemporary Concerns*, Majlis, 2003.
36. It is a well established principle of constitutional jurisprudence in our country that fundamental rights can not be waived.
37. Under the influence of this doctrine police, prosecution and the complainants often artificially link dowry harassment to domestic violence and vice a versa. and such cases often crumbled for lack of evidence.
38. According to Madhu Kishwar, domestic violence is about using brute force to establish power relations in the family whereby women are taught and conditioned to accepting a subservient status for themselves. Supra note 11.
39. Glimpses of such a provision may be found in the new Domestic Violence Bill of 2005. The bill is yet to be cleared by the Parliament.
40. As a matter of fact, states may appoint them as dowry prohibition officers under section 8b of the DPA.

41. See generally "A brand called dowry" by Chitra Padmanabhan, *The Hindu*, 24–8–03.
42. Sections 37 and 39 of the CrPC should be suitably amended for this purpose.
43. See "National Perspective Plan for Women"1988–2000, at pp. 138, interestingly it is observed their that demand of the dowry must be recognized as aground of divorce. It also appreciates relevant amendment (rule 13 A) in the government servant conduct rules, 1976,which is to the effect that taking or giving dowry amounts to misconduct. However, this rule is observed in its violations.
44. A bill has already been passed by the parliament for this purpose, see for its critique, *combat law* human rights magazine, January 2005, pp. 34–38. A bill for making the registration of the marriages compulsory is also pending before the parliament.
45. See generally: "Legal strategies for curbing the dowry problem"; (97–150) by Werner Menski in *South Asians and the Dowry Problems*, edited by Werner Menski,1999.
46. Appellants: In Re-Enforcement and Implementation of Dowry Prohibition Act 1961 vs. Respondent: (2005) 4 SCC 565.
47. Para 5.
48. Para 9.
49. Para 10.
50. Para 10.
51. This direction is in the form of an advise.
52. Para 11 and 13.
53. Para 2.
54. Para 12.
55. Pawankumar v. State of Haryana, AIR 1998 SC 958.
56. Reema Agrawal v. Anupam and Others 2004 3 SCC c 199.
57. Shanti v. State of Haryana, AIR 1991 SC 1226.
58. Pratibha Rani v. Surajkumar AIR 1985 SC 628.
59. *An Eagle's Eye on Dowry Demand and Dowry Cruelty and Dowry Death* by ISH Kumar Mango, 2004, Capital Law House. See particularly chapter 2.
60. See supra.
61. See, Rani Jethmalani and P.K. Dey, "Dowry Deaths and Access to Justice" Jethmalini (ed.) *Kali's Yug, Empowerment, Law and Dowry Deaths*: at pp 36.New Delhi: Kali for Women. Jethmalini reports that already in Neelam Varma and others v. Union of India, a Supreme

Court writ petition of 1983, seven dowry victims and two women's organizations had moved the Supreme Court of India, alleging that their rights under Articles 21 and 14 of the Constitution of India had been violated. The petitioners submitted that the police authorities had not complied with their statutory obligations under the criminal laws and under the Constitution, by refusing to register their complaints regarding dowry harassment, thereby not carrying out the necessary investigation enjoined upon them under the CrPC. It was contended that the right to life included the right to live with human dignity.

62. See Sakshi v. UoI, 2004 (6) SCALE And Delhi Domestic Working Women's Forum v. UoI,1 SCC 14, 1995.
63. Vishaka v. State of Rajasthan 1997, 6 SCC, 241.
64. See Article 1 of the CEDAW defining discrimination.
65. See Article 51–A(e) of Constitution of India. This article was employed by Supreme Court in Visakha's case, to deprecate sexual harassment of women at their workplaces.
66. There is a growing demand from a section of society that section 498 A of IPC is being abused as a weapon against husbands and in laws by the wives and family member. In fact, constitutional validity of the section was challenged in Sushil Kumar Sharma v. Union of India AIR 2005, SC 3100. Although a petition was dismissed, what is important is the fact that issue afterall reached SC. See generally, *Digest on Wife Subjected to Cruelty by Husband and his Relatives Under Section 498–A* by T. Mohan Rao, National Law House, Hydrabad, 2001.
67. It is instructive to refer a six point's programme to eradicate dowry and dowry deaths which is evolved by Dr. Himendra Thakur, Director, International Society Against Dowry. It was discussed in 5th International Conference on Dowry in Delhi, available at http://www.1worldcommunication. Yet another important initiative is Dowry Project, evolved by Dr. Julia Lesley and under this project six international conferences have been organized to generate constructive research on the various dimensions of the problem of dowry.

CHAPTER SIX

# Family violence with special reference to Section 498A of Indian Penal Code

*Meena Gokhale*

## Family violence

Family violence is a global issue that requires global response. The violence within family is manifested in various forms, such as physical violence, emotional violence or economic violence. Sexual violence, although a form of physical violence, is closely related to emotional as well as economic violence.

Family-based violence, gender-based violence and domestic violence are three different terms and it is necessary to develop clear understanding of these three terms. Family-based violence refers to violence that takes place between two family members, gender-based violence implies violence manifested by person belonging to one sex to other sex and domestic violence takes place at domestic front, but the two parties involved may not be related to each other (e.g., violence towards domestic servant). These three groups overlap each other but in any case it is related to the power relationship between the two parties involved. In any form of violence, the aggrieved party has no or less power compared to the perpetrator.

At international level, the two conventions that address the issue of family violence are Convention for Elimination of Discrimination Against Women (CEDAW) and United Nations Convention on the Rights of Child (CRC), 1989. The Indian state has dealt the issue by framing special laws such as Child Marriage Act, 1929, which prevents child marriage, Pre-Natal Diagnostic Technique Act, 1994, which prohibits identification of sex fetus, and Juvenile Justice Act, 2002, which ensures protection and care to children and Section 498A (IPC) that deals with violence manifested towards women within the family. This study is primarily focused on Section 498A of IPC as a legal tool to address the issue of family violence.

## Section 498A

Section 498A of Indian Penal Code (IPC) is the first piece of law in India that stressed that Indian women have right to violence-free life. The emergence of this law is rooted in the initiatives by feminist movement between 1970–80, which threw light on dowry deaths as well as rape, and demanded concrete action. As a response, the 91st Law Commission Report recommended introduction of legal reforms as a preventive measure and also strengthening the existing laws. This led to insertion of Section 498A in IPC and certain changes were introduced in other laws, namely, Hindu Marriage Act and Evidence Act, 1972 as well as in Criminal Procedure Code (CrPC). Ever since its introduction, this is one of the most debated laws and many myths prevail in the society related to this piece of legislation.

The salient features of the section are:

- This is a criminal law that deals with a issue that mostly takes place within the closed walls.
- It deals with cruelty by husband or relatives of husband towards the wife or the woman.
- Cruelty or harassment considered as a "willful" conduct with a view to meet unlawful demand. (It does not specify that the unlawful demand as dowry.)
- This offence is cognizable, bailable and triable by Judicial Magistrate First Class.
- It is specified as non-compoundable. However, only the High Court can give permission for compounding the case in exceptional situation.

This is a landmark in the history of Indian law as it is a unique section that deals with criminal and matrimonial matter simultaneously. This is the law that deals with two major institutions in society: marriage and family. It gives a new dimension to the concept of cruelty. This law challenges the power equation between matrimonial relationship, and gives power to the aggrieved woman against the husband or his relatives. With the introduction of this law, a new era in Indian society has began. The state has been granted powers to intervene in the personal and family relationship of its citizens.

## The study

A research team of ILS Law College, Pune conducted a study 'Efficacy of Section 498A of IPC' during 1998–99. The details of the study are as follows:

### *Objective*

To study socio-legal dimensions and the efficacy of the section, with respect to purpose of the law and its implementation.

### *Scope*

The primary data was collected from the Pune district, which included study of 933 FIRs, interviews, and discussions with all stakeholders: families, police, lawyers, magistrates, and representatives of women and men's organizations. The sources of secondary data were crime data by Department of Police at national and Maharashtra state level and cases in JFMC and High Court.

## Findings

- There is a high correlation between the declining rate of dowry deaths and increasing rate of cases under Section 498A. As mentioned above, this section was introduced as a preventive measure and it has largely succeeded in achieving this objective.
- The rate of registration of cases increased steadily till 1996 and then there was a sudden drop. This implies that the law was easily accessible and women have availed of it.

- Out of the total cases registered under this section, in most (around 70%) of the cases, the decision is still awaited as either the cases were pending in the court or the proceedings were on-going when the data was collected for the study.
- Out of the cases for which the court has passed the verdict, in majority of cases, the accused was not found guilty and hence acquitted. The incidences where the charge was proved and the accused party was convicted were very few. The ratio between the acquitted and convicted cases is 8: 1.
- Although the section is non-compoundable, in reality, the cases are compounded without the permission of the court. Cases were either withdrawn or settled outside the court. This highlights the gap between the books of law and the ground realities.
- The section was found more effective when used with other sections of grave cruelty (304B, 306). It helped to prove the guilt of the accused, proving that it has definitely strengthen the existing law.
- It was found equally useful as taking timely steps to avoid the cruelty that a woman might have faced in the absence of it.
- It was equally effective as a deterrent on the individuals who abide by it.
- However, the law has failed considerably to provide protection and relief to the aggrieved women who accessed to it.

## Limitations of the law

The limitations of the law that emerged from the study are of two kinds: firstly, legal and secondly, socio-cultural.

### *Legal*

- Due to certain inherent deficiencies of the section, such as absence of guidelines for protecting the victim, the law failed in providing the protection to women.
- Besides, due to the absence of supportive law, cruelty of less gravity (other than danger to life) could not get proved.

- Although the law was introduced as a preventive measure and to strengthen the then existing law, in practice, it was also used for purposes other than specified above. The aggrieved women accessed to this law with a purpose of getting rid of the harassment or to improve her family life etc.
- The gap between 'genuine complaint' and 'genuine case' was unbridgeable. As the law deals with issues within the four walls getting proofs was most difficult aspect.

### *Socio-cultural*

- The inequality between men and women in Indian society is deep-rooted and just one piece of law is insufficient to eliminate or change, social evils. Cruelty or harassment between the relationship of husband and wife was in a way an accepted norm and this law has attempted to shaken this. However, there is a long way to go before a right to violence-free life is ensured to Indian women.
- Ignorance about the law in general and the legal procedures as well as misconceptions about it are yet other causes that affected the efficacy of the section. The study revealed that the society in general, including the legal machinery, especially the police force, believed that dowry is a necessary component for filing a case under Section 498A. This compelled them to mention demands of dowry in the FIR, even though that was not the fact in each case. During the court proceedings and the cross-questioning by the magistrate, the demand of dowry could not be proved in many cases. This resulted in making the case more weak leading to acquittal of the accused. So, although the accused had committed cruelty and harassment towards the victim, it could not be proved due to the style and pattern of writing FIRs.
- The biases/prejudices and attitude of the implementing machinery (particularly, the police department as well as lawyers) have affected adversely. The police department considered this a family matter and an extra burden to their

already busy schedule. Hence, filing a case under this section received least priority and was also treated as a routine matter. This was reflected in the stereotyped writing of FIR. The weak presentation in FIR ultimately impacted the verdict in favour of the accused party.

## Recommendations

- The researchers felt that, family violence is a complex issue and this section is just a beginning to address this age-old practice. Cruelty is manifested even beyond the matrimonial relationship and for reasons other than dowry. Hence, the study recommended introduction of a comprehensive law with wider perspective, which will go beyond matrimonial relationship and incorporate all aspects of family violence.
- Besides, it was realized that the term 'cruelty' needs to be defined more precisely making room for cruelty of less gravity.
- A separate mechanism on the line of family courts needs to be established to deal with family violence.
- This mechanism should incorporate provision of counselling to both parties before the case is presented in the court.
- Sensitization of implementing machinery, the police and the judiciary, is essential for improving efficacy of any law and it is equally true for this section as well.

It is heartening to note that most of the recommendations of this study have been taken into consideration in the newly introduced bill on domestic violence.

## Law as a tool

At the end, it is very essential to note that the law against violence although, necessary, is just a first step. It offers no guarantee of elimination of violence. Children and women need to know their rights and the society in general needs to be sensitive towards the issues of rights of the aggrieved. Laws need to be enforced effectively and ongoing efforts are required in order to make the law work.

CHAPTER SEVEN

# Violence against women in the family

## A human rights violation?

*V.S. Elizabeth*

Violence against women in human society is quite all-pervasive: be it a society in India, Nigeria, Argentina, Japan, United Kingdom or the USA, women in every country, irrespective of the class, culture, level of economic and political development, face violence on the streets or within their homes.[1] Research carried out by various groups in India shows that quite a high percentage of Indian women face domestic violence in some form or the other – physical, mental, financial or emotional.[2] Family violence against women is a violation of fundamental human rights. It is not only discrimination against women but results from discriminatory beliefs, systems and institutions that perpetuate and reinforce the inequality between men and women. It is thus a form of gender-based violence and a human rights violation. The Vienna Accord of 1993 and the Beijing Platform for Action, 1995 together have made it clear that women's rights are human rights. The legal framework provided by documents like these have made it possible to articulate violence within the family, considered till now as a private matter, as human rights violations of public concern. Human rights discourse has begun to dissolve the public-private divide and has provided a legal and moral background for national governments and NGOs to make a direct response to issues of violence against women in the family.

Violence against women in the family is not only pervasive across various cultures, classes, castes, etc., it is quite deeply embedded and contributes to the low status of women, in spite of the constitutional and human rights guaranteed to women in most countries of the world today. Though we increasingly live in a world that emphasizes individualism and individual rights, women's right to their individuality and rights as individual citizens are yet to be recognized widely by most cultures. Women are seen as mothers and wives, but whether all women are in reality wives and mothers is irrelevant for most people. What is relevant is the acceptable roles for women and the fact that gender stereotypes are largely still prevalent. As a consequence, it is difficult for most women and men to recognize the fact that women are first individuals and persons in their own right and only then come their social roles as mothers and wives. Any recognition of women as individuals is immediately seen as a threat to the institution of family, which is the foundation of society, and therefore the logic and the reasonableness of women's legitimate claims to their human rights goes unrecognized or is blatantly violated.

In many cases, the cause of the violence is laid at the women's door, and the victim becomes responsible for what has been done to her. She is somehow to blame for the abuse, the idea of "she asked for it" or that "she must have done something to provoke that violence". With that, society is no longer responsible even vicariously for the violence perpetrated on its girls and women.[3]

The high level of tolerance of violence against women is unimaginable. Women have internalized these notions and values and, therefore, often do not think that they deserve or have a right to a life without violence and it is seen by others as small price to pay for the preservation of the family. In discussions with many people in the context of the new Domestic Violence Act, which has come into force in India this year, most people, especially men, cry out that this is the end of the family – "the foundation of society" – because now women on frivolous grounds or false grounds will break up the family and the children will be lost.[4]

Generally people do not seem to reflect on the fact of how women, who have been socialized into considering marriage and family as their natural destiny and to consider the purpose for their existence as serving their husbands and in-laws and taking care of their children, are going to abuse a law meant to provide protection to women in distress. This is just a reflection of the reason why even in the 21st century and the era of liberalization and globalization women's lives are little better than those of their sisters several thousand years ago. Economic and technological revolutions may have taken place over all these thousand years liberating some men from drudgery and exploitation but for the rest of society and especially women little has changed in terms of their status or their rights. Women have only duties and responsibilities and that is why despite various national legislations and international guarantees they continue to experience violence in their lives.

Some reasons for family violence identified by sociologists and feminist scholars[5] are unequal distribution of power in society leading to women occupying positions inferior or subordinate to men. Historical and social acceptance of gender stereotyped roles, which legitimize and justify aggression against women, contribute to family violence against women. Socialization of men and women is such that women's rights as individuals entitled to live their lives without violence is not recognized. Therefore, what is acceptable in society at large gets reflected in the relations within the family as well. Thus, though there may be some superficial reasons for immediate provocation for violence against women in the family as being husband's drunkenness, wife's disobedience, not serving hot food, talking to other men, talking back to their husbands etc., generally speaking, every act of violence against a woman has some characteristic or other that identifies it as gender-based violence.

Gender-based violence is defined as violence that reflects the existing imbalance in the power relations between men and women and that perpetuates the subordination and devaluation of the female as opposed to the male. "The difference between this kind of violence and other forms of aggression and coercion lies in the fact that in this case the risk factor or source of vulnerability is the mere fact of being a woman."[6]

The Committee on the Elimination of Discrimination Against Women, in its general recommendation 19, adopted at its 11th session, in 1992, defined in para 6 gender-based violence as "violence that is directed at a woman because she is a woman or that affects women disproportionately. It includes acts that inflict physical, mental or sexual harm or suffering, threats of such acts, coercion and other deprivations of liberty…."

The gender-based division of labour, the differential socialization processes, and the roles and characteristics culturally assigned to women restrict their options and their autonomy and are based on a repressive and symbolic form of violence that is expressed in the limitations imposed on them in terms of employment, social participation, decision-making and power at all levels; this is what is known as invisible violence, which includes objective situations of aggression, either physical, psychological or sexual, direct or indirect.[7]

Studies on family violence have established clearly the causal link between women's inferior status in family and society and the violence perpetrated on them. Popular culture in the form of television serials in the vernacular languages and fictions reflect this well-accepted position of women. Even today, there is the perpetuation of the idea that a man and his family have a right to expect certain kinds of conduct within the household from the woman and her family and failure to this justifies the use of violence against the woman. Even though studies have brought to light some of the consequences of family violence for women and children, there is still little appreciation of the extent of its impact or the fact that such acts are criminal acts and gross violation of human rights.

Some consequences of family violence are as follows:[8]

- *Physical injuries:* fractures, burns, cuts, bruises, wounds, headaches, temporary or permanent disability, sexual abuse, gynaecological problems, unwanted pregnancies, premature births, miscarriages, sexually transmitted diseases, transmission of HIV virus, and the abusive consumption of alcohol, drugs and tobacco.

- *Psychological damage:* depression, anxiety, anguish, eating disorders, stress, phobias, obsessions, compulsive behaviour, toxic substance, abuse, insomnia, hypersomnia, frigidity, low self-esteem, sexual dysfunctions, emotional instability, decreased productivity and reduction of cognitive and intellectual capacities, suicide and homicide.

Family violence also prevents women from playing a role in decision-making within the household, at work and in the political, economic and social spheres and therefore directly influences their participation or the lack of it in public activities and hence, the exercise of their citizenship.

In the case of children, it causes nervousness, irritability and fearfulness, poor performance in school, abuse by parents, imitate parental behaviour – grow up to be violent men and battered women – have greater tolerance for social and political violence.

When the above is viewed in the light of the Indian Penal Code, the Indian Constitution and international human rights standards, we find that family violence is a serious criminal offence and violation of basic constitutional and human rights: Under the Indian Penal Code following are some of the crimes which family violence entails:

- Offences affecting the public health, safety, convenience, decency and morals – Sections 268, 290–294.
- Offences affecting life – Sections 299–309.
- Offences of the causing of miscarriage, of injuries to unborn children etc. – Sections 312–318.
- Offences of hurt – Sections 319–330 and 334–338.
- Offences of wrongful restraint and wrongful confinement – Sections 339–348.
- Offences of criminal force and assault – Sections 349–352, 354, 357–366, 372–374.
- Sexual offences – Sections 375–377.
- Offence of cruelty by husband or relatives of husband – Section 498–A.
- Offences of criminal intimidation, insult and annoyance – Sections 503, 507, 509 and 510.

We also find that the rights enshrined in the Indian Constitution too stand violated in this context – Fundamental Rights:

- Article 14: Right to equality before the law and to equal protection of the law.
- Article 15: Right against discrimination.
- Article 19: Right to freedoms.
- Article 21: Right to life.

When viewed in the context of international human rights regime, we find that all of the acts of family violence are human rights violations. Article 1 of the United Nations General Assembly Declaration 48/104, adopted on 20th December, 1993 defines violence against women as "any act of gender-based violence that results in, or is likely to result in, physical, sexual, psychological harm or suffering to women, including threats of such acts, coercion or arbitrary deprivation of liberty, whether occurring in public or private life". Article 2 states that violence against women shall be understood to encompass, but not be limited to, the following: *physical, sexual and psychological violence occurring in the family*, including battering, sexual abuse of female children in the household, dowry-related violence, marital rape, female genital mutilation and other traditional practices harmful to women, non-spousal violence and violence related to exploitation.

A quick overview of some of the international covenants will enable us to appreciate this fact better. In the light of the Universal Declaration of Human Rights violence against women in the family entails: violation of the right to life, liberty and personal safety (Art. 3); right to not be subject to torture or to cruel, inhuman or degrading treatment or punishment (Art. 5); right to equality before the law and equal protection of the law (Art. 7); right to a fair trial (Arts. 8 and 10); right to freedom of movement (Art. 13); freedom of assembly and association (Art. 20).

Internationally, it has come to be recognized that gender-based violence is a violation of the right to identity, right to affection, right to peace and enriching personal relations, right to protection, right to personal development, right to social and political participation, right to freedom of expression and right to an optimum state of physical and mental health.

Further, Article 6 of the ICCPR provides that "every human being has the inherent right to life". While Article 7 states that "no one shall be subjected to torture or to cruel, inhuman or degrading treatment or punishment". Both the UDHR and the ICCPR guarantee that states shall provide an effective and adequate remedy for acts violating fundamental rights guaranteed by constitution or by law.

The Convention on the Elimination of All Forms of Discrimination against Women forbids discrimination against women. The Committee on Elimination of Discrimination against Women has explained that violence against women constitutes discrimination and "...seriously inhibits women's ability to enjoy rights and freedoms on a basis of equality with men". It also affirmed that violence against a woman constitutes a violation of her internationally recognized human rights – regardless of whether the perpetrator is a public official or a private person. In the same general recommendation [para 24 (t)], the Committee has asked states parties to take all the necessary measures to prevent gender-based violence. All necessary measures in this context mean not just legal and civil remedies, but preventive measures like public information and education programmes, in order to create awareness and sensitize the general population to various forms of gender-based violence. General Recommendation 12 recommends that all parties to the Convention report to CEDAW on the existence of support services for victims of family violence, relevant legislation, statistical data and measures adopted to eradicate violence against women in the family. Regional Courts of Human Rights have also interpreted state action to include the failure of the state to prevent violence.

The Declaration on the Elimination of Violence against Women includes explicit directions to member countries to "...not invoke any custom, tradition or religious consideration to avoid their obligations with respect to its elimination". It sets forth specific steps in Article 4 for a member-state to take in combating domestic violence. These steps include:

- investigating and punishing acts of domestic violence;

- developing comprehensive legal, political, administrative and cultural programmes to prevent violence against women;
- providing training to law enforcement officials; and
- promoting research and collecting statistics relating to the prevalence of domestic violence.

Article 4(g) of the Declaration directs that states should work to ensure that women subjected to violence and their children receive specialized assistance, health and social services, facilities and programmes as well as support structures, and should take all other appropriate measure to promote their safety and physical and psychological rehabilitation.

Thus, the violence may be by the state but it may also include violence in the community and in the family. According to this criterion, the state becomes a de facto accomplice if it does not offer women the necessary protection from violations of their rights, or when it acts in discriminatory fashion by not preventing or punishing acts of gender-based violence, thereby denying women equal protection under the law. In fact, in its forty-seventh session, the United Nations General Assembly agreed that "the violation of human rights of women was not limited to acts perpetrated or directly condoned by governments, but rather that governments bore a social and political responsibility for acts committed by third parties if they had not taken the necessary measures to prevent, investigate and punish acts of violence."[9]

Scholars and human rights groups have argued that a state's failure to prosecute individuals who are violent against women constitutes a violation of equal protection in the implementation of law. Using the same argument it would mean that the incapacity of the state to put an end to social, economic and cultural conditions that expose women to gender-based violence means that it is responsible for such violence, since it should actively contribute to eradicating injustices and inequalities that manifest themselves in gender relations.

Not only can family violence be viewed as human rights violation, it also comes within the purview of the definition of torture under Convention against Torture and Other Cruel

Inhuman or Degrading Treatment or Punishment, 1987, Part 1, Article 1 wherein "the term 'torture' means any act by which severe pain or suffering, whether physical or mental, is intentionally inflicted on a person for such purposes as obtaining from him or a third person information or a confession, punishing him for an act he or a third person has committed or is suspected of having committed, or intimidating or coercing him or a third person, or for any reason based on discrimination of any kind, when such pain or suffering is inflicted by or at the instigation of or with the consent or acquiescence of a public official or other person acting in an official capacity. It does not include pain or suffering arising only from, inherent in or incidental to lawful sanctions".

Scholars have argued that certain forms of human interaction in which women are the victims, such as domestic violence and marital rape, would qualify as torture. International debate has led to the conclusion on human rights violations where the infliction of pain is evident, in marital rape, domestic violence, sexual harassment at the workplace etc., with their short-term as well as long-term consequences that injure and dehumanize women, should not be excluded on the ground that it occurs in the private realm.

Despite these national and international legislations and directions to states to prevent, punish and prosecute domestic violence against women, we find that due to the deep-rooted nature of the patriarchal values little or nothing has been done to eliminate such violence. It is not that we do not have laws to punish such acts of violence, we find that the problem lies in the way in which such violence is perceived by law-enforcement agencies and the judicial officers and even the state. In a study that we conducted in 1998–2000, we found that while judges of the Family Court in Bangalore had been willing to consider certain acts of family violence as cruelty and grant relief to the women who had filed for divorce or maintenance before them, however, when it came to punishing acts of violence resulting in the death of the victims did not elicit the same response. The deaths are more often than not dismissed as 'unnatural deaths' and the accused acquitted for want of evidence.[10] The very sections under which complaints of family violence are filed and the perception of Section 498A by lawyers, policemen, judges and even the general public give us an indication of the enormous task of sensitizing all concerned to consider family violence as a criminal, illegal and unconstitutional act as well as violation of human rights.

Given that family violence is not confined to a particular economic class, social caste or religious group or even that it is not confined to the developing countries but to be found even in the developed countries like the UK, the USA, Canada etc., reflects the fact that family violence cuts across class, region, culture and countries. The deep-rooted nature and the pervasiveness of patriarchy in all institutions is largely the reason for the wide prevalence of family violence and the failure of the state despite legislations and institutions to prevent and eliminate it. Religion, culture and tradition have been used to reinforce the values that justify family violence and the resistance to any kind of steps for the empowerment of women to enable them to access their human rights and live a life of dignity.

In the light of both national and international law it is absolutely clear that violence against women in the family is a human rights violation. The fact that various governments too recognize this fact is evident from the national legislations enacted by them to punish those who perpetrate acts of family violence and at the same time to provide relief to victims of such violence. However, little has been done to disseminate this information or to make women aware of the available relief. States are satisfied that they have enacted laws in this context and plead helplessness in eradicating this problem because of the duty to protect minority rights in the context of culture and religion.

Theoretically, it is acknowledged that every human being is entitled to enjoy human rights and to have them protected by the laws and practice of his/her country of residence. As we have seen, international human rights law is applicable to women and men alike without regard to their sex and race. Besides, cultural practices, religious beliefs and levels of economic and social development should not hinder the enjoyment and exercise of these human rights. However, the practical situation is far different. Few women are aware of their rights and therefore rarely exercise them or use the national and international human rights systems to demand protection. Through the use of human rights language it is possible to recognize cultural practices and national laws that violate their human rights.

In this context, taking the approach that violence against women in the family is human rights violation enables activists and law-enforcement agencies to take a strong position against the continuation of such practices that legitimize violence against women and at the same time bring pressure on national governments to enact appropriate legislations or to pursue such policies as will end such violence and prevent their practices through the use of the media and educational policies. For historically human rights practice has failed to recognize rights violations that are gender-based. Some of these violations are justified on the basis of biological differences, gender, culture, religion etc., as we have already examined and as a result have not gained full international recognition as human rights violation. Through the use of the human rights language we can bring visibility to violation of women's human rights within the family and also put pressure – national and international – upon state and human rights agencies to act against such violence and use all available mechanisms and where necessary create new ones in order to enable women to enjoy their human rights and be able to live a life of dignity.

## Notes

1. Severe, repeated and systematic violence occurs in at least five of every hundred marriages in Britain; between 40 and 45 per cent of murdered women are killed by their male partners: UK Statistics on Domestic Violence (1993). According to available statistics from around the globe, one of out of every three women has experienced violence in an intimate relationship at some point in her life: World Health Organization, 1997.
2. There is not enough statistical evidence available on the actual prevalence of domestic violence in India. The few studies available indicate that it is quite high, anywhere from 22 per cent to 60 per cent of surveyed women (Rao, 1997; Mahajan, 1990). The records of the National Crimes Record Bureau, Ministry of Home Affairs,

Government of India suggest that there has been a 71.5 per cent increase in cases of torture and dowry-related deaths between 1991 and 1995.

3. Recently, while watching a Christian channel on TV, I was appalled to hear the speaker stating that if things are not right in the family, it is because women are not doing what they should be as wives, viz., obeying their husbands. Not for one moment did the preacher while talking about family relations examine how men by failing to obey God-given command "to love their wives as they love themselves" were the ones actually contributing to the violence in their homes and the lack of a peaceful environment within the family. This state of things I know are common to most if not all the religious leaders. Women are to blame for the wife beating, for the rape, sexual abuse, and sexual harassment by their failure to conform to gender norms as prescribed by society.
4. In private discussions as well as those aired through the TV channels indicate that quite a few men hold this view regarding the Domestic Violence Act, 2005 that has come into force in October 2006.
5. Eve S. Buzawa and Carl G. Buzawa, *Domestic Violence: The Criminal Justice Response, Studies in Crime, Law and Justice,* Vol. 6, Sage Publications, New Delhi, pp. 15–19. Here, the authors discuss the various theories put forward by sociologists, psychologists and feminists viz., individually-focused theories, family-oriented theories and theories that critically review the legal, religious and economic basis of how violence is structurally based in society (feminist theories).
6. Nieves Rico, *Gender Based Violence: A Human Rights Issue,* United Nations, Santiago, June 1997, p. 8.
7. Giberti and Fernandez, 1989.
8. Ibid., p. 25.
9. United Nations, 1994, as cited in Nieves Rico, op. cit., 1997, p. 15.
10. "Domestic Violence: A Study through Court Records", carried out by the Centre for Women and Law, National Law School of India University, 1998–2000, sponsored by the International Centre for Research on Women.

CHAPTER EIGHT

# Child sexual abuse

## A violation of human rights?

*Shalini S. Phansalkar-Joshi*

In India, even in the 21st century, family is a closely knit, compact unit, a sort of fortress where any intervention of outsiders is almost resented and rejected. The culture of silence surrounds it so tightly that any third person has no means to know what is happening therein. Though the problem of domestic violence or battered women is being acknowledged now, there is blissful unawareness about other forms of abuse that occur in the family. At the same time, there is also refusal and reluctance to talk about the intra-familial violence, particularly towards the children. Child sexual abuse is one such issue, which is the most closely guarded secret of the family. Irony of it is that of all the forms of violation of human rights, child sexual abuse is the most blatant, heinous and worst form of violation of human rights because it is perpetrated on the most helpless, vulnerable and defenceless class of society, i.e., the children, who are not knowing their rights, cannot speak or complain about violation of such rights and in case of girl child, it is committed by someone close to her like father, brother or uncle, who owes a duty to protect her. In such cases abuser is none else but her protector.

Abuse of any person in any form is always bad. If such abuse is sexual in nature, it is worse and if it is of a small child, particularly girl child, it becomes the worst. There are, therefore, no words to condemn and no laws to cover it if such sexual abuse is committed by her own family member in her own house; it becomes an out-and-out criminality and brutality. This malady then takes the form of a scar on humanity and civilization. The most precious section of our society, which requires utmost protection, is now being most abuse and offended by the very section of society, which is supposed to protect it. It is the most agonizing and serious problem currently surfacing though existing in all societies since time immemorial. It is a disease, which is affecting all strata of society the world over, irrespective caste, creed, sex, religion etc., and is spreading widely. It is a matter of regretful introspection that crimes against children are increasing all over the world. As observed by the apex court, in *State of Punjab v. Gurmit Singh,*[1] "It is noticed that of late crimes against children in general and of sexual abuse in particular, are on the rise. It is an irony that while we are celebrating children's rights in all spheres, we show little or no concern for his/her honour and right. It is a sad reflection on the attitude of indifference of the society towards the violation of human dignity of the victims of sexual abuse, especially when victims are children."[2]

It is shocking but true that abuse of children, whether male or female, has become now a widespread phenomenon, in both developing and developed countries. The very thought that a human being can stoop so low as to invade the person of an innocent child is most reprehensible. It not only militates against all canons of good social behaviour but also leaves deep-rooted physical as well as psychological scares on the child victim. It is the worst possible crime that a man can imaginably perpetuate as there cannot be comparable situation where the criminal causes the maximum damaged to the victim, who is more innocent, most defenseless and is least responsible for the provocation, if at all there is any. It is a violation, with violence, of the private person of a child, an outrage by all means. Here momentary pleasure of one causes devastating effect on another. Apart from the individual suffering, the society as a whole is compelled to suffer as it creates an incurable dent in fabric of milieu.[3] It is despicable enough when the attack is on an adult female but the situation becomes far more gory when the victim is a minor and virtually crosses the limits of depravity in cases where the offence is directed against infants and tender children.[4] The most pathetic situation is that such heinous and abhorrent cases of sexual assault and abuse of child victims are on increase. And, in most of the cases, such assaults are committed in the house and that too by member of the family. Though all sexual assaults on female children are not reported and do not come to light, yet there is an alarming increase in sex offences committed on children. This is due to the reasons that children are ignorant of the act of rape or sexual abuse and are not able to offer resistance and become easy prey for lusty brutes who display the unscrupulous, deceitful and insidious act of luring female children and young girls.[5]

### How widespread it is?

In a traditional country like India, the very idea of "child sexual abuse" is never found to be readily believable. One often feels and presumes that parents value their children very much. Every father is supposed and expected to be the protector of his children. The child owes an inherent right in himself/herself to be given the best treatment on this earth. Therefore, one finds it difficult to accept or admit that such an innocent child, who deserves nothing but only love, care, protection and affection, can be the victim of such a heinous crime like sexual abuse. Some relations are presumed to be so sacred that it is not easy to accept that such relationships can also be tarnished. In India, because there is emphasis on cultural and ethical values, there is total disbelief among the judges, lawyers or police officers who routinely deal with the perverse side of human nature that child sexual abuse cannot occur.

Though of late these crimes against children are on increase and more cases are being reported in law journals and newspapers, there is an appalling ignorance as to how widespread child sexual abuse is. Surprisingly, however, from the society's point of view, sexual abuse of child is not something new or a totally strange area. It has been known through the ages. In every society, at any given time, child sexual abuse has been ubiquitous. It is a common belief or myth that having sex with child can increase man's sexual powers or sex with a virgin can cure sexually transmitted diseases. Therefore, children are often subjected to such abuse. However, the subject of child sexual abuse is shrouded in mystery to such an extent that there is total disbelief and denial about its existence. Moreover, in India, sex itself is a taboo topic. Secondly, as the social stigma is attached to the sexual abuse, the reaction of family and society, in general, is of denial of its existence. The various studies also show that, in the first place, children themselves do not find language, expression, capacity or ability to disclose such incidents. Secondly, the shame and secrecy surrounding sexual abuse is such that even if the child discloses about the incident, family is not ready to acknowledge it. They do not want to discuss openly about it. Further, as abuser in such cases is mostly some one from the family itself, that too, closely related to the child, the family becomes reluctant to discuss it, even if anonymity is assured. Thus, the child is forced into silence given the culture of privacy, family prestige and family unity.[6]

Therefore, statistics in this area are often proved to be elusive, flawed and not real. Such sexual abuse of child occurs everywhere from mansions to slums. It cuts across all the barriers of social, economic and educational status and reduces it to a 'sameness'.[7] Neither caste nor religious background matters. As per the study conducted by International Statistics on Child Sexual Abuse, at least two out of four girls and one out of six boys are victims of child sexual abuse.[8] The pioneer study in the field was conducted in 1994 by Samvaada, an NGO based in Bangalore. The survey of about 348 college-going girls was conducted by this organization and it revealed that,

1. 83 per cent of the girls had been subjected to eve-teasing.
2. 13 per cent of them had been vocally, visually and sexually harassed when they were less than 10 years old.
3. 47 per cent had been molested.
4. 15 per cent of these when they were less than 10 years old. They were used for overtures mostly by male relatives.
5. 15 per cent had been seriously sexually abused.
6. 31 per cent of them, when they were less than 10 years old, had been raped, forced into oral sex or penetrated with some in animate object.[9]

Sakshi, a Delhi-based organization, which spearheaded work on child sexual abuse in the early 1990, has conducted a study of 357 school-going girl children and found that,

- 63 per cent have been victims of some form of child sexual abuse.
- 22 per cent have indicated experience of serious form of child sexual abuse.[10]

Another Delhi-based organization RAHI has also conducted a survey specifically addressing non-lower class women. It was conducted among 600 English-speaking middle and upper class women living in Delhi, Mumbai, Kolkata, Goa and Chennai, of the ages ranging from fifteen to sixty-six. It was transpired that

1. 76 per cent of the women had been sexually abused in childhood.
2. Out of these, 457, i.e., 40 per cent had been sexually abused by the nearest family member.
3. 71 per cent had been sexually abused by relatives and family friends.
4. 2 per cent of these 457 women were sexually abused before they were four years of age.
5. 17 per cent between four and eight years of age.
6. 28 per cent between the ages of eight and twelve years.
7. 35 per cent between twelve and sixteen years.

In its 1999 report, the World Health Organization (WHO) says that one of every ten children in India is being sexually abused at any given point of time. Even now, if child sexual abuse sounds alien to one, Devika Nading, Principal of the Shyamrao Kalmadi School in Pune, urges one to think again, because as a teacher for the last nearly two decades, she has encountered several kinds of child sexual abuse where some family members, sometimes drivers, who drop children to and fro school and home and sometimes strangers have been taking undue advantage of the child's innocence, at times leaving deep emotional scars within his or her tender heart.[11]

The study made of reported cases published in the law journals like *All India Reporter*, *Criminal Law Journal* and *Supreme Court Cases*, of the last 10 years, indicates that whereas in the year

1991, in *Criminal Law Journal,* the reported case of rape on children below 12 years was only one, in the year 2000, there were 13 such cases. This increase in the reported cases is not only constant and persistent but these are also rising continuously. When there used to be hardly one or two cases in the year, now, the number is increased significantly and noticeably. The things have come to such an extent that hardly a single volume of any of these publications passes without reporting of such cases.

As per the latest figure, in the year 2004, in Maharashtra, 1,392 cases of rape were reported reflecting 10 per cent increase compared to 2003 and out of that more than 45 per cent cases were reported of girls below the age of 18. In as many as 419 cases the victims was in the age group of 14–18, while 85 cases were reported of girls who were below 10 years.[12]

### Who are the victims?

The age of the victims or the offender is also no decisive factor. A female of any age is susceptible to high risk of being sexually abused. From a small child in cradle to the girl or lady of any age sexual abuse is committed. One may feel ashamed to think that as young a child as two to three years is also not spared from such sexual attack.[13] What will send shivers in the spine of any person is that even an infant of four or eleven months is also subjected to such vicious and heinous crime for no fault of her. What one can say of the obnoxious act if accused committing rape on a child of 21 months, resulting into profuse bleeding from her private parts, and child succumbing to death. There is no immunity to children from not being subject of crimes of sexual assaults for which they are neither physically prepared or mature nor mentally capable of being susceptible of such attack. The girl child is never safe even from her infancy to puberty and thereafter.[14] She is always in the danger of being defiled and deflowered. What is shocking to conscious is that even handicapped and the deaf and dumb child is also not spared from the lustful attack.[15] The male children are also susceptible to such sexual abuse. According to an international study, statistics on child sexual assault show that at least one out of every six boys is victim of sexual abuse.

### Who are the abusers?

The peculiarity of the offence of child abuse is that perpetrators of such offences hail from all strata of society. As in the case of victims, in case of offenders also, there are no barriers of social or economical status, caste or religious background. Such abusers are also not monsters but ordinary human beings. The statistics show that, regardless of its financial or social status, each family is susceptible of presenting harm and abuse to child and in some cases, a child may face greater risk of abuse within four walls of her home than would be the outside. The abuser can be uncle, grandfather or horrifying, even a father. No relationship is sacred anymore. A child is not safe even at home. As a matter of fact, statistics defy the myth that child can be exposed to such abuse only at the hands of a stranger. The statistical data show that the perpetrator is, in 90 per cent of cases, a person known to the victim or from within the family.

The study conducted by Sakshi, a Delhi-based organization, confirms the fact that majority (75%) of the abusers fall in the category of close relatives like father, grandfather or family friend. The findings of survey conducted by Samvaad, a Bangalore-based organization, in the year 1994, of the girl students from 11th standard in Bangalore, also show that around 65 per cent child sexual abuse cases involved family members and close relatives, and these cases happened, within the four walls of 'Sweet Home' Abusers are also from the people moving behind the facade of respectability. More secure place for the child often becomes insecure.

At international level also it is well recognized that the majority of sexual abusers are known to their victims. The study by Kennedy and Manwell, on the pattern of child sexual abuse in Northern Ireland (1992), also confirms that in 85 per cent of the cases, abuses were committed by relatives or a person known to the victim. Most cases of child sexual abuse are not the cases, where a child is abducted from the street and attacked by an unknown assailant. Instead, they typically involve the abuse, sometimes carried on over several years and increasing in severity, by person whom the child trusts. The study in the UK (1983) discloses that 74 per cent of the victims already knew their abusers and 58 per cent were abused by family members. The picture in the USA is more or less similar. Finkelhor, on the topic of 'sexually victimized children' (1979), reported that of a group of 530 female college students, 17 per cent had been abused before puberty and out of those approximately 50 per cent had been abused by a relative. In cases involving stranger abuse, the majority had single encounters, whereas in the case of abuse by a known or family figure, the abuse was repeated.

The study conducted by a Delhi-based organization RAHI, of middle and upper class women, in respect of incest and childhood sexual abuse, supports this finding. It reveals that perpetrators in 71 per cent of cases were someone known to the victims or close to the victims; majority of abusers in the family were maternal and paternal uncles and cousins; father and brothers came next; and in the category of known persons were included male family friends and servants. Age of the victim howsoever tender could not keep the abuser away from the crime. The survey by the Central Social Welfare Board has also found that most of the child prostitutes in our country have already been subjected to child sexual abuse by their own family members and to escape from that, they have run away or have been forced into this trade.

H.D. Shourie[16] of the Common Cause has also found that in 70 per cent of the rape cases, the rapists are found to be known to the victims. There is hardly any city or town where heart-rending cases of atrocities against girls are not taking place, which makes one hang his head in utter shame. One wonders whether we have any right to be included among civilized people. Sydney Brandman was, therefore, constrained to observe that, "statistically it is safer to be on the streets after dark with a stranger than at the home in the bosom of one's family. For it is at home most accidents of murders and violence are likely to occur".

The study of about 100 reported cases by this author confirms that the common categories of perpetrators are the father or uncle, cousin or family friend and in other cases, either he is a school teacher, principal or even the priest, the neighbour, or servant. The blood relationship has no more remained a guarantee of safety or purity of relation. However, on account of family 'izzat' and so-called prestige such cases do not see the light of the day or get reported. The 99 per cent of such cases remain unreported to any one and hence unknown to the public, therefore, the myth prevails that child is safe in the family with relatives, neighbours or friends.

## Which is the place of occurrence?

Even the most secure and protected place on the earth, like one's own home is not free from sexual abuse for the child. As a matter of fact, in 70 to 80 per cent of the reported cases, the assault is committed on the child, either in her own house or in the house of perpetrator. Four walls of the house, which were considered as fortress, have no more remained so. When the insiders in the family are acting under the lustful feelings, how any relation or any place can remain secure? This research supports the statistical data collected so far, that home is the worst place, where such incidents took place most often and the relatives are the first persons, who subject the child to assault. The reasons for the same may be two-fold. One, because the house or the home is a place, where whatever happens is hardly known to the others. Within four walls of the house, even if one shouts, screams or cries, the stranger or any outsider is not expected to know about it and even if he comes to know about it, rarely will any person intervene in the private affairs of the house. The perpetrators take the advantage of this very security and privacy that the house provides. Here, the child is easily accessible and within reach, without anyone suspecting or coming to known about it. Therefore, the very security, which the house provides, becomes a liability as far as the protection of child is concerned, from such attacks.

Another reason, why such attacks are found to be committed more in the house, is that the child places implicit reliance, faith and trust on the person, who comes to the house. House is meant for close acquaintances with all the family members. Therefore, the child is not only easily accessible in the home but is more prone to such attacks because she is not in a position to resist and is greatly confounded. Even somewhat mature girls, aged 10 to 12 years, found it difficult to make disclosure about these incidents, because of being accused or being suspected of making such eerie allegations against someone, known to the family or someone, from the family. This is one reason, of which the perpetrator is fully aware and takes advantage to its full limits.

### Incest

Of all the forms of child sexual abuse, incest is the most heinous and serious because, it is perpetrated by one family member against another, by someone having the blood relationship and in the position of authority and trust like father, brother and uncle. It is betrayal of the trust of child and it has got serious impact on the victim child. Incest, as is said, is almost a state of lifetime condemnation for child. Yet, its existence in our society is rarely acknowledged. Incest has been forbidden by almost every religion and society with some variations. However, though all societies have had some type of taboo, it is believed that incest has existed throughout all ages in all known societies.

### Factors responsible for child sexual abuse in general and for incest in particular

Though there are several factors responsible for such sexual abusive or incestuous behaviour, the first and foremost factor may be the inability of the person to control impulse and lust overpowering the person to such an extent that he loses the sense of distinguishing right from the wrong. But, then, why of all the persons, they select the child? The reason is simple. The child is an easy prey, the most vulnerable, not in a position to protest and disclose, and therefore easily pliable. Abuse may go on for years together but no one will come to know about it; no one will suspect also, the relationship being so close that any sexual component in it is expected to be devoid of. The age difference between the victim and perpetrator is also such that even if child dares to disclose it, no one will believe. In case of incestuous abuse, the perpetrator being in a position of trust, the guardian of the child, like father, elder brother, uncle, etc., the child is easily available and accessible. The concept of family honour and unity being so strong that such abuse always remains a closely guarded secret. Therefore, here, the easy availability of child and her helpless dependency upon adult – the perpetrator – acts as an important contributing factor for such sexual or incestuous abuse. Lack of religious education and degradation of the moral standards also lead to such crimes.[17] With an increase in permissiveness, the concepts of morality and family norms are also being changed. The ill-effects of TV, cable, and films are also pervading in family life, in one form or other. Apart from these factors, the increase in occurrence of such incidents may also be appearing on account of reporting of non-these incidents. Sexual abuse has existed in families for ages but was shrouded in silence because of women's and children's dependency and subservient role. The women and children have suffered sexual abuse in families and outside but have not voiced their humiliation because the social system wants to ignore it, in order to save the honour of the families and the prestige of the family institution. However, now, with the advanced education and the economic independence, the social acceptability, which the women are getting, is empowering or enabling them to raise voice and report about these incidents of sexual abuse of their children to police and therefore one finds the increase in the reported cases. Even then, one must not forget the documented figures are only proverbial tip of the iceberg. To repeat, it has to be stated that behind one reported case, there are at least ten unreported cases.

The newspapers, day in and day out, carry the reports of incestuous relationships, as still today they have the sensational value. The statistical data shows that every third or fourth day, a case of incest is reported in the paper. These figures again do not reflect exact rate of incidents. Only a fraction of child rape cases are reported. But, the cases of continuous sexual abuse within the families, as in the case of incest, are seldom reported. In case of incest, the statistics are often elusive in the sense that, actually less than 1 per cent of such cases are reported than the incest committed by family members. Loyalty to the family unit seems to discourage filing of formal complaints. Moreover, the offender is someone to whom the child relates emotionally as well as economically. Therefore, there is very less possibility of child reporting about it.[18]

The existing laws do not reflect the specific and peculiar aspects of the child sexual abuse. They do not reflect the violation of child's bodily integrity and her inability to defend herself from such intrusion. It is still the deepest secret, jointly held by the family. There is also no law in India which recognizes it as an offence. Moreover, child sexual abuse is also not a single incident like rape; it is a repeated and continued act. Therefore, it has far-reaching impact on the physical and psychological well-being of the child. The physical damage is not restricted to injuries and scars alone but the child may succumb to death or intentionally put to deliberate death in the process. It is not only the violation of physic alone but of the childhood and innocence also.

## Psychological impact

The incest leaves behind a devastating impact on the entire life of the child. It destroys the entire psychology of the child and pushes her into deep emotional crisis. It violates the victim's most cherished values and basic rights. It causes trauma and agony, with which the child has to live rest of her life. The immediate and the predominant impact of sexual abuse on a child is that of shock. The child is utterly perplexed as to what is happening to her. As the offender is known to the victim or is one of her family members, she is further confounded with utter disbelief.

As per the survey carried out by Samvaad, the pre-dominant feelings amongst the victims are of utter sadness, frustration, helplessness, guilt, fear, humiliation and anger, coupled with distrust of men, disgust and confusion. They are also prone to a variety of psychological and behavioural disturbances caused by trauma of abuse. These could include bed wetting, nightmares, sleep disorders, depression, anxiety, running away from home, multiple personality disorders, precocious sexual behaviour or its reverse, extreme inhibition and low self-esteem caused by a sense of guilt and shame.

Then comes the feeling of guilt, especially when the abuser is some elder member of the family, which happens in most of the cases. The child starts self-blaming, holding herself responsible for whatever has happened. Her anger and rage turns in words. She starts having the feeling of being accused of participation or provocation and fear of loved ones' reaction: a fear of being ridiculed.

From all this agony and mental trauma, the child victim nurtures the fear of disclosure. Not only is she being engulfed with the feeling of shame and desire to protect herself from the ridicule but is most worried of reactions of her close ones. She is not sure whether her family members will believe her, or whether they will hold her responsible for it. The fear of being maligned forces the child to keep quiet and then the secret shame and pain becomes too tremendous a burden for a young mind to carry, leading at times to self-contempt and self-destruction. What happens is that in most cases when abused child turns to her mother for help, mothers themselves are not only powerless but also sometimes victims of abuse themselves and therefore unable to protect the child. Pressure is brought on the mother forcing her not to break the silence, as this would mean loss of face for the family. Therefore, even if the child gathers courage to disclose about abuse to the mother, she is forced to keep quiet saying that such things do not happen.[19]

There may be several other reasons also why the children do not disclose about such abuse. Sometimes, the children are coerced into participation and sometimes are even made to believe that, what is happening is okay. Very often, the abuser builds a special relationship with the child. He is often the favourite uncle or parent or even the only adult around, who does not neglect the child. The child is showered with presents and affection. But, when the abuse begins, the abuser withholds his affection. If the child refuses to do as he says, abuser tries to portray the abuse as a special secret between the child and him.

He exploits the fact that child loves him deeply and is emotionally dependent upon him. This also affects the chances of disclosure.[20]

## Inadequacies of laws

The laws are also inadequate to deal with the problem as such abuse is neither rape nor violation of modesty and does not come within the purview of any existing provision of law. In the existing laws there is neither the definition of 'sexual abuse' nor is there any separate provision or chapter dealing exclusively with these offences. The definition of rape is too restrictive as it does not cover sexual violation by any other object or part of body except the male organ, whereas the concept of violation of modesty is quite obscure and it carries moral overtones, hence, rarely applicable to children. There is also no law, which recognizes the offence of incest, which is so widespread and has serious implications on the child. It is treated like ordinary offence of rape, though its gravity is enhanced on account of such abuse being committed by close family member and hence it also amounts to betrayal of trust. Moreover, it is also repeated over the years. The existing laws do not address the specific features of the sexual abuse perpetrated on children. Sexual abuse of child has its own characteristics, which require separate and different treatment than that of the sexual abuse on adult person.

The irony is that the Constitution of India, which is the source of all laws, contains several provisions and mandates to safeguard the interests of children and to afford them special protection, which they require and deserve. For example Article 15(3) permits the favourable discrimination, as regards women and children. Similarly Article 39(e) and (f) of the Directive Principles for State Policy deals with the duty of state towards prevention of exploitation of children.

The crucial question is how the society and criminal justice system respond to this plight of the child, the trauma and life crisis faced by such victims? The answer is very sad. Response of the society and criminal justice system is not only unsatisfactory but instead of reducing this trauma, working of the system only aggravates the same, which leads to further victimization of the child. This victimization of child may not be purposeful or intentional but it occurs unknowingly, not being fully aware of the trauma faced by child. Sometimes police and courts also face some difficulties in recording details with such child victims. Thus, from the victim's, police's and judge's points of view, these cases pose serious and difficult proposition. Lack of adequate laws and absence of special court or separate procedure, as in the case of juvenile delinquents under Juvenile Justice (Care and Protection of Children) Act, 2000, seriously hamper the trial of such cases. No special training, no guidelines or fixed parameters, no awareness and no research to deal with these cases make the investigation and trial of such cases a difficult task both for the police and the court, which again works as a disadvantage to the child victim, as these factors go to add to the secondary victimization of the child in this entire process.

### What constitutes child sexual abuse?

There is neither the legal definition of the 'child', nor any standard definition of the term, 'sexual abuse'. From common man's point of view, the 'child' may be someone, who has not attained majority and 'sexual abuse' generally and only means rape, i.e., forcible sexual intercourse or violation of modesty and hence victim of such abuse has to be always a female. However, it is not always so. Child sexual abuse can take place in various forms and degrees, entailing different consequences and impacts. Just as, it can be brutal, it can also be subtle! Just as it can be physically violent, it can also be even without touching the child; it can be oral or even by facial expressions and body language. Mere engaging the toddler in pornographic material also amounts to sexual abuse. Just as use of criminal force for violation of modesty of a woman is an offence involving sexual abuse, fondling or touching the child in a suggestive manner is also no less a sexual abuse. The experiences/instances of child sexual abuse may also vary from person to person and include:

- An adult exposure of genitals to the child or to persuade the child to do the same.
- The adult touching the child's genitals or making the child to touch his own.
- Involving the child in pornography both printed and visual which includes showing a child pornographic material.
- Using the child for his own satisfaction even without touching, just by ejaculating on the private parts of the child.
- Having oral, vaginal or anal intercourse with the child.
- Making verbal or other sexual suggestions or indecent overtures/gestures.
- Fondling, fingering or touching the private parts of the child or any such attempt.
- Inserting foreign objects in the private parts of the child for own sexual gratification.
- An adult persuading child to engage in sexual activity.

As sexual abuse is the outcome of pervert mind, there is no limit how many varied forms it can take but one thing is certain that it is an all-pervasive abuse of the physic, mind and emotion of the child. It is violation of the child's dignity and basic human right, entailing life-shattering long-term effects on the child.

### Measures for prevention

Given the long-term scars child sexual abuse leaves behind, the best approach is to prevent the abuse. It is necessary to stop such abuse before it happens. Prevention of such abuse can be achieved mainly through awareness-raising. As the offence of child sexual abuse is shrouded in mystery and surrounded by silence, only the awareness about it will help to prevent it. The children being small, unable to understand it or to speak about it, this awareness has to be created in their parents, teachers and the society at large. For that the media can play a vital role. To some extent the children should also be given some basic information on sexuality. They should be made aware to know the difference between good touch and bad touch. That will save the children not only of being subject of such sexual abuse but it will also help address some basic barriers in children disclosing their abuse thereby getting help for themselves. Voluntary organizations can and do play an active role in public awareness and prevention by conducting awareness programmes in schools and colleges with children, teachers and parents by organizing workshops and seminars. Such subject can be introduced in the college syllabus.

It is necessary to make amendments in the law, casting a mandatory duty on the people like doctors, nurses, social workers, psychologists, marriage and family counsellors, hospital administrators, coroners, clergymen, teachers, librarians, school counsellors and attorneys to report any suspected abuse, if they have a 'reasonable suspicion' about it and their failure to report, resulting in criminal sanctions. This is a crucial issue, especially as all those identified as having an obligation to report must invariably be coming across cases of abuse and ignoring it as a private matter. In case of incestuous sexual abuse, as family members are most reluctant to disclose or lodge any report about it, the provision of mandatory reporting of the incidents will be the only and best alternative, otherwise these offences will never be made known or reported and victim will keep on suffering. In such cases, provision should be made for protecting the identity of the person who has reported the abuse. In this respect, the assistance of the organizations and individuals who work as helpline will be of utmost importance. The helplines are in the nature of doctors and counsellors who are experienced professionals in the handling of childhood – female and male. There is thus a need of adopting multidisciplinary approach.

In this direction, there is also much scope and need for appointment of National Commission for Children on the line of National Commission for Women. It will be necessary for the overall development of our future citizenry.

Ultimately, only by our dedicated and sustained efforts and by becoming accountable and answerable to our children, we can protect our future.

## Notes

1. (1996) 2 SCC 384 at p. 403.
2. Mangilal v. State of M.P. 1998 Cri.L.J. 2304 (M.P.).
3. Saddik Singh v. State of Maharashtra 1993 Cri.L.J.2919 (Bom.)
4. Madan Gopal Kakkad V. Naval Dubey (1992) 3 SCC 204.
5. Javita Narang, "Children sexual abuse, 'NGO's perspective", Women's Link, (New Delhi), (2000 July–September), pp. 20–24 at p. 22.
6. Pinki Virani, *Bitter Chocolate,* (Penguin Books, India 2000), p. 17.
7. Surekha Raman, "Violation of Innocence: Child Sexual Abuse", The Cover Story, From the Lawyers Collective (New Delhi), Vol. 10, (October–November 1995) pp. 4–7 at p. 6.
8. Preliminary report of a workshop series and surveys on childhood sexual abuse of girls, Ms. Anita Ratnam Ganesh (Samwad, Bangalore 1994).
9. Child Sexual Abuse: A preliminary report based on school workshops in Delhi, (Sakshi, 1996)
10. "The children we sacrifice", *The Times of India,* Pune News Line, 11 December 2000.
11. *Times of India,* Pune Edition, Dt. 9–1–2005.
12. See the cases of, The Child Victim – of 2 years: Kakoo v. State of H.P. A.I.R. 1976 S.C. 1992. State of Delhi v. Pannalal 1993 Cri. L.J. 852 (Delhi). The Child Victim – of 2 ½ Years Ramesh v. State of Maharashtra 2001, Cri. L.J. 1579 (Bom.). Bhawani Giri and Deo Kumar v. State of Rajasthan 1995 Cri. L.J. 983 (Raj.) The Child Victim – of 3 years: Jagdish Pandit Sharma v. State 1994 Cri. L.J. 774 (Bom.).
13. Vir Bahadur V. State 1995 Cri. L.J. 2501 (Delhi). The Child Victim of 11 months.
14. See the cases of – R.K. Agarwal v. State of Orissa A.I.R. 1976 S.C. 1774. Riyasat v. State of U.P. 1993 Cri. L.J. 2834 (All), etc.
15. See the case of, Public Prosecutor, Andhra Pradesh High Court v. Lingi Setty Sreena, 1997, Cri. L.J. 4003 (A.P.) where prosecutrix was a dumb girl of 14 years left alone in the house by her mother and when mother returned, she found the offender lying naked on the body of prosecutrix. See also the case of Mango v. State of Haryana 1979 Cri. L.J. 939 (P&H) where 12 to 13 years deaf and dumb girl subjected to sexual assault.
16. Shourie, H.D. "Atrocities against women are our national shame", *The Times of India* (Mumbai), 3 May 1999.

17. Abdul Wahid v. State of Maharashtra, 1996 Cri. L.J. 29 (Bom.).
18. Legal Corner, Woman's Link (New Delhi) (January–March 2000), p. 60.
19. Lalita Panicker, "The Cruelty that begins at Home", *The Times of India*, (Mumbai), 20 August 1999.
20. "Silent Suffering", cover story, *News Week* (Delhi), 7 June 1997.

CHAPTER NINE

# Cruelty and physical torture against children in family

## Socio-legal dimensions

*Durgambini Patel*

Family is a social institution and child is the most integral, important, sensitive and vulnerable component of it. For proper and wholesome development of child's personality, it is essential that the family atmosphere is supportive and conducive, wherein supreme welfare of child can be achieved. The family conditions must provide an atmosphere of happiness, love and understanding for the realization of the child's talents and potentials. The family must essentially provide for all the emotional, physical and material security necessary for the proper development of the child and must prevent situations associated with abuse, violence and exploitation.

Children are considered as the nation's supremely important national asset and its living malleable potential. The future of any nation is largely determined on how its children grow and develop. The issues relating to the rights of child, care and welfare have been constantly engaging the attention of the world.[1] These factors emphasize the need of suitable family atmosphere for a child. A responsibility lies on a family to prepare a child to be a responsible and good citizen and human being. It is essential for this purpose to provide care and nurture a child in the atmosphere of understanding, peace and tolerance. Use of corporal punishment is antithetic to these values. We cannot subject the child to torture and still expect him/her to act with understanding, peace and tolerance towards others and be a protagonist of peace and love. It was probably for this reason Mahatma Gandhi said that "if we are to reach real peace in this world, and if we are to carry on a real war against war, we shall have to begin with children. And if they will grow up in their natural innocence, we won't have to struggle, we won't have to pass fruitless idle resolutions, but we shall go from love to love and peace to peace, until at last all the corners of the world are covered with peace and love for which consciously or unconsciously, the whole world is hungering."[2]

## Violence against child a social phenomenon

Each year, thousands of children are cruelly beaten by their parents, and some are even killed in the process of such harsh and irrational beating. Physical cruelty commonly takes the form of prick, punch, facial bruises, cigarette burns, head injuries and fractured bones. Gunshots and knife injuries are also reported. According to an estimated report, thousands of children die each year in India due to parental assaults and many others are permanently paralyzed, physically deformed or mentally retarded. The newspapers have always reported that the babies and young children have had scalding water poured on their faces. They have been strangled, stomped and burned with cigarettes, matches and hot irons. They have been shut in closets for several days without food. Many times they have been beaten again and again by intoxicated, drugged parents.[3]

Cruelty and physical torture against children in the institution of family is a widespread phenomenon and exists in one form or other.[4] Corporal punishment, as mode of maintaining discipline among children in schools and at home, is common to all societies. Recently, we have understood the evils of these practices and adopted more scientific and reformed approaches to tackle problems of discipline and moulding behaviour patterns of children, namely, counselling, correction and therapeutic approaches, psychological treatments etc. Modern society has become sensitive towards children's issue. However, there still prevails widespread violence against children due to their weak, vulnerable status.

## Laws in India

The Constitution of India inter alia extensively deals with child protection and welfare. Having identified them as disadvantaged section of society, they are entitled for protective discrimination under Article 15 (3) of the Constitution of India.[5]

An elaborate interpretation given to the Article 21 of the Constitution by the Indian judiciary have brought revolution in understanding the fundamental rights. The sum total of judicial dicta emphasized that right to life and personal liberty does not mean mere physical existence or being medically alive, but it includes the right to essential means and facilities, which makes life worth living with comfort and dignity. It contemplates an atmosphere where a person can grow physically as well as mentally without fear and restriction. It means more than mere survival or animal existence and protection against deprivations, which are essential for all those limits and abilities through which life is enjoyed.

Right to life and personal liberty is the most precious, sacrosanct, inalienable and fundamental of all the fundamental rights of citizens/persons. It is one of the most essential basic human rights in a democratic state. It is the backbone of human right movements, both at national and international levels. The human rights are a direct progenitor of doctrine of natural law.[6]

The courts have construed right to life widely. On a larger canvas right to life includes all that which gives meaning to life and makes it wholesome and worth living.[7] Article 21, in its expanded horizon, confers the medley of rights on a person, including the following:

1. A life of dignity.
2. A life, which ensures freedom from arbitrary and despotic control, torture and terror.
3. Life protected against cruelty, physical or mental violence, injury or abuse, and exploitation, including sexual abuse.

All these rights are available to the children and they cannot be deprived of the same just because they are small. Being small does not make them a less human being than a grown up. Whatever rights are available to the former are also available to the latter. Imposition of corporal punishment on the child is not in consonance with the right to life guaranteed by Article 21 of the Constitution. It is violative of child's dignity and human right. It is, therefore, cruel to subject the child to physical violence in school and in family in the name of discipline.[8]

The child being a precious national resource is to be nurtured and attended with tenderness and care and not with cruelty. Subjecting the child to corporal punishment for reforming cannot be part of education and discipline. It causes incalculable harm to both body and mind. In *F.C. Mullin v. Administrator, Union Territory of Delhi*,[9] the Supreme Court held that Article 21 protects every limb or faculty through which life is enjoyed. This would include the abilities of thinking and feeling. Freedom of life and liberty guaranteed by Article 21 is not only violated when physical punishment scars the body, but that freedom is also violated when it scars the mind of the child and robs him/her of his/her dignity. Any act of violence, which traumatizes, terrorizes a child, or adversely affects his/her faculties falls foul of Article 21 of the Constitution.[10]

Article 39 of the Constitution imposes positive mandate on the state to strive to achieve better conditions of living for children devoid of exploitation and abuse. Under sub-clause (e) of Article 39, the state is to frame and follow policies and laws towards securing conditions wherein the tender age children are not abused and forced by economic necessity to enter vocations unsuited to their age or strength. Similarly, sub-clause (f) states that children are given opportunities and facilities to develop in a healthy manner and in conditions of freedom and dignity and that childhood and youth are protected against exploitation and moral and material abandonment.

## International scenario

As early as in 1924, the need to extend special care was set out in the Geneva Declaration on the Rights of the Child. In December 1948, the Universal Declaration on Human Rights proclaimed that childhood is entitled to special care and assistance. This has also been affirmed in the International Convention on Civil and Political Rights, the International Convention on Economic, Social and Cultural Rights and in the statutes and relevant instruments of specialized agencies and international organizations concerned with the welfare of children. Yet another declaration on the children was adopted by the U.N. General Assembly in 1959. The Convention on the Rights of the Child (CRC), adopted by the U.N. General Assembly, in November 1989, provides a comprehensive framework of rights of the children at global level, so that they can have right to live with dignity and human existence. The Government of India ratified CRC on November 12, 1992, and has once again reaffirmed its commitment to child welfare and protection.

The CRC draws attention to four sets of basic rights:

1. *The Right to Survival:* which includes the right to life, the highest attainable standard of health, nutrition and adequate standard of living.
2. *The Right to Protection:* which includes freedom from all forms of exploitation, abuse, inhuman or degrading treatment and neglect, including the right to special protection in situations of emergency and armed conflicts.
3. *The Right to Development:* which includes the right to education, support for early childhood development and care, social security and the right to leisure, recreation and cultural activities.
4. *The Right to Participation:* which includes the respect for the view of the child, freedom of expression, access to appropriate information and freedom of thought, conscience and religion.

The Convention provides the legal basis for initiating action to ensure the rights of children in society. The CRC Charter has 54 articles divided into three parts. While Part I (Articles 1–41) deals with rights of child, Part II (Articles 42 to 45) and Part III (Articles 46 to 54) deal with the implementation of CRC.

The detailed rights recognized under CRC are as follows:

1. Every child is entitled from birth to nationality and name.
2. He/She has the right to develop his/her personality to the fullest and to participate in play, cultural and artistic activities.
3. He/She has the right to nutritious food, safe drinking water and a secure home.
4. He/She has the right to be protected from abuse and neglect.

5. He/She has the right to family and if the family is not there, he/she has the right to institutional care, placement and treatment.
6. The child, who is handicapped, has the right to special care, education and training.
7. He/She has the right for protection from any form of dangerous work, which might affect his/her health, education or development in any way.
8. He/She has the right to be protected from sexual exploitation and abuse.
9. Every child has the right to be protected from torture, cruel treatment, punishment, capital punishment, unlawful arrest and restriction of their freedom.
10. Every child has a right to education (Article 21A of the Indian Constitution recognizes this right as a fundamental right)
11. The child has also the right to have the highest level of health possible and access to medical facilities.
12. All children shall enjoy their rights without discrimination of race, colour, sex, religion, nation, property, birth or status.

## Child rights as human rights

The Protection of Human Rights Act, 1993, under section 2 (d), defines 'human rights' as the rights relating to life, liberty, equality and dignity of the individual guaranteed by the constitution or embodied in the international covenants and enforceable by courts in India.

Since childhood is the foundation of human life, ensuring child rights is the first step towards ensuring human rights. Further, children are the most vulnerable group, as they do not have a political constituency in any system to represent their interests. Hence, there is every possibility of violation of child's rights, which in turn becomes violation of human rights. In India, children in the age group of 0–14 years constitute a little over one-third of the country's population, constituting around 307 million. In spite of the constitutional guarantees and enactment of laws for care and protection of children and their rights, prevalence of high infant mortality rate, high illiteracy, abundant child labour, malnutrition, etc., are the indicators which show that children's rights are not taken care of.[11]

Children all over the world are victims of human right violation – whether it is sexual exploitation of minors in the United States, bonded labour in Pakistan or child labour in India.

There is no way to enumerate thoroughly the various ways in which children around the world are economically exploited and physically mistreated. Their sufferings are great and widespread. The adult being in stronger position exploits and uses violence, that compromises children's humanity and subjects them to physical and emotional tortures (hostility towards their problems, omission of praise, continuous criticism, humiliating etc.)

There has been great concern for the welfare of children at the international level culminating in the Declaration of the Rights of the Child adopted by the General Assembly of the Untied Nations. The Declaration, in its Preamble, points out that the child by reason of his physical and mental immunity needs special safeguards and care, including appropriate legal protection, before as well as after birth, and that mankind owes to the child the best it has to give and formulated several principles. It provides that the child shall enjoy special protection and shall be given opportunities and facilities, by law and by other means, to enable him/her to develop physical, mentally, morally, spiritually and socially in a healthy and normal manner and in conditions of freedom and dignity. In the enactment of law for this purpose, the best interests of the child shall be the paramount consideration. Child shall also be protected from all forms of neglect, cruelty and exploitation.[12]

Children's programme should find a prominent place in our national plans for the development of human resources, so that our children grow up to become robust citizens, physically fit, mentally alert and morally healthy, endowed with skills and motivations, needed by society. Equal opportunities for development to all children during the period of growth should be our aim, for this would serve our larger purpose of reducing inequality and ensuring social justice.[13]

The Government of India, in pursuance of the constitutional provisions of clauses (e) and (f) of Article 39, evolved a national policy for the welfare of the children. In a civilized society, the importance of child welfare needs to be over emphasized because the welfare of the entire community, its growth and development, depends on the health and well-being of its children. There is a growing realization in every part of the globe that children must be brought up in an atmosphere of love and affection and under the tender care and attention, so that they may be able to attain full emotional, intellectual and spiritual stability and maturity and acquire self-confidence and self-respect and a balance view of life with full appreciation and realization of the role which they have to play in the nation-building process without which the nation cannot develop and attain real prosperity because a large segment of the society would then be left out of the developmental process. In India, this consciousness is reflected in the provisions enacted in the Constitution[14] as well as policies, programmes and schemes adopted by the government for integrated development of child. However, the truth and reality is that, today's child is exposed to many forms of abuses and torture both within and outside home.

Various forms that tantamount to exploitation, cruelty and physical torture are:

1. Child labour, domestic workers.
2. Child prostitution.
3. Child sexual abuse within the family (offence of incest) or by an outsider.
4. Depriving educational facilities or overburden with educational stress.
5. Denial of adequate nutrition and health care.
6. Use of children for committing crimes, drug trafficking.
7. Child battering and corporal punishments.
8. Sexual molestation.
9. Verbal abuse.
10. Problems of destitute and neglected children.
11. Female infanticide.
12. Use of juveniles by adults to commit crimes.
13. Absence of proper medical facilities.
14. Child marriage.

The focus of this paper is to deal with physical torture and cruelty against children and to examine the legal aspects pertaining to the same.

## Corporal punishments

Several times this form of torture goes unnoticed, as there is passive acceptance to this as a method of discipline in the society and is not considered as objectionable. The corporal punishment can be defined as a "discipline method in which the supervising adult deliberately inflicts pain upon a child in response to a child's unacceptable behaviour and/or inappropriate language."[15] The immediate aims of such punishments are usually to halt the offence, prevent its recurrence and set an example for others. The purported long-term goal is to change the child's behaviour and to make it more consistent with the adult's expectations. In corporal punishment, the adult usually hits various parts of the child's body with hand, or with canes, paddles, yardsticks, belts, or other objects expected to cause pain and fear. Corporal punishment is the intentional inflicting of pain upon a child because he or she has exhibited unacceptable behaviour. Slapping, punching, kicking and choking are also included under the definition of corporal punishment.

## Ill-effects of physical torture and corporal punishment

Hitting children teaches them to become hitter themselves. In many cases of so-called 'bad behaviour', the child is simply responding according to his/her own experience of violence and torture. Corporal punishment distracts the child from learning to resolve conflicts in an effective and humane way. Punishment interferes with the bond between parent and child, as it is not human nature to feel loving towards someone who hurts them. The true spirit of cooperation, which every parent desires, can arise only through a strong bond based on mutual feelings of love and respect. Punishment, even when it appears to work, can produce only superficially good behaviour based on fear, which can only take place until the child is old enough to resist. In contrast, cooperation based on respect will last permanently, bringing many years of mutual happiness, as the child and parent grow older.

Research has revealed that physical torture has psychological effect on children. Corporal punishment is ineffective and non-productive. It makes children defiant, rebellious and hostile. Anger and frustration gets stored in the mind of the child and such children grow up to become spouse beaters, molesters and rapists. They believe that might is right and violence is the answer to most of the problems.

## Gender perspective

In patriarchal society there is blatant discrimination between the male and female child. The plight of the female children is worse and they are always treated inferior to male children within the institution of family. Even before being born, the girl child is denied the right to be born. The modern science and technology is misused to detect the sex of the foetus and if it is female foetus is destructed. In spite of passing the statutes like the Pre-Natal Diagnostic Techniques (Regulation and Prevention of Misuse) Act, 1994, the law is incompetent to control the falling rate of girl children. Female infanticide is a great problem in India. The girl child, if born, is maltreated in terms of nutrition and education. There is high rate of child marriages leading to early motherhood and poor health conditions among the females in India.

There are several forms of domestic violence against women within the family. They are more prone to all types of sexual abuse. The laws and the institutions operating in the legal system are insensitive towards women's issues and there is wide prevalence of gender bias.

## Concluding remarks and suggestions

It is pertinent to note at this juncture that corporal punishments have been condemned as a mode of dealing with the criminals with the emergence of modern criminology. It is considered as barbaric and uncivilized practice and is outdated. It is, therefore, important to discard this kind of inhuman practices while dealing with innocent children in case of so-called deviant behaviour which does not match the thinking of the adult. The problems of conflicting nature in children shall be dealt by using modern scientific techniques such as counselling, psychological approach as well as reorientation techniques.

Though India has framed several national policies and programmes, and identified the children as the 'supreme national asset', they have remained on paper and are not effectively implemented. For effective implementation and to monitor and supervise the same, the government should formulate a National Plan for Children and issue a White Paper to implement it. The Commissions for Protection of Child Rights shall work effectively and efficiently to achieve their objectives and aims. Corresponding amendments should be carried out in the substantive and procedural criminal laws to make it child-friendly and sensitive and to implement programmes and policies adopted by the government for the benefit of the children.

There shall be a comprehensive code for children that shall define cruelty to child and physical torture in an exhaustive manner. The code must also identify voluntary organizations of the citizens and NGOs working in the field as authorities to identify child-related problems in society and to aid and assist the state machinery to fulfil their duties towards children.

Besides, social skill training should be imparted to parents and teachers to tackle problems of deviance and other disciplinary matters relating to child, scientifically, without indulgence in any form of torture. It may be noted that Article 4 of CRC, 1989 recognizes inter alia that states parties shall undertake all appropriate legislative, administrative and other measures for the implementation of the rights of the child recognized in the Convention. Article 6 of the Convention recognizes right to life as an inherent right of the child and imposes duties on the states parties to ensure to the maximum extent possible, the survival and development of the child. Article 19 also requires states parties to take all appropriate legislative, administrative, social and educational measures to protect the child from all forms of physical or mental violence, injury or abuse, neglect or negligent treatment, maltreatment or exploitation, including sexual abuse, while in the care of patent(s), legal guardian(s) or any other person who has the care of the child. It further imposes duties on states parties to adopt social programme to provide necessary support to child. Therefore, it is necessary to make laws to give full effect to the Convention on the Rights of the Child.

The violators of the rights of the child must be punished severely and absolute nature of liability shall be imposed in this regard. Vigilance committees, similar to that of Human Rights Watch, shall be appointed in various parts of the society to identify atrocities against the children and various forms of cruelty and torture towards the children. Machinery should be established to give social-legal remedies and relief to the victim child and his/her rehabilitation, wherein he/she is free from physical torture and cruelty. The machinery should be empowered to take *suo moto* action without hindrance of the doctrine of *locus standi*. This may be especially required when the child is not able to raise voice or complain because of the pressures of hostile, drunken or drugged parents. The social work organizations and judiciary should be sensitized to give appropriate relief to the victim child.

## Notes

1. See, Justice Palok Basu, *Law Relating to Protection of Human Rights under the Indian Constitutional and Allied Laws* (2002, Modern Law Publication, Allahabad), p. 137.
2. *Parents Forum for Meaningful Education* v. *Union of India*, AIR 2001, Del. 212, p. 218.
3. Subhash Chandra Singh, "Growing Problem of Child Abuse and Neglect", referred in 2001 Cri. LJ. Journal Section 50 at p. 51. (Referred from Palik Basu, (op. cit.), p. 143.
4. There may be various forms of abuses and exploitation such as child labour, child sexual abuse, emotional and physical tortures, depriving the child from proper physical and mental development, child prostitution, use of children to commit crimes, denial of right to education etc.
5. Nothing in this Article shall prevent the state from making any special provisions for the women and children.

6. Sunil and Kiran Deshta, *Fundamental Human Rights (The Right to Life and Personal Liberty)*, 2003, Deep and Deep Publications (P) Ltd., New Delhi, p. 1.
7. This view finds support from the various decisions in *Munn* v. *Illinois* (1876–78) 94 US 113. *Maneka Gandhi (Smt.)* v. *Union of India*, AIR 1978 SC 597. *State of Maharashtra* v. *Chandra Bhan*, AIR 1983 SC 803, *Kharak Singh* v. *State of U.P.*, AIR 1963 SC 1295, *C. Masilamani Mudaliar* v. *Idol of Sri Swaminathaswami Swaminathaswami Thirukoil*, AIR 1996 SC 1697, *Glan Kaur* v. *State of Punjab*, AIR 1996 SC 946. All cases referred in *Parents Forum for Meaningful Education* v. *Union of India*. AIR, 2001 Del 212, p. 217 (DB).
8. *Parents Forum for Meaningful Education* v. *Union of India*, AIR 2001 Del 212, p. 217 (DB).
9. AIR 1981 SC 746, p. 753: *referred in Parents Forum for Meaningful Education* v. *Union of India*, AIR 2001 Del 212, p. 218 (DB).
10. *Parents Forum for Meaningful Education* v. *Union of India*, AIR 2001 Del 212, p. 217 (DB). Article 24, dealing with prohibition of employment of children in factories and Article 23, dealing with traffic in human being and forced labour establishes the rights of children of freedom from exploitation and violence. Also see, generally, Justice Palok Basu, op. cit.
11. K. Venugopala Rao, PGDHR 422, University of Hyderabad, Hyderabad.
12. Sathyavan Kottarakkara v. State, AIR 1997 Ker 133, p. 137; (1997) 1 Ker LT 130: (1996) 2 Ker LJ 576: see also Vishal Jeeth v. Union of India, AIR 1990 SC 1412.
13. Sathyavan Kottarakkara v. State, AIR 1997 Ker 133, p. 137.
14. Ibid., p. 136 and p. 137.
15. Article 28 of the CRC provides that "state parties shall take all appropriate measures to ensure that school discipline is administered in a manner consistent with the child's human dignity."

SECTION TWO

# Contextual Issues in Indian Family Violence

CHAPTER TEN

# Declining sex ratios in Maharashtra

## Gift of technological advance

*Sanjeevanee Mulay*

India is a predominantly a patriarchal society. The perception that the family line runs through a male makes men a precious commodity that needs to be protected and given a special status. The dominance of men is reflected also in our marriage practices. Because of the practice of dowry, the daughters are cursed to an extent that even the birth of a girl child in a family is sought to be avoided. We are ashamed to find instances of female infanticide occurring regularly. Female infanticide has been replaced by female foeticide and more sadly, female foeticide has made inroads into areas, where earlier there were no instances of female infanticide. Further, we find that it has also crossed the class boundaries.

### Son preference in Maharashtra

Maharashtra is one of the states with fairly high amount of son preference. It has been observed that the effect of son preference on fertility is most pronounced in regions, which are in the middle of the fertility transition. We give below some simple indicators of son preference for India and Maharashtra:

| | *India* | *Maharashtra* |
|---|---|---|
| Ratio of ideal no. of sons/daughters | 1.4 | 1.33 |
| Proportion wanting no more children (2S/2D) | 1.13 | 1.14 |
| Proportion using contraception (2S/2D) | 1.68 | 2.26 |
| Proportion fully vaccinated (S/D) | 1.05 | 1.06 |
| Mean duration of breastfeeding (S/D) | 1.07 | 1.05 |
| Prevalence of childhood diarrhoes (S/D) | 1.03 | 0.94 |
| Proportion taken to health facility (S/D) | 1.05 | 1.03 |
| Proportion severely undernourished (stunted) (D/S) | 1.12 | 0.99 |
| Excess female child mortality (%) | 47.00 | 29.00 |

Data Obtained in 1998–99.

It can be observed that although, on an average, the extent of son preference does not differ much between India and Maharashtra, but in case of the contraception the difference is significant. Maharashtra has 40 per cent higher value of son preference indicator. Thus, the conclusions of Mutharayappa et al. (1997) about son preference in Maharashtra (NFHS, 1992–93) get a support from the data in 1998–99. They had concluded that the excess percentage of births due to gender preference is 14.6 per cent for Maharashtra as against 8.4 per cent for India.

As mentioned earlier, when the state is in the middle stage of fertility transition, the impact of son preference is substantial. In Maharashtra, in majority of areas, the norm of total children has come down to about two. However, among those two, at least one has to be a son. The dilemma arises particularly when the first-born child is a girl. In such circumstances it is possible that the couples go for sex determination, although banned, and if the foetus is of a girl child, they get the child aborted. The recent SRS (2003) estimates of sex ratio at birth (M/F) for Maharashtra is 113 as against 105 as a biological norm. This is a clear indication of sex-selective abortions. The child sex ratios revealed by 2001 census are one more evidence of declining proportions of girl babies.

### Child sex ratio in Maharashtra

Sex ratio is an important social indicator to measure the extent of prevailing equality between men and women in a society and mainly reflect the sex differentials in mortality. Contrary to the universal pattern, sex ratio is unfavourable to women in India. Several reasons are cited for the consistently low levels of sex ratio and their further decline over the decades in India. Some of the important reasons discussed in the literature for the decline of sex ratio in India are: (1) neglect of girl child resulting in their higher mortality at younger ages, (2) high maternal mortality, (3) sex-selective female abortions, (4) female infanticide, and (5) change in sex ratio at birth.

### *Sex ratio of children in the age group 0–6 years*

During the last decade (1991–2001), India and all the neighbouring states of Maharashtra have shown rise in sex ratio of the total population but Maharashtra has shown a decline indicating worsening position of women in the state. As per 2001 census, the sex ratio of the total population of Maharashtra (922 females per 1,000 males) is not only lower than all-India sex ratio (933) but it has been declining from 936 in 1961 to 922 in 2001. It is, however, the sex ratio of the child population which causes more concern in Maharashtra, as this group is not affected by migration. A decline in the sex ratio in the age group 0–6 years points towards the attitude and outlook towards the girl child. Universally, the sex ratio at birth is favourable towards males and usually falls between 943–952 girls per 1,000 boys (or 105–106 male babies per 100 female babies). As per the 2001 census, sex ratio of the child population in India (927 girls per 1,000 boys) is much lower than the universal sex ratio at birth. In Maharashtra, the child sex ratio has declined by 29 points from 946 in 1991 to 917 in 2001. It is not only much lower than the universal child sex ratio, it is also much lower than those for the all four South Indian states (Kerala 963, Andhra Pradesh 964, Karnataka 949 and Tamil Nadu 939) and Madhya Pradesh (931). Of course, it is much better than the states like Punjab (793), Himachal Pradesh (897), Haryana (820) and Gujarat (878). The drastic decline in sex ratio of child population suggests the possibilities of neglect of girl child leading to higher mortality among girls than boys and practice of female foeticide (Parasuraman, 2001; Kulkarni, 2001; Premi, 2001; Bhat, 2002).

District-wise sex ratio of the child population shows that it varies between 974 in Gadchiroli and 850 in Sangli (Table 1). The districts with higher sex ratio mainly come from eastern and central regions of Maharashtra and most of the low sex ratio districts come from western Maharashtra. Mainly, the prosperous districts/areas of Maharashtra have worst sex ratios, e.g., Sangli (850), Kolhapur (859), Jalgoan (867), Aurangabad (884), Satara (884), Ahmednagar (890), Solapur (897), Beed (898), Mumbai (898), Pune (906) and Dhule (907). The sex ratio of children in the entire Pune region is very much unfavourable to females (below 900). On the contrary, the backward/tribal districts like Gadchiroli (974), Nandurbar (966), Gondiya (964) and Bhandara (958) have higher sex ratios in the state.

District-wise sex ratios of child population, in rural and urban areas, are also given in Table 1. It shows that the sex ratio in urban areas of Maharashtra (908) is 15 points lower than in rural areas (923). Except five districts, in all districts of Maharashtra, the urban sex ratios are lower than the rural sex ratios. In 15 districts of the state, the urban sex ratio is 25 points lower than the rural sex ratio.

### *Decline in child sex ratio between 1991 and 2001*

Comparison of sex ratios of total population of 1991 and 2001 in the state shows that 23 districts have registered a decline in sex ratio and 10 districts have registered an increase (Directorate of Census Operations, Maharashtra, 2001). But, the comparison of sex ratios of child population shows that every single district had experienced a decline except Akola where it increased by 7 points (Table 2). The extent of decline is more than 40 points in eight districts and in all these districts sex ratio is below 900. The districts, which have experienced higher magnitude of decline, already had a lower sex ratio in 1991. The range between the highest and the lowest the child sex ratio has increased significantly between 1991 and 2001 in the state. The range between highest (Gadchiroli, 980) and lowest (Sangli, 924) child sex ratio in 1991 is 56 points whereas this range has increased to 124 points in 2001 (Gadchiroli, 974 and Sangli, 850). Gadchiroli experienced a decline of 6 points and Sangli experienced a decline of 74 points

**Table 1** Sex ratio of child population in the age group 0–6 in Maharashtra, 2001

| | *District* | *Total* | *Rural* | *Urban* |
|---|---|---|---|---|
| 1. | Nandurbar | 966 | 976 | 895 |
| 2. | Dhule | 907 | 914 | 888 |
| 3. | Jalgoan | 867 | 865 | 871 |
| 4. | Buldana | 915 | 921 | 890 |
| 5. | Akola | 936 | 941 | 927 |
| 6. | Washim | 921 | 917 | 945 |
| 7. | Amrawati | 947 | 953 | 935 |
| 8. | Wardha | 934 | 946 | 898 |
| 9. | Nagpur | 949 | 964 | 939 |
| 10. | Bhandara | 958 | 961 | 939 |
| 11. | Gondiya | 964 | 966 | 946 |
| 12. | Gadchiroli | 974 | 976 | 941 |
| 13. | Chandrapur | 944 | 965 | 897 |
| 14. | Yavatmal | 942 | 948 | 910 |
| 15. | Nanded | 944 | 948 | 929 |
| 16. | Hingoli | 935 | 938 | 919 |
| 17. | Parbhani | 926 | 931 | 915 |
| 18. | Jalna | 914 | 913 | 917 |
| 19 | Aurangabad | 884 | 886 | 82 |
| 20. | Nashik | 936 | 948 | 916 |
| 21. | Thane | 933 | 971 | 915 |
| 22. | Mumbai (Suburb) | 919 | — | 919 |
| 23. | Mumbai | 898 | — | 898 |
| 24. | Raigad | 943 | 952 | 914 |
| 25. | Pune | 906 | 912 | 900 |
| 26. | Ahmednagar | 890 | 892 | 878 |
| 27. | Beed | 898 | 897 | 898 |
| 28 | Latur | 923 | 926 | 912 |
| 29. | Osmanabad | 927 | 933 | 895 |
| 30. | Solapur | 897 | 890 | 914 |
| 31. | Satara | 884 | 888 | 857 |
| 32. | Ratnagiri | 954 | 959 | 911 |
| 33. | Sindhudurg | 946 | 948 | 925 |
| 34. | Kolhapur | 859 | 870 | 832 |
| 35. | Sangli | 850 | 850 | 851 |
| | Maharashtra State | 917 | 923 | 908 |

*Source:* Directorate of Census Operations, Maharashtra, 2001.

**Table 2** Change in child sex ratio between 1991 and 2001 by districts

| | *District* | *Sex ratio of child population in the age group 0–6* | | *Change between 1991 to 2001* |
|---|---|---|---|---|
| | | *1991* | *2001* | |
| 1. | Sangli | 924 | 850 | –74 |
| 2. | Kolhapur | 931 | 859 | –72 |
| 3. | Ahmednagar | 949 | 890 | –59 |
| 4. | Jalgoan | 925 | 867 | –58 |
| 5. | Satara | 941 | 884 | –57 |
| 6. | Aurangabad | 933 | 884 | –49 |
| 7. | Mumbai | 942 | 898 | –44 |
| 8. | Beed | 939 | 898 | –41 |
| 9. | Dhule | 947 | 907 | –40 |
| 10. | Solapur | 935 | 897 | –38 |
| 11. | Jalna | 951 | 914 | –37 |
| 12. | Pune | 943 | 906 | –37 |
| 13. | Parbhani | 956 | 926 | –30 |
| 14. | Buldana | 945 | 915 | –30 |
| 15. | Latur | 947 | 923 | –24 |
| 16. | Chandrapur | 965 | 944 | –21 |
| 17. | Osmanabad | 947 | 927 | –20 |
| 18. | Washim | 941 | 921 | –20 |
| 19. | Yavatmal | 961 | 942 | –19 |
| 20. | Thane | 952 | 933 | –19 |
| 21. | Raigad | 961 | 943 | –18 |
| 22. | Nashik | 954 | 936 | –18 |
| 23. | Hingoli | 953 | 935 | –18 |
| 24. | Wardha | 952 | 934 | –18 |
| 25. | Sindhudurg | 963 | 946 | –17 |
| 26. | Nanded | 960 | 944 | –16 |
| 27. | Gondiya | 978 | 964 | –14 |
| 28. | Nandurbar | 977 | 966 | –11 |
| 29. | Mumbai (Suburb) | 930 | 919 | –11 |
| 30. | Ratnagiri | 961 | 954 | –7 |
| 31. | Gadchiroli | 980 | 974 | –6 |
| 32. | Bhandara | 964 | 958 | –6 |
| 33. | Amrawati | 950 | 947 | –3 |
| 34. | Nagpur | 951 | 949 | –2 |
| 35. | Akola | 929 | 936 | +7 |
| | Maharashtra | 946 | 917 | –29 |

*Source:* Directorate of Census Operations, Maharashtra, 2001.

from 1991 to 2001. The decline in sex ratio from 1991 to 2001 generally goes down if one travels from west to east of the state with few exceptions (Sindhudurg and Raigad). The developed districts of the state had experienced higher magnitude of decline compared to the less developed districts. The magnitude of the decline in the entire Pune region is alarming.

### *Sex ratio of child population in the Municipal Corporations*

Maharashtra has 15 Municipal Corporations (MCs) in the state. Sex ratios of child population in the MCs are given in descending order in Table 3. Out of the 15 MCs only three (Amrawati, Nagpur and Nanded) are from the central and eastern regions of the state and the remaining 12 are from the western regions. It shows that the child sex ratio for the MCs is 910, which is lower

**Table 3** Sex ratio of child population in the Municipal Corporations of Maharashtra, 2001

| | *Municipal Corporations* | *Sex ratio of child population (0–6)* |
|---|---|---|
| 1. | Amrawati | 943 |
| 2. | Nagpur | 939 |
| 3. | Nanded-Waghala | 932 |
| 4. | Solapur | 930 |
| 5. | Navi Mumbai | 926 |
| 6. | Thane | 915 |
| 7. | Mumbai and Mumbai Suburb | 913 |
| 8. | Pune | 906 |
| 9. | Nashik | 905 |
| 10. | Pimpri-Chinchwad | 893 |
| 11. | Ulhas Nagar | 890 |
| 12. | Aurangabad | 885 |
| 13. | Kalyan-Dombivali | 881 |
| 14. | Sangli-Miraj-Kupwad | 857 |
| 15. | Kolhapur | 815 |
| | All Municipal Corporations | 910 |

*Source:* Directorate of Census Operations, Maharashtra, 2001.

than the child sex ratio for the entire state (917) and much lower than the child sex ratio for rural areas of the state (923). Child sex ratio of MCs is comparable with the urban child sex ratio of the state (908). Except Amrawati, the child sex ratio in all the remaining 14 MCs is below 943. In six MCs the child sex ratio is below 900. Child sex ratio is below 930 in all the MCs from western regions. Child sex ratios in MCs indicate the severity of the discrimination against female children in the bigger cities of the state, which goes contrary to the expectations.

The information presented till now is clearly indicative of the female foeticide taking place in Maharashtra. In fact, Maharashtra was the first state to frame a law against the sex determination either by amniocentesis or ultra-sound sonography. It was named as Pre-natal Diagnostic Techniques Act and was passed in 1989.

## Pre-Natal Diagnostic Techniques (PNDT) Act

In 1978, the Government of India issued a directive banning the misuse of amniocentesis in government hospitals. Thereafter, due to the efforts of activists, a law to prevent sex determination was passed in Maharashtra, known as the Pre-natal Diagnostic Techniques Act, 1988. Finally, after a public debate all over India, the Central Parliament enacted the Pre-natal Diagnostic Techniques (PNDT) Act on September 20, 1994. It provides for the regulation of: (i) use of pre-natal diagnostic techniques for the purpose of detecting genetic or metabolic disorders or chromosomal abnormalities or certain congenital malformation or sex linked disorders; (ii) for the prevention of the misuse of such techniques for the purpose of pre-natal sex-determination leading to female foeticide; and (iii) for matters connected there with or incidental thereto. This Act came into force in 1996. Some amendments in the Act were suggested later on. The amended rules have come into effect from February 14, 2003.

Some important provisions of the PNDT Act are:

- No genetic counselling centre, genetic laboratory, or genetic clinic (including clinics or laboratories or centres having ultrasound or imaging equipment), unless registered under the Act, shall conduct, associate with, or help in conducting activities relating to diagnostic techniques that can be used to assess the sex of a foetus.

- No person, including specialist in the field of infertility, shall conduct or cause to be conducted or aid in conducting a pre-conception sex-selection technique on a woman or man or both or on any tissue, conceptus, fluid, or gametes derived from either or both of them.
- No prenatal diagnostic technique shall be used or conducted unless the person qualified to do so is satisfied that at least one of the following conditions is fulfilled: (i) the age of the pregnant woman is above 35 years; (ii) the pregnant woman has undergone two or more spontaneous abortions; (iii) the pregnant woman has been exposed to potentially teratogenic agents such as drugs, radiation, infection, or chemicals; (iv) the pregnant woman has a history of mental retardation or physical deformities such as spasticity or other genetic desease; and (v) any other condition as may be specified by the Central Supervisory Board designated by the Act.
- No person conducting prenatal diagnostic procedures shall communicate to the pregnant woman concerned or her relatives the sex of the foetus by words, signs or in any other manner.

Following bodies are appointed for the supervision of enactment of PNDT Act:

1. Central Supervisory Board
2. State Supervisory Board and Union Territory Supervisory Board
3. Appropriate Authority and Advisory Committee

The appropriate authorities at district/tehsil level are the immediate supervisory authorities. They have powers in respect of the following matters:

1. summoning of any person, who is in possession of any information relating to violation of the provisions of this Act or the rules made thereunder;
2. production of any document or material object relating to clause (a);

3. issuing search warrant for any place suspected to be indulging in sex selection techniques or pre-natal sex determination; and
4. any other matter which may be prescribed.

Every Genetic Clinic/Ultrasonography Centre/Genetic Counselling Centre/Genetic Laboratory has to have a registration with the Appropriate Authorities and shall be required to pay prescribed fees. Every such centre has to apply within 60 days of commencement of the Act. The Appropriate Authorities, after holding an enquiry and satisfying itself that the applicant has compiled with all the requirements of the Act, shall grant a certificate. The certificate shall be displaced in a conspicuous place at the centre. Every certificate shall be valid for five years.

There is a prohibition of advertisement relating to pre-natal determination of sex and punishment for contravention on any person or organization involved in such advertisement shall be punishable with imprisonment for a term extending to three years and a fine which may extend to Rs 10,000. Any subsequent conviction will lead to imprisonment of five years and the fine of Rs 50,000.

The centre needs to maintain records in terms of different forms to be submitted to Appropriate Authorities. Form 'F' containing the information on the men/women subjected to any pre-natal diagnostic procedure, and Form 'G' containing the consents of the men/women need to be maintained by the centre. Appropriate Authorities should maintain the record of Form 'H' containing the details about the application by centres. The centres should send monthly report to the concerned Appropriate Authority. Every centre need to display prominently a notice in English and local language to effect that disclosure of sex of the foetus is prohibited under law.

There is a code of conduct to be observed by persons working at the centre. It includes mainly: (i) not engaging oneself or helping in sex determination; (ii) not employing unqualified people; and (iii) not conducting the tests in place other than that registered to conduct or cause to conduct female foeticide.

The Appropriate Authorities have a power to inspect the centre and seal and seize any ultrasound machine capable of detecting sex of foetus used by any organization, if it has not registered with them. The machines could be released if the organization pays five times the registration fees to Appropriate Authorities. However, Retherford and Roy (2003) observe: "The law contains loopholes. Government laboratories and clinics are monitored much more closely, than private laboratories and clinics, which are only required to register under the Act. Also genetic tests are monitored much more closely than ultrasound tests."

The law is easy to circumvent for both physicians and clients. The PNDT Act seems to have little impact on sex-selective abortions. Arnold, Kishor and Roy (2002) estimate indirectly that more than 1,00,000 sex-selective abortions, following ultrasound or amniocentesis, have been performed annually in India in recent years. Even, if there are no data available directly on sex-selective abortions, there are number of indirect indicators on the basis of which one could estimate the extent of sex-selective abortions. The NFHS-II data on use of ultrasound facility and on sex ratio at birth provide useful clues pointing to existence of substantial number of sex-elective abortions (IIPS and ORC Macro, 2000).

## Sonography centres in Maharashtra

As on September 30, 2004, Maharashtra had 4,345 registered ultra-sound sonography clinics/centres in the entire state and this number is increasing continuously as the new centres are being registered regularly throughout the state. Getting the total number of registered sonography centres in the state in one place was a difficult job. The information was not readily available with the State Family Welfare Bureau (SFWB), and the State Appropriate Authority, for implementing the PNDT Act, when we approached them. This indicates the lack of importance given for maintaining the data related to the registered sonography centres at one place. Upon our request, the letters were sent by the State Appropriate Authority to all District Appropriate Authorities to supply the data on number of sonography centres with the qualifications of the owner of the centre and the operator of the sonography machine, and the type of centre. For this purpose, (MOHFW) the format supplied by the Ministry of Health and Family Welfare, was sent along with the letter to collect the above data. We have received the necessary data from the district Appropriate Authorities in September 2004. Five districts (Chandrapur, Bhandara, Washim, Buldana and Nandurbar) did not send the details till we completed this report in spite of the reminders by the SFWB. These five districts together have 124 sonography centres (2.9%) and also come from the region where the number of sonography centres is very less in the state. The following section analyzes the distribution, type and qualifications of the owners and operators of the sonography centres in Maharashtra supplied by the District Appropriate Authorities.

The sonography centres are unevenly distributed in the 35 districts of the state. Maharashtra's districts are further grouped into eight health circles by the Directorate of Health Services for administrative purposes. Table 4 shows the uneven distribution of the ultrasound centres in the state by health circle. More than three-fourth centres (78%) are registered in just four health circles (Mumbai, Pune, Nashik and Kolhapur). These four circles together have 16 out of 35 districts of the state, forming a contiguous region of western Maharashtra. It means that 78 per cent of the sonography centres are located in just 46 per cent of the districts of the state – a highly concentrated distribution. It would be worthwhile to mention here that many of the low child sex ratio districts in the state come from this region. Also, the decline in child sex ratio between 1991 and 2001 is higher in this region compared to the rest of the regions in the state. Mumbai health circle alone has one-third of the centres. Mumbai and Pune circles together have nearly half of the (48%) centres. Twenty-two per cent of the sonography centres are evenly distributed (5–6%) in rest of the four health circles (Nagpur, Akola, Aurangabad and Latur) located in central and eastern parts of Maharashtra. These four health circles together contain 19 districts of the state. It means that 22 per cent of the sonography centres are located in 54 per cent of the districts of the state.

**Table 4** Number and percentage of registered ultrasound sonography centres in Maharashtra by health circles as on September 30, 2004

| | *Name of the health circle* | *No. of districts in the health circle* | *No. of registered ultrasound centres/clinics* | *Per cent* | *Cumulative percentage* |
|---|---|---|---|---|---|
| 1. | Mumbai Circle | 5 | 1421 | 32.70 | 32.70 |
| 2. | Pune Circle | 3 | 656 | 15.10 | 47.80 |
| 3. | Nashik Circle | 5 | 864 | 19.88 | 67.69 |
| 4. | Kolhapur Circle | 3 | 441 | 10.15 | 77.84 |
| 5. | Nagpur Circle | 6 | 229 | 5.27 | 83.11 |
| 6. | Akola Circle | 5 | 220 | 5.06 | 88.17 |
| 7. | Aurangabad Circle | 4 | 238 | 5.48 | 93.65 |
| 8. | Latur Circle | 4 | 276 | 6.35 | 100.00 |
| | Total | 35 | 4345 | 100.00 | 100.00 |

*Source:* State Family Welfare Bureau, Pune.

Table 5 gives the distribution of the ultrasound centres in the districts and Municipal Corporations of Maharashtra. It shows that in central and eastern Maharashtra (Nagpur, Akola, Aurangabad and Latur circles) the number of centres is far less than the districts in western Maharashtra. Also, the sonography centres are concentrated in the bigger cities of the state. In the state, as a whole, half of the sonography centres are located within the Municipal Corporation limits.

## Regression analysis

Having examined the data on child sex ratios and availability of sonography centres, it was anticipated that there was some kind of association between the two. Wherever the availability of sonography centres was higher, the sex ratio was lower. A scatter (Graph 1) showed that there was a strong relationship. This led us to express the relation in the form of a linear regression:

$$Y = a + bx$$

where x is the availability of sonography centres and y is the child sex ratio. The fitted regression is

$$Y = 955.9 - 913.6x \qquad R^2 = 0.46$$

The results show that the availability of sonography centres has definitely played a major role in bringing down the child sex ratio.

**Table 5** Number of registered ultrasound clinics/centres in the districts of Maharashtra as on September 30,2004

| *Health Circle* | | *Name of the district/MC* | *No. of registered centres* | *Total in health circle* |
|---|---|---|---|---|
| Mumbai | 1. | Raigad | 106 | 1421 |
| | 2. | Ratnagiri | 56 | |
| | 3. | Thane | 170 | |
| | 4. | Mumbai and Mumbai Suburb Municipal Corporation | 833 | |
| | 5. | Navi Mumbai Municipal Corporation | 71 | |
| | 6. | Thane Municipal Corporation | 86 | |
| | 7. | Kalyan Municipal Corporation | 77 | |
| | 8. | Ulhasnagar Municipal Corporation | 22 | |
| Nashik | 9. | Ahmednagar | 211 | 656 |
| | 10. | Dhule | 54 | |
| | 11. | Jalgoan | 163 | |
| | 12. | Nashik | 84 | |
| | 13. | Nandurbar | 15 | |
| | 14. | Nashik Municipal Corporation | 129 | |
| Pune | 15. | Pune | 160 | 864 |
| | 16. | Solapur | 99 | |
| | 17. | Satara | 209 | |
| | 18. | Pune Municipal Corporation | 276 | |
| | 19. | Pimpri-Chinchwad Municipal Corpn | 45 | |
| | 20. | Solapur Municipal Corporation | 75 | |
| Kolhapur | 21. | Kolhapur | 107 | 441 |
| | 22. | Sangli | 106 | |
| | 23. | Sindhudurg | 47 | |
| | 24. | Kolhapur Municipal Corporation | 104 | |
| | 25. | Sangli Municipal Corporation | 77 | |
| Aurangabad | 26. | Aurangabad | 27 | 229 |
| | 27. | Jalna | 34 | |
| | 28. | Parbhani | 36 | |
| | 29. | Hingoli | 12 | |
| | 30. | Aurangabad Municipal Corporation | 120 | |

contd...

contd...

| | | | |
|---|---|---|---|
| Latur | 31. Beed | 61 | 220 |
| | 32. Nanded | 17 | |
| | 33. Latur | 67 | |
| | 34. Osmanabad | 27 | |
| | 35. Nanded Municipal Corporation | 48 | |
| Akola | 36. Akola | 64 | 238 |
| | 37. Amrawati | 20 | |
| | 38. Buldhana | 47 | |
| | 39. Yawatmal | 37 | |
| | 40. Washim | 14 | |
| | 41. Amrawati Municipal Corporation | 56 | |
| Nagpur | 42. Bhandara | 19 | |
| | 43. Chandrapur | 29 | 276 |
| | 44. Gadchiroli | 5 | |
| | 45. Nagpur | 24 | |
| | 46. Wardha | 23 | |
| | 47. Gondia | 10 | |
| | 48. Nagpur Municipal Corporation | 166 | |
| Total | | 4345 | 4345 |

*Source:* State Family Welfare Bureau, Pune.

**Graph 1** Relationship between child sex ratio (total) and number of sonography centres per 1,000 population in the districts of Maharashtra (n=35)

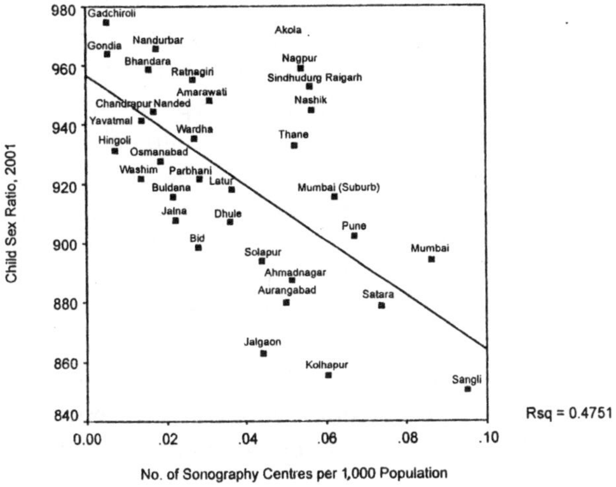

### Findings of the survey of ultrasound sonography centres

The survey was carried out in 372 sonography centres during August–November 2004. The questionnaire supplied by the MOHFW was looked into for the survey and it contained questions on type of machine, registration number, qualification of the operator, number of referrals by both allopathic and non-allopathic doctors, the purpose (obstetric/non-obstetric) of sonography, the classification of obstetric sonographies by trimesters, etc. With a purpose of assessment of observance of PNDT Act, we had prepared a check-list about the maintenance of records, sending timely reports, supervisory visits, etc. In all, the survey was conducted in 69 sonography centres owned by the trained doctors/persons, 275 centres owned by untrained persons and another 28 centres owned by not properly trained/qualified persons.'

Although, the prescribed objectives of the survey and the questionnaire did not contain anything related to sex determination, we have analyzed the available data to look for the relationship of sonography centres and the significant declines in child sex ratios in selected districts of Maharashtra. During the survey, one could not ask openly about the sex determination tests, since there is a ban on the same. However, we used to address a simple question, "Do couples come to you asking for the sex determination?" and the reply always would be, "Yes, they come, but I do not do the test. There are many, who do the tests". This indirectly hints at the possibility of sex determination tests being carried out in non-negligible proportion.

The information regarding the type of machine, cost of machine, performance, referral etc. enabled us to have an assessment about the functioning of the sonography centres. Type and cost of machine tells us about the investment incurred by the owners. It is observed that 80 per cent of the owners have a fixed machine, whereas only 12 per cent are using the mobile machine. Although a small proportion, its variation between 'trained' and 'untrained' category of centres provides an interesting observation. For 'trained' centres, it is just 7 per cent, which increases to 25 per cent for 'untrained' centres, indicating the untrained owners' tendency to make use of the 'mobile' facility in absence of capacity to invest. In this context, it is further more interesting to observe the trend in 'untrained ownership'.

The data on the 'year of installation' show that the untrained ownership has increased remarkably after 2002. It means that these people must be operating even before registration and new people must have taken the benefit of the 'mobile' facility and registration with the help of an appointed person. For untrained owners, many of them being AYUSH doctors with limited earnings, the cost of machine could be unaffordable and hence the 'mobile' facility becomes helpful. At the same time, those 'untrained' owners, who have bought the machines at the rate of Rs 5–6 lakh must have done so, looking to the treatment benefits and monetary benefits emerging from this investment. It should be noted down that 40 per cent of the sample of 'untrained owners' came from the AYUSH systems of medicine. The returns to this investment would be substantial if the utilization of the machine is adequate enough. In this context, it is necessary to examine the data on the performance of these centres.

Data pertaining to the performance of the centre are collected in terms of both obstetric (three trimesters) and non-obstetric cases. It is observed that 63 'trained' centres have carried out on a average 620 sonographies in an year, while the performance of 'untrained' centres is 380 cases per year. Assuming 300 working days in a year, the average turns out to be around two for 'trained' centres and around one for 'untrained' centres. Is it not an indication of 'underutilized capacity'? Yes, if the figures are to be believed. In fact, the experience of our field team does not suggest such low averages. For 'untrained' centres, there are reasons to believe in the reported figures, for example, limited availability of operators, majority of the centres being attached to hospitals and hospitals having limited needs and dominance of the AYUSH doctors with still lower needs of sonography facility. However, what about the 'trained' centres? Attachment to a hospital has affected this category of centres also. Our actual field experience and our expectation lead us to conclude that the performance is underreported. Then, the question arises, "what could be the reason for underreporting? Does it smell of 'sex-determination cases'?" It seems plausible, because by not reporting, chance of getting caught is nil and with exorbitant fees for the same, the centre runs in spite of inadequate performance. One remark by a busy sonologist is worth noting down. While discussing about sex determination, he said, "Sometimes, when a woman with 3–4 daughters comes to me asking for sex determination, I am tempted to satisfy her demand. However, I know that, if I do it, I shall not be able to have a sound sleep and as far as money is concerned, why should I do it for money? For a simple case of 'Thrombosis', I get Rs 1,000. Why should I bother? But I know, there are many doctors, who are doing sex determination". The money-mindedness has overpowered the moral values. Less said the better.

Improvement in obstetric care is one of the significant advantages of sonography. A number of gynaecologists reported that sonography has brought revolution in the treatment of the pregnant women. They themselves wonder as to "how they could treat pregnancy-related problems when sonography did not exist". If the doctors do this religiously, one is willing to accept the possible impact of the sonography facility. How to test this? One way is to examine observance of some broad norms regarding the sonographies in the three trimesters. It is understood that there is no norm regarding the number of sonographies needed during pregnancy. It depends upon the need of the case. However, we came to know that sonography in the second trimester is essential, since it, for the first time, reveals deformities, if any, with the foetus. Similarly, sonography during the third trimester reveals the growth of the baby and retardation, if any. Generally, the first trimester sonographies are relatively less in proportion. Assuming that there should be some time-schedule in carrying out obstetric sonographies, we tried to examine the schedule followed by the centres and we observed that the sonographies carried out by the 'untrained' category of centres do not follow the time-schedule. Thus, the centre with 'untrained' owner fails both in quantity and quality.

In order to assess the need of the centres of different types, a question was addressed about the referrals by allopathic/non-allopathic doctors. As expected, more than three-fourths of the referrals are by allopaths. Further, It is observed that for centres with untrained owner, the proportion of referrals from allopathic doctors is slightly lower (70%). This indicates that particularly, the AYUSH doctors still not that conversant with the utility of sonography and hence do not refer patients for sonography. This phenomenon is also reflected in the responses of 53 AYUSH doctors desirous of using the machine. Only one-third of them want to use the machine by themselves. They have, on an average, referred only 17–18 cases per month. Community of the AYUSH doctors, as a whole, does not seem to be that keen on having the facility.

As mentioned earlier, we had attached a check-list along with the questionnaire in order to assess the observance of the PNDT Act. There are few lapses in some matters. But, the worst situation is about the maintenance of records. Nearly 15 per cent of the centres have failed in this. Similarly, at the level of Appropriate Authorities, the lapses are observed and they are more serious. In only 45 per cent of the cases, the supervisory visits are regular.

Private doctors have literally no check. PNDT Act is one such tool to have a check. If it is implemented properly, misuse of sonography could be avoided and the doctors will not be able to use it only as a money-making machine.

## Recommendations

1. An important finding has emerged from this study. There is a strong correlation between availability of sonography centres and decline in child sex ratio during 1991–2001. This is a clear revelation of the sex-determination tests being carried out in spite of the PNDT Act, 1994. It is further observed that the districts with sharp declines in the child sex ratio and higher availability of sonography facilities are mainly from western Maharashtra, particularly, the sugar-belt of Pune division. Clearly, the declining sex ratio is the consequence of availability of sonography centres, persistent son preference and capacity to pay. As the well-known demographer, Dr. Ashish Bose has said, "The unholy alliance between tradition (son complex) and technology (ultrasound sonography) has played havoc in Indian society. One recommendation, naturally emerging from this type of scenario, is "stop the expansion of

sonography centres". However, this may not be a practical suggestion. One way-out could be a recommendation in terms of disallowing registration to an untrained owner (AYUSH doctors or MBBS doctors with no experience or training). Further, it is also suggested that expansion in western Maharashtra should be discouraged. Our study has observed that the performance of centres with untrained owners is quite low – one sonography a day – implying that there is ample idle capacity. In this connection, one thinks that there is no need of increasing this idle capacity.

2. The Form 'F' supposed to be submitted by the centres has a column on sex composition of the children. The data should be analyzed along with the information on MTPs. It would definitely help identifying centres where sex-determination tests are being carried out.
3. Column on owner's qualification should be added to the application form. In absence of this it becomes difficult to assess the extent of untrained ownership.
4. The study has also pointed out to the lapses in supervision. The condition in non-corporation areas is worse. The Appropriate Authorities should look into it seriously.
5. In spite of the provisions in the Act, records are not maintained by the doctors. The Appropriate Authorities should appraise the doctors about the legal provisions.
6. We have doubt about the reporting of performance. The Appropriate Authorities have to have some machinery to avoid under-reporting. From the point of view of utilization of the machine, new machines should not be allowed, if the performance is poor.
7. There should be standardization in training. Sometimes registration is given on the basis of a certificate given by some doctor.
8. The functioning of doctors with multiple attachments should be carefully examined. Sometimes, this attachment could only be for completing the formality for registration.
9. The centres owned by cardiologists, logically, should not come under PNDT Act. A serious thought needs to be given.
10. In spite of the PNDT Act, there is evidence of sex-determination test being carried out. This makes us

think about the supervision, not only in quantitative terms, but also about "who should supervise?" A slight doubt regarding the supervision of a doctor by doctor only.

## References


Directorate of Census Operations, Maharashtra, 2001.

International Institute for Population Science (IIPS) and ORC Macro (2002). National Family Health Survey (NFHS–2), India and Maharashtra, 1998–99, Mumbai.

Mulay, Sanjeevanee and R. Nagarajan (2005). *A Study of Ultrasound Sonography Centres in Maharashtra,* Population Research Centre, Gokhale Institute of Politics and Economics, Pune.

Rangamuthia Mutharayappa, Minja Kim Choe, Fred Arnold and T.K. Roy (1997). 'Son preference and its effect on fertility in India', *National Family Health Survey Subject Reports,* No.3, International Institute for Population Sciences, Mumbai and East-West Centre Program on Population, Honolulu, Hawaii, USA.

CHAPTER ELEVEN

# Globalizing India and domestic violence against women

*Ranjana Kumari*

The process of globalization sweeping the world is exerting its unnoticed forces to redefine 'marriage' and 'family'. The forces of globalization and market are influencing the family structure and marriage norms to a large extent. Institution of marriage and the existence of a 'family' as a unit have found a new meaning. This new meaning is very often dictated by the market forces. The notion of family is shrinking, from large joint families, to nuclear families to individual or 'autonomous family' constituted by single person.

This move that has been precipitated by the process of globalization has both positive and negative fallouts. On the one hand, this new-found freedom promotes acceptance for such a process and allows the nuclear family to democratize and negotiate better living conditions. Women find their freedom to enter job market and earn enough for buying all material needs. Modernity has promoted women's empowerment through education, legal reforms, political power, economic and personal autonomy, and social mobilization for gender justice.

Women, though allowed to earn, are incapacitated by lack of control over their own resources and earnings and suffer discrimination and violence. Thus, the changes are more superficial than penetrating. The women may have entered the public arena, but the family values dominate and family violence is kept as a closely guarded secret. In the private arena, at the level of the family, the family is still dominated by patriarchal norms.

Many traditional values and norms take new forms, which may be detrimental to old social arrangements, such as providing family support systems to women. According to studies, one of the definite fallouts of globalization and marketization has been growing incidence of domestic violence on women.

In East Asia, while national economies grew, the human costs of the gain included continued social stress and fragmentation. Increasing domestic violence, street crime and suicides have been reported in Malaysia, Thailand and Korea. In Korea, a hotline for women received an escalating number of calls from women suffering from domestic violence – seven times as many as during the year 1998 (UNDP, 1999: 40).

According to a WHO study, violence against women exists in epidemic proportions in many countries around the world. The study further reports that domestic violence rates varied between 15 per cent of women having been a victim or domestic violence during their lifetimes in Japan to 71 per cent in Ethiopia. Previous research has found rates of about 20 per cent in the United States and Sweden and 23 per cent in Canada and Britain.

In surveys conducted in various countries, between 10 and 69 per cent of women reported having experienced domestic violence. By region, 10–35 per cent of women in Latin America and 13–45 per cent of women in Sub-Saharan Africa have experienced physical violence by intimate partner at some time or other in their lives.

The important questions at this point are whether the process of globalization and the market forces and changing societal structures are inducing more violence into the lives of women, or they provide a new power in hands of women to come out of the patriarchal dominance and exert their rights to fight violence.

This paper shall analyze the impact of globalization and market forces on changing nature of family and marriage and its relationship with growing domestic violence in India. To understand the change in society and its influences on domestic violence in the context of globalization, some references have been drawn from studies and researches in Europe, the United States, India and Japan. The paper also attempts to put across a model for combating domestic violence against women in the new era of globalization.

## Prevalence of domestic violence in Indian society

Crime against women in India touched a new high in 2003 with 1,32,720 cases registered. The dowry deaths alone totalled at 6,285 with 2,532 other cases registered under the Dowry Prohibition Act. There were 40,287 cases of cruelty by husband or relative against the married women. In a recent study conducted by Centre for Social Research, it has been found that nearly 5 crore married women in India suffer from domestic violence. Just one out of 1,000 cases of domestic violence case gets reported. And, out the 100 cases that are investigated under 498A of the Indian Penal Code (IPC), the accused gets conviction only in two cases.

The reported cases of domestic violence in India represent only the tip of the iceberg, which means vast majority being socially institutionally invisible.[1] As the 'iceberg' image suggests, recorded or official cases represent only a minimal portion of the problem of family violence in society. The majority of cases of violence fall "below the water line", invisible both socially and institutionally. In India, this iceberg theory has been reiterated by several studies, research papers and experience of NGOs working for the victims of domestic violence. For example, according to NFHS–2 Study,[2] which was conducted in 1998–99, where 90,000 married women in the age group of 15–49 years were interviewed, 18.9 per cent, i.e., 17,102 experienced domestic violence from their spouse. In the same study, it was reported that more than one in five women report having experienced at least some from of violence at some time or other in their married life. In Indiasafe 2000 multi-site study of nearly 10,000 households, 40 per cent of the women reported experiencing at least one form of physical abuse and 26 per cent reported severe physical abuse, including being hit, kicked, or beaten. UNFPA also reports that 40 per cent of the women in India suffer domestic violence and abuse from their male partner. Those that come forward often do so only after abuse have escalated to a point of severe, life-threatening violence. Records from the Special Cell for Women and Children in Mumbai, established by the Police Commission, to provide a range of support services to women and their families, revealed that 43 per cent of women endured domestic violence for 3–17 years before complaining to police (Dave and Solanki, 2000).

According to the 2001 census data, a total of 2,367,72,617 women are married and according to NFHS–2 data, if one out of five women suffers domestic violence, then we can infer that at least 4,73,54,523 must be suffering some form of domestic violence. Also, NCRB 2003 data shows that approximately 50,000 cases of domestic violence were reported in India in year 2003.

## Changing institution of marriage in India

Indian marriage systems are going through a major transition due to the impact of globalization on basic social values and institutions. The institution of marriage can be assessed by comparing and contrasting traditional and contemporary marriage patterns. The traditional pattern was marked by prominence of arranged marriages which were primarily oriented towards creating alliances between two families through 'classical matchmakers' such as family priests and relatives. In such a marriage, there was only a minor role for the bride and bridegroom in the context of decision-making regarding the marriage.

Contemporary marriage, however, is based more on an understanding between the about-to-be-married man and woman along with attention to the views of family elders. New 'mediators' such as the media (matrimonial columns) and marriage bureaus have also emerged, contributing to the rise of a nationwide, and sometimes transnational, system of information and choice-making in the context of marriage. Similarly, there is a noticeable shift from an exclusive focus upon the physical attributes of the bride and economic assets of the bridegroom to the intellectual and economic characteristics of the bride and personality-related attributes and career prospects of the bridegroom.

Today, we see a slight shift in the way traditional marriages are arranged. The strong presence of the audio, video and print media, supported by the internet, has influenced the marriage scene tremendously. Open any newspaper on a Sunday and you will see hundreds of advertisements of prospective brides and grooms. Type the word 'matrimonial' in any search engine, and see the list of countless websites for Asian marriages, Indian marriages, Hindu marriages, Muslim marriages and Christian marriages. These matrimonial advertisements may sound amusing to the west but they are pervasive not only in India but in the entire South Asian region.

In earlier times, people tended to live in joint families and it was easier to find the prospective bride or groom from amongst the relatives of the family members. For example, the eldest daughter-in-law of the house could suggest her maternal aunt's daughter as a match for her younger brother-in-law. However, as traditional families started breaking up, and people started moving to cities for work, this form of arrangement started to break down. So, there was a need for an alternative system of finding the ideal bride or groom. And, the print media, such as newspapers and magazines, came to the rescue. The audio-visual media soon followed. Today, the print media and the internet provide the easiest and fastest method for finding a suitable partner. The role of 'marriage arranger' who used to be a priest or a relative, has been taken over by the new media.

Marriage bureaus are popping up like mushrooms. Depending on how much you are willing to pay, they do anything from giving the 'right advertisement' in the media, scrutinizing the resumes, sending the selected resumes for your approval, arranging the meeting of the two families, and also undertaking private investigation to check for the character and the details mentioned in the resume of the prospective candidate. They plan the weddings and take commission as a percentage of the amount spend on the marriage! Needless to say, their businesses are booming because they keep themselves updated with the latest trends in the marriage markets.

A glance at the marriage advertisements confirms that religion, caste and sub-caste continue to dominate as criteria for spousal selection. The advertisements are arranged according to the castes and sub-castes and invite responses from families belonging to the same class or caste. The only change, over time, is in the method by which marriages are arranged, and not in the parameters by which a suitable match is evaluated.

## Marriage, market and dowry-related violence

The major influence that has been cast by globalization is an over-exposure to, and increased presence of worldly pleasures and luxury items, which are now essential items of dowry. The markets are flooded with household goods such as refrigerators, televisions, audio systems, DVD players etc. The bride's family is expected to give the latest model of these branded items as dowry or gifts at the time of marriage. It is an issue of prestige and the status of the family depends upon it. Dowry (or bride price in certain communities) has always had a universal presence in Indian marriage. The list of items in dowry or items given as gifts to the groom's family has changed over the years according to the market trends. But they are all there in some form. The more educated the boy, the more the demand for dowry and the more lavish the party. The dowry can vary from household items to fancy cars and apartments.

The story does not end here. The bride's family is also expected to throw a lavish and extensive marriage party, which may be preceded by cocktail dinners and 'Ladies Sangeet' (a day when songs of marriage are sung), and the 'Mehndi Night' (where henna is put on the hands and feet of the bride and may be her friends and relatives). The bride's family has to spend a huge amount to call the party to sing the marriage songs and the henna could cost anywhere from Rs 100 to Rs 10,000 for a hand depending upon the social status and the family's ability to pay. Beauty parlours would charge anywhere between Rs 2,000 and Rs 20,000 for the bridal make-up. There are "month before marriage" beauty packages available that could cost anywhere between Rs 5,000 and Rs 20,000.

The bride's family is also expected to pay for all the rituals that precede the marriage and that happen at the time of marriage. This includes the fee of the priest, the arrangements made for the rituals, and the gifts to be given to the boy's family and the relatives.

Polishing schools are also flourishing, and it is the fashion to attend these schools before marriage. Since most households are large families, where the boy shall be staying with his parents even after marriage, the innovators in the marriage market have started training schools for prospective daughters-in-law, where the girls are being trained on how to get along with their mothers-in-law and how to fit exceptionally well into the traditional role of an ideal daughter-in-law. These schools are gaining tremendous popularity amongst the middle class.

The Indian daily soap opera industry is highly influenced by the marriage institution, and barring a few TV serials, which have few takers, and the entire visual media is dominated by the mother-in-law and daughter-in-law episodes. These TV daily soaps on one hand show the 'new woman', who is independent, intellectual and a decision-maker, and on the other hand, show women as traditional, homemaker and the ideal daughter-in-law. This new image of women, for which the serial directors are largely responsible (though they would say that they make films only about what the people want to see), puts them in a double-edged bind. A woman is supposed to work and earn for the family as well as do the household chores with the same vigour and enthusiasm as their non-working mothers-in-law display or used to display.

This double jeopardy is a result of the new marriage norms that have been slowly evolving. The boy looks for a girl who is beautiful, smart, intellectual and sporty because she has to accompany him at all company dinners and parties and yet she should be traditional because she has to gel with his mother and father and fit into the traditional role.

The roles of men are also changing, but for women they are causing an excess burden. A look at the marriage advertisements shows that the boys' families look for a fair, slim, convent-educated, professional girl from a respectable family. Some even hint at the expected dowry. They also want a working girl. In addition to all this, the girl should also be homely and should know cooking and be able to manage the house. Moreover, there is no decrease in the amount of dowry, even if the girl possesses all the desired characteristics.

The latest National Crimes Record Bureau (NCRB) data shows that dowry deaths and torture by husband has been increasing. If we include all the marriage-related violence, the data shows that there is a consistent increase in cases related to dowry deaths and violence by husband and his family on the bride. Moreover, among all categories of crimes against women, cruelty by husband and relatives has shown an increase of 10 per cent between the years 1998–2003.

**Table 1** Incidence of crime against women in India

| *Crime* | *Incidence* | | | | | |
|---|---|---|---|---|---|---|
| | *1998* | *1999* | *2000* | *2001* | *2002* | *2003* |
| Dowry death | 6975 | 6699 | 6995 | 6851 | 6822 | 6208 |
| Torture (cruelty by husband and his relatives) | 41376 | 43823 | 45778 | 49170 | 49237 | 50703 |
| Dowry Prohibition Act | 3578 | 3064 | 2876 | 3222 | 2816 | 2684 |

*Source:* NCRB, 2003.

Thus, the globalization and economic power in fact are precipitating domestic violence because there is a greater demand of resources. There is an increasing need of commodities and luxuries.

## Domestic violence in other industrialized nations

When one looks at the highly industrialized nations, such as the United States, where consumerism has been able to induce changes in the family structures leading to extreme forms of individualism, it is estimated that every year, approximately 3 million women are assaulted by their partner. Many of these incidents go unreported to authorities due to the shame and fear associated with domestic violence. In 1998, of the approximately 1.5 million violent crimes committed between intimate partners, over 876,000 of the victims were women, and over 835,000 were men. Of the approximately 1,830 murders committed against intimate partners in 1998, three out of four of the victims were women. In 2001, according to the Bureau of Statistics, there were 691,710 non-fatal domestic violence acts committed and 1,247 fatal incidents. In homes where domestic violence occurs, children in the home are at a 300 per cent greater risk of being abused. Between 3 and 5 billion dollars are spent annually for medical expenses related to domestic violence. Also, approximately 100 million dollars is lost by businesses annually though lost productivity, sick leave and absenteeism due to domestic violence.[3]

Nearly one-third of American women (31%) report being physically or sexuality abused by a husband or boy friend at some point in their lives, according to a 1998 Commonwealth Fund surveys.[4] One-third of all police time is spent responding to domestic violence disturbance calls.[5]

While Sweden sticks out internationally as a nation with maximum number of women representatives in parliament, and its progressive laws in the gender arena, still, the application of domestic violence law has still not reached its potential. In Sweden, according to the National Council for Crime Prevention, 22,500 cases of domestic violence were reported last year – an increase of 10 per cent since the year 2000. But, the report also showed that as many as 80 per cent of cases are not even reported to the police. Of all the cases, only 22 per cent were solved. This means that a report had led to prosecution, a conviction or the prosecutor has declared trial neglect. In the cases, where the man and woman knew each other, 24 per cent were cleared up.[6]

The health-related, economic and social costs of violence against women – on women themselves, on their families, and on social and economic development – are substantial. Most of the data that exist on the costs of violence refer to the experiences of western industrialized countries such as Canada, United Kingdom, Finland, Australia and New Zealand, where systems of information and services are well-developed. A few recent studies have, however, estimated the costs of violence against women in countries in Latin America. Canada has estimated, for example, that the direct costs of violence against women – criminal justice and police costs and counselling and training costs – amount to over $1 billion per year. This does not include the non-monetary costs of suffering, morbidity and mortality; the broader economic effects of absenteeism, decreased labour market participation and decreased productivity, or the broader social effects on interpersonal relations, such as the disempowering effects on the women themselves and the serious impacts on children.[7]

In Japan, the closed family system and the strong patriarchal values that dominate the household did not allow the women to come out and speak about her mental and physical trauma for years. The concept of domestic violence as a social problem did not even exist in the Japanese language.[8] The Japanese translation of domestic violence is 'kateinai boryoku', but 'kateinai boryoku' refers to the violence of children against their parents. To date, there has been little social comprehension of violence against women in Japan and the problem has therefore remained invisible, sometimes being trivialized as an individual problem Domestic violence as an issue started surfacing in 1990s, and the term 'DV or domestic violence' began to be used by the media around 1998 in Japan.[9] Before this, the issue of domestic violence was a family affair and no women were allowed to speak about it in public. However, the recent statistics in Japan indicate that one in every 20 women surveyed felt her life was in danger due to violence from her spouse or boy friend.

According to the Japan's Cabinet Office's *Survey on Domestic Violence* (2002), 15.5 per cent of women have suffered physical assault from their spouse or boy friend, 5.6 per cent have suffered frightening threats from their spouse or boy friend, and 9 per cent have suffered sexual coercion from their spouse or boy friend in their lifetime. In total, almost one out of five (19.1%) women has experienced one or more of these types of violence.

Chart 1 shows the incidence of domestic violence in Japan.

**Chart 1** Domestic violence in Japan

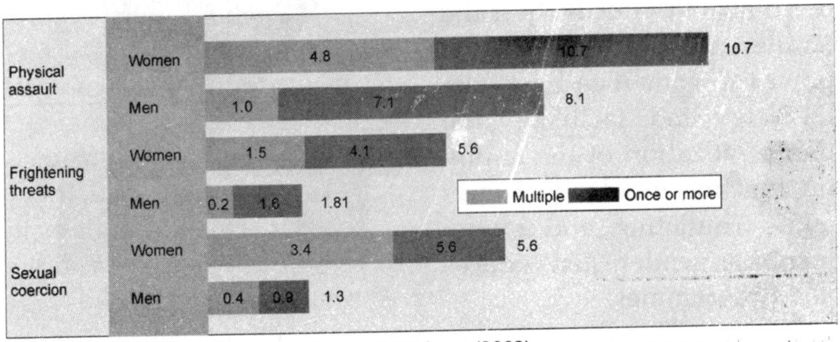


From Cabinet Office *Survey on Domestic Violence* (2002).

In Japan, domestic violence is so pervasive that it is considered a normal part of marriage, never recognized as a serious social problem, and lacking even an appropriate term in the Japanese language. Moreover, battered women have been deprived of any social institution where they can confront domestic violence.[10]

Concomitant with globalization over the last two decades in Japan, however, the rate of serious crimes, juvenile misdeeds, and domestic violence has been rising sharply, as has the risk of becoming the victim of a criminal offense.[11]

It is now being felt that violence against women is a social issue that should be apprehended and tackled as a structural problem rooted in the circumstances into which women and men are placed by society, such as hierarchical relations in family, disparities in economic power, and a fixed division of roles.

### Democratization for combating domestic violence

In order to effectively combat domestic violence, we must closely examine why our society has ignored or denied this issue. The most important reason is that in world men and women are not equal – socially, economically or politically – in both private and public life. This inequality reflects the strong patriarchal structure of the family and society as a whole. This unequal status continues despite a constitution which clearly guarantees equality between the sexes.

The fallouts of the process of globalization and market forces on growing domestic violence against women can be combated effectively if the family and society give equal power to women and the state mediates and facilitates the democratization of the family by enacting gender just laws and formulating and implementing gender just polices and programmes.

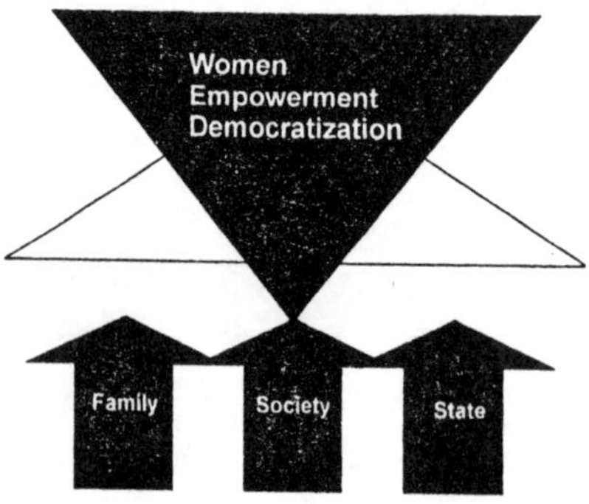

Women participation and access to resources is actually a manifestation of the democratic processes that exist within the family, the society and the state. The more democratic the structure, the more is the power given to women.

There are three steps to democratization for combating domestic violence:

1. Democratize of family to allow women to be equal partner in decision-making.
2. No discrimination between sexes in society.
3. Equal representation of women in state.

These three conditions must co-exist to eliminate violence against women. If one of these conditions is missing, violence remains in the life of women. For example, in the United States, the family is individualized, the society apparently does not discriminate between sexes, but the violence persists because the women are not equally represented in parliament and decision-making bodies.

In Sweden, as stated earlier, women have reached in appreciable numbers in the parliament and other decision-making bodies. They are more or less equally represented in state structures. But, this alone has not been able to curb violence.

In closed family system of highly industrialized nation such as Japan, women form an appreciable part of the workforce. However, the family is not democratized and women are also not represented in equal number in state institutions. They continue to suffer violence.

Looking at India, the Indian family is highly undemocratic, women representation at state and national structures is negligible and the society is devoid of gender justice. However, in the wake of globalization, which is throwing new challenges, is there also a hope or a possibility of moulding the market forces to the advantage of the women? Possibilities such as where the family structures start to democratize, women come forward to participate in the political process and the society starts valuing the contribution of women.

## Conclusion

The process of globalization is not new. The globalization of the economic, social, cultural and political structures happened in all ages. Earlier, the pace of such a process was so slow that we hardly noticed it. However, today, with the advent of the information technology, newer means of communication have made the world a very small place. Not only the pace of the globalization process, but the penetration and integration of the changes induced in our day-to-day life has made the impact of globalization manifold higher. With this process the world has become one huge market place.

However, fallout of such a process is that increasing domestic violence has been reported in most of the countries including industrialized nations, as a result family fragmentation and loss of social support systems in marriage. Accompanying the increased burden for women is an increase in the level of all forms of violence, including domestic violence.

It has been seen that when the society imposes sanctions against the perpetrators of violence, the women are empowered to exert for their rights. Only when the family and the society are democratized, the status of the women is strengthened. At this time, it becomes the duty of the sate to facilitate and strengthen the process. The solution lies in the fact that women empowerment approach to combat violence against women should be well-integrated and interwoven into in all polices and programmes of the governments. Women should be equal partners not only at the public places but should have adequate control of their own resources.

## Annex 1

**Table 1** Domestic violence against women[12]

| | |
|---|---|
| | *Industrialized Countries* |
| Canada | 29% of women (a nationally representative sample of 12,300 women) reported being physically assaulted by a current or former partner since the age of 16. |
| Japan | 59% of 796 women surveyed in 1993 reported being physically abused by their partner. |
| New Zealand | 20% of 314 women surveyed reported being hit or physically abused by a male partner. |
| Switzerland | 20% of 1,500 women reported being physically assaulted according to a 1997 survey. |
| United Kingdom | 25% of women (a random sample of women from one district) had been punched or slapped by a partner or ex-partner in their lifetime. |
| United States | 28% of women (a nationally representative sample of women) reported at least one episode of physical violence from their partner. |
| | *Asia and the Pacific* |
| Cambodia | 16% of women (a nationally representative sample of women) reported being physically abused by a spouse; 8% report being injured. |
| India | Up to 45% of married men acknowledged physically abusing their wives. |
| Korea | 38% of wives reported being physically abused by their spouse, based on a survey of a random sample of women. |
| Thailand | 20% of husbands (a representative sample of 619 husbands) acknowledged physically abusing their wives at least once in their marriage. |
| | *Middle East* |
| Egypt | 35% of women (a nationally representative sample of women) reported being beaten by their husband at some point in their marriage. |
| Israel | 32% of women reported at least one episode of physical abuse by their partner and 30% report sexual coercion by their husbands in the previous year, according to a 1997 survey of 1m826 Arab women. |

contd...

contd...

| | |
|---|---|
| | *Africa* |
| Kenya | 42% of 612 women surveyed in one district reported having been beaten by a partner; of those 58% reported that they were beaten often or sometimes. |
| Uganda | 41% of women reported being beaten or physically harmed by a partner; 41% of men reported beating their partner (representative sample of women and their partners in two districts). |
| Zimbabwe | 32% of 966 women in one province reported physical abuse by a family or household member since the age of 16, according to a 1996 survey. |
| | *Latin America and the Caribbean* |
| Chile | 26% of women (representative sample of women from Santiago) reported at least one episode of violence by a partner, 11% reported at least one episode of severe violence and 15% of women reported at least one episode of less severe violence. |
| Colombia | 19% of 6,097 women surveyed have been physically assaulted by their partner in their lifetime. |
| Mexico | 30% of 650 women surveyed in Guadalajara reported at least one episode of physical violence by a partner; 13% reported physical violence within the previous year, according to a 1997 report. |
| Nicaragua | 52% of women (representative sample of women in eon) reported being physically abused by a partner at least once; 27% reported physical abuse in the previous year, according to a 1996 report. |
| | *Central and Eastern Europe/CIS/Baltic States* |
| Estonia | 29% of women aged 18–24 fear domestic violence, and the share rises with age, affecting 52% of women 65 or older, according to a 1994 survey of 2,315 women. |
| Poland | 60% of divorced women surveyed in 1993 by the Centre for the Examination of Public Opinion reported having been hit at least once by their ex-husbands; an additional 25% reported repeated violence. |
| Russia (St. Petersburg) | 25% of girls (and 11% of boys) reported unwanted sexual contact, according to a survey of 174 boys and 172 girls in grade 10 (aged 14–17). |
| Tajikistan | 23% of 550 women aged 18–40 reported physical abuse, according to a survey. |

## Notes

1. Director, Centre for Social Research, 2, Nelson Mandela Road, Vasant Kunj, New Delhi 110 070.
2. Social Visibility and Tolerance to Family Violence. Enrique Gracia. *Universitat de Valencia Psychology in Spain* 2003, Vol. 7 No. 1, pp. 39–45.
3. National Family Health Survey–2, 1999, International Institute for Population Sciences, Mumbai, India.
4. http://en.wikipedia.org/wiki/Domestic_violence#Cause
5. The Commonwealth Fund, Health Concerns Across a Woman's Lifespan: 1998 Survey of Women's Health, May 1999.
6. National Center on Women and Family Law, *Battered Women: The Facts*, 1996.
7. *The Local*, Sweden's National Daily: Domestic violence kills 16 women a year: 26th November 2004 10:53 CET.
8. Women's Rights and Empowerment: Gender Equality in the New Millennium. Presentation by Carolyn Hannan, Director United Nations Division for the Advancement of Women United Nations Day Banquet Organized by the Dallans Chapter of the United Nations Association October 24, 2004.
9. *Journal of the International Institute*, Vol. 3, Number 1: Fall 1995 University of Michigan International Institute, Japanese Women Confront Domestic Violence By Yukiko Tsunoda, Attorney and visiting research scholar at the University of Michigan Law School.
10. IKEUCHI, Hiromi, Head of Tokyo Kazoku Labo, Tokyo Family Laboratory, an organization that provides divorce consultation, http://wom-jp.org/e/JWOMEN/work.html.
11. *Journal of the International Institute*. University of Michigan International Institute, Japanese Women Confront Domestic Violence By Yukiko Tsunoda, Attorney and visiting research scholar at the University of Michigan Law School.
12. Safety and Security in Japan: Creating Crime-Free Communities Through Government-Citizen Collaboration, Akira Nakamura, Ph.D., Dean of the Graduate School, Meiji University Tokyo, Japan (August 2004). A paper prepared for presentation in the Eastern Regional Conference for Public Administration From October 6 to 8, 2004.

CHAPTER TWELVE

# Married men's perspective

## Attitude towards wife beating

*Savita Kanade*

The World Health Organization (WHO) defines violence as "the intentional use of physical force power, threatened or actual, against oneself, another person, or against a group or community, that either result in or has a high likelihood of resulting in injury, death, psychological harm, mal-development or deprivation" (WHO, 2002).

The issue of domestic violence has been brought into the forefront in the last decade receiving international recognition and attention because of its documented physical mental and reproductive health consequences. In 48 populations-based surveys worldwide 10–70 per cent of women reported being hit or otherwise physically harmed by an intimate male partner at some point in their lives.

Home is perhaps a dangerous place for a woman-to-be, since husbands, fathers-in-law or other male relatives within this "safe haven" perpetrate much of the violence. This very fact has also ensured that the issue remains shrouded within a culture of silence and denial. The very term "domestic violence" relegates it to the realm of a private and personal family matter that does not brook outside interference.

Literature suggests a growing body of evidence highlighting the magnitude of the problem in India also. In three states in India (Punjab, Rajasthan and Tamil Nadu), about two-third of men aged 15–24 and 43 per cent aged 36–50 had perpetrated violence on their wives in the 12 months preceding the investigation (http://www.who.int/). One study, conducted among women and men in Jullunder district, Punjab in North India, reports that about 75 per cent of scheduled caste women reported being beaten frequently by their husbands; and likewise, about 75 per cent men reported beating their wives. There has been little research in recent years into those who perpetrate domestic violence.

Available evidence suggests that 46.3 per cent men themselves or some other members of the family beat their wife. In most of the cases husband himself beats her. Situations leading to wife beating are as follows: wife does not listen to her husband (48.3%), suspicion of extramarital relationships (30.9%), wife insult family members other than husband (17.4%), husband is addicted to liquor and returns home intoxicated (31.5%) etc. (Sharma and Singh, 2004). Other determinants of violence included shortfalls in dowry payments, female sterilization and the number of male children etc. (Mahajan, 1990).

The proportion of respondents, who considered wife beating justifiable in at least one situation, ranged from 36 per cent (in Malawi) to 89 per cent (in Mali); among men the range was from 25 per cent (in Malawi) to 75 per cent in (Ethiopia). In general, the women and men were least supportive of wife beating as a response to a woman having burnt the food or refused sexual relations with her husband; they often considered the practice acceptable as chastisement for a woman who had neglected her children or gone out without informing her husband. In the multivariate analysis income and level of school had the most consistent association with women's acceptance of wife beating (Digests: International Family Planning Perspective, 2005)

Men were consistently less likely to justify wife beating than women in all six countries. Mean number of scenarios out of five presented in which wife beating was justified ranged from 0.54 in Malawi to 2.46 in Ethiopia for men (Manju Rani et al., 2004)

A strong association between the consumption of alcohol and drugs and domestic violence has also been documented as alcohol is known for provoking aggressive and violent male behaviour towards women and children (Koenig, 2003; Sethulakshmi et al., 2002).

To summarize, the available literature indicates that 10–70 per cent women worldwide report that their husbands beat them and 20–50 per cent men are admitting that they are perpetrating violence. Determinants of violence include dowry, alcohol, children or wife behaviour. Both men and women justify violence in situations like wife not listening to her husband.

## Aim of this study

The aim of this paper is to study prevalence of domestic violence and attitude of currently married men's towards wife beating. The paper also looks into the association between wife beating and socio-demographic factors, dowry and alcohol habit of the male respondents. The data used for this paper is a part of a larger set of the data for the project carried out by KEM Hospital Research Centre on "Gender Based Domestic Violence and its Implications on Reproductive Health" during 1998–2001.

This paper will focus on the findings only from the married men's survey, as it will give men's perspective to domestic violence and also some insights into the intervention strategy, e.g., raising awareness amongst men.

## Background of the project

The original project was undertaken following population-based studies on maternal mortality, which identified violence-related deaths to be the second largest cause of death in pregnancy, hence, the aim of the KEM study was to explore the link between violence and reproductive health issues. The objective of the study was to explore gender-based violence within the studied community with regard to prevalence, determinants and consequences of violence.

## Study methods

The study, conducted in 31 villages in Shirur and Haveli tehsils of the Pune district, was designed to integrate both qualitative and quantitative data collection methods. In the initial qualitative phase, a mixture of methods and information sources was administered, to collect data. Group discussions were undertaken mainly to generate information on norms, attitudes towards violence and to understand the local vocabulary used in relation to violence. Free listing exercises were done on a number of topics to gain an understanding of the definition, norms and perceived consequences of violence from the perspectives of both men and women. In-depth interviews with men and women from the community, which included 23 women who were separated/divorced, 41 women who are currently married, 12 men who are separated from their first wife (most have remarried) and 33 currently married men. Of the 43 key informants interviewed, 16 were offering legal services, 21 health and medical services and 14 counselling services. Only thee were involved in training and rehabilitation services for women and two organizations were additionally offering de-addiction services.

All interviews were conducted in the local language (i.e., Marathi) field notes expanded and transcribed and then translated into English. The interviews were analyzed using ATLAS-TI.

### Survey of currently married women and men

In the final phase of the project, a survey of a random sample of both men and women in the study area was undertaken. Sample size for each village was calculated in proportion to population size. Within each village sample was distributed equally between the central village and the hamlets. Individual households were selected using cluster sampling. Only one woman was interviewed in one household. If there was more than one married woman in the same family, the interviewee was selected using a random lottery. The male respondents were drawn from other clusters in order to avoid the potentially threatening context of a man and woman from the same household being selected in the sample. Thus, a total of 526 currently married women and 216 currently married men were interviewed by same sex interviewers using a structured data collection instrument. A smaller sub-sample was also interviewed in depth.

The male and female samples were selected independently as this could put some women at risk of further violence within their homes.

Data from the preceding qualitative phase guided the development of separate structured questionnaires for both men and women. Questionnaires were extensively pre-tested prior to actual use. Respondents were interviewed only if they consented and were free to discontinue the interview at any point. The research team strictly maintained confidentiality of data and identification information on individual respondents was not recorded at all.

## Results

To understand the attitude of the male respondents to violence, six specific situations were presented to them and asked whether they feel that it was justifiable to beat wife under some specified situations. Situations were grouped into trivial and serious for analysis purpose. The grouping (serious/trivial) was done after reviewing literature and taking into account their implications in the future. The serious situations were: if wife insults her husband in front of others, if wife disobeys her in-laws, and if husband is under influence of alcohol. The trivial situations included: if wife disobeys husband, if wife is negligent in her housework, and if wife goes to her natal home too frequently. Beating never justified was considered as independent variable and thus analyzed separately.

An open-ended question was asked to beaters to know the reasons for beating. The reasons mentioned clubbed together into 19 issues and then classified into serious and trivial. Serious reasons were due to family quarrels, insult husband in front of others, neglected children, hit children, alcohol related etc. Trivial reasons included answered back, lazy by nature, did not come from 'maher' (parental home) on time etc.

To explore the opinion of male respondents on family conflict and gender disparities, 11 statements were asked and took their opinion as whether they agree or disagree to each statement. The statements asked were: family quarrels should remain within the family, man beats wife when angry, man takes out his anger on wife, quarrel between husband and wife are more than between mother-in-law and daughter-in-law, daughter-in-law gets harassed by mother-in-law, if quarrels between husband and wife goes to extreme then wife either goes to natal home or commit suicide, if quarrels between husband and wife goes to extreme then man either gives divorce to wife or gets remarried, family breaks if did not control the wife, wife should always listen to her husband, wife should be punished if does not listen, and wife should behave as per husband's opinion.

Attitude score was calculated for six situations and first five statements directly linked to violence. T-test was performed for significance. Remaining six statements were grouped as men's opinion towards family conflicts, which was not considered for this paper.

## Prevalence of wife beating

Of the 216 married men interviewed, while 105 (49%) reported that they had beaten their wife, 173 (32.9%), out of 516 married women, reported that their husband had beaten them. It reflects that women are underreporting domestic violence due to culture of silence deeply ingrained in them.

**Table 1** Prevalence of wife beating

| *Beating* | *Married men surveyed (216)* | *Married women surveyed (516)* |
|---|---|---|
| Yes | 105 (49%) | 173 (32.9%) |
| No | 111 (51%) | 353 (67.1%) |

### *Profile of respondents and their partners*

Table 2 shows the comparative profile of the two groups, i.e., beaters and non-beaters. It shows that there is no significant difference between the groups as family type (nuclear, joint/extended), mean age, education, occupation, years of marriage of respondent and his partner are concerned. A total of 21.9 beaters, in comparison with 10 per cent non-beaters, stay out of the town for work-related reasons; 17.1 beaters were married in relation as compared to 32.4 per cent non-beaters; and 66.7 per cent beaters and 45 per cent non-beaters took dowry in their marriage.

**Table 2** Profile of married men

(in %)

| | *reported perpetrating DV (n=105) (beaters)* | *Reported not perpetrating DV (n=111) non-beaters)* |
|---|---|---|
| Gaothan | 22.9 | 25.2 |
| Wadi/Wasti | 77.1 | 74.8 |
| Hindu | 93.3 | 95.5 |
| Married in relation | 17.1 | 32.4 |
| Taken dowry | 66.7 | 45.0 |
| **Type of Family** | | |
| Nuclear | 36.2 | 35.1 |
| Joint/extended | 63.8 | 64.9 |
| Mean Age<br>Respondents | 32.5 | 32.7 |
| Respondents partner | 27.17 | 27.32 |
| Mean Education<br>Respondents | 8.10 | 7.79 |
| Respondents partner | 5.16 | 5.07 |
| Years of marriage | 10.39 | 10.13 |
| **Respondents' occupation** | | |
| Paid work | 30.5 | 30.6 |
| Unpaid work | 69.5 | 69.4 |
| **Respondents' partners' occupation** | | |
| Paid work | 45.7 | 35.1 |
| Unpaid work | 54.3 | 64.9 |
| Stay out of town for work | 21.9 | 10 |
| Men reported alcohol | 23.0 | 16.4 |

### *Attitude of men respondents towards wife beating*

Men justified violence under varying situations or circumstances and those who beat their wife were also more likely to justify the use of violence as seen in the following table:

**Table 3** Men's attitude towards wife beating

| | *Beating Justified* | |
|---|---|---|
| | *Beaters (105)* | *Non beaters (111)* |
| If wife disobeys husband | 41.0 | 18.0 |
| If wife is negligent in her housework | 31.4 | 9.0 |
| If wife goes to her natal home too frequently | 44.8s | 22.5 |
| If wife insults her husband in front of others | 76.2 | 45.0 |
| If wife disobeys her in-laws | 64.8 | 32.4 |
| If husband is under influence of alcohol | Nil | Nil |
| Family quarrels should remain within the family | Nil | Nil |
| Man beat wife when gets angry | 54.3 | 49.5 |
| Man takes out his anger on wife | 28.6 | 29.7 |
| Quarrels between husband and wife are more than between mother-in law and daughter-in-law | 41.9 | 41.4 |
| Daughter-in-law gets harassed by mother-in-law | 60.0 | 55.9 |

Survey findings show that attitude to violence was positively correlated with wife beating (t=3.84) as attitude score increases so does the risk of beating wife.

Following table shows the significance level and the chance of wife getting beaten under six situations:

**Table 4** Situations of wife beating

| | *Relative Risk (RR)* | *Significance* |
|---|---|---|
| If wife insults her husband in front of others | 2.1 | *** |
| If wife disobeys her in-laws | 2.0 | *** |
| If wife is negligent in her housework | 1.8 | *** |
| If wife disobeys husband | 1.7 | *** |
| If wife goes to her natal home too frequently | 1.6 | *** |

***(p<0.001)

Similarly, while 20 per cent men justify violence at least in one situation, 75.2 per cent in more than one situation and only 4.8 per cent in none of the situations.

### *Serious/trivial attitude/reasons and wife beating*

Out of 146 men, who justified violence for serious situations, 62.3 per cent were beaters and out 15 men who justified violence for trivial situations 40 per cent of them were non-beaters. This highlights the fact that generally men who have lenient attitude towards violence are more likely to beat their wives.

### *Serious/trivial reasons and wife beating*

Likewise, out of 105 beaters, 23.1 per cent men reported beating wife for serious reasons and 76.9 per cent for trivial reasons. Similarly, among men who beat their wives, reasons for beating is not combined to serious reasons. They beat for very trivial reasons like not coming back from parental home on time.

### Association between socio-demographic factors and wife beating

While examining the association between socio-demographic factors like age, education, occupation, type of family (nuclear, joint/extended), years of marriage, married within or out of relation and wife beating, it was found that none of the factors is significantly associated with wife beating.

However, factors like dowry and men staying out of the town for work were highly significant with beating wife. With men taking dowry, there is 1.6 times more likely chances that they justify beating wife and men staying out of the house for work, there is 1.5 times more likely a chance that they justify beating wife.

### *Association between men's addiction and wife beating*

So far as the association between men's addiction and wife beating is concerned, it was found that 23 per cent beaters and 16.2 per cent non-beaters drank alcohol. Though most studies show the positive association between alcohol and wife beating, our study does not show any such correlation. The reason might be men less likely to admit that they drink alcohol (in the same study, survey conducted with 526 married women, 52.6 per cent who get beaten by their husband reported that their husband drink alcohol).

## Conclusions and recommendations

Physical violence is a part of the daily lives of the women in the rural areas. The study shows that, wife beating is widely accepted and justified under many situations or circumstances by men. Two, more lenient the attitude of the man towards violence, more likely he is to beat his wife. Three, physical violence is not confined to any particular type of issues. Once a man becomes a beater, he is likely to beat his wife for least of the reasons. Though alcohol is not correlated with beating in this study, it is likely that it is being underreported. These findings plead for evidence-based interpretation to create awareness among both men and women regarding violence and for support.

## References

Digest: International Family Planning Perspective, Vol. 31, No. 3, September 2005.

Koenig, M.A., Iryna Zablotska et al. (2004). "Coerced First Intercourse and Reproductive Health Among Adolescent Women in Rakai, Uganda", *International Family Planning Perspectives:* 30 (4).

Mahajan, A. (1990). "Instigators of Wife Battering". In S. Sood (ed.), *Violence Against Women,* Jaipur: Arihant Publications.

Manju Rani, Sekhar Bonu and Nafissatou Diop-Sidibe (2004). "An Empirical Investigation of Attitudes towards Wife-Beating among Men and Women in Seven Sub-Saharan African Countries", *African Journal of Reproductive Health,* Vol. 8, No. 3, December 2004, pp. 116–136.

Sharma, A.K. and Rita Singh. (2004). "Men's Understanding of Women's Health Issues in Kanpur City, India: A Preliminary Research Report", *Population Review,* Vo1. 43, No. 2, Section 2.

Sethulakshmi, V.F, C.J. Bentley, M.E. Sivaram, S. Srikrishnan, A.K. Celentano, D.D. Solomon (2002). Marital Violence in India: Women's Heightened Vulnerability to HIV/AIDS. *Int Conf AIDS.* 2002 July 7–12; 14: Abstract No. WeOrE1284. Johns Hopkins University, Bloomberg School of Public Health, Baltimore, United States.

World Health Organization (2002). *World Report on Violence and Health,* Geneva.

# CHAPTER THIRTEEN

# Ending domestic violence

## Self-help groups can help

*Milind Bokil*

The world around us is besieged by many issues – poverty, unemployment, social inequality, economic disparity, crime, terrorism and so on. Many of these issues have specific regional and temporal dimensions. However, the issue that is really universal is gender-based violence. Discrimination on the basis of gender has remained a painful characteristic of human societies and gender-based violence, especially violence against women, has been a historical and all-pervading feature.

In recent years, a great deal of discussion and subsequently a great deal of literature has been generated on the issue of violence against women (VAW). This literature has taken cognizance of the various forms and dimensions of VAW and the role of law, state and society in it. In the U.N. Declaration on Elimination of Violence Against Women (December 1993), VAW is defined as "any act of gender-based violence that results in, or is likely to result in physical, sexual or psychological harm or suffering to women, including threats of such acts, coercion or arbitrary deprivation of liberty, whether occurring in public or private life and includes physical, sexual, and psychological violence perpetrated or condoned by the state, wherever it occurs."

Violence can be viewed as a never-ending phenomenon in the lives of the women. Before birth, it could be in the form of coerced pregnancy or sex-selective abortion. During infancy, it is in the form of female infanticide or deprivation of female infants from food and medical care. As a girl child, it could be in the form of genital mutilation, child prostitution, child marriage, and physical or sexual assault by strangers or family members. As adults, women are subjected to eve-teasing, molestation, prostitution, trafficking and sexual harassment of many forms. Marriage against will is also a form of violence. After marriage, apart from suffering from violence at home, women's reproductive rights are seriously challenged. This may again take various forms. In India, the preference for a male child often violates women's reproductive rights. In the later life, elderly abuse is also a possibility, especially for widows, destitute and single women. Outside the realm of family, women are vulnerable to sexual abuse and discrimination in the community spheres and at work places. The fear of molestation and rape is never completely ruled out. Women continuously face one or the other type of violence at various stages in their life.

Within this broader context of VAW, the issue of domestic violence or violence within the family is explored. The United Nations Commission on the State of Women, in its Vienna Summit, noted that from the existing empirical evidence regarding causation of violence, four generalizations could be drawn:

- Violence in the family is primarily by men against women.
- Most victims of violence within the family and society are the weakest owing to their sex (women have been considered to be weaker sex), age (children, youth, elderly) and physical fitness (disabled). It can also be in terms of dependency relationships of various natures (economic, employment status in an organizational setting, and so on).
- Violence occurs when the imbalance of power is challenged and the perpetrator fails to recognize and respect the victim's basic human rights, fundamental freedom, dignity and right to peace and security, and acts accordingly.
- Violence has always existed in various forms but it is only during the last decade that violence against women has been

increasingly acknowledged to be a serious issue in terms of both magnitude and effect (Dave et al., 2001: 430–31).

As domestic violence has been an all-pervading phenomenon, a good deal of discussion about its forms and magnitude as well as about the remedial measures has been made in the concerned literature (Krishnaraj, 1991; Karlekar, 1998). The fact that clearly emerges from the review of literature is that domestic violence is related to two institutions, namely, marriage and family; and it occurs within the framework of patriarchy. The institution of marriage, especially the way it is operated in today's Indian society, has a close bearing on the pattern of domestic violence. Similarly, the institution of family, which is considered as the social and cultural ideal, shapes the occurrence of domestic violence. Patriarchy serves as both the foundation as well as the roof for these two institutions.

The issue of domestic violence is eminently the issue of human rights. The Criminal Law Amendment Act, 1983 and Section 498A of the Indian Penal Code (IPC) have been designed to deal with domestic violence. However, as noted by researchers, "the legal system gives pre-eminence to the notion of homogenous family, thus disregarding the subordinate status of women within the family, and of her experience of violence that this entails....Preservation of the family continues to be of primary concern to the State. The physical and mental abuse experienced by women at home is still not recognized as violation of her human rights" (Mitra, 2000: ii).

The subtle and complex phenomenon of domestic violence has not only called for various analytical perspectives but also various approaches for its resolution. The analytical perspectives have dealt with the sociological factors affecting domestic violence, the economic dependence of women and their consequential vulnerability and the issues of sexuality. The practical approaches, on the other hand, have dealt with the role of law, judiciary, state and social policy. Specifically, the role of police and the state welfare system is analyzed in this context. The broad conclusion is that the resolution of domestic violence becomes difficult because marriage and family are considered as institutions in the private domain and beyond a limit the state or the judiciary cannot intrude upon them. Specifically what is realized is:

- The present policy framework is not sufficiently equipped to handle the incidence of domestic violence. Although the bill on the prevention of domestic violence has been passed in the parliament and although it is an improvement over the previous legislation, it has not met the expectations of lawyers, practitioners and feminist organizations.
- Although the state administration, especially the police machinery, has adopted a progressive stand on these issues, their practice is not very satisfactory. The police force is still not gender-sensitized and has plenty of prejudices and biases. Their actual behaviour is also not women-friendly.
- The present system of social welfare is inadequate to cater to the needs of women affected by domestic violence. There is a dearth of counselling centres as well as shelter homes for women. The state social welfare departments do not provide the necessary security to the victims.
- Judicial resolution of the problems of domestic violence is a time-consuming and strenuous process. The victims do not necessarily possess the courage and resources to fight legal battles.
- Although impressive efforts are made by voluntary organizations, especially feminist groups and women's support centres to provide various types of support to the victims, their reach is quite inadequate compared to the extent of domestic violence.
- The resolution of domestic violence needs immediate, location-specific and women-centred strategies, which at present are not in place.

This situation has prompted for the search of alternate sociological approaches. In this regard, the area that is not sufficiently researched into is how domestic violence can be addressed through women's collectivities. At present, most of the assistance consists of providing counselling and legal services to the victim and helping her overcome the problematic situation. This assistance is mostly provided by the feminist groups or welfare-oriented, non-governmental organizations. Recently, the police department has also started assistance centres at many places. However, the scope and outreach of such services is limited against the gigantic nature of the problem. Most importantly, they are not pro-active centres. Unless a woman approaches them, they do not provide assistance. Secondly, they treat the incidence of domestic violence as a 'case' and try to solve it individually. This approach is useful but its applicability is limited. Hence, an attempt needs to be made to find alternate ways and arrangements which could tackle the problem at the societal level.

This brings us to the institution of self-help groups (SHGs). At present, SHGs have emerged as the best and most efficient means of organizing women for their empowerment. The SHGs are primarily oriented towards savings and credit activities but their broader goal is social and economic empowerment of women. The process of empowerment commences with bringing economic self-reliance through savings and credit activities and supporting livelihood ventures. The social aspect of empowerment begins with making the women aware about their rights and making them equal partners in decision-making at the family and community levels. Overcoming domestic violence and realizing one's development potential fully is an important step in the process of empowerment. Most importantly, these groups cater to the poor and underprivileged sections for whom empowerment is not a hypothetical condition but a necessity of life. They are not only the most vulnerable sections to domestic violence but also the most deserving in terms of community support, legal assistance and socio-economic security.

From the academic or sociological perspective also the importance of SHGs is significant. As noted at the outset, the phenomenon of domestic violence takes place within the institution of 'family'. Much of it is also related to the institution of marriage. Most of the methods and approaches used by the state or society become ineffective because of the 'familial' setting. The issues related to family could be tackled only by an institution which is on the same plane and has the same degree of potency. Earlier, such institutions existed in the form of kinship organization, caste council (*jati panchayat*) or village council. As these institutions are no longer valid, we need to search for alternatives. Such an alternative is provided by the SHGs. An SHG is nothing but a collectivity of neighbouring women who share a common habitat and similar life conditions. This is an informal community group, which is bound by a sense of purpose and having a set of rules and norms. It has a mandate of helping the fellow women. It alone can tackle the distortions in the family as the family is nestled in the wider world of the community.

The SHGs thus intrinsically present a better option in dealing with the incidence of domestic violence. However, at present, their full potential is not realized. This is partly because there are two schools of thought behind the organization of SHGs. One type of organization emphasizes the hard core, micro-finance model in which a group is organized solely for micro-finance activities. Here, the economic or financial functions are prominent. The NGOs organizing such groups are professional micro-finance institutions emphasizing links with formal banking and finance sector. A group is formed basically to provide micro-finance to individuals and to make use of peer pressure for prompt repayment of loans. The second type of organization emphasizes empowerment of women. Here, the SHGs are organized first for improving the economic conditions of women and secondly for their social empowerment. The NGOs organizing such groups are change-oriented voluntary agencies. Their primary concern is gender issues.

Among the two categories of organizations, the second category has the potential of tackling the issue of VAW in general and domestic violence in particular. This does not mean that the first type of collectivities cannot do so but they are not motivated in that direction. 'Motivation' is the dividing line between these two types.

Although it is a sound hypothesis that SHGs are best suited to address the issue of domestic violence, its validity needed to be tested in the field. Community-based approaches to fight against domestic violence have been discussed in the present literature (Mitra, 2001) but the cognizance of SHGs is not taken. This has happened because the SHGs are a new reality and, hence, their full potential is not assessed as yet.

The present study was undertaken to fulfil this gap. The goal of the study was to explore whether the SHGs could become the means to tackle the incidence of domestic violence, especially in poor rural and urban communities. While doing so, the study aimed at documenting and analyzing the incidence of domestic violence. Specifically, the aim was to draw lessons regarding how and by what means domestic violence could be stopped and how the victim could be supported.

The study was undertaken by the Programme Support and Research Unit at the Development Support Team (DST). DST has been associated with the SHGs movement for more than ten years. Besides helping a number of organizations in promoting and strengthening the SHGs in rural areas, it has made pioneering efforts in organizing SHGs in an urban area (Pune city). Its efforts are also directed towards increasing the synergies of urban SHGs by forming their federations and building their financial capacity towards community banking. DST has also been active in research and documentation in this field. Prior to the present study, DST had undertaken the following studies:

- Women's Empowerment through SHGs: A Case Study of DST (1999)
- A Comparative Study on the Cost-Effectiveness of Promoting SHGs (2000)
- SABALA – Community Banking for Women's Empowerment (Study of a Federation of SHGs in Pune City) (2002)
- Micro-enterprises and Gender Division of Labour: An Empirical Study of Self-Employed Women in Maharashtra (2003)

DST's familiarity and experience with the SHGs, indicated that these groups could become an important and essential medium to address the issue of domestic violence. This was not a hypothesis alone, as in reality a large number of enlightened groups had not only tackled the issue in their groups but had also solved the problem with collective efforts. The ingenious means and innovative methods used by these groups were noteworthy.

The study was also deemed appropriate in the context of the WE CAN (We Can End All Violence Against Women) campaign, launched by Oxfam International. As an active associate of Oxfam-Australia, DST though it fit and timely to channel the findings of the study into the WE CAN campaign.

## Objectives

1. To collect and analyze the experiences on solving the issue of domestic violence from among the SHGs across different localities, communities and cross-sections of society.
2. To draw lessons from these experiences regarding the effective methods of tackling domestic violence through collective means.
3. To disseminate the findings nationally and internationally.

## Methodology

Considering the magnitude of the problem and also the diversity of the social context, it was essential that the study should cover as many diverse situations as possible. Hence, the study universe needed to be that of a state which consisted not only of various types of habitats – metropolitan, urban, suburban, rural and tribal – but also various types of castes and classes.

Considering the strategic location and experience of DST and considering the language and cultural familiarity, the state of Maharashtra was ideally suited for this purpose. Maharashtra has been known for its long tradition of civil society movements and feminist thought. Raising the awareness of women and organizing them in different collectivities has been a dominant activity of community development in Maharashtra. Lately, a large number of NGOs and action groups have mobilized rural and urban women through SHGs. Unlike other parts of India, the basic orientation of the SHG movement in Maharashtra has been towards women's empowerment and, hence, tackling domestic violence has been an important agenda before the groups.

Maharashtra also has the dubious distinction of belonging to the category of 'high crime rate against women'. This is partly because the reporting of the cases of domestic violence is better in Maharashtra but partly also because the crime rate is high. Cruelty at home constitutes a large share in the aggregate of crimes against women and Maharashtra ranks very high in this regard (Mukherjee et al., 2001: 4077). The *Crime in Maharashtra* report of 2003 indicated that the proportion of IPC crimes committed against women to the total IPC crimes was 7.68 per cent and among the total crimes against women, cruelty by husband and relatives constituted the most (43%).

The socio-economic composition of the disadvantaged sections in Maharashtra could be broadly divided into following categories:

1. Metropolitan communities – as in large metropolises like Mumbai, Pune, Nagpur
2. Urban communities – as in towns like Miraj, Ahmednagar, Satara
3. Irrigated rural areas – as in Srirampur, Sangamner, Sangli talukas
4. Dry rural areas – as in Latur, Aurangabad, Parbhani districts
5. Tribal areas – as in Raigad, Chandrapur, Gadchiroli districts
6. Fringe areas and communities – transient population and nomadic communities

Although these habitats do not entirely cover the state, nevertheless, they fairly represent the diversity within the state. Needless to mention, the aim was not to make a representative study of the society but to gather insights from as many diverse communities as possible which would enrich the understanding about the different socio-economic contexts and the approaches used therein.

For collecting the actual information, an appeal was made to various organizations who were partnering with DST in the SHG movement. Most of them had stories about how domestic violence was tackled by the SHGs. The collection of these stories and their subsequent analysis formed the core of the methodology. The approach adopted by each organization while tackling the problem was particular but their collection and analysis paved the way for drawing generalizations. It was decided to collect at least five stories/cases from each area mentioned above. The actual distribution of cases is shown in Tables 1 and 2.

**Table 1** Region-wise distribution of cases

| | *Area* | *No. of cases* |
|---|---|---|
| 1. | Metropolitan communities | 9 |
| 2. | Urban communities | 8 |
| 3. | Irrigated rural areas | 5 |
| 4. | Dry rural areas | 11 |
| 5. | Tribal areas | 2 |
| 6. | Coastal areas and fringe communities | 7 |
| | Total | 42 |

**Table 2** Agency-wise distribution of cases

| | *Name of the NGO* | *No. of cases* |
|---|---|---|
| 1. | Chtean Sanstha (Belgaum) | 2 |
| 2. | Jyoti Mahial Vikas Sanstha (Kolhapur) | 3 |
| 3. | Ramamata Mahila Vikas Sanstha (Sangli) | 2 |
| 4. | Swapna Mahila Vikas Sanstha (Sangli) | 5 |
| 5. | Development Support Team (Pune city) | 13 |
| 6. | Yuva (Nagpur city) | 4 |
| 7. | Amhi Amuchya Arogyasathi (Gadchiroli) | 2 |
| 8. | Shramik Janata Sahayak Mandal (Satara) | 1 |
| 9. | Chaitanya (Pune) | 3 |
| 10. | Chetana (Sindhudurg) | 7 |
| | Total | 42 |

Although it was intended to cover equal number of cases from each zone, in actual practice, this did not materialize. Firstly, because the cases were identified purposively. The SHGs were contacted after receiving preliminary information from the respective agencies. Only those SHGs which had tackled the issue were contacted. Secondly, the incidence of domestic violence and the efforts taken by individual SHGs and the NGOs differed considerably from region to region. Hence, it was not possible to cover equal number of cases from each region.

A noteworthy feature of these NGOs was that excepting two, all of them were promoted by women. It was therefore natural that the promoters were concerned with the issue of domestic violence and put in their energies towards resolution of cases.

Field level inquiry was conducted by Ms. Rashmi Khot. An attempt was made to gather first-hand information by meeting the victim of violence. Alongside, her family members were also contacted. As this study was directed towards understanding the role played by the SHGs, an attempt was made to meet the members of SHGs and solicit their feedback. Key functionaries of the NGOs promoting the SHGs were also contacted.

## The nature of domestic violence

We begin by presenting some of the demographic features of the women interviewed. The average age of respondents was 30 years (29.64). There were three ladies who were 60 and above (60, 62, 62) and one was 50. Excepting these four, all the rest belonged to their late twenties. Barring these four cases, the average age of the respondents was 26.34 years. This finding vouchsafes the fact that domestic violence is mostly committed against young women.

However, the most perturbing fact was the age at marriage. The average age at marriage of these women was just 17 years (16.61). As we will see later, one of the main reasons behind marital problems and subsequent domestic violence was the practice of early marriage.

The average education of the respondents was only 7.57 standards which meant that a majority of women had studied only up to seventh standard. Although nobody was illiterate, only one woman was graduate. Needless to mention, the low level of education contributed to the secondary status of women in their households. Lack of education also meant lesser awareness about the surrounding world and inadequate socialization through schools. This resulted into a lack of self-reliance in earning livelihoods and subsequent dependence on the husband's family.

The average number of daughters of respondents was 1.88 whereas the average number of sons was 1.52. This difference, although small, is significant as lack of male issues has been a reason for marital discard. Taken together, this means three children to the family on the average.

Before we discuss the role of SHGs in helping the victims of domestic violence, it would be useful to present the nature of domestic violence as observed through these cases. Although each case was different and unique, nevertheless a pattern was discernible.

- Although the causes behind each case of domestic violence varied, the basic factor was the power relationship in the matrimonial home, i.e., the clash between the weak and strong. The present-day institution of marriage is characterized by unequal power relationships founded on the basis of patriarchy. The newly wedded bride is powerless not only against her husband but also against the in-laws. This basic inequity in power is the root cause of violence. The male acquires power because he is the main livelihood earner, he owns the property, his side is numerically stronger, he is physically dominating and is backed by the traditions of patriarchy. The unequal power relationship encourages the powerful parties to commit violence and continue with it. At the same time, it forces the powerless to become submissive and suffer subsequently.
- One of the features of the cases studied was the incompatibility of spouses. This gave rise to marital discord which culminated into physical and mental abuse of the weaker party. Incompatibility came about because marriages were made hastily. It appeared that the girls' parents were bent upon marrying their girls as early as possible. As mentioned earlier, a majority of the girls were married before the age of 18. Secondly, in most of the marriages, a proper investigation of the groom was not made. Conventionally, marriages are arranged by the parents with the help of relatives. Although the cases of blatant cheating were a few, in many situations, the bride's side did not make sufficient inquiries about the character and financial condition of the groom.
- Husband's alcohol addiction was a prominent contributing factor. Other vices like gambling and womanizing also played a role. Jealous and suspicious husbands also caused violence.

- The addictions had a two-way relationship with poverty. They were both the cause and effect of poverty. Frustrations in earning a livelihood or lack of work led to addictions. Consequently, an addiction resulted into a loss of livelihood.
- Insufficient dowry has also been a cause behind domestic violence.
- Women's looks mattered. Women with dark complexion and with so-called ordinary looks suffered the most. Dark complexion was both an explicit and subtle cause of domestic harassment. However, in some cases, fair looks also brought the women in trouble.
- The incompatibility in marriage was also caused by the so-called misbehaviour of women. Domestic violence was caused because women were thought to be foul-mouthed, unkempt, bad cooks and ill at work.
- Joint family, especially in the agrarian setting, was found to be a major factor in domestic violence. The incidence of violence was relatively small in nuclear families. This is again related to the balance of power. In large, joint, agricultural families, the balance of power is heavily tilted against the victim.
- In confirmation with the traditional stereotype, it was noticed that the mother-in-law was a contributory factor in perpetuating domestic violence.
- Habitats or social categories did not much matter. Domestic violence was reported across all regions, castes and communities. There was not much difference between urban or rural habitats regarding the incidence of violence. Almost all the cases belonged to poor households, hence income comparisons were not relevant. As for ethnic indicators, it was noticed that domestic violence was relatively higher in Muslim families.
- In most of the cases, initially, the women suffered the violence patiently. They reported it to their parents or neighbours only when it became unbearable. Reporting to police occurred only when the violence reached an extreme form of cruelty.

- The first and foremost resort of the affected women was their parents' place. This was followed by sister's or brother's homes. The incidence of using women's shelter homes, run either by the government or by private agencies, was nil.
- A majority of the affected women did not want to break the marriage. Their plea was to have a non-violent, peaceful and trouble-free domestic life. Only in extreme cases the marriages were dissolved.
- One of the traumatic aspects of domestic violence was the impact on children and their subsequent separation from the parents. In many cases, the affected women had to part with children as a cost of avoiding violence. Reclaiming the children then became a strenuous enterprise. Husbands were oblivious of the impact of domestic violence on children.
- In the case of adamant husbands and extreme cases of cruelty, recourse to police was the only solution. Brutal husbands could be tamed only by police force. Reconciliation and counselling worked only when both the parties were amenable and where marital discord was triggered by misunderstanding or by petty reasons.

## Summary of case studies

As it is not practical to present a narrative of all 42 cases, a summary table is presented in the following. This will give the reader an idea about the nature of domestic violence and its resolution.

**Table 3** Summary of case studies

| | *District* | *Age* | *Nature of domestic violence* | *Resolution* |
|---|---|---|---|---|
| 1. | Belgaum | 35 | Muslim family. Illiterate. Landless labourer. Husband's addiction to alcohol and gambling led to violence. Now, stays separately with her parents and five daughters. | SHG and the local NGO tried to reconcile with husband but failed. Now, the SHG is trying to get her a house under the public housing programme. |

contd...

contd...

| | | | | |
|---|---|---|---|---|
| 2. | Belgaum | 35 | Devadasi woman. Husband, an army man, rebelled against his family to marry her. However, after his retirement, developed liaison with another woman and deserted her after considerable abuse. He provides for two children but stays separately. | Counselling by NGO is on going. Husband came for counselling but laid down certain conditions. Matter unresolved. |
| 3. | Pune city | 19 | Wife's preoccupation with maternal family angered the husband. NGO intervention failed. Police were approached. A local counselling centre helped. | SHG women provided firm support and also helped with the police. Husband conceded in front of police and SHG. Now, no violence but sporadic ill-treatment occurs. |
| 4. | Kolhapur | 21 | Muslim family. Incompatible marriage. Dowry harassment. Husband's illicit affairs. Extreme cruelty. | Divorce obtained with the help of SHG. The group was also helpful in dealing with the police. |
| 5. | Kolhapur | 28 | Harassment started because of failure of contraceptive operation of the wife. Poor economic status, negative attitude towards girl child. | Local NGO and SHG intervened, provided support. Amicable settlement. |
| 6. | Kolhapur | 18 | Muslim family. Husband an alcoholic, suspicious person and a gambler. Wife's desire to study further was opposed. Violence occurred in connivance with mother-in-law. | Victim's mother was a member of SHG which provided support with police intervention. Husband and mother-in-law were locked up in police custody. Violence stopped. |
| 7. | Sangli | NA | Hasty marriage. Husband got addicted to alcohol and violence started. Later, he died. | Lady stays with her mother with children. Poverty increased due to husband's death. SHG provided moral support but cannot help with shelter and livelihood. |
| 8. | Sangli | 62 | Elderly lady. Troubled by the behaviour of her daughter-in-law. Psychic ill-treatment in the old age. | Matter not resolved. SHGs unable to resolve the basic incompatibility between spouses which causes the harassment of the old lady. |

contd...

contd...

| | | | |
|---|---|---|---|
| 9. Sangli | 24 | Hasty marriage. Dark looks of the wife not acceptable to mother-in-law. Husband addicted to alcohol. Lady was thrown out of the house a number of times, frequently beaten. | SHG tried to reconcile the matter initially but they were afraid lest the husband trouble her more. When violence became unbearable, police help was sought with assistance from the NGO. Husband was reprimanded and kept in police custody for a few days. Violence stopped. Now, live amicably. |
| 10. Sangli | 25 | Physically handicapped girl. Was cheated in marriage. Mother-in-law and sister-in-law were in prostitution. They tried to coerce the lady to join the trade. Harassment started after her refusal. Husband had an illicit affair. | Intervention by SHG and NGO not successful. Lady came back to her parent's house and started studying D.Ed. Legally not yet separated. |
| 11. Sangli | 42 | Widow being harassed by a local goonda, instigated by the ill-willing kin. | SHG stood by her and pressurized the police to curb the menace. The goonda was put in police custody. Problem solved with women's unity. |
| 12. Sangli | 30 | Young lady troubled by father-in-law and his mistress (not wife). Husband used to harass her but died under mysterious circumstances. Custody of son denied by in-laws. | SHG and the NGO provided due moral and organizational support. Became a community organizer of the NGO. Son's custody received. Stays with parents. |
| 13. Sangli | 38 | Married at the age of 13. Family had to spend lavishly on the marriage. The lady was troubled by lecherous father-in-law, who also tried to burn her house. | Started staying separately with husband after trouble became unbearable. SHG helped her to take the matter to police. Father-in-law was reprimanded. SHG also helped her to get a share in property. |

contd...

contd...

| | | | |
|---|---|---|---|
| 14. Pune city | 50 | Elderly lady harassed by daughter-in-law, who was practicing mysterious occupation (probably prostitution). No physical violence but the family was mentally and socially troubled by the daughter-in-law who had extravagant ways of life. | The SHG stood by the lady and provided moral and organizational support. Fate of marriage undecided. |
| 15. Pune city | 26 | The lady committed love marriage against the wishes of her brother, who was aware about the bad character of her husband and his family. Her father-in-law was a drunkard and an abusive person. Husband was careless. No physical violence but mental abuse was committed. | SHG and the local community leader helped her to reestablish her house and restore relationships with the in-laws. Joint family continues. Lady is mentally insecure. |
| 16. Pune city | 32 | Muslim woman. Husband was indifferent and neglected her. He complained that she had a nagging nature. He married another woman. | SHG members intervened and removed the misunderstanding. Husband visits her periodically and provides for the upkeep. |
| 17. Pune city | 30 | The lady was married at the age of 10. Abusive husband. All types of cruelty. The woman persisted on staying in the husband's house. Worked as a landless labourer. | SHG provided credit support to the victim to start vegetable vending. Built her confidence. Have shown readiness to stand by her as and when she takes the necessary decision against the husband. |
| 18. Pune city | 27 | Husband frustrated due to repeated failures in business. Started drinking and used to abuse his other family members but never the wife. Misunderstanding developed over an unwanted pregnancy. Other family members used to harass the lady. | SHG stood by her and intervened between the quarrel. Provided the necessary arbitration and counselling. Matter was resolved amicably. |

contd...

contd...

| | | | |
|---|---|---|---|
| 19. Nagpur city | 30 | Case of marital discord, no physical violence. Muslim family. Wife was supposedly negligent. Husband had one more wife. | Arbitration and reconciliation provided by SHG members settled the matter. |
| 20. Nagpur city | 25 | Husband was raised by his sisters. He was addicted to alcohol. Would abstain from the house for days. Sisters-in-law harassed the victim. | SHG members helped the victim to file a case to the police. The husband was reprimanded. SHG members warned the sisters-in-law. Matter resolved. Victim started living separately with her husband. |
| 21. Nagpur city | 60 | The victim had two marriages. First married when she was 15. Husband was infidel and abusive. Used to bring other women in the house. Somehow she continued, till her sons became older. Then, she left the house and after a few years, married the second time. The second husband was also abusive and drunkard. | SHG members provided repeated arbitration between husband and wife. Consoled the victim and developed her confidence, who had become emotionally insecure. The present marriage continues but relationship is strained. |
| 22. Pune city | 37 | Husband was suspicious because the lady was good looking. He was a drunkard as well. Abusive atmosphere for a long time. Lady made a suicide attempt. | The local SHG saved this stranger lady at the railway tracks. Provided all sorts of support, then took up the case with police and stood by her. Husband repented. Matter amicably settled. |
| 23. Pune city | 28 | Case of marital discord. Husband was very docile, wife was arrogant and ill tempered. Wife wanted to stay with her maternal family. | The husband was the nephew of one of the SHG members. They tried to reconcile the marriage but failed. Divorce was obtained by mutual consent. |
| 24. Nagpur city | 30 | The lady's in-laws were suspicious and abusive. They stole her jewelry for sister-in-law's marriage. Later, her husband became mentally unstable. | SHG members helped her in the criminal proceedings filed against the in-laws and provided moral support but could not actively alter the physical conditions. |

contd...

contd...

| | | | |
|---|---|---|---|
| 25. Gadachiroli | 28 | The lady and her husband were troubled by the in-laws. She was ridiculed due to her dark complexion. Father-in-law was drunkard and abusive. Brothers-in-law were greedy and ill-minded. Sisters-in-law also abused her after they were separated. Later husband became abusive. A classic case of how patriarchy subjugates a woman. | The victim stood her ground only because of the support from her SHG where she was an active member. SHG women helped to change the attitude of the husband but did not succeed with the in-laws. Quarrels with in-laws continue but husband has been pacified. |
| 26. Gadachiroli | 27 | This was the lady's husband's second marriage as he did not have a child from the first wife. She was compelled to marry because of parent's poverty. Suspicious husband, did not allow her to carry on the community work through the SHG. No physical abuse but mental torture. | SHG gave strong support. Repeatedly acted as mediators. Husband was pressurized to behave well. Now live together but small problems persist. |
| 27. Pune city | 20 | Husband was unable to earn his livelihood and was dependent upon his father, who kept on intervening in the family. He wanted them to shift to the rural area to work at the rain-fed farm. No physical violence but continuous tension resulted into the lady coming back to her parents place. | SHG members arbitrated and pressurized the father-in-law not to trouble them. Husband was urged to find suitable work and shelter. Amicably settled. |
| 28. Pune city | 20 | Husband was a complete drunkard and did not earn anything. The lady was cheated at marriage. Mother-in-law and sister-in-law were extremely abusive. Physical violence forced her to go to mother's place. | The SHG women were quite supportive and helped her in seeking legal support. Maternal family is very supportive. Legal separation awaited. |

contd...

contd…

| | | | |
|---|---|---|---|
| 29. Pune city | 8 | Case of child rape. A girl of six, raped by neighbouring youth. | Some of the SHG leaders who had come to promote the SHG concept, took up the case and helped the mother. They built her confidence and helped her file a police complaint. Also facilitated speedy justice without affecting the girl's psyche. The culprit was convicted for seven years of rigorous imprisonment. |
| 30. Pune city | 15 | Case of juvenile abduction. Young girl of ninth standard (15) fled away with the neighbourhood boy of 23. Went to Mumbai. No physical violence but the boy's side did not cooperate. They helped the crime. The girl became pregnant. Got aborted. | The local feminist NGO helped to initiate police action. Got the girl back. Now resides at home and has resumed school. Not much involvement of SHG as the matter was sensitive and was solved at the domestic level. |
| 31. Pune city | 25 | Case of juvenile abduction and extreme form of cruelty. The boy married her but ill-treated and abused her. Had two children. After 21, husband sent her as a housemaid to USA. Wages were confiscated. Violence continued after she came back. Husband had another woman in the meanwhile. Then sent her to Chennai to work as housemaid. Lives there in almost captive condition. | Matter not resolved due to legal complications. SHG could not do much except provide mental support to victim's mother, who was a member of the SHG. The mother's life was also charred due to domestic violence. |
| 32. Satara | 18 | Case from a tribal community. The girl, from an extremely poor family was married at the age of 8 to a boy of 15. The boy used to drink and beat her. The boy's family migrated out in search of livelihoods, leaving the girl at her mother's place. Came back after seven years and took the girl home. Now leaves amicably. | The SHG was not actively involved as it was newly formed but the promoting NGO helped the girl's family to get over the problem. |

contd…

contd...

| | | | |
|---|---|---|---|
| 33. Pune rural | 26 | Husband was a bit hot headed person. Considerable interference by the sisters-in-law. Husband beat the lady and threw her out of house in Mumbai over a quarrel when she was pregnant. | Police complaint filed by a relative under Section 498A. Husband and sister-in-law were arrested but the problem was not resolved. SHG was not active but the community organizers of the promoting NGO took lead and effected reconciliation. Now stays separately from the in-laws. |
| 34. Pune rural | 20 | Poor farming family. Husband completely addicted to alcohol. Extreme form of cruelty. Was thrown out of house a number of times at night, even while pregnant. Had to come and stay at parent's place. Husband refused to comply despite intervention by the NGO and police. | The lady went back to stay with the husband and later committed suicide. NGO activated the legal machinery. Husband was convicted to four years of rigorous imprisonment. |
| 35. Pune rural | 20 | The victim was married off at 17 with a big dowry and jewelry. Marriage was not consummated. The in-laws kept on asking for more dowry. Her mother was dead and father was mentally challenged. She came to her aunt's house. The in-laws refused to part with her jewelry (stree-dhan). | The SHG led by the aunt supported the lady. After trying moderate means several times, went together and fought with the in-laws. Later sought police help and got the jewelry back. Divorce awaited. |
| 36. Sindhudurg | 62 | Long history of domestic violence. Itinerant husband used to beat her frequently. She was abused also by the mother-in-law. The lady's body is deformed due to chronic beatings. Husband demands sex from her even in old age. Non-compliance results into physical abuse. | Lady joined the SHG very late. However, SHG members reprimanded the husband and pressurized him to stop violence. Mental abuse continues. |

contd...

contd...

| | | | |
|---|---|---|---|
| 37. Sindhudurg | 33 | The case of the daughter of the above lady. Married for 16 years. Husband incurred huge loss in the business. Had lent a big sum to a woman. He used to drink and beat wife out frustration. | The SHG members helped the family to find a legal solution and helped to get the money back. Domestic life improved considerably. |
| 38. Sindhudurg | 37 | Case of goonda trouble and police atrocity. Widow brewing liquor for livelihood. Stopped after the local goondas and police began to harass. Started rearing goats but police falsely implicated her and looted her money. | The SHG group took up the matter with police. Made use of the legal training imparted to them. Made the event public through media. Waged a long struggle. Got justice. Police officials fined. |
| 39. Sindhudurg | 27 | Tragic victim of superstitions. Mother-in-law considered this lady as inauspicious and abused both physically and mentally. Husband was absconding. The lady disappeared mysteriously. | SHG members were trying to help her but before it could materialize, the tragic incident happened. SHG did not act promptly. |
| 40. Sindhudurg | 29 | Fisherman husband. Used to drink and beat her cruelly. Domestic violence continued for six years. | SHG was not effective but local NGO provided legal assistance and help. Lady stays at her mother's place. Problem not solved as the husband not responsive. |
| 41. Sindhudurg | 22 | Fisherman husband older by 11 years than the lady. Love marriage. Turned sour because husband became suspicious of wife's past relationship. Started drinking and beating her. | Local women gathered together and held a community meeting. Persuaded the husband to stop harassing her. Drinking did not cease but violence stopped. |
| 42. Sindhudurg | NA | Widow staying with sister-in-law (brother's wife) who was also a widow but who used to trouble her. Physical violence was committed by the sister-in-law in collaboration with her paramour. | SHG women took action in cooperation with local villagers and tamed down the sister-in-law. |

## Findings: The role of SHGs

The pattern of domestic violence, as observed in the present study, is not much different from the one observed contemporarily. However, the aspect to be noted here is the intervention made by the groups of women organized as SHGs. The different tasks undertaken by various SHGs and the roles performed by them can be comprehended from the above matrix.

In broad terms, following roles were performed by the SHGs:

1. Arbitration in domestic quarrels and disputes
2. Preventing the perpetrators and pressurizing them to stop the violence
3. Counselling, especially of the women involved in committing violence
4. Assistance in seeking police support
5. Facilitation of legal action
6. Moral and motivational support to the victim

### *Arbitration*

Many of the domestic quarrels and disputes, which result into domestic violence, are triggered by misunderstandings, prejudices, lack of information, suspicion, superstitions and attitudinal problems. These can be sorted out if proper arbitration by a third party, especially by senior, mature and elderly person, is provided. The SHG members could play this role effectively.

### *Prevention*

The SHG members could prevent the violence by physically intervening into the scene. However, they were more effective when the violence was committed by the women of the matrimonial family. They were effective against the men in a limited manner. Secondly, they were effective when the violence was committed in the immediate neighbourhood. Where the victim lived distantly and when the violence occurred at night, the SHGs were less effective.

### *Counselling*

This was the associated function of arbitration. Again, counselling was more effective in the case of women in the matrimonial family. Men seemed to be less amenable to such inputs. Counselling of the victim was also necessary for training her to avoid the probable instances of violence.

### *Police action*

To the extent possible the victim and SHG members avoided going to the police. However, police support was sought when physical violence reached its extremes. The SHG's involvement was highly useful at this juncture as no individual woman could/would dare to contact the police on her own. The police also seemed to listen when a group of women approached them. Although the police machinery is broadly sympathetic with the victims, in actual practice, individual police personnel were not sensitive enough to comprehend the issue. Their patriarchal attitudes also posed a problem.

### *Legal support*

In cases where separation was the best option, legal support was solicited and the SHG members provided necessary help. However, such instances were few as in a majority of the cases, the orientation was towards preventing the violence and living amicably with the spouse.

### *Moral and motivational support*

During the whole traumatic process, the SHG members were useful in providing moral and motivational support to the victim. This was the most notable assistance as it could not be provided by any other external agency. The incidence of domestic violence and the long process of its resolution demanded substantial patience, perseverance and moral boosting measures.

## The merits of SHG action

The first important thing is that the SHGs do not face the problem of *locus standi* or the 'Who Are You' question. One of the major obstacles in preventing domestic violence is that it is considered a private affair of the family and, hence, except for the immediate kin, other people are not allowed to intervene. The SHG being a group of close, neighbouring women can overcome this barrier because it is a primary group like the family. Whenever a member of the group is victimized, the SHG can rightfully intervene and stop the violence. Similarly, where an immediate relative of the member is concerned, the SHG can rightfully express their concern. Above all, the SHG, being a group of women, can always intervene in solidarity with a fellow woman. They need not have to seek anybody's mandate for this purpose. The mandate is earned by the very nature of the group.

Secondly, SHGs are founded to foster human relationships. This feature has the potential to make SHGs an institution, which can redress the aberrations in the primary institutions of marriage and family. The state, the police or the judicial system cannot undertake this task as they cannot operate at the micro-level and their nature is not compatible to deal with social institutions. They can only create a policy framework but cannot govern the subtle, complex and emotive human relationships. Domestic violence is the culmination of domestic relationships. Hence, a micro-level social institution alone can prevent it.

Intervention by an SHG has two advantages. The women perpetuating violence in the matrimonial family (mother-in-law and sisters-in-law) can be effectively confronted only by a group of women in the neighbourhood. Secondly, the men committing violence (especially the husbands) are powerless against a group of women. If other men confront them, then, the matter is taken otherwise. The pressure of the women in the neighbourhood and the fear of social ridicule works as a deterrent against domestic violence. In comparison, law and police have not been much effective. It has been found by researchers that "Section 498A of the IPC has been largely ineffective in criminalizing acts of domestic violence and in punishing the male abuser" (Mitra, 2000: ii). In such circumstances, it is essential that alternate mechanisms become available in society.

Another notable feature is that the SHG members aim at prevention of violence rather than legal separation. In doing so, they emphasize the right of the victim to reside in her matrimonial home. Although the SHG members do not necessarily have the understanding of the rights framework, nevertheless, their action implies the assertion of rights. The legal solution to end domestic incompatibility is separation, i.e., divorce. However, it is not necessarily the ideal solution in Indian context given the helpless situation of single women in society. This common sense is perhaps well understood by the SHG members and, hence, they emphasize the stoppage of violence and the right to reside in the matrimonial home. Of course, when the conjugal relationship is broken, divorce is the only solution but as could be seen from the above cases, reprimanding and/or penalizing the abuser appeared to be the course adopted by the majority.

The strength of the SHGs is that they can provide livelihood support to the victim if she is a member of the group. They can provide micro-finance with which she could earn her livelihood. In the present context, no other agency has this potential. This fact is important because a majority of victims come from poor households and are in need of livelihood support once they declare independence from their husbands.

Another merit of the SHG action is that these groups, being spontaneous community entities, do not carry any ideological baggage. The NGOs, tackling cases of domestic violence, often perpetuate the ideology which they are imbued with. Ideological orientation is good to achieve certain ends but dogmatic preoccupation with it often blurs the comprehension of reality and hampers the effectiveness of action.

Finally, SHGs being neighbourhood groups have the potential to provide continuous support to the victim. No other agency has this faculty. The sustenance of support is an important factor as resolution of domestic violence is often a long-term process.

## Limitations

There are, however, some limitations also, consideration of which underscores the various dimensions of the role.

- Marriage and family are still considered as private affairs. Hence, SHG members are inherently reluctant to intervene.

As women, they are also a bit afraid to take the first step. Initially, domestic violence is treated as 'natural quarrels' between the spouses. The intervention usually starts with counselling the victim and correcting her lapses, if any. The SHGs require definite motivation to overcome this basic reluctance. Then alone a positive action becomes possible.

- The SHGs are most effective when their member is directly affected. It then becomes a part of the mandate to care for her well-being. But, they are less effective when a non-member is concerned. Relatives of members (like daughters or nieces) do become a matter of concern but then there are practical limitations to action.
- Relationship between the SHG members, i.e., cohesion within the group matters. If the group is marred with internal quarrels, jealousies, squabbles or misgivings, then, their inclination to take action and potential to actually do so is jeopardized.
- SHGs lack legal training and do not necessarily have the competence to deal with the police machinery. They are seldom aware of the Section 498–A of the Indian Penal Code, which deals with mental and physical torture. The lack of information and training affects the efficacy of action. Many a time they are not aware about the exact steps to be taken when a case is referred to them.
- The SHGs do not have a control on the institution of marriage although they have the potential for good match-making. As mentioned earlier, faulty or mismatched marriages are one of the main sources of domestic violence.
- The promoting NGOs are often stronger than individual SHGs. Hence, women tend to seek help from them rather than the SHG. The NGOs often tend to redress the cases themselves rather than developing the capacity of SHG members. The women also have greater faith in the promoters of NGOs who are charismatic personalities.
- Although the members of SHGs can potentially prevent the act of violence, in actual practice, there are a number of limitations. Physical abuse usually takes place within the

four walls of the household and mostly at nights. Only when it turns violent or when the victim is driven out of the house, the neighbours come to know of it. Moderate violence often goes unnoticed. Secondly, it takes place not in a series but in spurts and bouts. Although it is predictable (as in the case of drunkard husbands), it occurs without a warning. Hence, although it is not impossible, most of the times it is difficult to prevent it on the spot.

- The SHGs cannot provide livelihood support to non-members although they can prevent the violence against them.
- One limitation, which has come about due to the newness of SHGs, is that the SHGs cannot provide shelter to the victim. This is a dire need when the parental home is far away or when the parents are apathetic or helpless. It is understandable that SHGs being small and informal organizations may not have the infrastructure to provide shelter but the need is apparent.

## Conclusions

1. Women's SHGs, being closely knit, neighbourhood groups, are most strategically placed to tackle the issue of domestic violence. They have the potential to rectify the distortions occurring in the institutions of marriage and family.
2. The SHGs can serve as a 'help line' in the event of domestic violence. A neighbourhood SHG can be a reliable force to prevent physical abuse.
3. The SHGs can provide livelihood support to the members who are affected by violence. They are the most potent agency in this regard.
4. The SHGs are a useful medium of arbitration and counselling in marital discords. The arbitration and counselling are essential to pre-empt and prevent domestic violence.
5. The SHGs can serve as useful facilitators in seeking police intervention and resorting to legal action.
6. The SHGs are best suited to provide moral and motivational support in a sustained manner to the victim of domestic violence.

Despite these strengths, at present, the potential of SHGs is not fully realized. This is due to following reasons:

(i) The SHGs are not geared to serve as a structure to combat domestic violence. This orientation is lacking due to their preoccupation with savings and credit activities.

(ii) They are afraid to venture into the delicate and sensitive issue of domestic relationships.

(iii) They do not have the legal and technical knowledge to address the issue.

(iv) They are dependent upon the promotional NGO for motivation and guidance.

(v) They do not possess the organizational and financial means to support the victim. In particular, they are unable to provide shelter support to the victim. They are also handicapped to provide livelihood support to non-members.

## Recommendations

1. Although SHGs are primarily organized for savings and credit activities, the promoting agency needs to motivate them to address the issue of domestic violence. Such orientation needs to become a part of the overall mandate of women's organization and empowerment.
2. The promoting agency also needs to develop the capacity of SHGs to tackle the issue at various levels. In particular, they need to impart knowledge regarding human rights, marriage laws, Indian Penal Code and legal rights of women. The SHG leaders can be trained as 'Community Counsellors' or 'Barefoot Lawyers'.
3. The SHGs need to act as 'watchdogs' while marriages are arranged and performed. In particular, they should inform about the groom, and advise on the suitability of marriage. They should also discourage the practice of dowry and early marriages.
4. If not SHGs, at least, the federations of SHGs need to set aside a fund for the welfare of the victim of domestic violence, irrespective of whether she is a member. To the extent possible they should also make some arrangements for providing shelter-homes to the victims. This could be possible at the federation level.

5. Campaigns to end domestic violence need to involve all the SHGs, irrespective of who has promoted them. The SHGs should become key stakeholders and main rallying points to end domestic violence.

## Some cases from the study*

### *Case study 1*

This case happened in one of the suburbs of Pune city where the Tulaja Devi Self-Help Group was operational. The victim Asha's mother was a member of the SHG. Asha was married in 2001. This was a properly arranged marriage and was also performed in a proper, conventional manner. The boy came from the same locality. No dowry was given and demanded. Asha stayed with her husband in a joint family. First six months passed smoothly and then the trouble started. Asha's mother-in-law did not like her going to her maternal place very frequently. She started scolding Asha on this issue. Asha's sister-in-law also added fuel. Initially, Asha's husband did not take part in it but later on he also sided with his mother and sister. First, the harassment was restricted to verbal abuse, then, it turned physical. Once her husband used a stick to beat her. Knowing this, Asha's mother became furious and went to her son-in-law's house and gave him a decent thrashing. Asha came to her mother's house for her delivery. After delivery, her babygirl was taken away forcibly by her in-laws and she was left alone at her mother's house.

Asha's mother took the case to a local, family counselling NGO. This organization made some arbitration but was not successful. She then turned to her SHG for support. The members of the SHG talked to the husband and warned him for his misbehaviour. The husband did not pay heed and, hence, they decided to file a police complaint and accompanied Asha's mother in doing so. The police took due action and brought Asha's child back to her. Next day, the husband came to take Asha back into his house but her mother refused. The SHG members made him to sign a written pledge that thenceforth he would not misbehave with his wife. Subsequently, he partitioned his house and started

---

* The names of the victims have been changed.

staying separately. Asha's life became easier although occasional wife-beating continued.

In this case, the role of the SHG was to stand firmly behind their member and provide the requisite solidarity and group support. Their collective pressurization made Asha's husband realize his mistake and make amendments.

### *Case study 2*

Parvati Kudale was a widow of around 50 and lived in a small drought-prone village in Sangli district. Her husband had died 20 years ago due to jaundice. He was a drunkard and used to abuse her a lot. Parvati had four sons and two daughters. She began facing hardships since the demise of her husband. She somehow raised her children who later sought employment in Mumbai. None of her relatives helped her. Parvati stayed at the village with her daughter and a daughter-in-law. She lived by wage labour. Seeing her single condition, one local gunda started harassing her. He had been notorious as a drunkard and abusive man. Her ill-willing relatives actually instigated him against her. He used to frequent her house in a drunk condition and abuse her and make advances towards her. Once she had a guest in her house who was a teacher and a decent man. The gunda started spreading the word that Parvati was having an illicit affair with him. Parvati was embarrassed as she had had grown-up children. On another occasion her younger son was playing with a drum at her doorstep when this gunda came and started abusing him. He also started beating him. Parvati tried to intervene but he became more aggressive. She then took out her chappal and started heating him.

After the incident, Parvati was terrified. She reported the incident to her SHG and asked for help. The SHG members realized that there was no one to help her and unless they provided due support she would be victimized. Hence, all of them went to the taluka police station and filed a complaint against the gunda. The police were reluctant to register the complaint. The women then requested the parent NGO – Swapna Mahila Vikas Sanstha – to intervene. The police took cognizance of the matter once Swapna Sanstha stepped in. The gunda was taken into the police custody and kept there for four days. After this, the local villagers came forward and assured the women that they would ensure that the man did not harass Parvati. Upon this assurance, the women withdrew their complaint. Then onward the man did not trouble Parvati and her misery came to an end.

The SHG members opined that they did not have enough resources to go to the taluka police station and also did not have enough knowledge about the handling of the case. Hence, they had to depend upon the Sanstha (NGO) for guidance.

### *Case study 3*

Hasina belonged to a poor Muslim family in a small town of district Kolhapur. Her father was a peon in a private company. Her mother was a member of the SHG promoted by Jyoti Mahila Sanstha. She had bought a sewing machine by taking a loan from the SHG and used to stitch garments. Hasina was married off in a neighbouring village. The marriage cost Rs 70,000 to her family as dowry in gold was given and it was conducted with pomp and ritual. The groom was in the distant relation of Hasina. He had seen Hasina at a cousin's wedding and liked her very much. He was insistent on marrying her and hurried for the marriage. Hasina's family was not financially prepared. They had to mortgage their farm. It was told to them that the boy did farming and his family had a ration shop. But, after the marriage, it was realized that he was a gambler and a drunkard.

The problem started after a couple of months of marriage as Hasina came to know about the habits of her husband. The domestic life was not peaceful. The problem was further aggravated when Hasina desired to take admission to 12th standard. She was opposed by her in-laws and her husband gave her a bashing. He started drinking heavily and wife-battering became a daily affair. Her jewellery was grabbed by the in-laws and kept in a bank locker.

Hasina's mother then went to see her with some of the relatives and spoke to her husband. He behaved well for a couple of days,[4] but later the violence was resumed. The mother-in-law and the husband taunted Hasina for her desire to study further. The mother-in-law also told her that her son would do everything – drink, gamble, have affairs with women – but she would have to endure with it.

On 14 October 2004, Hasina spoke to her mother for almost an hour on the phone and told her about the miseries. Later that day, her husband accused her of having some affair and said that it was not her mother but her boy friend, whom she spoke with. She was then mercilessly beaten by her husband. Her clothes were torn. He poured kerosene on her. While he was searching for a match, she escaped and ran out of the house. She somehow managed to reach her mother's house and told her what happened.

The mother came to see Ms. Shewanta Sasne of Jyoti Mahila Sanstha. She also contacted the fellow members of the SHG. Then, they filed a complaint at the local police station. The police went to Hasina's place and rounded up the mother-in-law as the husband was not available. She created a big fuss at the police station and had to be made quiet by two lady constables. She was kept in the lock up for two hours and was made to give an undertaking that next day she would reappear in the police station along with her son. But no one turned up. So, again on 16 October, the police constables went to fetch them. Hasina's husband had four brothers. When the police reached their place, one of the brothers told Hasina's husband in front of the police that he should take a sword and cut her into pieces as its no use having a wife who complained to police against her husband. The police then brought him also to the police station along with Hasina's husband and mother-in-law. The husband was locked up for the day at the police station.

Then, some of the prominent persons from the village, including the Sarpanch, came and guaranteed that thenceforth Hasina would not be ill-treated. The other two brothers of the husband also guaranteed Hasina's well-being in their house. Hasina was ready to go back and give her in-laws another chance but her mother wanted a divorce. The police took a written affidavit from her in-laws that if anything happened to Hasina, her husband and in-laws would be held responsible. Hasina then went with them and has been reported to have peace.

When Hasina was being beaten, the neighbours did not dare to intervene. The members of the SHG of her mother had decided to take out a Morcha, had the police failed to take the necessary action. But, the need did not arise.

### *Case study 4*

Meera Kamble from district Sangli was married when she was 15. She went to stay with her husband's family in Mumbai. She had a son when she was 18 and a daughter when she was 21. Her in-laws were a controversial family. Her father-in-law had an affair with another woman who stayed next door. It was rumoured that the father-in-law and his mistress had killed her husband so that they could stay together. Meera's mother-in-law was a docile woman and raised her son patiently. Meera's husband was a hot tempered person and occasionally beat her and the children. However, he did not make them starve. When Meera's father-in-law retired, he received a large provident fund amount. Meera's husband asked him a part of the money which he refused. His mistress got angry with this request and tried to kill Meera. Sensing the trouble, Meera's husband sent her to her maternal home in Sangli. This was during her second pregnancy. Her son stayed with his father. After a year, Meera heard that her husband died due to burns. Meera was apprehensive that her father-in-law's mistress might have killed him.

After this, she was scared to go to Mumbai. She learnt nursing and started working in a private hospital at her mother's place. Later on, she became a member of an SHG and got interested in the work of organizing women. Considering her interest, the local NGO – Swapna Mahila Vikas Sanstha – enrolled her as a community organizer. This measure brought stability to her life but the real issue was that of bringing her son back. In this regard, the SHG members helped her. They built her confidence and provided various types of support to reclaim her son. Meera went to Mumbai and challenged her in-laws and got the son back. She then lived at her parents' house and raised her children alongside continuing to work as a community organizer.

### *Case study 5*

Maya Patil was married at 17. She belonged to a very poor landless family in Pune district. Her husband was a small farmer. He drank a lot and beat her every night. He never bothered to get the daily necessities for the household. After getting beaten, Maya was thrown out of the house and had to spend the nights sitting at the doorstep. She put up with this abuse for a long time but one day she was thrown out, not to be taken back. She came to her parents' place. She had a son of one-and-a-half year old but the husband retained the boy.

Maya then approached Chaitanya, the NGO from Rajgurunagar, as she wanted the custody of her son. Chaitanya sent many notices to summon the husband. Maya used to come and sit all day but her husband never turned up. Then, they filed a case for maintenance. Still, he did not respond. They even alerted the police of his place but they did not cooperate. Then, Maya stopped coming to the organization. When Chaitanya's social workers called her relatives, it was told that she had gone back to her husband.

After two months the news came that Maya was dead. The organization made enquiries and came to know that after post-mortem, poison was found in her viscera. They appeared before the court and gave their statement. Because of their testimony, Maya's husband was convicted for four years of rigorous imprisonment. Maya was not a member of SHG but her relatives were and, hence, the case was taken up by Chaitanya.

### *Case study 6*

When she was just 15, Susheela ran away with a neighbourhood boy. The boy supposedly married her and brought her back to their locality, a suburb of Pune. The marriage was accepted by both the parents. After some days, however, the boy showed his true colours and started beating her on flimsy grounds. The physical and mental abuse increased day by day. Susheela's parents left the locality as they could not withstand their daughter's abuse.

Susheela lost her first child and almost became mentally imbalanced due to the shock. She was hospitalized and after a traumatic recovery was brought back to her house. By the time she was 20, she had two children – a boy and a girl. When she was 21 years old, her husband got her passport made and sent her to the United States to work as a housemaid on a contract of four years. She used to earn Rs 12,000 per month but never got a penny of that money. All her salary was sent to her husband.

During this period, her husband got another girl and the girl's mother in the house. He had sexual relationship with both of them. Susheela came back after four years only to find these strangers in her home. The physical and mental abuse started all over again. It was reported that Susheela's husband had even sent that other girl's mother to work as a housemaid in Mumbai.

One day, Susheela spoke with somebody on the phone. Her husband suspected of an affair and beat her mercilessly with a thick iron rod. Susheela got bruises all over her body and the wounds had swollen. The neighbours informed her mother who came and took Susheela away from the husband. After some days she was sent home. Later, Susheela's husband sent her to Chennai to work in the house of the relatives of the people she worked for in the US. She was staying there when the case was reported. Meanwhile, Susheela's mother had approached a women's organization to check whether her daughter can get a divorce but this did not materialize as there was no marriage certificate. They asked Susheela's employers in Chennai to send her back but they refused saying that she owed them money.

Susheela's mother has been a member of the SHG who tried to give her moral support. But they could not do much as Susheela's husband manipulated the matters. The women also could not comprehend the legal mess and did not know what action to take. Susheela had to suffer all these years simply because proper legal advice was not received.

### *Case study 7*

Regina D'souza (62) belonged to the coastal district of Sindhudurg. She was married at 15 and lived in a joint family. Her husband used to work in a outstation hotel and used to come home only on holidays. Her mother-in-law received the money sent by him but never treated her well as he sent less money compared to his brothers. Regina had to work at home and also in the farms. Whenever her husband came home, he used to beat her mercilessly. Regina's body got deformed due to the beatings. Her legs were bent and she could not walk properly.

Her husband came back to his village after retirement and they stayed together. Their children were married but none of them stayed with them. Regina therefore had to carry out all the domestic work. Her husband did not extend any help and continued abusing her. He demanded sex from her even at the old age, failing which invited his wrath.

Regina became a member of a local SHG and reported the harassment to the fellow women. Initially, they did not respond, fearing that this would increase her troubles. However, when situation did not improve, they talked with the husband and asked him to stop the abuse. When he did not concede, they reprimanded him and threatened to take the matter to police. This action sobered him down and the physical violence stopped. However, ill-treatment and mental abuse continued. Regina felt that it would end only after his or her death.

## Note

This paper was earlier published by Development Support Team, Pune.

## References

Dave, Anjali, Gopika Solanki and Pekham Basu (2001). 'Journey from Violence to Crime: A Research Study on domestic Violence', *The Indian Journal of Social Work*, Vol. 62, Issue 3, July, pp. 430–445.

Karlekar, Malavika (1998). 'Domestic Violence,' *Economic and Political Weekly*, Vol. 33 (27), July 4, pp. 1741–1751.

Krishnaraj, Maithreyi (ed.) (1991). *Women and Violence: A Country Report*. SNDT Women's University, Mumbai.

Mitra, Nishi (2000). *Domestic Violence as Public Issue: A Review of Responses*, Tata Institute of Social Sciences (Unit for Women's Studies), Mumbai.

— (2001). 'Community Based Initiatives in the Struggle Against Domestic Violence', *The Indian Journal of Social Work*, Vol. 62, Issue 3, July, pp. 414–429.

Mukharji, Chandan, Preet Rustagi, N. Krishnaji (2001). 'Crimes Against Women in India: Analysis of Official Statistics', *Economic and Political Weekly*, Vol. 36(43), October 27, pp. 4070–4080.

CHAPTER FOURTEEN

# Battered and bound in their own homes

## Does family violence have an answer?

*R. Indira*

The joy that those concerned with women's well-being felt when the Domestic Violence Prevention Act finally came into force on October 25, 2006 is often blurred by the realization that a large number of women are still experiencing a sense of insecurity in their homes. A recent study came out with the shocking finding that nearly 70 per cent of women in India are victims of domestic violence (the two terms 'family violence' and 'domestic violence' are used interchangeably in this paper). Elaborating the issue further, the author noted that 15,000 women die every day due to different forms of domestic violence (Ramanna, 2006). Whether or not we take these figures at their face value, the hard truth is that the largest number of crimes against women is committed in their homes. How could this be possible? Isn't the home considered the safest place for a woman? In a culture that has been extolling the virtues of the 'family' as a centre of human bonding and human welfare, it is difficult to swallow the bitter pill that this paradise is actually the most insecure place for a woman to live (see Yllo and Bogard, 1988).

The family, be it the parental home or the marital home, constructs 'ideal types' of women that are actually internalized both by men and women. By upholding such traits as 'self-denial' and 'submission to male authority' as virtues that a woman must imbibe, families prepare women to not only expect male violence but also tolerate it. Women are also deliberately socialized to believe that the family is a private domain that must be kept away from the public sphere. By glorifying the notion of 'family honour', the family creates the feeling that it is the woman's prime responsibility to protect this honour even if she has to lay down her life for it. The dependence syndrome that most women have to endure further renders them vulnerable to violence. The feeling that family violence has to be tolerated and not contested is passed on from mother to daughter with the tacit approval of other relatives. The home actually sows the seeds of violence against women. For many women, "home is where they face a reign of terror and violence at the hands of somebody close to them – somebody they should be able to trust. Those victimized suffer physically and psychologically. They are unable to make their own decisions, voice their own opinions or protect themselves and their children for fear of further repercussions. Their human rights are denied and their lives are stolen from them by the ever-present threat of violence" (UNICEF, 2000).

Violence against a woman may start at any point of time in her life, for that matter even before she is born. Though family violence is widespread and cuts across barriers of race, region, religion, class and caste, until recently it went largely unrecognized by society. While reliable data may be hard to get, studies estimate that from country to country, between 20 and 50 per cent of women have experienced physical violence at the hands of an intimate partner or family member (WHO, 1996).

It is now very important to raise the question "how does family violence also referred to as domestic violence manifest itself?" *The Innocent Digest*, a UNICEF publication, provides one of the most comprehensive definitions of family violence, which is given below:

"Domestic violence, as defined for this Digest, includes violence perpetrated by intimate partners and other family members and manifested through:

- *Physical abuse* such as slapping, beating, arm-twisting, stabbing, strangling, burning, choking, kicking, threats with an object or weapon, and murder. It also includes traditional practices harmful to women such as genital mutilation and wife inheritance (the practice of passing a widow and her property to her dead husband's brother).

- *Sexual abuse* such as coerced sex through threats, intimidation or physical force, forcing unwanted sexual acts or forcing sex with others.
- *Psychological abuse* which includes behaviour that is intended to intimidate and prosecute, and takes the form of threats of abandonment or abuse, destruction of objects, isolation, verbal aggression and constant humiliation.
- *Economic abuse* includes acts such as the denial of funds, refusal to contribute financially, denial of food and basic needs, and controlling access to health care, employment etc." (UNICEF, 2000).

The definition of domestic violence cited above gives us an idea of the entire gamut of oppressive situations that a woman could face in her own family. Violence against women is often a cycle of abuse that manifests itself in many forms throughout their lives. In fact, there is no place that is safe for a woman including the mother's womb. Identified as one of the major causes for India's declining sex ratio, female foeticide is a fast spreading virus that refuses to be curbed by the Pre-natal Diagnostic Technique Act of 1994. Female infanticide, the practice of killing a new born, is nothing short of murder, which is a punishable act and yet goes without even the slightest of punishment. What underlies the practices of female foeticide or infanticide is a cost-benefit calculation. Parents justify their action by quoting the proverbial dowry as the root cause for the decision to wipe out their daughters even before they see the light of the day.

According to a report published recently in *Times of India,* as many as "80 per cent of India's districts have recorded a decline in sex ratios of children since 1991"(Dhawan, 2006). The sex ratio in the age group 0–6 years has declined from 962 girls per 1,000 boys in 1981 to 927 girls per 1,000 boys in 2001. It is even needless to mention that this skewed sex ratio is the direct consequence of female foeticide and infanticide.

Forcing a woman to undergo tests for screening the sex of the unborn child and then coercing her to abort the foetus if it is diagnosed a female is only the beginning of a cycle of violence that a family can let loose against her. In a cultural milieu, where son preference is almost an accepted norm, sex determination tests and sex-selective abortions prevent the very birth of female infants. Though female foeticide is described as an act of violence by one female against another, in reality, it might actually be the powerlessness of a mother-to-be that hinders her from protesting against the murder of her unborn daughter. The decision to abort a female foetus or a new-born daughter is the family's collective decision and not that of the mother per se. Those who look at foeticide or infanticide as a crime against one female by another must realize that this phenomenon has to be examined in the context of the choices which are available to a woman to decide the course of her life.

Even before a female child sees the light of the day if she could become a victim of family violence one can imagine the extent of control her family could have on her life even "if she manages to be born and survive". This violence need not always take on the form of physical abuse. Depriving female members of the family from enjoying their rights as human beings is one of the ways in which family violence manifests itself. Not sending a daughter to school or a college, preventing her from seeking or utilizing opportunities for gainful employment, preventing her free movement both within and outside the home are but some of the ways by which family acts as the 'silent suppressor'.

Economic abuse is another form of family violence that most often goes unnoticed. There is a widespread belief that economic independence liberates women from violence, but the case is not always so. While it is true that economic dependence forces many women to tolerate violence, economic independence does not necessarily prevent family-induced oppression. Economic independence must never be interpreted as the capacity to earn money only, the more important factor being the liberty that one enjoys to make decisions relating to its usage. But, in many families, women are forced to handover all their earnings to the husband or parents-in-law, failing which they have to face both verbal and physical abuse. It is also possible that a woman might be forced to work only to cater to the demands of her family members.

The most abusive form of family violence that causes harm to both the body and the mind is of course physical assault. Wife battering that is almost considered a husband's right over his wife is the most common form of family violence. In a survey of 969 men conducted in three states of India, eight out of every 10 men accepted that they had physically tortured their wives (see Action India, 2004). In many Indian families the single most important cause of physical abuse is the dowry demand. The fact that there is a history of dowry in Indian society is corroborated by the fact that the Dowry Prohibition Act was passed as way back as in 1961. With an amendment in 1984 and another in 1986, the anti-dowry law became more stringent but the gravity of dowry-related offences did not decline. Though hard figures are difficult to get, it is reported that in India today every two hours there is a dowry-related death.

In the case of a large number of women domestic violence has become a way of life. But, why does a woman tolerate this humiliation? The desire to hold a family together, fear of the future of her children and herself, threat of homelessness, economic and emotional dependence on the abusing spouse, short-lived apologies from abusers and of course familial and social pressures are some possible explanations. There is also a lack of support structures that could provide shelter to women who want to exit from abusive homes. In many parental homes there is no place for a married daughter, because of the widely prevalent norm that once married her place is her husband's home.

## Is there an answer to family violence?

Family violence stems from a man's attempt to prove his power over a woman. In a social set-up where marriage is viewed as a relationship between unequal partners notions of male superiority and female subordination dominate. A woman is seen as her marital family's property and is coerced into a situation where she internalizes violence as an inevitable consequence of marriage. Even to this day most girls are under pressure to keep the family honour intact. 'Question' and 'protest' are not encouraged but 'tolerance' is a virtue.

In a recent seminar on domestic violence the panelists who deliberated on the options that victims of family violence had reached the conclusion that "women in crisis have no where to go". A police officer, who was one of the panelists, was of the view that the police force, and women in particular, were not able to help women in crisis because they pleaded for protection of perpetrators of violence, who in most cases happened to be their kins. In her own words, "in atleast 95 per cent of the cases, the accused is a male relative – a husband, father or a brother. The complainants themselves plead with the police not to initiate action against the men". Another panelist, who was a psychologist, took the matter a little too far when she said that "women could not be blamed for not complaining about violence because the man would be the only breadwinner. If he is convicted, he will be jailed for three months and the family would be in distress. Worse when the man returns, the complainant is once again victimized" (*Times of India*, August 20, 2006).

These expressions that leave a note of depression invariably throw up the following questions:

- Does it mean that victims of family violence have reached a wall beyond which there is only a vacuum?
- Does such a situation of hopelessness encircle the lives of women who face violence in their families?
- What are the law-enforcing agencies that are supposed to be protecting women from violence doing?

It is a pity that even after a quarter century of the women's movement and a plethora of legislation that is considered 'pro-women', we have to be asking such questions. There are a number of laws to protect women from abuse and cruelty that can actually be termed family-specific. These include Section 304B (dowry death), 406 (punishment for criminal breach of trust), 498A (cruelty by husband or relative of husband), 323 (punishment for voluntarily causing hurt), 324 (voluntarily causing hurt by dangerous weapons and means), 325 (punishment for causing grevious hurt) and 306 (abetment of suicide). Besides these, there are women's police stations and family courts that have been specially created to address the problems of women who are suffering from family violence (see Prasad, 2006). The Dowry Prohibition Act is another law that can be used to protect women from dowry-related family violence. The most recent addition to this long list is the Domestic Violence Prevention Act. Do we really need more laws to safeguard women from domestic violence? Where does the problem actually lie?

It is not the law per se that is problematic, but it is the style of functioning of the law-enforcing machinery that leaves a lot to be desired. Besides the delays and tiring and lengthy procedures, the patriarchal mindset of those involved in running the criminal justice system severely hampers a fair trial. Even, the law seems to make a clear distinction between 'public spaces' and 'private spaces'. The home is a private domain and a woman is supposed to put up with what happens behind closed doors. The experiences of many women, who have gone to police stations to complain about ill-treatment, are not encouraging. It is not uncommon to meet a police person who says "after all, it is your husband who is beating you, doesn't he have a right over his wife?" So, women are expected to comply and not complain. Even, the hidden agenda of the family courts is that at any cost a marriage must be protected. Serious lapses on the part of the husband such as bigamy, wife battering or denial of property are expected to be tolerated by a woman.

Nevertheless, the recent times have seen courts passing many landmark judgements that have actually shown that a proactive judiciary can make a difference to the lives of women. As opposed to this, there are retrograde judgments that have brought forth severe protests and sent the wrong messages. One classic example is a judgment of the Delhi High Court upholding the marriage of those who had not reached marriageable age. There are also a large number of dowry cases where the guilty have been let off without any punishment. This only shows that there is no gender-sensitive judicial system that is yet in place, but it is the mindset of those who are in charge that is going to make a big difference.

## Giving a voice and a face to victims of family violence

### *Role of women's organizations*

For over twenty-five years autonomous women's organizations have been relentlessly struggling to bring justice to women who are abused by their families. In fact, the major credit for busting the myth of the family as a woman's paradise goes to women's organizations. These civil society institutions have given women the confidence to report family violence and seek interventions for combating abuse. Women's organizations have been acting as pressure groups not only for demanding effective implementation of existing policies but also for sensitizing the law enforcing machinery to be proactive.

That women's organizations have provided the most effective answer to family violence was echoed by the Innocent Digest when it observed: "For nearly a quarter of a century, women's organizations have provided leadership in boosting the visibility of violence against women; giving victim-survivors a voice through tribunals and personal testimonies; providing innovating forms of support to victims of violence; and forcing governments and the international community to recognize their own failure to protect women. From local, collective action, women have transformed their struggle against violence into a global campaign."

Women's advocacy has prompted the formal sectors (legal and judicial system, criminal justice system, and the health sector) to begin to respond to the needs of women who suffer violence. Women have pushed for policy change and institutional mechanism to set up – be it legal reform, training of police, or providing shelter to women and their children. In attempting to address the structural causes of such violence, women's organizations have sought to empower women through human rights education, credit programmes, and linking women to larger networks (UNICEF, 2000).

By giving victims of family violence a platform for airing and sharing their grievances, women's organizations have shown the world that family violence has an 'answer'. These groups have often braved threats and grueling circumstances to stand behind women who are seeped in situations of helplessness and self-pity. Progressive women's groups have questioned what psychologists describe as 'battered women's syndrome' or 'learned helplessness' and have helped women to see a pathway, even when they have reached a situation when they think that all roads are closed.

There is, however, a note of caution that needs to be sounded here. Family violence is a complex issue that needs to be handled from a holistic perspective. It is true that women's organizations have shown the way for women to question, protest and challenge violence. But throwing the entire burden of violence management on women's organizations is not the right approach. It is very important to create gender conscious men and women, families and a social order all of which will learn to treat family violence as a violation of human rights and not just, another family quarrel.

## References

Action India (2004). *National Consultation,* New Delhi, p. 2.

Dhawan, Himanshi (2006). Skewed Sex Ratio in 80 per cent Districts, *Times of India,* December 10, p. 1.

Prasad, Shashi (2006). A Long Wait, *Sunday Vijay Times,* November 26, p. 2.

Ramanna, Anjali (2006). *Sudha,* November 30, p. 19.

UNICEF (2000). Domestic Violence Against Women and Girls. *Innocent Digest,* No. 6, June, 2000.

World Health Organization. 'Violence against Women' *WHO Consultation,* Geneva: WHO.

Yllo, Kersti and Michele Bograd (1988). *Feminist Perspectives on Wife Abuse,* Sage Publications Inc.

SECTION THREE

# Special Topics for Indian Research

CHAPTER FIFTEEN

# Witchcraft, witches and social exclusion

*Kanchan Mathur*

Naming/labelling of women, as witches, is a violation of women's human rights and right to life and dignity. It is a complex phenomenon having various dimensions. Labelling and ostracizing women and subjecting them to various forms of violence is prevalent in different parts of the world. The United Nations has named Africa, Asia and South America as high-incidence zones for witchcraft-related killings (Religion News blog.com, 2004).

Recently, India has witnessed a spurt in reporting of cases of labelling women as witches. Though incidents of witch-craft-related crimes have been reported from most states, the highest incidence has been reported from Andhra Pradesh, Bihar, Jharkhand, Chattisgarh, Maharashtra, Orissa, Gujarat, Assam, West Bengal and Rajasthan (ibid.).

Historically, belief in witches and witchcraft dates back to the 13th century and has been part of the historical development of most countries in the world. These beliefs not only harm women's psyche but also impact their physical health. Belief in witches and witchcraft, labelling women as *dayans/dakans*,[1] is one such belief which impacts women's status. It has been used as a means of subjugating women and subjecting them to extreme physical torture and mental violence ostracism and social exclusion. Women, who are branded/ labelled as, witches are often stigmatized for life. The mental and physical torture may range from battery to brutal murder. The forms of torture in most parts of the world are somewhat similar. They include stripping and parading the victim, tonsuring, blackening the face, and slashing her with knives or any other sharp instrument. Women are often made to eat human and animal excrement. They are also stoned, drowned, hanged or burnt to death, their teeth smashed, heads shaved and breasts chopped off.

In Rajasthan, labelling women as witches is common, as it is mostly women who are believed to be practising witchcraft and are consequently persecuted and subjected to various forms of violence.

The present paper attempts to share the findings of a recent study[2] undertaken to analyze the causes, nature and forms of violence meted out to women so labelled. Part I of the paper is based on a review of literature and attempts to understand the phenomenon and the nature of the problem as it exists in India and Rajasthan. Part II draws on the analysis of the primary data focusing on the causes of labelling and the forms of violence including different forms of social exclusion that a woman is subjected to once she is branded a *dayan/dakan*. The concluding part suggests measures and intervention strategies that can possibly be used to counter this form of violence.

## I

### The Indian context

Witchcraft in India can be traced to the *Atharvaveda,* which has justifiably been described as "the earliest book of Indian priestly magic", and one may add, of witchcraft too (Saletore, 1981). Witchcraft in ancient times played an important role in royal as well as public life. In the 4th century BC it had permeated court life. A prince under training was expected to look after those who were experts in witchcraft (Kautilya). The king had to look to the business of those practising austerities as well as those who are expert in sorcery and yoga. Witchcraft was an act of employing magical spells or supernatural powers to produce certain effects for attaining specific objectives. The beneficial and evil effects of witchcraft were distinguished in the 4th century BC though later people associated it only with evil practices. The belief in witches was common and witches were persecuted whenever they were identified. Belief in witchcraft was also widespread in colonial India. In the early 19th century, one official speculated that around a thousand women had been killed as witches in the plains of Central India alone. According to another, the number of women killed as witches far exceeded those who died as *satis*[3] (Skaria, 1997). Even today, many a life is lost on this count. According to official figures, 2,556 women were branded as witches and killed in India between 1987 and 2003 (Religion News Blog.com, July 2004).

People of different regions of the country use different names such as *'dakan'*, *'dayan'* *'banamati'*, *'chetabadi'*, *'chillangi'* *'hawa'* or evil eye or *'halka'*, *'dahani'*, *'tonhi'* etc. The names may be different but the practice seems to be taking more or less a similar form. In interior rural India many lives are lost on this count.

In Orissa, crimes against women branded as witches occur mostly in the tribal districts of Sundergarh, Mayurbhanj, Keonjhar and Phulbani. The tribal-dominated Sundergarh district has recorded at least fifty deaths due to suspicion of witchcraft since 2001. The local word for witch, *Dahani,* has powerful repercussions for the tribal population and almost invariably it is the women who are at the receiving end. Ironically, such incidents have not been confined to tribal dominated and backward regions of the state. One hears of this crime even in some of the coastal districts.[4] Mayurbhanj district has recorded fifteen deaths related to belief in witchcraft since 2003. In this district, even men become victims of this crime.

In the state of Jharkhand too the problem is widespread in tribal areas where women accused of practising witchcraft are ostracized and even tortured by superstitious tribal members. Nathan and Kelkar (1998) have shown that in the Santhal and Munda tribes of Jharkhand the phenomenon of denouncing women as witches is on large scale. They have advanced two major reasons behind such accusations. According to them, at some point of time, the Santhal women participated in ritual practices. Subsequently, men established a monopoly over the higher ritual sphere. Women's participation in these higher rituals then became a sign of their possessing evil powers, being witches. Secondly, the Santhal women had certain definite rights in land, and witchcraft accusations were an attack on women's land rights and the strengthening of men's domination over land.

Chhattisgarh is well known for the existence of *tonhi* (witches). In south Bastar, 50 per cent of men in prison on murder charges are for witch-related killings (Nathan and Kelkar, 1998). Grison, in 1938, called Bastar a land of "potent practitioners of magic and witchcraft" (as quoted in Nathan and Kelkar, 1998). Since 1996, 73 women have been murdered on charges of being a *tonhi* in the state. The Raipur district is well known for witch-craft-related crimes.

The problem is even more serious in the state of Bihar. According to a report of the Free Legal Aid Committee (an NGO), 536 women have been slain in the past ten years in just two districts of Bihar. Severe form of violence and punishment are meted out to women who are branded as witches in the state.

The belief is prevalent even in southern regions of the country. The practice of persecuting witches exists in Andhra Pradesh with Telangana region, Warangal, Mahbubnagar, Ranga Reddy and Medak districts of the state being the worst affected areas.

Witchcraft accusations were very common in certain tribal areas of Gujarat in the 19th century. According to Skaria (1997), the late 19th century was a time of considerable stress and transformation for *adivasi* societies and this was the reason for a rise in the number of witchcraft accusations. The British government banned witch-killings in the Dang and surrounding regions around 1847. The practice of naming and branding women as witches continues in tribal areas of Gujarat even today. Cases of witch-hunt have also been reported from Maharashtra and West Bengal.

Though different states have their own cultural context, yet the phenomenon of witch-hunting seems to be taking more or less a similar form. The causes of accusations and the kind of violence meted out under this practice in the different regions are also somewhat similar.

### The Rajasthan context

In Rajasthan, the local name for a witch is *dakan* or *dayan* and a *dakan* is always a living woman, quite unlike a *churel*, a dead woman, who manifests herself as an evil force. It is believed that a *dakan* has a capacity to harm others by the evil eye, evil word or sometimes by simply praising anything (Bharucha, 2003). Another belief surrounding the *dakan* is that she consumes children's livers (*kaleja*). If many children happen to die in a village, it is assumed that a *dakan* may be operating there, and this assumption very often leads to a general consensus in the village community that such a woman is a *dakan* and should be killed. Women who are old, widowed, unprotected are regarded as far more likely to be *dakan*s than others. A woman's personality also affects her chances of being considered a *dakan*. The *dakan* "usually happens to be the most notorious, quarrelsome and troublesome woman in a family, or one gifted with the longest, broadest and sharpest tongue in a family" (Skaria, 1997).

According to Bharucha (2003), if such a woman asks for a simple thing, like water, for example, all the people around her would start running to get her water, just to keep her happy. The basic view of the villagers is to placate her and keep her happy at all costs, and not to allow their children to be anywhere near her.

It is believed that there are certain involuntary practices by which women get initiated as *dakan*s. An existing *dakan*, for instance, could ask a woman in the village to listen to one of her stories, while providing the response to a story through onomatopoeic sounds (*'hu'*, *'ha'*, *'hmm'* and so on). On finishing the story, the *dakan* will tell the *hunkario* (respondent), *"Jaisi main hun, vesi tu ho ja"* (Just as I am, so you become). At this point, the woman feels compelled to take on the role of the *dakan* and proceed with her life accordingly. Another source of initiation arises when any woman wears the discarded clothes of a *dakan* after her death. Witchhood is also considered to be something hereditary. It is passed on from mother to the daughter. These are involuntary practices in so far as the initiated do not actually choose to become *dakan*s. Of course, there are other folk tantric practices in which *dakan*s play on fears, by throwing grains, or seed, or chili on people's bodies, or by making an effigy of a person's body out of flour and sticking pins into it, or by chanting mantras, and so on (Bharucha, 2003).

According to local folklore, witches can temporarily discard their human form and turn themselves into cats or ants. In this form, they can slip out of their house unseen in order to foregather with other witches at a burning-*ghat* at midnight on a Saturday. Here, they resume human form and ride naked on the backs of hyenas. If a witch is engaged in 'devouring the liver' of a victim, she could only be appeased by the slaughter of a kid or a lamb: part of this sacrifice would be placed in a broken pot and left at a place where three paths meet (Carstairs, 1983: 15).

In the 19th century the belief in the existence of witches was very common in certain regions of Rajasthan such as Mewar, i.e., Dungarpur and Banswara. Many witches were executed during the 19th century. The Bhils and Garassia tribes staunchly believed in *dakan*s and subjected them to extreme torture. The Commander of Bhil Core J.C. Brookes has said that when the Bhils suffered from indigestion or pain in any part of the body they branded that part and, on getting relief, felt that there was some *dayan* who was the cause of their ailment and who by fear of fire left them (as cited in Bhatt, 2001). Many Bhils protected themselves from the consequences of being bewitched by not marrying into a family in which there was not a reputed witch (Skaria, 1997).

Generally, if a person fell severely ill, he was taken to a *bhopa* (witch doctor), who was easily available in every village. It was believed that he possesses divine powers and is capable of curing the affected person. He was the one who disclosed whether the concerned person's ailment was due to magic of some *dayan* and he also identified the *dayan*. The *ojha*s were important persons within the local community. For their work they were paid in cash or in "eatables and drinks in the shape of poultry, goats, coconuts, rice and *mohwra* liquor" (made from the flowers of the *mohwra* tree) (Skaria, 1997).

If any woman was dubbed as a witch, she had to be tested before she could be declared as real. She was put to different trials ascertaining her guilt or innocence and if she was found guilty, she was burnt alive or beheaded or beaten mercilessly. But, if she was found innocent, she was sent back to her home. The trials were varied – she could be forced to dip her hand in boiling oil and take out a rupee coin – if she was innocent, then, her hand would not be burnt. Another was the water test, where an arrow was shot into the distance and, in order to prove her innocence, she had to keep her head under water until a runner returned with it. On other occasions, she was tied in a bag and thrown into a pool where sinking was the only proof of her innocence. If her struggle kept her afloat, she was inevitably condemned and punished (Gaur, 1998). Another method was dropping grain into a vessel of water with a copper coin at the bottom thereof and calling out a name at the same time. If the grain fell on the coin, the woman was declared a witch or else she was let off (ibid.). In addition, however, there was swinging test, an exclusive form of sanction against *dakan*. The eyes of the suspected *dakan* were first covered up with a cloth filled with chilies, since 'a single glance' of an enraged witch could be certain death to him or whom it might alight. Besides, her eyes would smart if she were not a *dayan*. She was then strung up by her feet from a tree and a slow fire was lit on the ground below her. She was swung just above the fire through most of the day and taken down only at night, when her feet were kept tied. This usually continued upto three days, or until the woman confessed to being a *dakan* and promised to release the sick person. Another method was to rub their eyes with a well-dried capsicum: if they withheld their tears, they were justly deemed witches (Gaur, 1998; Skaria, 1997).

Historically, several rulers and chiefs of the state indulged in persecuting witches. Zalim Singh, Rajput Chief of Jaipur, the Rana of Udaipur and even Diwan like Tantia Jog, were virtual witch-hunters. During the reign of Zalim Singh of Kota, more than 1,000 women were arrested and a majority of them killed as witches, under his orders. In Udaipur, in 1854, the Maharana imposed a penalty of six months imprisonment on witches if they caused anyone's death from torture (Saletore, 1981). The evil practice became so oppressive as to attract the attention of the British government who banned witch-killings in Rajputana around 1853. The ban caused gradual decline of cases though the crime could not be suppressed completely.

Even today, in certain districts of the state such as Udaipur, Bhilwara, Tonk, Sirohi, Kota, etc., women are humiliated and tortured on this account. It has become a common form of violence against women in the state. Most of the cases go unreported and even those that are reported are registered under laws for ordinary offence, as there is no law under which such cases can be registered.

## II

## Causes of violence

### *Profiling the women*

In order to get an in-depth understanding of the phenomenon of labelling women as *dayan/dakan*s in the state, a total of 63 case studies were documented from six districts selected for study. Out of the 63 cases documented, in 11 cases, branding took place nearly 20 years back. In 13 cases, it took place more recently, i.e., in the past two years or so.

Detailed profiles of women survivors were prepared on the basis of in-depth interviews with them as well as their family members. The profiles include age of women at the time of the survey as well as at the time of labelling, caste, marital status and occupational status both before and after labelling as well as residential status pre- and post-labelling. Some additional informations were also gathered, i.e., the person responsible for initiating the accusation and duration of violence faced. Both qualitative as well as quantitative methods were used to analyze the information collected.

The profiles of women revealed that the highest incidence of labelling/naming women as *dayan*s takes place on women in the age group of 41 to 55 years. The reason is that women in this age group acquire an assertive position in the family and society, having dispensed with their reproductive roles. The study highlights that poor, low-caste women are easy targets for naming/labelling with a majority of them belonging to the SC/ST and OBC groups. A large majority of the women interviewed were dependent on agriculture and animal husbandry, which is the main source of livelihood for the rural population. The second largest category comprised of women engaged in their traditional occupations such as sweeping and petty trade, making pots and lamps for festivals, performing certain rituals on death, birth and marriage functions, selling flowers, fruits and vegetables, selling bangles, conducting prayer and other religious ceremonies at the village temple etc.

The marital status of the women interviewed shows that contrary to our assumption that single women, i.e., widows or separated women, are more likely to be labelled as witches, a larger majority of the women were found to be married. In a majority of cases women labelled as witches are subjected to verbal abuse and physical torture as long as they live and many a time they are even murdered. The duration of violence faced by the women in our sample ranges from two years to more than 20 years. The process of labelling/branding women as witches in many cases was initiated by the husband's family and that once accusations begin from within the family these women are not left with any support structures to handle the violence.

### *Family as initiator of violence*

The process of labelling/branding women as *dayans* in 23.8 per cent of the cases was initiated by the husband's family. In a few cases the woman's husband accused her of being a *dayan*. Our study reveals that once accusations begin from within the family, these women are not left with any support mechanism to handle the violence. It also makes them more vulnerable to taunts and accusations of other community members who assert that if the family members themselves believe that a woman is a *dayan,* she actually 'must' be one. For instance, in one case of Chittoriya village in Bhilwara district, when the woman's own husband and family members began to accuse her of being a *dayan,* the villagers also started to blame her for all the mishaps that took place in the village. Even her natal family and community members in her natal village began accusing her. In the absence of any kind of support from her family and community, she now lives by the roadside. In some cases (22.2%) the initiation of the accusation has come from members of the women's own caste. In 46 per cent cases persons belonging to other castes were the first ones to accuse the women of being *dayans*.

The main *causes* of violence are as follows:

### *Superstition*

The study confirms the findings of the review that superstition is one of the main causes of labelling/naming women as *dayans* in the state. It is in fact at the root of all accusations. In most cases superstition forms the sole basis for accusation with several factors contributing to it. In a majority of districts selected for study low educational status and lack of quality health care have given rise to many superstitious beliefs. The belief in women's evil powers and their harmful effects is, therefore, universal. In times of any misfortune or mishap or for unforeseen happenings women bear the blame of being a *dayan*. The mishap leading to branding can be as petty as cattle falling ill or a cow not yielding milk, or the loss of cattle or it can be as grave as the sudden death of a child. Such is the extent of superstition that women are also held responsible for the infertility among other women.

In the state, there is another belief related to the concept of a witch. It is believed that the *dayan* enters the victim's body and speaks through his/her mouth. The possessed person acts in a hysterical way. In the state of trance (*bhava*), the 'possessed' person takes the name of that supposed *dayan*. The state of *bhava* is sufficient reason to declare/consider a woman a *dayan*.

The supposed *dayan* is then taken to a shaman or *ojha/bhopa* for consultation. The *bhopa* both identifies the *dakan* and tries to free the victim of her, either through charms and spells, or by torture. Thus, in identifying a *dayan* or in instigating people to accuse a woman, the *bhopa/ojha/pir* plays a major role. In the rural areas of the state there are many shrines of local deities such as Tejaji and Bhaioornji and it is at these shrines that the *bhopa*s are supposedly possessed by the deity who imbue them with power to heal sickness or to drive out the *dayan* from the person supposed to be afflicted with it. In the process, the *bhopa* becomes possessed with the deity getting into a state of trance and the deity promises that all would turn out well. The *bhopa* prescribes what action must be taken, and what offerings made in order to drive out the evil spirit. In exchange of these services the *ojha* generally gets liquor and goats. They brand women as *dayan*s simply for acquiring money or gifts. Since their claim is never challenged, they reinforce the powerlessness of the women so labelled. It is for their own selfish interests that the *ojha*s use their powers to exorcise evil spirits.

Another superstitious belief prevalent in Rajasthan, especially in Kota district, is that the women of Harijan community are more vulnerable to demonic temptations/malevolent forces. It is believed that since they perform menial tasks, they easily learn the base art of witchcraft.

One peculiar superstition is that witchcraft is passed intergenerationally. It is believed that the power of witchcraft is passed on from the mother to the daughter and even from the mother-in-law to the daughter-in-law.

### Property disputes

Property disputes have emerged as one of the main causes for branding women as *dayan*s. The easiest way to grab fixed assets of a woman, who is either a widow or a single woman and lacks male protection, is to brand her a *dayan*. Very often, when a widow tries to manage her land without adult sons, her brother-in-laws insist on sharecropping or managing her land themselves, or simply, attempt to deprive her rightful share of the land (Mathur, 2004). In our study, out of 63 cases, a total of 12 women were named/labelled as *dayan*s due to property disputes, land grabbing or encroachment.

### Political causes

In one case, that of Umli Devi who was a sarpanch in village Bagad (on the border of) Udaipur district an attempt was made to malign her as a *dayan* due to local politics.

### Infertility and childlessness

Women are also labelled *dayan*s on account of infertility and childlessness. Infertility in women is viewed as a 'disability' and a woman who is unable to produce a child is viewed with suspicion. This often leads to her being branded as a *dayan*. Even those women who lose their children due to lack of medical help are alleged as *dayans* and held responsible for their children's death. People believe that if they can devour their own children, they can do the same to other people's children.

### *Physical deformities and challenges*

Apart from women's inability to produce children, physical deformities as well as perceived low intelligence levels also become a cause for labelling/naming them as *dayans*.

### *Fear of ignominy/disgrace*

In three cases it was observed that women have been so labelled because people are scared that they will expose and disgrace them. In all the three cases, the culprits had indulged in extra-marital relations over a period of time.

### *Personal rivalry and caste rivalry*

The study revealed that women also become victims of this form of violence on account of personal rivalry. Some of women's husbands had indulged in extramarital relations and fearing ignominy had decided to defame their wives. On the other hand, caste rivalry is often the main cause behind labelling/naming women as *dayans*. It is not uncommon for upper caste men to victimize women belonging to lower caste.

### *Assertive nature of women*

Labelling is also a means to suppress those women who are bold, confident, articulate or assertive. Women who are sharp tongued, bad tempered and quarrelsome, traits which naturally involve them in disputes with neighbours and directs some resentment against them, are prosecuted. This clearly reflects the patriarchal structure prevalent in most parts of the state. Women, who do not adhere to the traditional norms of behaviour, become the targets of accusation. Assertion by women in any matter is not tolerated and such women incur the wrath of others.

Women's strong economic, social and political position is seen as a threat to the existing patriarchal power structures. It can lead to branding simply in order to damage their position. Kajri of Kasir village of Tonk district is the only Harijan family in the village. The family is economically better off and hence the villagers are envious of them and in order to put them down accused Kajri of being a *dayan*.

The various causes of labelling women as *dayan* reflects the complex nature of the problem. The causes may range from superstition to more critical issues like land and property disputes, personal and caste rivalry, infertility as well as assertive nature of women.

## Forms of violence

The research study highlights that once women are branded as *dayans* they are subjected to extreme torture/violence. In fact, labelling itself is a violent act against women's dignity and respect. A woman can be humiliated and harassed over a matter as trivial as a cattle falling ill which becomes reason enough for declaring her a *dayan* and assaulting her either physically or psychologically. As stated earlier, forms of violence range from verbal abuse to battery and even brutal murder. They are often locked in their homes and not permitted to interact with other people on account of being labelled as *dayans*. It is common for such women to be thrown out of their families and villages because of the labelling due to and lose their mental balance. Their hair are cut off, heads shaved, they can be stoned, beaten mercilessly, branded with hot iron rods, raped, made to eat excreta or even burnt and brutally murdered.

## *Social exclusion*

Once a woman is labelled as a *dayan*, she faces several forms of social exclusion. The concept of social exclusion is a multidimensional and dynamic concept. Social exclusion is a process by which individuals or groups are wholly or partially excluded from full participation in the society within which they live. It restricts the access of certain social groups to valued resources and entitlements, relegating them to the status of social outsiders.

To be socially excluded is to be deprived from social recognition and social value (Wikepedia; Prasad, 2003).

Social exclusion, according to Hilary Silver (1995: 60–61) is, "associated with a variety of terms like superfluity, irrelevance, marginality, foreignness, closure, disaffiliation, dispossession, deprivation and destitution". The concept is broadly synonymous with the concept of marginalization and is related to a number of other concepts, notably poverty, unemployment, withdrawal, underclass, alienation, lack of freedom, etc.

The above definitions suggest that alienation and deprivation are the major constituents of social exclusion. Exclusion generates adverse consequences in terms of human rights violation, deprivation and poverty (Thorat, 2006).

The violence and its various heinous forms impact women's psyche and well-being in varied ways, creating feelings of helplessness, fear and powerlessness. The impact and consequences are wide ranging. At times, the labelling has displaced them from their traditional occupations compelling them to lead a life of abject poverty. Labelling has also forced them to leave their houses and villages. Unable to bear the humiliation levelled on them by their own family/community members, many women experience severe depression and low self-esteem. In extreme cases, they have also been forced to end their lives by committing suicide. One of the commonest impacts of labelling is that a woman is socially excluded not only from the community but also from the family.

Social exclusion takes different forms, alienated not only by the community but also by their own families women so labelled experience a sense of powerlessness and helplessness. They are not allowed to participate in auspicious occasions and their mobility is restricted. In few cases, it was found that they had been held prisoners in their own homes and are not allowed to interact with anyone.

Labelling also adversely affects the economic status of many women labelled as *dayans*. Many of them have been compelled to lead a life of abject poverty. Those engaged in traditional occupation necessarily have had to leave their occupation since no one wishes to interact with them and receive services rendered by them. The economic dimension of exclusion also is visible in few cases.

Many women have been tortured to the extent of being ex-communicated from their families and communities. As mentioned earlier, in many cases, the initiators of labelling have been from the women's own family. The family members include not only distant relatives but one's own sons and, in few cases, even husband. Therefore, many a time, the family members themselves become instrumental in making them vulnerable to accusations and allegations by the village community.

It becomes evident that the phenomena of labelling women as *dayans* and the accompanying violence leaves the women in a distressing state. In the absence of support from families and communities women often have nowhere to go. They end up facing a life of hardship and ignominy. Exclusion from family and community is one of the most significant dimensions of social exclusion, which leads to deprivation in economic as well as political realm.

## III

### Conclusion

The system of social justice, by its very nature, is formidable and patriarchal in nature and approaching it in itself requires a lot of courage on the part of the women who are not literate and belong to economically and socially vulnerable sections of society. In the eventuality that women do get to approach the police, judiciary or the NGOs or caste panchayats, justice is most often denied to them.

The study attempted to analyze the role of the various agencies in either preventing or abetting the practice of naming/ labelling women as *dayans* in the state. It highlighted that different agencies can play a supportive role in combating violence against women so labelled. It also pointed out that countering the violence meted out to women branded as witches requires effort at various levels and by various agencies. Interventions have to be planned both in terms of countering the violence meted out to women survivors and also towards preventing it from happening in the future. In our study superstition has emerged as the major cause of all accusations. This belief cuts across caste/class, urban/rural/and educated/uneducated divides. Towards this end, one main step that needs to be taken is changing mindsets of people.

The research study put forth the following recommendations and intervention strategies:

### At the level of NGOs

- NGOs should include the issue of violence against women labelled as *dayans*/*dakans* as part of their development agenda.
- They should organize advocacy campaigns/rallies/ street plays/ puppet shows/posters to create awareness on the issue and support existing 'survivors' and to prevent the occurrence of such incidents in the future.
- They should undertake responsibility for conducting sensitization trainings amongst village community, *anganwari* workers, ANMs, *sathins*, PRI members, representatives of caste panchayats, police, judiciary and media.
- They should play an active role in simplifying the Draft Bill and disseminate it as widely as possible.

### At the level of police

- Expansion and strengthening of Mahila Salah Evam Suraksha Kendras to include identification of women labelled as *dayan*/*dakan* as well as their counselling and rehabilitation.
- The police department officials should be instructed to lodge FIRs of cases of *dayans*/*dakans* even in the absence of an Act as well as provide immediate redressal and relief to victims suffering acute mental and physical violence.

- Issue of labelling women as *dayans/dakans* should be included as a major issue while discussing the subject of violence against women in trainings of police personnel.

## At the level of state government

- The Department of Women and Child Development should take a lead role in identifying women survivors through various programmes/networks and the SHGs in various districts should provide support to women labelled as *dayans/dakans*.
- The Department of Social Welfare should take an initiative to rehabilitate women sufferers of violence, especially those who have no family/community support as well have lost their means of livelihood after the labelling
- The Panchayati Raj Department should make it mandatory that the issue is included in the regular agenda of district, block and village level meetings, especially in the ward and gram sabha.
- The Department of Education should initiate a public education programme. As a first step, this could be included as part of primary education.

## At the level of State Commission for Women

- Should initiate a dialogue with *bhopas and ohjas.*
- Involve women's groups/activists to lobby for getting the Draft Bill passed and enacted in the state.
- Initiate a well-planned advocacy campaign to prevent labelling women as *dayan/dakans.*
- Make efforts to sensitize various enforcement agencies, specially the police, to take action against the perpetrators of violence of women so labelled.

## Notes

1. Term used in Hindi and in rural India.
2. The study 'Local Customs and Practices in Rajasthan: An In-depth Study of *Dakan/Dayan*' was undertaken by the author along with a team of researchers from IDS-J in the year 2005–06. The contribution of the following team members in particular is gratefully acknowledged: Varsha Kalla, Etee Purohit, Kirti Sharma and Radheyshyam Sharma.
3. Widows immolating themselves on their husband's pyre.
4. In 2003, in Krushna Prasad block of Puri district, a woman branded as a witch was tied upside down and four of her teeth were broken after the local panchayat decided to punish her.

## References

Becker, Cantarino Barbara (1994). "Feminist Consciousness and "Wicked Witches". Recent Studies on Women in Early Modern Europe', *Signs,* Autumn, Vol. 20, No. 1, p. 170.

Bharucha, Rustom (2003). *Rajasthan: An Oral History: Conversations with Komal Kothari,* Penguin Books, India.

Carstairs, G.M. (1983) *Death of a Witch A Village in North India 1950–1981.* Hutchison and Co. (Publishers) Ltd.

Gaur, Meena (1989). *Sati and Social Reforms in India,* Publication Scheme, Jaipur, fn p. 69.

*Kautilya Arthasathra,* book II, ch. II.

Kittredge, George (1929). *Witchcraft in Old and New England.* Russel and Russel: New York, p. 26.

Levack, Brian P. (ed.) (1992). *Witchcraft, Women and Society,* Vol. 10 of A Twelve Volume Anthology of Scholarly Articles on Witchcraft, Magic and Demonology, Garland Publishing, New York.

Mathur, Kanchan (2004). *Countering Gender Violence Initiatives Towards Collective Action in Rajasthan.* Sage Publications: New Delhi.

Nathan, Dev, Kelkar Govind and Xiaogang Yu (1998). 'Women as Witches and Keepers of Demons: Cross-Cultural Analysis of Struggles to Change Gender Relations', *Economic and Political Weekly,* October 31, p. 59.

Prasad, R.R. (2003). 'Social Exclusion: Concept, Meaning and Scope' in A.K. Lal (ed.), *Social Exclusion: Essays in Honour of Dr. Bindeshwar Pathak*, Vol. I, Concept Publishing Company, New Delhi.

Religion News Blog. Com, Religious news about religions, cults, sects, world religions, and related issues, Item 8006, Posted 2004–07–26 09:02:29. 'India's Government may make witchcraft illegal'.

Saletore, R.N. (1981). *Indian Witchcraft*, Abhinav Publications, p. 120.

Skaria, Ajay (1997). 'Women, Witchcraft and Gratuitous Violence in Colonial Western India', *Past and Present*, May.

Thorat, S. (2006). Exclusion and Poverty Need for Socially Exclusive Politics and Development Approach, *People's Democracy: Weekly Organ of the Communist Party of India (Marxist)*, Vol. XXX, No. 5, January 29.

Wikipedia, The free encyclopaedia, 'Social Exclusion', en.wikipedia.org/wiki/Social_exclusion.

CHAPTER SIXTEEN

# Emotional abuse in family, an act of power play

## A human rights debate with special reference to scleroderma patients

*K. Asha*

Why is it that women cannot retaliate or fight back with men? Is it because of the biological differences or is it something beyond this? Why are women like what they are, at present? Why do women act like what they act? Why is there a stereo type regarding women?

Does the difference in human behaviour and social positions lie in biological differences – a point of great importance in achieving social equality? But biological differences may arise from behaviour or social difference. Stereotypes of masculinity and femininity – theories about women as nurturers – are these biologically based or based on social norms or people's behaviour?

In cases, rape, sexual assault, physical abuse, and emotional abuse of women by men, why cannot women fight back against men against this violence? What restricts them or what denies them of a fight back? Are women really weak or not strong enough to protect themselves from this cruel act? To put it straight, why cannot woman resist to protect herself from the cruelty of a man's act – physical and emotional.

This paper is an attempt to discuss the following and suggest a course of remedy for those sufferers of emotional abuse:

- Socio-biological theories
- Human rights: an overview
- What is emotional abuse?
- Focus on scleroderma
- Role of professionals

## Socio-biological theories

The crux of this whole argument lies on the following points related to socio-biology:

1. Sex differences are not completely determined by biological differences.
2. Biological differences lurk underneath.
3. Biological functions, viz., body size, strength, hormone, brain development, etc., can be changed by environment.
4. Social environment moulds behaviour – as environment changes – when they become more common for both men and women sex differences decrease.
5. Size and strength depend not only on in-born factors but also on environmental differences.

Women are unable to fight back or do not fight back because of the stereotypes present in the society. They are socialized in such a way that they are told aptly as to what they ought to do by the environment they live in. Acceptance of inevitable superiority of male strength on the part of both women and men contributes to men's violence against women and this explains women's hesitation to resist. The above statements are based on the sociological premise of socialization of the genders in our society. Could correction in socialization help women from abuse?

What are the stereotypes related to women with respect to strength, physical performance, motor development, height, weight and intellectual abilities?

The assumptions that women cannot do reinforces social roles, while at the same time producing some of the actual strength differences. Frailer women are more consistent with women's social role and lack social power. The greater the innate physical strength a woman has, she is called to possess greater male social power. Environment and the way one is brought up determines physical strength. Girls and boys are channelled in different roles which result in sex differences. Physically, both differ in height, weight, muscular structure, fat distribution, bone structure etc. more due to the environment and socialization but they do not correspond to the stereotypes. It is believed that the leg strength of women is more than men.

A proverb says:

"A horse sweats, a man perspires, but a lady only glows….."

This again is one such example of the norms of the society that aims at treating women in its own special manner. The sweat of the lady is exemplified!

Society encourages an average man to be more active than an average woman. Lack of strength in upper body in women subjects them to various kinds of physical assaults. If these are the reasons for women to be subject to physical violence, what could be the reasons for emotional and psychological abuses most of the women undergo?

For those who are against the radical feminists, thinking of both the sexes being equal, males and females are relatively and/or absolutely different biologically:

- in sexual organs,
- in sexual functions,
- in brain organization and activity,
- in form,
- in dimensions,
- in muscular strength,
- in energy production and energy expenditure,
- in heart pulse rate,
- in respiration rate,
- in cell composition,
- in maturation rate,
- in bio-chemical ratio,
- in muscle-fat ratio,

- in chemical ratio variability,
- in homeostasis,
- in weight variability,
- in red and white blood cell ratio,
- in internal influences on behaviour,
- in intrinsic tendencies of behaviour,
- in perceptual distractibility,
- in erotic perceptual arousability,
- in morbidity,
- in mortality, and
- and in other factors.

### *Totally different*

In fact, males and females are in one sense entirely different: each cell of the normal male has the XY sex chromosomes, while each cell of the normal female has the XX sex chromosomes.

## Emotional abuse

Emotional abuse is defined as actual or likely to have severe adverse effect on the emotional development of a child/person caused by persistent or severe emotional ill-treatment or rejection. All abuse involves some emotional ill-treatment.

### *Forms of emotional abuse*

- Neglect
- Verbal abuse
- Control of the victim's time
- Made accountable for all events
- Taunting, putting down, intimidating
- Jealousy, suspicion
- Inflicting pain that restricts space of interaction away from the shareable worlds

### *Signs of abuse*

1. Control of time
2. Accountability
3. Calling names
4. Confused mixed feelings
5. Putting you down, threaten, intimidator
6. Jealousy and suspicion

The prey bonds with the predator, the abusers. The abused suffers from restriction of space of interaction away from the shareable world. They get shunned from the shareable world. Invasion of the subject's body, pervasion of the psyche, and possession of the mind have a strong impact on the abused.

### *Who are the abusers?*

Emotional intelligence is the innate potential to feel, use, communicate, recognize, remember, learn from, manage and understand emotion. It has four components, viz., emotional sensitivity, emotional memory, emotional processing and emotional ability, which are in-born characteristics and which can be nourished by healthy family atmosphere and healthy relationships. Emotional quotient is person's healthy or unhealthy development of their innate emotional intelligence. Abusers lack or at very low level of emotional intelligence they fail to react to those nears and dears and build strong relations.

Most of them indulge in taunting or torture. There is no love or affection, which is traced to childhood insecurity, especially love of mother. It has been proved that lack of affection from mother during childhood leads to physical violence and mental abuse, neglect of partner and as such there is a constant disruption in the family life. Abusers could exhibit anything from silent neglect, verbal abuse, physical abuse, taunting or torture. All these isolated the act of bringing torment to partners and their physical, mental and emotional well-being is threatened and they are left to face life events problem alone added to the constant taunting torture from their partners.

High deprivation of mother's love in childhood could lead to high physical violence and could also be the origin of lack of human love, emotional stability and emotional sensitivity (Prescott, 1996). This needs to be checked as it involves social and economic costs that affect the development of society.

### *Effects of emotional abuse*

The abused experience a feeling of low self-worth, dignity, self-esteem, depressed, and many times, suicidal. Their thought process becomes threatened and in most cases their brain stops thinking, or paralyzed with fear, which makes them unsure of what they are doing. There is constant fear and tension, which is a cause for many other physical and mental problems. Stress and anxiety, combined with multiple tasks at family and office, affects their health in the long run.

In emotional abuse, overcoming the thought pattern, which has developed, is very difficult. Without counselling, most of the abused may divorce the partner emotionally. Women as nurturers and caretakers have their roles from time immemorial and it is just the extension of animal existence on trees. When the living form got down from the trees and started walking upright on two limbs, the more obvious exploitations of the female became more apparent!

The role of care provider takes on tremendous stress over the woman when she is abused and tortured. Who should be blamed: the abuser for all the eccentric behaviours of extremities, or the abused for her silent sufferings that she undergoes without making a hue and cry about it for getting justice?

How many women do really talk about the psychological stress they undergo? Do they talk within themselves, family, friends or self-help groups? In most of the cases, very few talk about this to family members for the fear of this becoming more obvious, which would become a stigma in their social life, and also because it instils worry in their parents, brothers and sisters. The woman prefers to suffer alone, and this adds to her misery. Also, putting on an act of 'no suffering' in actuality adds to more suffering.

### *Impact on children at home*

Children witnessing abuse of one of the parents by the other develop:

1. Fear
2. Confusion
3. Inferiority
4. Lack of confidence
5. Lose regard for the abuser

These are very detrimental to the growth of the children and there are mal-formations of their personalities and their emotional stability becomes very risky leading to the formation of inadequate personalities. They find themselves more at peace luring with single parent than both parents present as presence of both parents does not assure peace and happiness in their childhood and personality formation gets affected. Many children end up hating one of the parents thus parent-sibling exchange of love and affection is absent.

### *Interpersonal effects*

The abused undergo many interpersonal problems. The major problems faced by them are the following:

1. Cognitive impairment
2. Memory disorders
3. Sexual dysfunction
4. Social withdrawal
5. Phobias
6. Difficulty in managing long-term relationships
7. Presence of superstitions, delusions and hallucinations
8. Psychotic, neurotic episodes and emotional flatness
9. Depression and anxiety
10. Self-worth, self-esteem crippled and increase of self-directed aggression

### *Social effects*

1. Inability to communicate
2. Feels to forget torture/avoid emergence

3. Hyper-vigilance (paranoia), which is an enhanced state of sensory sensitivity, accompanied by exaggeration, inferiority of behaviours, whose purpose is to detect threats

*Impact on the personality of the abused*

1. Forgetful, changes in eating, sleeping, confused, low self-confidence and fear
2. Shame
3. Worthlessness
4. Dependency
5. Oscillate between psychological effects of emotional numbing and highly sensitive arousal, insomnia, irritability, restlessness and attention deficits
6. Post-traumatic stress disorder
7. Hate, rage, terror, guilt, shame, sorrow, cribbing, childhood abuse, domestic violence, rape and incest, helplessness, powerlessness, insomnia
8. Emotional imbalance
9. Recollections of events in the form of dreams, night terrors, flashbacks and distorting associations

At the risk of appearing to oversimplify a complex phenomenon, it would not be imprudent to say that in our country, the construct of masculinity is usually equated with patriarchy. In other words, masculinity is experienced not so much as a set of emotional or behavioural characteristics unique to the male gender, but more in terms of hierarchical domination over the feminine gender; so even the most 'feminine' man gets a socially dominant position over his female counterpart.

Gender segregation from childhood, lop-sided parental relationships as well as the representation of the man-woman relationship in literature and popular cinema – all serve to reinforce the patriarchal model of masculinity in the mind of the growing male child.

It may appear paradoxical that in a country where the mother is generally deified, the growing male child does not learn to respect members of his mother's gender. But, it is because of this deification that the boy finds it easy to slip into the patriarchal mode, for he does not relate to his mother as a woman, as a person, as a human being, but as a helpless and martyred dependent who needs to be venerated and cared for.

The vocal emergence of feminism has also pushed the contemporary male a little on the back foot, not only because women are threatening to encroach on his masculine dominion, but also because he does not have any idea about how he can counter-encroach on her's. So, he moves squarely into the adversarial position, something he is instinctively comfortable with and, during adolescence, focuses not just on how he can express himself sexually, but also on how he can claim his patriarchal right.

You do not have to be a biological scientist to figure out that testosterone does have a lot to do with this problem, for you never come across adam-teasing, at least not of a kind that assumes the proportions of a social phenomenon.

If physical abuse is terrible, then, emotional abuse creates much more damage psychologically. Dr. Vijay Nagaswami, psychotherapist and marriage consultant, says: "Emotional violence can be of two kinds – intellectual battering and emotional blackmail." He goes on to explain: "Men do not know how to handle their emotions well. Often, violence is displaced. For example, anger that is built-up, can explode in the form of physical abuse. Finally, it is all about controlling your partner." He adds that according to a study conducted on women in rural Tamil Nadu, "women did not mind a couple of 'taps' on the face if it was to 'correct' them or 'keep them in check'." But beyond that, they would not tolerate. Again, it is a myth that domestic violence is more prevalent in the lower strata of society. In fact, women with higher social status are as much victims. More often than not, it is the fear of losing their position in society that prevents them from taking their problem to court.

### *Men are from mars, women are from venus line*

The break in domestic bliss is due to the control games couples play: "Each tries to control the other perhaps unconsciously, creating fear in the spouse's mind." In a joint set-up, this fear would be absorbed while in a non-communicative nuclear family, the situation goes ballistic. He also talks of the constant tussle between intellect and emotions. "Women are closer to their emotions and so are at an advantage. But men retreat from displaying them. They replay parental parameters and count societal sanctions and patriarchal assistance as allies. Cornered when nagged by the wife they lash out. The woman may be justified in her demands but chooses the wrong method to establish her authority. If bullying is wrong, so is nagging," is his contention. What about unprovoked assault? "We follow ritualized patterns of behaviour. Aggression is in-built. Parents cling to their children. If the mother is willing to let go most mother-in-law vs. daughter-in-law wars will vanish. But, she has been a martyr in her own marital home." Translated, it means married men are mama's boys who take refuge in 'tradition' to justify abuse. And jump when there is an emotional 'boo'.

"The expectations from the institution of marriage are astronomical. My theory is that if you can get personal relationships right, you can also get relationships at work right. Often, what happens is that personal emotions are brought to the workplace. For example, if you have an unresolved problem with your father, you end up having an unresolved issue with your boss. And this continues." And sure enough, productivity suffers at the workplace. What's more, these days, people are beginning to face a mid-life crisis in the thirties itself. By the time they are in their forties, they are completely exhausted – physically, mentally and emotionally.

The sociopath is "aware of the discrepancy between his behaviour and societal expectations, but he seems to be neither guided by the possibility of such a discrepancy, nor disturbed by its occurrence" (Wisdom, 1976a: 614). This cold-hearted and selfish approach to human interaction at one time garnered for sociopathy the moniker "moral insanity" (McCord, 1983; Davison and Neale, 1990). Sociopaths are also sometimes known as psychopaths or anti-social personalities.

*Impact on women*

The impacts caused by emotional abuse are many. The abused suffer a sense of worthlessness and helplessness that bring down their self-esteem. They feel at loss to face the realities of life. Many of the victims suffer psychological breakdown and they are totally stressed out with the emotional trauma that they undergo. Many are unable to relate to normal life routine as they get into depression and their mind is always preoccupied with the trauma. When the frequency of taunting and abuse is more, they get into depression and in some cases inherit suicidal tendencies.

Every episode of emotional abuse leads them to a low self-esteem and it takes a very long time for them to continue with their responsibilities and they end up with lot of stress due to multiple tasking as the whole responsibility of the family's welfare falls on them. The symptoms are more severe for those who are home makers and stay at home the whole day as the emotional abuse becomes more often as the possibility of contact with the abuser partner is more than in the case of working women. If the emotional maturity of the victim is higher, then, the possibility of their facing the life's challenges becomes easier, otherwise, it becomes a great hindrance to manage with normal life. Most of the victims suffer a loss of belonging and deprivation. Many a time they are made to feel that they are unfit to live and manage relationships. Every episode casts doubts in the abused on their abilities to mange the situation.

## Special case of scleroderma patients

Scleroderma is a rare, chronic disease, characterized by excessive deposits of collagen in the skin or other organs. The localized type of the disease, while disabling, tends not to be fatal. Diffuse scleroderma or systemic sclerosis, the generalized type of the disease, can be fatal as a result of heart, kidney, lung or intestinal damage.

- Scleroderma is an auto-immune disease, which can affect virtually the whole body. It is more confusing as in some people they not only have scleroderma but cross with other auto-immune diseases. Lupus, sjogren's are a couple of these diseases. At the moment, there is no cure.

- Scleroderma is an umbrella name for two differing types of the diseases
- *Localized scleroderma:* This is restricted to skin involvement with two differing types: (i) Morphea: Irregular shaped patches of thickened skin, often surrounded by a dark edges. (ii) Linear: A line of thickened shiny skin, can be very disfiguring especially in children as the hard skin does not grow at the same pace as the rest.
- *Systemic sclerosis:* With systemic there is not only skin involvement, but as the name suggests, also internal involvement. It is also of two types: (i) Diffuse: Has the skin thickening as well as internal. Internal involvement can be quite rapid, happening in the first few years after diagnosis. (ii) Limited: This type has limited skin involvement, usually only the fingers, hands and face. The skin around the mouth can become puckered giving it a lined and protruding appearance. Organ involvement is slower, more likely to occur about 10 years after diagnosis. Limited patients are more at risk of pulmonary hypertension than those with diffuse. About 95 per cent of scleroderma patients will also have raynauds, which brings many problems to the circulatory system.

Scleroderma usually affects the skin, and in more serious cases, it can also affect the blood vessels and internal organs. The most evident symptom is the hardening of the skin and associated scarring. Typically, the skin appears reddish or scaly. Blood vessels may also be more visible. Where large areas are affected, fat and muscle wastage will weaken limbs and affect appearance.

The seriousness of the disease varies hugely between cases. The two most important factors to consider are the level of internal involvement (beneath the skin) and the total area covered by the disease. For example, there have been cases where the patient has no more than one or two lesions, perhaps covering a few inches. Less serious cases tend not to involve the internal bodily functions.

There is discolouration of the hands and feet in response to cold. Most patients (over 80%) have raynauds phenomenon – a vascular symptom that can affect the fingers and toes. Systemic scleroderma and raynauds can cause painful ulcers on the fingers or toes, which are known as digital ulcers. Calcinosis is also common in systemic scleroderma, and is often seen near the elbows, knees or other joints.

Diffuse scleroderma can cause musculoskeletal, pulmonary, gastrointestinal, renal and other complications. Some patients can develop pulmonary hypertension, or elevation in the pressures of the pulmonary arteries. This can be progressive, and lead to right-sided heart failure. The earliest manifestation of this may be a decreased diffusion capacity on pulmonary function testing. Other pulmonary complications in more advanced disease include aspiration pneumonia, pulmonary haemorrhage and pneumothorax. The most important clinical complication of scleroderma involving the kidney is scleroderma renal crisis.

### *Who gets scleroderma?*

It is believed that we are born with a genetic predisposition for scleroderma, but it may never be activated. It needs a trigger to activate and there are many theories to the nature of these triggers. Exposure to certain chemicals, the environment in which we live, stress, serious illness, pushing the body beyond its limit to often for too long. May be, it is one or more of these or may be none, hopefully, the research now being undertaken in America and Australia will tell us an answer to the why, and then may be we will find a cure. The symptoms of this disease are many and vary from patient to patient, also because there is more than one form of scleroderma the symptoms can differ from, mainly affecting the skin, to whole body involvement.

### *Symptoms of scleroderma*

- Skin thickening
- Tight or swollen skin
- Raynauds, ranging from just nuisance value to the loss of fingers and toes

- Reabsorption of end finger bones
- Calsinosis
- Stiffness in hands and feet
- Skeletal, muscle and joint pain
- Muscle wasting
- Weight loss
- Difficulty swallowing
- Impaired stomach motility (frozen stomach)
- GERD (Gastro Esophageal Reflux Disease)
- Mal-absorption of the small intestine
- Overwhelming fatigue
- Hair loss
- Fibrosis
- Renal failure
- Heart failure
- Lung fibrosis leading to pulmonary hypertension

### *Practical difficulties*

- Enormous pain and fatigue.
- Tests to be done once a month, very stressful and painful and if partners not cooperative and understanding, left alone to do the tests which causes more emotional distress.
- Suffer the pain of deterioration and the fear of death.
- Loneliness, depression and isolation.

### *Duration of the illness*

"We must just greet every day with joy and make the most of our lives, for if they are long, then they will be the richer for it, but if shortened then we will have placed greater value on what is ours" (as quoted by the scleroderma family group). Since there is no cure for this disease as on date, the patients have to suffer through the pain until the medical fraternity finds a solution for their incomparable suffering. Many of them put up with the disease with sheer will power and most of them commented that with more understanding of the life partner they would be able to put up with the sufferings better and live longer!

This is one of those rarest diseases, which is peculiar. They do not look sick and this puts them in the lowest category in receiving sympathy and attention from others. Being woman and being a scleroderma patient makes them doubly disadvantageous to face the humiliation, neglect and lack of sympathy. They feel neglected and no self-worth, taken for granted and they continue the silence without any response or recognition. The silence of torture can be very damaging to these women as they suffer so much physical pain already that this demonstration of no sympathy or care makes them lose all hopes in their lives in their already hopeless existence.

Most of these women suffer from very stressful and painful symptoms as listed above. They suffer the routine of their medical tests and treatments alone. Most of the scleroderma patients around the world are women. There could be some scientific reasoning emerging in the future regarding this fact. But, the reality remains that they suffer the disease and majority of them suffer alone, some unmarried, some if married, highly neglected by the partner, some divorced. They undergo the stress of taking the tests alone and suffering their screams for help inside the four walls. To the onlooker, the partner, the abuser it is "much ado about nothing" and life goes on for her mercilessly. The physiological misery of the pains and the added emotional neglect and abuse puts them in the highest rung of the ladder of suffering.

Now, where and how the human rights can step in to and bring justice to those women who are deprived of their emotional well-being, already crippled by physical well-being? How do they carry on the tasks of caregivers?

## Human rights: an overview

Dr. Samuel Johnson says, "Nature has given women so much power that the law has very wisely given them very little."

This section will deal into the aspects of human rights, what it means to an emotionally abused woman to lean on human rights. How much do the legal provisions provide justice to her? Is it really possible for an emotionally abused woman to prove her case in the court of human rights? What are the provisions available for an emotionally abused woman?

### *Article 5*

No one shall be subjected to torture or to cruel inhuman or degrading treatment or punishment.

### *Article 32*

Everyone, as a member of society, has the right to social security and is entitled to realization through national effort and international cooperation and in accordance with the organization and resources of each state of the economic, social and economic, social and cultural rights indispensable for his dignity and the free development of his personality.

## International Covenant on Civil and Political Rights

### *Part III (Article 7)*

None shall be subjected to torture or to the cruel, inhuman or degrading treatment or punishment. In particular, no one shall be subjected without his free consent to medical or scientific experimentation.

### *Article 14(3)*

In the determination of any criminal charge against him, everyone shall be entitled to the following minimum guarantees in full equality:

8. not to be compelled to testify against himself or to confess guilty.
9. We the people of the United Nations determined to reaffirm faith in fundamental human rights, in the dignity and worth the human persons in the equal rights of men and women and of nations large and small.

> "to be humiliated is to be rendered inferior or deficient in some respect by others in a deliberate and destructive way. It is therefore a deeply distressing way. It is therefore a deeply

distressing experience. It is something one cannot get over easily and those who have to face it everyday sense a constant to the sense of self-worth".

- The Declaration on the Elimination of Violence against Women provides a definition of gender-based abuse, calling it "any act of gender-based violence that results in, or is likely to result in, physical, sexual or psychological harm or suffering to women, including threats of such acts, coercion or arbitrary deprivation of liberty, whether occurring in public or in private life".

Home is not a refuge for many women across the world but a place of terror, where there is abuse, neglect, violence and assaults. The Russian government estimated that 14,000 women were killed by relatives in 1999. In South Africa, more women are shot at shore in acts of domestic violence than are shot by strangers on the streets or by intruders. If abuse/violence within home is a private matter and not treated by the authorities as crime, then, the state becomes part to crime and shares responsibility of the abuser.

### *Amnesty International*

- Violence in the family included battering by intimate partners and others sexual abuse of female children and young women, marital rape and traditional practices harmful to women. Abuse of domestic workers can also be considered in this category. Violence in the family is often physical, psychological and sexual. Women do not approach justice system because of

1. unaffordability,
2. fear of loss of children, and
3. fear of loss of security.

### *Role of the professionals*

The role of professionals is very crucial in this area of emotional abuse. There is a need to first of all create awareness on the problems resulting form emotional abuse so that the silent sufferes find some solace and solution to their problems. An educational awareness campaign is also important for educating masses about scelroderma – the rarest of the disease that affects women the most. The early diagnosis can save these women of some physical pain. Counselling is very much essential for those abusers who may have suffered from past emotional abuse themselves that may be the cause for their present behaviour. In a nutshell, what is needed is,

- Counselling to the abused
- Counselling to abusers
- Child counselling
- Support group of more listeners/volunteers
- Court of humanity, love and affection in the place of court of law
- Human love in the place of human rights

## References

Bleier, Ruth (1984). *Science and Gender: A Critique of Biology and its Theories on Women*. New York: Pergamon Press.

Caplan, Paula and Jeremy Caplan, "Thinking Critically About Research on Sex and Gender" (2nd. Ed.) by. *Sexuality and Culture*, 5.

Davidson, G.C. and Neale, J.M. (1990). *Abnormal Psychology: An Experimental Clinical Approach*. New York: Wiley Inc.

Dolen, Walter R., *Sex and Politics: Sex Differences v. Dogma*. BeComingOne Press.

Lowe, Marian, "Sociobiology and Sex Differences" *Signs: Journal of Women in Culture and Society*, Vol. 4, No. 1, (Autumn, 1978), pp. 118–125.

McCord, J. (1983). "A Forty Year Perspective on Effects of Child Abuse and Neglect". *Child Abuse and Neglect*. Vol. 7, Issue 3, pp. 265–270.

Prescott, James (1996). "The Origins of Human Love and Violence". *Pre and Perinatal Psychology Journal* 10(3): 143-188 Spring.

Watts, Meredith W., "Biopolitics and Gender". *Contemporary Sociology*, Vol. 15, No. 1 (January 1986), pp. 15–17.

Widom, C.S. (1976a) "Interpersonal and Personal Construct Systems in Psychopaths". *Journal of Consulting and Clinical Psychology*, 44(4): 614–623.

# CHAPTER SEVENTEEN

# Desh-Pardesh

## Indian immigrants and Canadian domestic violence policies

*Swati Shirwadkar*

The domestic violence field has, over the last decade, made substantial programmatic and policy advances to reduce violence against women. There is a realization on international level that the state should take measures to ensure that human rights should be protected. There is a growing recognition in the field of human rights that without social and cultural rights, enjoyment of civil and economic rights is not possible. Human rights conventions, adopted by the United Nations, such as Convention on the Elimination of All Forms of Discrimination against Women, represent social, economic, cultural and civil rights. Especially, the Committee on the Elimination of Discrimination Against Women (CEDAW) categorically states that violence against women is human rights violation. Most of the developed countries have adopted these conventions. These policy advances have been most pronounced in the western developed countries, particularly Canada, the United States and Britain. There is a growing awareness, however, that the programmes and policies in developed countries do not necessarily accommodate the diversity of cultures within those countries. This shortcoming is increasingly an issue given the influx of immigrants from less developed countries who bring very different cultural practices and family circumstances. It is especially apparent in Canada among the relatively large immigrant community of South Asian women. The limitations of Canadian policies in addressing this immigrant community, and in particular Indian immigrants who account for the largest portion of South Asians in Canada, warrants more attention and detail.

The Canadian example is potentially instructive because Canada's domestic violence policies are some of the most advanced in the world and are coupled with a well-articulated policy of multiculturalism. However, the established community of Indian immigrants appears to still encounter barriers to programme access and support. Many of these barriers are related to the cultural background of Indian women. As previous accounts of South Asian women have described, Indian women face oppressive gender roles and restrictive marriage relationships (Abraham, 2001; Dasgupta and Warrier, 1996; Singh and Unnithan, 1999). They also encounter intensified isolation and limited options as immigrants (Banerjee, 2000; Health Canada, 1999). In such a situation, what is the role of the policies with human rights framework to help them? More specifically, what do Canadian programmes and policies offer battered women, and what keeps many Indian women from benefiting from them? What modifications or alternatives would help Indian immigrant women suffering from domestic violence?

To answer these questions, I first review some of the existing studies on domestic violence against women in India and the experiences of immigrant Indian women in Canada. This research emphasizes the influence of the cultural, social and family context in domestic violence and the efforts to counter it. I also summarize the findings from an exploratory study with immigrant Indian women and social service workers in Ontario, Canada, and use these findings to expose limitations in Canadian policy and programmes and identify means to improve them. The conclusion suggests how bi-national research would help us better understand and improve the circumstances of Indian women both in their homeland and abroad.

## Domestic violence in India

Crime and violence against women in India is only a recent focus of research prompted in part by the Indian women's movement and concern about issues such as increasing dowry deaths (Kumar, 1993). The embedded nature of violence against women in Indian social structure is reflected in earlier studies about the status of women in India. These studies have brought out the regional variations in women's status as a reflection of differences in social structure and institutions (Karve, 1965; Madan, 1975; Srinivas, 1976; Committee on the Status of Women, 1974). They expose, moreover, the impact of the patriarchal, extended, joint family and imposing marriage customs in shaping the role of women.

An Indian woman traditionally faces a range of expectations associated with the principle of *'sewa'* (selfless service): efficiency in cooking elaborate Indian food, looking after in-laws, maintaining respectful and amicable relationship, entertaining guests, and providing a flow of gifts (Dube, 2001). The construct of femininity emphasizes submissiveness, inferiority, being docile and dependent, and the importance of the patriarchal family (Shirwadkar, 1998). Deviation from these gender role expectations are likely to meet with different forms of abuse, and give some justification to domestic abuse as an inevitable part of marriage (Busby, 1999; Rao, 1998).

With growing concern about the issue of domestic violence, recent research in India has highlighted several correlates of domestic violence such as young age at marriage, family hierarchies, poverty and economic independence (Ahuja, 1987; Fernandez, 1997; Karlekar, 1998; Kelkar 1992; Kumari, 1989; Mahajan, 1990; Rao, 1998). More recently, due to the lack of reliable official data, prevalence studies and surveys, clinical and health aspects of the issue have also been undertaken to examine and record the trends of domestic violence (Narayana, 1996; Poonacha and Pande, 1999; Visaria, 2000). Gender studies have brought out the class-caste context and the rural-urban variations of the problem of domestic violence.

This context helps to understand how and why development indicators, such as education or employment, may or may not work to reduce violence or dowry demands in some regions, and why strategies of women to subvert domination in different communities are more or less effective (Deolalikar and Rao, 1998; Liddle and Joshi, 1986; Mukharji, Rustagi and Krishnaji, 2001; Raheja and Gold, 1996). Whether economic development designed to create more employment opportunities for women and bring improvement in their quality of life needs further analysis (Dreze and Sen, 1998; Hadi, 2000; Kabeer, 1998; Nussbaum and Glover, 1995). At the same time, creating development opportunities without exploring the regional variation and social complexity of violence against women is likely to limit their impact on domestic violence.

Indian women are, moreover, faced with a scarcity of policies and programmes that deal with domestic violence in India. Whereas there are court-mandated counselling programmes for men in North America; in India, it is the women who primarily have to use the counselling available at family counselling cells, which, however, are hardly used. There are also some government-sponsored housing facilities set aside for women fleeing violent relationships. A Supreme Court Judge recently criticized that these facilities were being run like brothels (*Sakal* Daily, 2001), supporting the impression that most state-sponsored programmes are counter-productive. Domestic violence is not a priority for most non-government organizations and women's groups, because of the fear of losing public support by confronting traditional family structure. There is, however, some policy improvement because of recent legislative amendments and a proposed domestic violence bill. Women's organizations have raised several reservations against these. Apart from problems of definition of domestic violence, the proposed bill has not clearly given the women the crucial right to stay in her matrimonial home (The Lawyer Collective, n.d.). Women's organizations view the administrative set-up as inherently patriarchal and not gender-sensitive.

This cultural context of domestic abuse in India may help in analyzing the abuse experienced by Indian immigrant women. In the case of Indian immigrant women, the issue of violence within the family has to be situated in the context of Indian womanhood taking place in the Indian culture – albeit a culture undergoing turmoil, transition and reassertion. Indian immigrant woman's experience is complicated, however, by not only the woman's native culture, but also by her immigrant community and the new nation where she resides (Bhattacharjee, 1997). This social complexity and cultural specificity have led South Asian activists and researchers to voice their dissatisfaction with the mainstream battered women's movement which tends to focus on one dimension of these women's lives – the violent relationship (Alexander and Mohanty, 1997; Bhattacharjee, 1997).

### Indian women in Canada

The presence of the Indian immigrant community is strongly felt in some parts of Canada, especially Ontario and British Columbia. Toronto, which is in Ontario province, has the largest population of Indian immigrants (554,900 or 4.9% of Ontario's total population). Of the total Asian immigrants in Canada, 51 per cent are settled in Ontario (Asia Pacific Foundation of Canada, 2002). An Indian immigrant woman usually comes to Canada in a situation where she is totally dependent on a spouse and in most cases unaware of immigration laws. Her usual close-knit kin and extended family network, and her neighbourhood support and community resources, are suddenly lost or substantially reduced (Banerjee, 2000; METRAC, 2001). Consequently, she becomes very isolated. In some cases, this isolation results in compensating control by her husband that is psychological, physical, financial and even spatial. Owing to the cultural barriers, she cannot speak about her abuse in public or seek assistance elsewhere. Indian women, particularly those from middle-class backgrounds, are ashamed to admit domestic abuse because of the social stigma attached to it and the fear of 'gossip' (Johnson and Johnson, 2001; Raheja and Gold, 1996). They do not like to take help from shelters because of the Indian woman's preference to turn to the natal family for support instead of going to some outside agency (Desai and Raj, 1987; Pressier, 1999). Patriarchal joint family norms are predominant even in urban nuclear families in India, and, in the immigrant context, the community takes place of neighbouring kin group (Pillai, 2001; Segal, 1999; Uberoi, 2000).

An Indian middle-class woman is seldom educated about her legal rights as a 'wife'. Innumerable cultural symbols, such as the pan-Indian epic character of 'Sita' or 'Sati-Savitri' (idealizing the quiet suffering of women), ingrain the belief that the marital family home is a woman's only alternative (Epstein, 1996; Kakar, 1978; Segal, 1999). Indian immigrant women often stay in abusive relationships also because of few economic resources and language barriers, but social service workers generally do not have enough information or understanding of Indian immigrant women to effectively reach out to them (Status of Women Canada, 2002).

## Method

I recently conducted an exploratory study to identify more specifically the problems and needs of Indian immigrant women and the limitations of Canadian programmes and policy in addressing domestic violence against them. I did so by contrasting the current programme approaches and policy provisions against the actual experience and culture of these women. Official documents and manuals were reviewed to describe Canadian domestic violence policy. The policy description was substantiated and elaborated through interviews with battered women advocates and activists in the Toronto area. I then interviewed in-depth a snowball sample of Indian immigrant women to identify issues, barriers and problems that such women encounter when dealing with domestic violence in the Toronto area. Additional interviews with battered women advocates and activists were used to substantiate and elaborate the interviews with the immigrant women.

Since this was a short-term research project in a foreign land, there were some inevitable limitations. The descriptions about the Canadian system are based on a relatively small set of observations. They reflect perceptions and experiences of the small group of immigrants interviewed in for the study, and my own direct observations and review of documents. Consequently, the findings, especially with regard to Canadian policy and programmes, could be considered impressionistic and incomplete, but they are sufficient to outline the main issues facing immigrant women.

One of the main challenges in conducting research with immigrant communities is gaining access to its members and obtaining disclosure about sensitive issues. As an Indian native, I was more readily accepted by the immigrant community and visited a variety of formal and informal community activities. I was able to contact community residents and social workers in the functions held for celebrating Indian festivals and in informal get-togethers of community families. Discussions and observations with them helped me understand the cultural milieu of the immigrant community and the perception of the issue of domestic abuse within the immigrant community.

These gatherings also helped me to understand the attitude of the immigrant community about the problem of domestic abuse. The meaning that the community attaches to the issue of wife abuse is different than mainstream society. Certain forms of abuse are not only tolerated but may be considered legitimate (Rao, 1998). Though most immigrant women admitted that domestic violence was a problem, they tended to ascribe the problem to a regional Indian community other than their own. Prominent community social workers and activists, on the other hand, privately elaborated actual cases of abuse among all the Indian communities.

As a third source of information, eight domestic violence victims from the immigrant community of Toronto, who came from five different states of India, were drawn by snowball sampling and interviewed about their experiences. I had some advantage in developing trust with these women because of my being from India myself. Also, my short period of stay (three months) in Canada reduced their worry that I might eventually leak their 'family problem' to the community. The interviews with the victims were unstructured, and some of them were spread over the time of three months. Sometimes, the victims gave information about abuse on the telephone when the husband was not around or by e-mail. The joint family of one victim found out that she was talking to someone about domestic abuse and stopped her contact with the researcher.

In three cases, the abuse was physical, combined with psychological, spatial and financial abuse. In other cases, the abuse was more psychological and financial. However, it has to be noted that in the course of discussion most victims expressed that just a slap by the husband in the course of argument may be tolerated. None of these women had even sought help from service providers. One of the physically abused victims eventually confided to a community support group. Even, in the physical abused case, the victim did not want to end the marital relationship. (However, one victim had gotten a divorce.) In the case of one victim, the husband of the abused woman cross-checked if the wife was meeting with 'the researcher'.

## Results

### *Domestic violence policy in Canada*

#### *Canada and human development*

Canada has been at the forefront in social development in general and extended this development to its policies and programmes addressing domestic violence. It is among the leading countries on the Human Development Index, which measures not only economic growth but also social aspects such as education and health. It is also the first country in the world to clearly articulate policies addressing multiculturalism. These policies imply a secure life and equal opportunities for its citizens from a diversity of backgrounds, including immigrants. The Human Development Reports bring out Canada's good record on health and education policies that have created better 'life-chances' for people. Wider access to education has encouraged greater female participation in workforce.

Canada has, moreover, enacted legislation of policy and programmes to deal with domestic violence. Most Canadian government initiatives, as well as advocacy and activists groups, cite that the United Nations Charter of Elimination of Discrimination against Women (CEDAW) as the basis for their action. Article 1 in CEDAW refers to the 'violence against women' as "any act of gender-based violence that results in, or is likely to result in, physical, sexual or psychological harm or suffering to women, including threats of such acts, coercion or arbitrary deprivation of liberty, whether occurring in public or private life" (United Nations, 1993).

The Canadian government has developed several mechanisms to address this problem. The major policy interventions are the criminal justice programme and support services such as housing facilities or shelters for abused women, some of which also offer language services for immigrants. With all these facilities and active voluntary groups, the problem of abuse still persists. Though Statistics Canada 2000 has measured spousal violence on a smaller scale than 1993, women still accounted for 88 per cent of all reported domestic violence victims. Women victims are in the majority in all types of spousal violence, from battery to murder (Statistics Canada, 2000). In 1999, more than 27,000 cases of spousal violence were reported to police department (METRAC, 2001).

The government has recently begun to evaluate its domestic violence policy and programmes. The Violence against Women Survey collected data on different aspects of violence against women (Statistics Canada, 1994). However, it has been criticized for not providing a comprehensive understanding of the issue and for the method and sample used, failure to explain the context of abuse, deceptive statistics about violent women, and trivialization of women's experiences created by the General Social Survey data (Morris, 2002; Johnson, 1996; Sommer and Fekete, 1996). Some reports suggest that in addition to racist violence, women who are of minority, racial, ethno-cultural or linguistic backgrounds are likely to suffer violence at the hands of their partners (OAITH, 1996; Status of Women Canada, 1998). However, these women's access to the justice system and to services is not the same as other women's. In spite of constant flexibility in the policy and the criminal justice system to make improvements, many women still do not report violence to the police.

### *Major policy initiatives*

One of the important policy measures of the Canadian government is its Criminal Justice Programme. Several amendments were made to the Criminal Code to give better protection to women facing violence, including those within close relationship or marriage. Ontario opened two Domestic Violence Courts in 1997. The Canadian Judicial Council passed a resolution for a comprehensive in-depth programme for judges, training for Royal Canadian Mounted Police, prosecutors and correctional staff. These provisions, however, have limited impact on Indian immigrant women because of their reluctance to make the violence public and contact the police.

Usually, Indian women do not want to leave the marital relationship because marriage is seen as a relationship for the life or as a *'sanskar'* or sacrament (Agnes, 2000). In the immigrant context, the wife's perception of community support is as help to keep her marriage intact. In the case of immigrant Indian women, their legal illiteracy causes further submission to the abuse. Indian women do not have a clear understanding of the implications of their immigrant status in case the abuser decides to divorce the wife. There is also a fear that the woman will be blamed for the abuse or will not be believed by the police. The police force is not necessarily seen as protectors, as this is the general impression back home in India (Kapur, 2001). There is in Canada the double pressure of abuse and threat of deportation when the police are involved. The women fear racism and racial discrimination from the police and others, too.

A woman who takes the matter to the 'public' domain is, moreover, criticized and loses support of the community, especially in the middle and upper classes from where the immigrants come. One divorced woman interviewed for the study observed that she could not socialize among the community members nor could she attend the community gatherings to celebrate cultural-religious functions. Also, a woman doctor, who did not care to keep the public façade of a smooth relationship with her husband, got sneers and generated gossip in the community functions.

### *Housing facilities and its beneficiaries*

One of the crucial policy interventions has been to provide a secure place for women to stay if they need to get away from abused relationship. The national housing policy body, the Canada Mortgage and Housing Corporation (CMHC), designs assorted housing programmes, funds housing-related research, provides financial resources for some programmes, and supports traditional public housing and 'transitional housing' for survivors of domestic violence. Presently, in an attempt to place more responsibility on provincial and municipal governments, CMHC has eliminated many programmes. However, with all this provision of facilities, do Indian immigrant women feel secure to use them? The question remains unanswered.

The majority (80%) of the beneficiaries of this subsidized housing are Canadian-born. Social workers and counsellors corroborated that Indian immigrant women do not like to go to subsidized housing but prefer to buy a place of their own within a 'suitable' locality. This reflects Indian women's need to remain in a secure community network. One Indian immigrant woman told her impressions of her visit to a shelter home. All her fears of western 'loose' morals, lesbianism and racist discrimination surfaced, and she did not dare to even think of leaving her home again even if her husband was an abuser. A social worker of South Asian origin conceded that we have to fight against racism even within the social service organizations dedicated to helping women.

Even with this impressive record of policies and programmes, the present government is facing criticism against fiscally conservative economic policy and cuts to women's programmes. The social housing schemes of the government are shrinking, and the private sector is coming in to get the land. The existing subsidized housing is inadequate, considering the demand for housing and the 10-year waiting list for these houses. With the entrance of the private sector, there is no hope of expansion or upgrading affordable housing. The impact of funding cuts to the programmes is likely to affect the disadvantaged women most who need them most.

## Indian immigrants in Canada

### *The family constraints of Indian woman*

The most prominent factor related to the domestic violence among the immigrant Indian women interviewed for this study was the family constraints derived from Indian culture and tradition. A woman's identity in India is influenced by several complex and dynamic factors. It is influenced through primordial loyalties, such as religion, caste, language and history, combined with cultural specificities, such as particularized beliefs, customs, traditions and values. All these are ingrained in the process of socialization through local languages and literature, Hindi movies, and the invasion of satellite TV (Chanana, 1996; Dern'e, 1999; Kishwar, 1999; Segal, 1999). On one hand, the mystification of sexuality due to the rigid segregation of sexes in public life and, on the other hand, the elaborate of marriage ceremony, dowry and gifts both reinforce the subjugation of women within the Indian patriarchal social structure.

Browsing through the matrimonial columns of the major national daily *The Times of India* elucidates the importance of marrying into a 'status' family, preferably an NRI (non-resident Indian). These practices pressure women to keep the marriages intact. For example, two abused women interviewed in this study told of 'telephone marriages' of second generation South Asian Canadians of a particular religious community, where the actual presence of the bridegroom was not necessary. The young women said that they were happy about their family's decision to have them marry a person whom they had not even seen at the time of the wedding. "If something unfortunate happens then that is my fate", one of them said.

There are some practices in India that cross the boundaries of religion or caste. As an impact of consumerism, some castes and tribes are taking up the practice of dowry, which was never a part of their tradition. The spread of education and women's employment has not changed their dowry situation appreciably, but in some cases, educated boys carry a higher price tag. If a boy is already an immigrant, this will almost certainly cause an increase in his dowry price. Dowry has become a continuous source of extraction of cash, different forms of gifts that respond to the demand to acquire consumer goods, capital that continues even after marriage (Deolalikar and Rao, 1998; Jejeebhoy, 1998). The marriage ceremonies, among the rich, are increasingly competitive in terms of opulent expenditures.

Breaking such a marriage means returning to one's family not only with the shame and stigma of divorce, but also having wasted all the money spent on marriage. Even, in India, there is a tendency to encourage and almost force young women to suffer the abuse in the marital family and continue to live with their in-laws and the husband. The Canadian television telecast a Canadian Indian arranged marriage that was opulently celebrated, but sadly ended in the wife killing the husband in a scuffle. The woman's in-laws' attempted to control the son. Ending the marriage in divorce is not an easy option for Indian women, even when they are abroad.

Shelter workers reported that South Asian women do come for counselling, but they are reluctant to leave even a highly abusive situation and avail themselves of shelters. Acceptance of a failed marriage itself is extremely difficult; speaking about it in public is even more difficult. It can degrade one's self-image of being a 'good wife' and daughter-in-law. A 'failed marriage' is often accompanied by a loss of status and ties in the immigrant community, which serves as a support network for Indian immigrant women in an alien society. The fear of the losing one's immigrant status imposes an additional burden of having to face one's community back home in India.

Immigrant women's employment status does not necessarily ease these problems. Thus, employment status does not mean that housework and other service to duties for the relatives are shared by the husband. One of the middle-aged working interviewees stated that she still observes the Indian dress code because of her mother-in-law's dictates and her husband's disapproval of western culture. In-laws can maintain control even if they are living in India. The husband, in such cases, becomes the agent carrying out their wishes. One divorced woman told of her mother-in-law writing to her husband to not let her "get out of his control", on the incitement of her husband's sister who stayed with them for some time. As a result, the husband isolated and beat her.

Indian working women seldom have separate bank the accounts. They are not informed of financial matters, such as taxes, and as a result feel more dependent on the husband. In most cases, the immigrant woman earns less than her husband. The husband has the control over her pay and spending. The funds required for in-laws' air trips are typically drawn from the woman's resources. Women tend to accept such practices in fear of causing any conflict with family members or kin. Displeasure of in-laws may result in gossip and criticism within the immigrant communities. One agitated interviewee commented, "We are filling their (in-laws in India) 'boriyans' (food grain containers or coffers) with dollars, and here I cannot even buy underclothes for myself. It's not only that you invite husband's hostility if you don't comply but being a 'badi-bahu' (eldest daughter-in-law), the whole family-kin network expects you to do all kinds of sacrifices." In some cases, it becomes a thankless sacrifice.

## Isolation of abused migrant women

An elderly and physically handicapped woman brought out the role of another major factor related to domestic violence: isolation and dependency. Even though her abuse continued for years, she could not speak out for several reasons. The abuser, her husband, by virtue of his prestigious government post, threatened her with political reprisals if she spoke out. She suffered physical and financial abuse as well as the trauma of witnessing an illicit relationship of her abusive husband in her own house.

When she found out about her husband's infidelity, he became more violent. She described her humiliation when her husband not only thrashed her in front of the other woman, but also held her hands and asked the other woman to slap his wife. With tearful eyes, she said, "Somewhere being a woman, 'bai-pan' (this implied the common sufferings of women) was awakened in the other woman and thankfully for me she could not do slap me and at least further humiliation did not take place. But then they both made a practice of treating me as a mental case." Yet, she was not ready to consider leaving her husband: "I can't drive a car due to this handicap. So whom can I depend on for even simple things like getting groceries for livelihood, in this icy foreign land?" The abused woman expressed dreamily her wish that perhaps some day somebody will narrate her story in a film or a novel, and after watching that film, her husband will have a change of heart and will come back to her.

When this woman revealed her abuse to a small group of Indian immigrants involved in social work, the husband got worried about his own reputation in the community and stopped at least the physical abuse. This brings out the role of community pressure in stopping or reducing abuse. The Indian immigrant community in Canada is relatively close knit, but is now slowly changing due to the new influx of Indian immigrants from Gulf countries.

Another elderly abused woman, who spoke out about her own abuse as well as sexual abuse of her daughters by her abusive husband, reported that the community advised her to go back to India because the abuser was an important community leader and a fundraiser for community causes. In this case, there was pressure from the community to not speak out about the problems, because the community's reputation may suffer a setback. In some states of India, the control of joint family norms is rather strong. The exposure of sexual abuse is still suppressed in some Indian communities. Many younger men from such a community often assume security jobs that require night shifts. Their wives fear the father-in-law who stays at home with them. He may make sexual advances toward them. They feel helpless, face constant tension, and cannot speak out.

In extreme cases, Indian immigrant women prefer legal intervention than going to shelters, according to social workers and some victims. This is largely a result of their rigid ideas about being of middle class. The immigrants come primarily from the middle class, which implies caste-class status. Women tend to face the dilemma of losing their community status and support network if they leave their husband's house. Going to shelters or transition houses and then public housing means a woman has to move away from her community. This presents an additional setback to Indian women who are heavily dependent on their community and seek a network of immigrants from their home country. Immigrant women see social isolation as something that is seen very difficult to endure.

## Conclusion

### *Summary*

The policies of the Canadian government to counter domestic violence are more developed than those in many other nations, particularly India, where domestic violence law is yet to be passed. However, the Canadian policies do not appear to meet the complex needs of abused Indian immigrant women. Multiple layers of domination invariably subjugate these women. It is essential to understand the dynamics of this subordination process. Family hierarchy works to contain them along with historical gender inequalities. These factors are combined with the complexities of caste and community pressures. In the Indian context, the role and impact of community cannot be ignored. Some studies also caution against strategies that directly challenge existing structures and beliefs without being culturally sensitive. They may invoke a backlash (Garg, 2001; Kishwar, 1999).

This research reinforces the importance of family and community in the lives of Indian immigrants. The problems of immigrant Indian women carry this context. Therefore, policies need to create more awareness of domestic violence within the immigrant communities and establish networks of culturally-specific institutions to support immigrant women. Strategies, such as use of folk-dramas in the Ganesh festival (which was earlier used in India as a means to subvert the colonial regime) or reviving the reformist tradition through community-based organizations (as has been done in West Bengal or Maharashtra), can be useful in this regard. Active support from the Canadian government of progressive elements within the immigrant community is needed, as well. More immediately, abused Indian women need to be linked with facilities that provide social support and reduce isolation, rather than be 'rescued' or removed from their abusive situation.

### *Implications*

The current policies may, moreover, not be sensitive enough to the welfare needs of immigrant Indian women. The gender roles of South Asian women and the cultural barriers they face are not properly understood. As a result, Indian immigrant women find it difficult to access existing welfare benefits or shelter and transition houses. There is a need of developing more legal awareness and community support to counter the domestic violence these women face. The existing accepted channels such as those related to community cultural activities may be explored to ensure community support. This may be essential in the era of increasing budget cuts.

Several advocacy groups and activists are pressing for more changes in policies to counter the problem of violence against women. South Asian groups and activists, such as Poonam Khosla and Aruna Papp, have confronted the government about the domestic violence issue and highlighted it in the media. South Asian feminist leadership, such as Thobani, has also advanced the need to understand the diversity within the feminist movement. Though the Canadian domestic violence policy is laudable, there is a need to address the varied cultural experience of the Indian immigrant women.

### *Future research*

This exploratory research is limited by a small sample only from Ontario. A representative sample of Indian immigrants of all the regional ethnic background was not included, despite the apparent need to understand the variations of domestic violence among Indian immigrant from different regions of India. There is also a need to develop bi-national research to understand women's needs in both India and Canada. What are the differences and similarities between these two groups, and what do they tell us about policy and programmes for these women? How do Indian women's experiences of violence in Canada differ from those they may have had in their homeland, and why?

Furthermore, comparative policy analysis of domestic violence initiatives in Canada and India could benefit Indian policy makers to evolve interventions based on human rights framework. As mentioned, domestic violence policy in India is still in its infant stages in contrast to Canadian policies, which are linked to human rights framework and comparatively much more gender-sensitive and comprehensive. Sufficient documentation and research, sensitive legal provisions, and sociological and psychological research on the issue of domestic abuse are still lacking in India. A combination of quantitative and qualitative methods is needed to help build up a deeper understanding of the problem among Indian women. Finally, there is a need to link the problem of domestic violence with development issues. Women's access to economic opportunities ultimately needs to be improved in order to give Indian women more options, status and mobility.

## Notes

The research on which this paper is based was funded by the Canadian International Development Agency (CIDA) through the Development Studies Programme of the Shastri Indo-Canadian Institute (SICI). Neither CIDA nor SICI necessarily endorses the views expressed herein. The contents of this paper are based on the paper published in the journal *Violence Against Women*, Vol. 10, No. 8, August 2004 (Sage Publications), by the author. The author wishes to express her thanks to Sage Publications and Prof. Edward Gondolf, Indiana University of Pennsylvania.

## References

Asia Pacific Foundation of Canada (2002). Proportion of Asian immigrants in Canada and US. Vancouver, Canada: Asia Pacific Foundation of Canada; Retrieved November 19, 2003, from http://www.asiapacific.ca/data/people/immigration_dataset3_bycountry.cfm

Abraham, M. (2001). *Speaking the Unspeakable: Marital Violence among South Asian Immigrants in U.S.* Brunswick, NJ: Rutgers University Press.

Agnes, F. (2000). Community, gender and violence. In P. Chattarjee and P. Jeganathan (Eds.), *Subaltern Studies,* Vol. XI (pp. 106–137). New Delhi, India: Permanent Black.

Ahuja, R. (1987). *Crime against Women.* Jaipur, India: Rawat Publications.

Alexander, M.J. and Mohanty, C.T. (1997). Introduction: Genealogies, Legacies, Movements. In M.J. Alexander and C.T. Mohanty (Eds.), *Feminist Genealogies, Colonial Legacies, Democratic Futures* (pp. xii–xiii). New York: Routledge.

Banerjee, H. (2000). *The Dark Side of the Nation: Essays on Multiculturalism, Nationalism and Gender.* Toronto, Canada: Canadian Scholar's Press.

Bhattacharjee, A. (1997). The public/private mirage: Undomesticating violence work in the South Asian immigrant community. In M.J. Alexander and C.T. Mohanty (Eds.), *Feminist Geneologies, Colonial Legacies, Democratic Futures* (pp. 308–329). New York: Routledge.

Busby, C. (1999). Agency, power and personhood: Discourses of gender and violence in a fishing community in South India. *Critique of Anthropology, 19* (3), pp. 227–248.

Chanana, K. (1996). Introduction. In A.M. Shah, B.S. Baviskar, and E.A. Ramaswamy (Eds.), *Social Structure and Change: Women in Indian Society*. Vol. 2 (pp. 13–32). New Delhi: Sage Publications.

Committee on the Status of Women (1974). *Towards Equality: Committee Report on the Status of Women in India.* New Delhi: Government of India.

Dasgupta, S.D. and Warrier, S. (1996). In the footsteps of "Arundhati": Asian Indian women's experience of domestic violence in the United States. *Violence Against Women*, 2, pp. 238–259.

Dern'e, S. (1999). Making sex violent: Love as a force in recent Hindi films. *Violence Against Women*, 5, pp. 548–545.

Desai, N. and Krishnaraj, M. (1987). *Women and Society in India.* Delhi: Ajanta Publications.

Deolalikar, A. and Rao, V. (1998). The demand for dowries and bride characteristics in marriage: Empirical estimates for rural south-central India. In M. Krishnaraj, R. Sudarshan and A. Shariff (Eds.), *Gender, Population and Development* (pp. 122–140). New Delhi: Oxford University Press.

Dreze, J. and Sen, A. (1998). *Indian Development: Selected Regional Perspectives*. Delhi: Oxford University Press.

Dube, L. (2001). *Anthropological Explorations in Gender. Intersecting Fields.* New Delhi: Sage Publications.

Epstein, S. (1996). Culture, Women and India's Development. In A.B. Shah, B.A. Baviskar, and E. Ramaswamy (Eds.), *Social Structure and Change: Women in Indian Society, Vol. 2* (pp. 33–55). New Delhi: Sage Publications.

Fernandez, Marilyn (1997). Domestic violence by extended family members in India. *Journal of Interpersonal Violence*, 12, pp. 433–455.

Garg, A. (2001). Countering violence against women in Rajasthan: Problems, strategies and hazards. *Development*, 44, pp. 111–113.

Hadi, A. (2000). Prevalence and correlates of the risk of marital sexual violence in Bangladesh. *Journal of Interpersonal Violence*, 15, pp. 787–719.

Health Canada. (1999). *Canadian Research on Immigration and Health*. Ottawa, Ontario: Ministry of Health.

Jejeebhoy, S. (1998). Wife beating in rural India: A husband's right? Evidence from survey data. *Economic and Political Weekly, 33* (15): 855–862.

Johnson, H. (1996). *Dangerous Domains: Violence against Women in Canada*. Nelson, Canada.\: Scarbourough.

Johnson, P. and Johnson, J. (2001). The oppression of women in India. *Violence Against Women*, 7, pp. 1051–1068.

Kabeer, N. (1998). Money can't buy me love? Evaluating gender, credit and empowerment in Rural Bangladesh. IDS Discussion Paper, 363. Sussex, UK: University of Sussex.

Kakar, S. (1978). *The Inner World*. Delhi: Oxford University Press.

Kapur, N. (2001). Equality and truth of Brahma. *Violence Against Women*, 7, pp. 1069–1096.

Karve, I. (1965). *Kinship Organization in India*. Bombay: Asia Publishing House.

Karlekar, M. (1998). Domestic violence. *Economic and Political Weekly*, 33, pp. 1741–1751.

Kelkar, G. (1992). *Violence against Women: Perspectives and Strategies in India*. Shimla: Indian Institute of Advance Studies.

Kishwar, M. (1999). *Off the Beaten Track: Rethinking Gender Justice for Indian Women*. New Delhi: Oxford University Press.

Kumari, R. (1989). *Brides are not for Burning: Dowry Victims in India*. New Delhi: Radiant Publishers.

Kumar, R. (1993). *The History of Doing: The Illustrated Account of Movements for Women's Rights and Feminism in India 1800–1990*. New Delhi: Kali for Women.

Liddle, J. and Joshi, R. (1986). *Daughters of Independence: Gender, Caste and Class in India*. London: Zed Books.

Madan, T. (1975). Structural implications of marriages in North India. *Contributions to Indian Sociology*, 9(2): 1–81.

Mahajan, A. (1990). Instigators of wife battering. In S. Sood (Ed.), *Violence Against Women* (pp. 1–10). Jaipur: Arihant Publishers.

METRAC (2001). Statistics sheet: Sexual assault. Toronto, Ontario: Metropolitan Action Committee on Violence Against Women and Children (METRAC); Retrieved November 19, 2003, from http://www.metrac.org/new/stat_sex.htm.

Morris, M. (2002). *Factsheet: Violence against Women and Girls*. World March of Women, Canadian Research Institute for Advancement of

Women (CRIAW); Retrieved November 19, 2003, from http://www.criaw-icref.ca/factSheets/Violence_fact_sheet_e.htm

Mukharjee, C., Rustagi, P. and Krishnaji, N. (2001). Crimes against women in India: Analysis of official statistics. *Economic and Political Weekly*, 36, pp. 4070–4080.

Narayana, G. (1996). Family violence, sex and reproductive health behaviour among men in Uttar Pradesh, India: Policy Project. New Delhi: The Futures Group.

Nussbaum, M. and Glover, J. (1995). *Women, Culture and Development*. New Delhi: Oxford University Press.

OAITH (1996). *Home Truth: Exposing the False Face of Equality and Security Rights for Abused Women in Canada*. Toronto, Canada: Ontario Association of Interval and Transition Houses.

Pillai, S. (2001). Domestic violence in New Zealand: An Asian immigrant perspective. *Economic and Political Weekly*, 38, pp. 965–974.

Poonacha, V. and Pande, D. (1999). *Responses to Domestic Violence in the State of Karnataka*. Mumbai, India: Research Centre for Women's Studies, SNDT University.

Preisser, A. (1999). Domestic violence in South Asian communities in America. *Violence Against Women*, 5, pp. 684–699.

Rao, V. (1998). Wife abuse: Its causes and its impact on intra-household resource allocation in rural Karnataka: A 'participatory' econometric analysis. In M. Krishnaraj, R. Sudarshan and A. Shariff (Eds.), *Gender, Population and Development* (pp. 94–121). Mumbai, India: Oxford University Press.

Raheja, G. and Gold, A. (1996). *Listen to the Heron's Words: Reimagining Gender and Kinship in North India*. Delhi: Oxford University Press.

*Sakal* Daily (2001). Government shelters are like brothels: Justice Usha Mehra's comments. (February, 23, p. 3). Pune, India: Sakal Papers Ltd.

Segal, U. (1999). Family violence: A focus on India. *Aggression and Violent Behaviour*, 4, pp. 213–231.

Sev'er, A. and Gokcecicek, Y. (2000). Culture of honor, culture of change: A feminist analysis of honor killings in rural Turkey. *Violence Against Women*, 9, pp. 966–1000.

Shirwadkar, S. (1998). *Women and Socio-cultural Changes*. New Delhi: Gyan Publishing House.

Singh, R.N. and Unnithan, N.P. (1999). Wife burning: Cultural cues for lethal violence against women among Asian Indians in the United States. *Violence Against Women*, 5, pp. 641–653.

Sommer, R. and Fekete, J. (1996). How statistics Canada distorted the public perception of the violence against women. Paper presented at the 4th International Family Violence Conference; Retrieved November 19, 2003 from http://www.reenasommerassociates.mb.ca/.a_new.html

Srinivas, M.N. (1976). *The Changing Position of Indian Women.* Delhi: Oxford University Press.

Statistics Canada (2001). Provinces and territories. (modified: 2003–01-21); Retrieved November 22, 2003 from http://www12.statcan.ca/english/census01/products/analytic/companion/etoimm/provs.cfm

— (1994). *Family Violence in Canada: A Statistical Profile.* Ottawa: Statistics Canada.

— (2000). *Family Violence in Canada: A Statistical Profile.* Ottawa: Statistics Canada.

Status of Women Canada (1998). Report by the Government of Canada to the UN Commission of Human Rights Special Rapporteur on Violence against Women. Ottawa, Canada: Status of Women Canada; Retrieved November 22, 2003, from http://www.swc-cfc.gc.ca/pubs/unreport/ unreport_e.html

— (2002). Assessing Violence against Women: A Statistical Profile. Ottawa, Canada: Status of Women Canada.

The Lawyers Collective (n.d.). Women's rights initiative: The campaign for a civil law on domestic violence. Delhi, India: The Lawyers Collective; Retrieved November 15, 2003, from http://www.lawyerscollective.org/wri/activities/research_documentation/domestic_violence/wri_domesticviolence_campaignforcivillaw.htm

Uberoi, P. (2000). The family in India: Beyond the nuclear versus joint debate. *Occasional Papers in Sociology.* Delhi: Institute of Economic Growth.

United Nations General Assembly (1993). Declaration on the elimination of violence against women. Resolution A/RES/48/104 (February 23, 1994). New York: United Nations.

Visaria, L. (2000). Violence against women in India: Evidence from rural Gujrat. In L. Visaria, N. Mitra, V. Poonacha, and D. Pande (Eds.), *Domestic Violence in India: A Summary Report of Three Studies* (pp. 1–49). Washington, DC: International Centre for Research on Women.

SECTION FOUR

# International Campaigns

CHAPTER EIGHTEEN

# A sociological overview of the domestic violence field in the United States

*Edward W. Gondolf*

The domestic violence field in the United States has grown tremendously in terms of social services, academic research, and public awareness over the last thirty years. It has also contributed to a substantial reduction in domestic violence incidents during the 1990s. The development of the field, however, has received only cursory examination. Yet, an overview of this history is likely to hold some useful lessons for institutional reform and social change, and may identify issues and directions for other societies to consider. Of course, the domestic violence field in the United States has benefited from existing institutions, such as established social services, the criminal justice system, and governmental funding. The nature and responses to domestic violence will differ substantially across societies as a result of cultural, social, political, and economic circumstances. In India, for instance, there is the practice of so-called "bride burning", and in the United States there are incidents of suicidal gun-murders of female partners. Nonetheless, there may be some fundamental principles and issues that translate to other countries, regions or locales.

This paper presents an overview of the domestic violence field in the United States in an effort to identify the interaction of social forces that contributed to the development of the field.

("Social forces" refers to the aggregate of abstracted institutions, organizations, or groups in a society that influence individual behaviour and social change.) In the process, it also identifies the emergence of as yet unresolved controversies that beset the field. Three major social forces appear to have converged and reinforced one another over the last thirty years: the battered women's movement, social science research, and clinical psychology practice. Most impressively, these social forces have brought about reform of the criminal justice system, the expansion of intervention, designated government funding, and programme evaluation research. The national surveys on domestic violence show a 30 per cent reduction in the incidence of domestic violence during the 1990s that has been attributed to these advances, and the public awareness that has accompanied them (Dugan, Nagin, Rosenfeld, 1999; Gelles and Straus, 1988; Tjaden and Thoennes, 2000). However, the different assumptions, which influence these three forces, have also led to some inevitable conflicts and resultant controversies. As discussed below, debate continues over the nature of domestic violence, the role of therapy for perpetrators, and the limits of criminal justice intervention. "Domestic violence" refers here to physical abuse between adult male and female partners in an intimate relationship.

## Main social forces

### *Battered women's movement*

The battered women's movement has been credited with establishing the domestic violence field starting in the late 1970s (Schechter, 1982). It grew out of the feminist movement that asserted women's rights in the face of inequality and what was identified as subjection within the marriage (Friedan, 1963). As part of this movement, women met in consciousness-raising groups to talk about common experiences. Domestic violence emerged as an experience for a substantial portion of women, but one that had not been discussed in part because of the privacy associated with marriage relations and the sense of isolation many women felt. "Safe houses" were first established by these groups in private homes where women could go to escape violence, and during the mid-1970s to the 1980s over 1,000 women shelters and centres were established to house battered women. It was the largest and swiftest social service achievement since the rise of the "settlement houses" for the poor and indigent led by women like Jane Adams in the early 1900s. The striking thing about the women's shelters is that they emerged as grassroots efforts. Coalitions of local volunteers led by battered women advocates organized and raised money for these shelters in their respective communities. (Battered women's "advocates" here refers not to lawyers, but to women dedicated to helping battered women get protection, legal assistance, and social support. They are activists who also attempt to change the institutions in their communities and society to address the needs of battered women and ultimately to prevent domestic violence.)

In the 1980s, battered women advocates began to also improve the response of police and the courts to battered women. There was a clear need not only to help women escape violent relationships, but also to protect them by apprehending their violent male partners. Police tended to view domestic violence as a private matter and therefore to ignore or take no action on domestic violence calls. Moreover, the courts generally put domestic violence perpetrators on probation or dismissed the charges against them, thus conveying the message that domestic violence was tolerated and even acceptable. Battered women's advocates began to educate police about the seriousness of domestic violence and to press for policies that would increase arrests of and penalties for the perpetrators. The idea was that such policies would give women more leverage in their relationships – that is, help counter the men's sense of power and control – and also make the work of the police easier by reducing the number of calls for repeated incidents of domestic violence.

One of the most notable accomplishments of the battered women's movement was establishment of the Violence Against Women Act in 1994. Battered women's advocates lobbied the United States Congress for legislation that formally criminalized domestic violence and assigned funding to improve legislation. The legislation was conveniently incorporated into a major crime bill supported by conservative politicians who promoted stricter law enforcement and stronger families in general. These politicians might otherwise have opposed legislation that supported what conservatives perceived as a liberal and even radical movement. The bill helped to fund further police training, women's shelters and social services, and programme evaluation research. It also required the formation of domestic violence councils in communities that received funding. These councils were designed to bring together representatives from the women's shelter, criminal justice system, and human services agencies to develop and maintain procedures for domestic violence intervention.

## Social science research

Social scientists made a decisive entry into the field with the National Family Violence Survey conducted by Murray Straus and Richard Gelles in the late 1970s (Straus, Gelles and Steinmetz, 1980). This survey assessed the prevalence of domestic violence in a random sample of over 2,000 couples in the United States and established domestic violence as an extensive social problem. The survey results reinforced and documented the claims of battered women's advocates. It was repeated in the late 1980s and 1990s to help identify trends in the extent of domestic violence, and survey questions regarding domestic violence have been incorporated in the National Crime Victimization Survey of nearly 80,000 households, which is conducted annually by the US Department of Justice (Bureau of Justice Statistics, 2004).

In the mid-1980s, one of the most influential social science studies was completed. The Minneapolis Police Study (Sherman and Berk, 1984) was a field experiment in which police in the city of Minneapolis, Minnesota, responded to domestic violence calls with randomly assigned actions: (1) the man was told to leave the house until he calmed down; (2) the couple was advised about domestic violence and the conflict mediated; and (3) the perpetrator was arrested. According to a six-month follow-up study, which used both arrest records and interviews with the victims (N=314), the men who were arrested were 50 per cent less likely to repeat the violence. Replication in other cities confirmed the original findings (Garner, Fagan and Maxwell, 1995). Thus, the effectiveness of arrests in reducing domestic violence was substantiated and the ideas of battered women's advocates were proven to be correct.

The last decade has seen a spate of programme evaluations examining the effectiveness of battered women's advocacy, police interventions, court actions, and especially so-called batterer programmes (i.e., counselling and education programmes for men who are violent toward their female partners). Funding from the Violence Against Women Act helped to encourage and develop this line of research, as well as publicize and distribute it to practitioners in the field through conferences and summary publications. Most notably four experimental evaluations of batterer programmes have been conducted that suggest little improvement over open probation or other types of supervision (without batterer programme participation). Even though these evaluations are popular among researchers because of their experimental design, methodological problems have raised serious questions about their results (see Gondolf, 2001).

Our longitudinal follow-up of batterer programmes in four cities across the United States demonstrated a more positive picture of domestic violence intervention in general (N=845 men; Gondolf, 2001, 2004). In this study, the female partners of men, who were arrested and sent to batterer programmes, were interviewed every three months for a period of four years. With a response rate of 70 per cent for two-and-a-half years and 60 per cent for full four years, the women's answers showed that 42 per cent of the men had repeated their violence during the four-year follow-up, but nearly 90 per cent had not been violent in the previous year. In other words, it took some time for the men to stop their violence but the vast majority did stop. Eighty-five per cent of the women also reported feeling "very safe" at this point and two-thirds noted that they were "better off" overall than they had been prior to the initial arrest. Moreover, our complex statistical modelling showed that the men who completed at least three months of weekly programme sessions were 50 per cent less likely to reassault their partners than equivalent men who dropped out of the programme. The batterer programmes contributed to the reduction of domestic violence beyond the arrest and court action.

### Trends in clinical psychology

Clinical psychology has similarly evolved during this time frame, partly in response to the promotion of psychological counselling through television talk shows and self-help books. It has become one of the most popular areas of study in graduate schools across the country and an expanding profession overall as a result of increased insurance coverage for psychological treatment. Clinical psychologists have brought their perspective and expertise to the problem of domestic violence as well, and in the process are shaping the treatment of victims and perpetrators. They have developed, in particular, trauma research and treatment for battered women (Jasinski, 2005). Women who have been assaulted or abused often experience depression, anxiety, flashbacks, shame, distrust, and isolation as a way of adapting to abuse. Therapies that help to rebuild connections, trust, and confidence are increasingly a part of the work of women's centres and shelters that were once devoted primarily to protection and advocacy (Dutton, 1992; Herman, 1992).

Research by clinical researchers has also examined the psychological characteristics of men who are violent toward their partners. A variety of psychological tests for men who are arrested for domestic violence indicate a variety of personality profiles. Some researchers suggest that these comprise three separate types of violent men (i.e., the family-violent only; dysphoric-borderline, violent-antisocial), and that each type warrants a different kind of treatment (Holtzworth-Munroe and Stuart, 1994). Other clinical psychologists argue that an emotional explosive disorder is behind most violence and requires special psychiatric treatment (Kessler et al., 2006). Even though these conceptions are not fully accepted in the field, they have reinforced interest in conducting therapy with violent men that would "heal" their psychological disorders, as well as contain their violent behaviour.

An additional contribution from the research of clinical psychologists has been the development of risk assessment instruments (Dutton and Kropp, 2000). These instruments are a series of items that may be administered to men arrested for domestic violence. They are intended to help identify the men who are most likely to continue their violence and therefore warrant heightened supervision, containment, or treatment. Their partners are likely to need further safety planning and protection. The research on domestic violence intervention shows that a portion of arrested men (perhaps as many as 20%) continue to engage in severe violence toward their partners (Gondolf, 2000; Gondolf and White, 2001), but the instruments in themselves still fall short of correctly identifying these men. They improve the identification of the most violent men over clinical judgment, but still are only correct about 70 per cent of the time (Heckert and Gondolf, 2004).

## Impacted areas

These social forces – the battered women's movement, social science research, and clinical psychology trends – have had an impact on three major areas. One, they have helped to establish the extent and nature of domestic violence, and in the process elevated it to a social problem – one that warrants social policy, community programming, and public support. Second, they have brought about institutional reform, especially in the criminal justice system, which previously neglected domestic violence cases. Today, the criminal justice system is the primary source of intervention into the problem of domestic violence in the United States, along with women's shelters and centres. Third, we have seen the development of a coordinated community response to domestic violence. Training and procedures have been established for a variety of social services, such as medical facilities, mental health clinics, and alcohol treatment programmes, along with the police, judges, and prosecutors. The objective is to increase the involvement and responsiveness of these services and the criminal justice system to domestic violence cases. As discussed below, these accomplishments have also brought with them controversies that draw continued attention and debate.

### *Extent of domestic violence*

Prior to the early 1980s, domestic violence was largely treated as a private matter, and at worst one that was isolated to a few exceptional and usually poor households. A host of "myths," as battered women's advocates refer to them, further diverted attention to the problem: notions such as "women like to be beaten". As a result, battered women were portrayed as "undeserving of special help and public support" (DeKeseredy, 1999). Activists in the battered women's movement are largely responsible for establishing domestic violence as a social problem rooted in society's patriarchy rather than in the tendencies of individual women. They began organizing meetings and conferences at the local level to raise public awareness and increase services for battered women. In the 1980s, popular books, such as *The Battered Woman* (Walker, 1980), and TV movies, such as "The Burning Bed," put the issue further into the public mainstream. The ultimate media education was to come a decade later in the mid-1990s with the O.J. Simpson trial. (O.J. Simpson is a famous football player who later became a movie star and a celebrity in his own right.) The nationally televized trial of Simpson's alleged brutal murder of his wife, Nicole, featured the long history of O.J.'s abuse and violence toward Nicole, and with it a dramatic lesson on the potential escalation of abuse.

The groundbreaking research of Murray Straus and Richard Gelles, mentioned above, reinforced the rising awareness of domestic violence. The publication of the National Family Violence Survey in the book, *Behind Closed Doors* (Straus, Gelles and Steinmetz, 1980), and later in *Intimate Violence* (Gelles and Straus, 1988), documented the extent of the problem in very readable prose and statistics. The more current surveys indicate a substantial decrease of nearly 30 per cent in the incidence of domestic violence during the decade of the 1990s, but the level is still unsettlingly high. Approximately, 11 per cent of wives have been physically assaulted by their intimate partners in the year prior to the survey; 4 per cent have been assaulted repeatedly over many years; 30 to 40 per cent are physically abused in their lifetime; and nearly 1,200 women are murdered by their husbands annually (Bureau of Justice Statistics, 2004).

The controversy that looms to this day is over the extent of the violence committed by women. The National Family Violence Survey and subsequent surveys in other countries (e.g., Gelles and Straus, 2004; Moffitt and Caspi, 1999) show that conflict tactics used by women against their male partners (e.g., pushing, slapping, hitting, punching, etc.) are similar to men's tactics. These findings have led critics of the battered women's movement to assert that women are as violent as men, and that domestic violence is more accurately characterized as "mutual combat". The on-going debate over this issue was recently discussed in a workshop on "gender symmetry" funded by the US Department of Justice (Rosen, 2006). The workshop highlighted the long-standing counter-arguments, which claim that the conflict tactics used to measure domestic violence must be interpreted in light of the injury caused to women and the fear experienced by women as compared to men. The constellation of male behaviours against women, including control, subjugation, abuse, and sexual assault, distinguishes men's violent acts from women's, who appear to act primarily in self-defense. Additionally, women are more likely to disclose their violence than men, who are shown to minimize, excuse, or deny their violence.

A methodological question, moreover, persists about the measurement approach used in surveys on domestic violence (Saltzman, 2004). Other crime victimizations surveys show, for instance, that the incidence of men's violence toward women is as much as six times higher than women's violence toward men (Bureau of Justice Statistics, 2004; Tjaden and Thoennes, 2000). The weight of these counter-arguments has convinced many battered women's advocates that the attention given to women's violence is a backlash from political conservatives – that is, those who resist the changes initiated by the women's movement (DeKeseredy, 1999).

### *Criminal justice intervention*

The second area impacted by the social forces associated with the domestic violence field is criminal justice intervention. As mentioned earlier, the lobbying and training of police and later, of judges and prosecutors, and the research conducted on police response to domestic violence calls, contributed to substantial reform in the criminal justice system. This was a significant accomplishment given the male-dominated and hierarchical structure of the criminal justice system. Essentially, the battered women's movement along with social science research showed that it was in the interest of the criminal justice system to intervene more decisively and consistently in domestic violence cases, ultimately resulting in reduced recidivism and increased safety for battered women.

The most notable institutional reforms include probable-cause arrest laws, specialized domestic violence courts, legal advisors for battered women in the courtroom, and counselling and education programmes for the men arrested for domestic violence. As mentioned above, the Minneapolis Police Study and lawsuits against police departments helped to establish policies requiring police to make arrests in response to evidence of a domestic violence assault (i.e., a "probable-cause" arrest). Despite concerns that women would be more reluctant to report domestic violence, domestic violence reports increased around the country. For instance, in the city of Pittsburgh with a population of 500,000, arrests rose to over 4,000 a year in the mid-1990s (Gondolf, 2000).

To make the prosecution of the cases more efficient and effective, specialized domestic violence courts were established. These courts were comprised of officials who were familiar with the dynamics and nature of domestic violence and who could help avoid the mishandling and inappropriate dismissal of cases occurring in the general criminal courts. Legal advisors were hired, supervised, and trained by battered women centres and placed in the courts to support and advise the battered women of their rights and of court procedures. With so many battered women in a state of crisis and under threat from their partners during court appearances, the support from legal advisors ultimately helped to increase their cooperation with the prosecution (Fleury-Steiner, 2006).

The question of how to handle the arrested perpetrators then became an issue. In the late 1980s, "voluntary" counselling programmes for men began to expand to accommodate perpetrators sent by the court. Today, almost every major city has a so-called "batterer programme" that offers weekly sessions of about two hours each for groups of 10–15 men. Generally, the men are taught the nature of domestic violence, the consequences for it, techniques to avoid violence, and attitudes to replace the beliefs which support domestic violence. The men are required to attend these sessions for three months to one year depending on the requirements of the programme and the charges against them (see Etiony and Mederos, 2002, for an overview of batterer programmes and approaches)

The evaluation of batterer counselling programmes that has confirmed their effectiveness in reducing domestic violence also discusses ways to improve programme outcomes (Gondolf, 2001). For one, programme attendance and a cessation of violence are related to a swift and certain response to the initial offense or to non-compliance to the court order. In our multi-site study of domestic violence intervention, the highest programme completion rate (70%) was associated with a court that mandated men into the counselling programme within two weeks of their arrest, and also required a monthly review of attendance and payments. There is also much work being done to develop risk management. Risk assessment tests are increasingly being used to identify men who are not likely to respond to batterer programming and most likely to severely re-assault their partners. The ideal programme would include mental health and alcohol treatment for such men and increased supervision and oversight through case management. Additionally, safety planning and supportive counselling are being extended to female victims of such men.

The main controversy in this area relates to the effectiveness of batterer programmes and how to improve them. A few experimental evaluations of batterer programmes suggest very little effect compared to probation without batterer programming (Davis, Taylor and Maxwell, 1998; Feder and Dugan, 2002). Despite the limitations and shortcomings of these studies, some clinical psychologists argue that a more therapeutic approach is therefore warranted (Geffner and Rosenbaum, 2002). According to these professionals, the psychopathology of batterers, including the effects of trauma they may have experienced in their lives as children or adults, requires specialized treatment. Furthermore, each man should be individually assessed for such problems and ideally referred to specialized therapy or combinations of treatment.

The interesting counter-finding from our multi-site study is that the vast majority of men eventually stopped their violence, and this occurred within programmes using the conventional cognitive-behavioural approach which focuses on interrupting the violent behaviour and modifying the beliefs that support it (Gondolf 2000, 2001). The men in our study, furthermore, displayed a variety of psychological profiles; over half showed no evidence of psychopathology. The striking commonality was the narcissistic and anti-social tendencies among the men – that is, the sense that "I am right and everyone else is wrong." Treatment manuals indicate that a cognitive-behavioural approach is the most appropriate for these tendencies (e.g., Choca and Van Denburg, 1997), and reviews of interventions with other violent criminals and alcohol abusers suggest that cognitive-behavioural programmes are the most effective in changing the problem behaviour in these areas (Wilson, Bouffard and MacKenzie, 2005; MacKenzie, 2002).

### *Coordinated community response*

A third area of development has been coordinating the community response to domestic violence. The battered women's movement emerged with the objective of bringing about community and social change, as well as developing services for battered women. Several studies suggest as well that the effectiveness of the criminal justice intervention is improved by having a variety of services and agencies provide extended accountability, protection, and support (Clark et al., 1996; Gamache, Edleson and Schock, 1988; Shepard, 2005). Examples include the close relationship between domestic violence courts and batterer programmes in the form of court review of programme compliance, and the courts' relationship with battered women's centres whose legal advisors assist women in court. As mentioned above, domestic violence councils, comprised of representatives from a variety of community services (including police, courts, prosecutors, and probation officers), have played a central role in developing this sort of response. They have established and monitor specific procedures and protocols to help ensure that a battered woman's needs are met. This may include procedures for the hospital emergency room, as well as the types of evidence police are expected to collect in an arrest, and the information they are to give the battered woman.

Our research evaluation of two projects designed to further coordinate community services have exposed the need for additional steps. One project assessed men as they entered a batterer programme for a variety of needs, such as employment and parenting skills, and then referred men to services that addressed these needs (Gondolf, in press). A second project tested men for psychological problems and required those men who showed evidence of such problems to obtain psychological evaluation and treatment at a cooperating mental health clinic (Gondolf, 2006). In both cases, a very small percentage of men complied with the referrals even when they were required to do so as part of the batterer programme. There were also numerous other problems including insufficient funding and staffing at the referral services, and lapses in the court's enforcement of the requirements. The men's compliance, however, did increase when a case manager was added. The case manager called the men to urge them to comply with the referral and to address any reluctance to do so. She also obtained verification of the men's compliance from the cooperating agencies and checked whether the batterer programme reported the verification to the courts.

The controversy that remains in this still-developing area is over its emphasis and extent: does the coordination of services go far enough? For one, the coordinated community response is not tailored to the racial and ethnic diversity represented in the court cases. In the major cities included in our multi-site study, at least half of the men were African-American or Latino (Gondolf, 1999). These men tend to have more resistance to and suspicion of the criminal justice system and services associated with it. The services, moreover, do not sufficiently address the poverty, gang violence, and drug use that accompany and reinforce the domestic violence of many arrested men. The community coordinated response has, furthermore, focused primarily on the criminal justice system and services associated with it. The cases appearing in domestic violence court represent only a small percentage of the couples who are in violent or abusive relationships. In order to broaden the scope of intervention and services, a greater outreach is needed to couples who contact services with related problems – through hospitals, schools, workplace, or beauty salons. Beyond expanding intervention, more must be done throughout the process to prevent domestic violence. Finally, there are those who sound warnings about the overall levels of violence in society: the sexual assault, bullying in schools, gang violence, shooting homicides. Domestic violence work needs to join the efforts to stop violence in general and build a more peaceable society, free not only of domestic violence, but also of war towards other nations and peoples.

## Conclusion

Our overview of the domestic violence field reveals an encouraging but still challenging picture. In a relatively short time span of three decades, battered women's services have been established, the criminal justice system has been reformed, and a coordinated community response is being developed. A corresponding reduction in the prevalence of domestic violence has followed. The activism of the battered women's movement has been reinforced by social science research, and interventions for battered women and the men who batter them have been enhanced by contributions from clinical psychologists. A role for social science research in documenting the extent of the problem and the effectiveness of interventions is particularly noteworthy amidst public resistance to the claims of activists and suspicions about the ability to impact the problem. The controversies that remain, however, warrant more decisive analysis and resolution in order for the domestic violence field to progress in the United States. They also raise cautions to other countries where the field of domestic violence is in earlier stages of development.

The sociological perspective used in our overview does, however, have its limitations. The focus on aggregate and abstracted social forces obviously neglects the complexity of the field's development. On a more personal level, the field has been shaped by many strong personalities and dedicated individuals. Numerous factions pose further and more nuanced controversies. Some battered women's activists have, for instance, been accused of being too ideological and dogmatic in their approach and using misleading information to promote their cause, while activists and clinicians often view researchers as self-serving, detached from the realities of domestic violence, and insensitive to the impact of context and experience when interpreting data. One might also argue that developments summarized above have been very uneven across different jurisdictions, regions, and racial and ethnic communities.

The relevance of this overview to other countries remains uncertain. The extent of women's services, social research, and additional services reflects in part the formalized services and funding resources available in the United States. Disease, malnutrition, and poverty stand out as priorities in so many less wealthy countries. The criminal justice system, as well, may be under-funded and especially vulnerable to corruption and politics. The activism in such countries tends to address a broader range of women's oppression and hardship of which domestic violence is only a part. Furthermore, differences in cultural norms and traditions may warrant different understandings and approaches. Women in many societies are bounded by kinship networks that contain and even isolate them. Reporting or even talking about domestic violence may be taboo in some rural communities, and moving to the safety of a women's shelter is often an impractical and unavailable alternative.

Developments in the domestic violence field in the United States demonstrate the possible impacts that can be achieved through social change and clarify the role of diverse social forces in achieving that change. They also suggest the utility of looking for alliances from other sources, even unlikely ones such as social researchers and clinicians. Reflecting on the broader picture of the field may, furthermore, help to sustain direction and hasten impacts. In a field of such urgency and crisis, it is easy to focus on the moment, on immediate challenges and potential tragedies. The US example demonstrates that change and progress are possible.

## References

Bureau of Justice Statistics (2004). *National Crime Victimization Survey*. Washington, DC: US Department of Justice (available at http://www.ojp.usdoj.gov/bjs/cvict.htm#ncvs).

Carr, A. (2005). Contributions to the study of violence and trauma. *Journal* of *Interpersonal Violence*, 20, pp. 426–435.

Choca, J.P. and Van Denburg, E. (1997). *Interpretive Guide to the Millon Clinical Multiaxial Inventory*, Second Edition. Washington, DC: American Psychological Association.

Clark, S., Burt, M., Schulte, M. and Maguire, K. (1996). *Coordinated Community Responses to Domestic Violence in Six Communities: Beyond the Justice System*. Washington, DC: Urban Institute (Available at http://www.urban.org/url.cfm?ID=406727).

Davis, R., Taylor, B, and Maxwell, C. (1998). *Does Batterer Treatment Reduce Violence? A Randomized Experiment in Brooklyn*. Final report to the National Institute of Justice, Washington, DC.

DeKeseredy, W. (1999). Tactics of the antifeminist backlash against Canadian National Woman Abuse Surveys. *Violence Against Women*, 5, pp. 1258–1276.

Dugan, L., Nagin, D. and Rosenfeld, R. (1999). Explaining the decline in intimate partner homicide: The effects of changing domesticity, women's status, and domestic violence resources. *Homicide Studies*, *3*, pp. 187–214.

Dutton, D. and Kropp, R. (2000). A review of domestic violence risk instruments. *Trauma, Violence and Abuse*, 1, pp. 171–182.

Dutton, M.A. (1992). *Empowering and Healing the Battered Woman: A Model for Assessment and Intervention*. New York: Springer.

Etiony, A. and Mederos, F. (Eds.) (2002). *Programs for Men Who Batter: Intervention and Prevention Strategies in a Diverse Society*. Kingston, NJ: Civic Research Institute.

Feder, L. and Dugan, L. (2002). A test of the efficacy of court-mandated counseling for domestic violence offenders: The Broward experiment. *Justice Quarterly*, 19, pp. 343–375.

Fleury-Steiner, R., Bybee, D., Sullivan, C., Belknap, J. and Melton, H. (2006). Contextual factors impacting battered women's intentions to reuse the criminal legal system. *Journal of Community Psychology, 34*, pp. 327–342.

Friedan, B. (1963). *The Feminine Mystique*. New York: W. W. Norton.

Gamache, D., Edleson, J. and Schock, M. (1988). Coordinated police, judicial and social service response to woman battering: A multi-baseline evaluation across three communities. In G. Hotaling, D. Finkelhor, J. Kirkpatrick, and M. Straus (Eds.), *Coping with Family Violence: Research and Policy Perspectives*. Newbury Park, CA: Sage.

Garner, J., Fagan, J. and Maxwell, C. (1995). Published findings from the spouse assault replication program: A critical review. *Journal of Quantitative Criminology*, 11, pp. 3–28.

Geffner, R. and Rosenbaum, A. (Eds.) (2002). *Domestic Violence Offenders: Current Interventions, Research, and Implications for Policies and Standards*. Binghamton, NY: Haworth.

Gelles, R. and Straus, M. (1988). *Intimate Violence: The Causes and Consequences of Abuse in the American Family*. New York: Simon and Schuster.

Gondolf, E. and White, R. (2001). Batterer program participants who repeatedly reassault: Psychopathic tendencies and other disorders. *Journal of Interpersonal Violence, 16*, pp. 361–380.

Gondolf, E. (1999). Characteristics of court-mandated batterers in four cities: Diversity and dichotomies. *Violence Against Women*, 5, pp. 1277–1293.

— (2000). Mandatory court review and batterer program compliance. *Journal of Interpersonal Violence*, 15, pp. 438–437.

— (2000). Reassault at 30 months after batterer program intake. *International Journal of Offender Therapy and Comparative Criminology*, 44, 111–128.

— (2001). Limitations of experimental evaluations of batterer programs. *Trauma, Violence, and Abuse*, 2, pp. 79–88.

— (2001). *Batterer Intervention Systems: Issues, Outcomes, and Recommendations*. Thousand Oaks, CA: Sage Publications.

— (2004). Evaluating batterer counseling programs: a difficult task showing some effects. *Aggression and Violent Behaviour*, 9(6), pp. 605–631.

— (2006). Supplemental psychological treatment for participants in domestic violence counseling. Paper presented at International

Association of Forensic Mental Health Services, Amsterdam, Netherlands, June 13–16.

—— (in press) Implementation of case management for batterer program participants. *Violence Against Women.*

Heckert, A. and Gondolf, E. (2004). Battered women's perceptions of risk versus risk factors and instruments in predicting repeat reassault. *Journal of Interpersonal Violence,* 19 (7), pp. 778–800.

Herman, J.L. (1992). *Trauma and Recovery: The Aftermath of Violence from Domestic Abuse to Political Terror.* New York: Basic Books.

Holtzworth-Munroe, A. and Stuart, G.L. (1994). Typologies of male batterers: Three subtypes and the differences among them. *Psychological Bulletin,* 116, pp. 476–497.

Jasinski, J. (2005). Trauma and violence research. *Journal* of *Interpersonal Violence, 20,* pp. 412–417.

Kessler, R., Coccaro, E., Fava, M., Jaeger, S., Jin, R. and Walters, E. (2006). The prevalence and correlates of DSM-IV Intermittent Explosive Disorder in the National Comorbidity Survey Replication, *Archives of General Psychiatry,* 63, pp. 669–678.

MacKenzie, D. (2002). Reducing the criminal activities of known offenders and delinquents: Crime prevention in the courts and corrections. In L. Sherman, D. Farrington, B. Welsh, and D. MacKensie (Eds.), *Evidence-based Crime Prevention* (pp. 330–404). London: Routledge.

Moffitt, T. and Caspi, A. (1999). *Findings About Partner Violence From the Dunedin Multidisciplinary Health and Development Study* (NCJ 170018). Research in Brief Series. Washington, DC: National Institute of Justice (available at http://www.ojp.usdoj.gov/nij/pubs-sum/170018.htm).

Rosen, L. (2006). Origin and goals of the "Gender Symmetry" workshop. *Violence Against Women, 12,* pp. 997–1002.

Saltzman, L. (2004). Definitional and methodological issues related to trans-national research on intimate partner violence. *Violence Against Women,* 10, pp. 812–830.

Schechter, S. (1982). *Women and Male Violence: The Visions and Struggles of the Battered Women's Movement.* Boston: South End Press.

Shepard, M. (2005). Twenty years of progress in addressing domestic violence. *Journal of Interpersonal Violence, 20,* pp. 436–441.

Sherman, L.W. and Berk, R.A. (1984). The specific deterrent effects of arrest for domestic violence assault. *American Sociology Review, 49,* pp. 226–272.

Straus, M., Gelles, R. and Steinmetz, S. (1980). *Behind Closed Doors: Violence in the American family.* New York: Doubleday.

Tjaden, P.G. and Thoennes, N. (2000). Full report of prevalence, incidence and consequences of violence against women: Findings from the national violence against women survey (NCJ 183781). US Department of Justice, *National Institute of Justice & Centres for Disease Control and Prevention Research Report,* Washington, DC.

Walker, L. (1980). *The Battered Woman.* New York: Harper.

Wilson, D., Bouffard, L. and MacKenzie, D. (2005). A quantitative review of structured, group-oriented, cognitive-behavioural programs for offenders. *Criminal Justice and Behaviour, 32,* pp. 172–204.

CHAPTER NINETEEN

# Domestic violence

## Comparative analysis of German and British research findings

*Helmut Kury and Ursula Smartt*

It has long been established that the 'family' is seen as the most essential socialization constituent and of central significance for the development of the next generation. The notion of the family is partly defined in recent editions of Webster's Dictionary as "parents and their children considered as a group" sharing the same blood, i.e., a group in which persons are together under the same identity. "Blood is thicker than water" is a famous proverb, and blood ties should unite a family in an emergency. Older dictionary entries are: the collective body of persons who live in one house, and under one head or manager; a household, including parents, children, and servants, and, as the case may be, lodgers or boarders; the group comprising a husband and wife and their dependent children, constituting a fundamental unit in the organization of society (Webster's Revised Unabridged Dictionary, 1913; 2005). Social scientists have put 'the family' on top of social hierarchies as a strong power uniting all its members. The literature tells us that, for at least 30 years, the 'family' has been vitally important for the development of the individual, especially as a child. The family is seen as a vitally protective unit in which the state should not interfere. This manifests itself for instance in the German Constitution of 1949 (*Grundgesetz* - GG) and its fundamental human rights. Article 6(1) GG states: "Marriage and family enjoy the special protection by the state."

'Home' is another word for a family. Even though all the members are not in the same place, they each keep the home in mind as the only and the very best place for each family member. Despite the industrialization of the early 19th century, scattering each family member all over the place, home still takes its firm place as the family unit. Christian religions have attributed an additional and special role to the family, often expressed in paintings that depict the 'holy family' – especially during the Middle Ages in Europe. The Roman Catholic Church has long symbolized itself as 'the family'; this was recently expressed in Pope Benedict XVI's 'First Encyclical Letter' of December 2005 stating that, "The Church is God's family in the world. In this family no one ought to go without the necessities of life… today as in the past. The Church as God's family must be a place where help is given and received, and at the same time, a place where people are also prepared to serve those outside her confines who are in need of help" (*'Deus Caritas est'*, 2006, at 25a–32). This confirms the religious image of the family as being a supportive and positive unit.

But, we know only too well that the idealistic image of the family has changed in modern times, that the notion of how such a family *ought* to be and function is no longer existing, though there is no precise distinction between what constitutes a 'modern' and 'premodern' family. Some authorities – like *Encyclopaedia Britannica* – consider the modern family to be identical with the Western family since the Industrial Revolution. Others take the notion of modern in a more literal sense, meaning the family as it is today in any part of the world. Certainly, there is no reason to exclude the entire Third World and equate modern only with Western society. In cases where we are confronted with a contradicting picture, it is generally understood that the overall mythical notion of the family must never be put into question. There is no doubt that a well-functioning family is of central importance during adolescence, for the (psychological) development and successful socialization of an individual, as we have learnt from Sigmund Freud's psychoanalytical works of the 1890s–1930s (e.g., *Abriß der Psychoanalyse*, 1939; 'Outline of Psychoanalysis'). It was the general belief (see also Freud) that it was the parents' sole responsibility to enhance the child's formative individual development, whereby the father – as the 'head of the family' – had to ensure that 'societal functioning' were adhered to and took place.

The historical notion of domestic violence dates back to antiquity where civil legislation regarding gender inequality is largely founded on 'legitimate' violence between consenting adults; in short, the male was allowed to exercise dominant chastisement over his female partner (see Leuze-Mohr, 2001: 7ff.). The basis for such legitimate conventions of permitted 'wife beating' was the protection of the 'weaker sex' feeble woman and the semi-scientific justification that women and children were seen as 'inferior' and 'incomplete' beings compared with the male. Möbius (1900) still referred to the "psychological madness of the woman" in his book reprinted in its 12th edition in 1922. The notion that the woman had to be supervised "resulted in administrative law regarding the husband's supervision of the marital (combined) wealth, which maintained the wife's subordination and curtailing of her freedom within marriage up until the 1970s" (Leuze-Mohr, 2005: 144). Legislation and conventions allowing chastisement of the woman and children in the home were relatively recently abolished in Western civilizations from the first quarter of the 20th century onwards.

Because of these accepted laws and conventions, people did not really care or wanted to know what happened behind closed doors. What we understand today as 'domestic violence' never really reached the public domain and was not actually part of public law enforcement. If there were noticeable problems in a family, it was the norm to turn a blind eye. One instinctively knew that the solution to any problems would simply lie within the family, and that the (male) head of the family was responsible for solving any problems or discord. It was best to keep well away. Only in very extreme cases would the police intervene in order to protect the vulnerable (women and children). A 1998 survey by the British Zero Tolerance Charitable Trust found that of 2,039 young people (13–19 years old), one in five young men and one in ten young women thought violence against women was acceptable. Almost one in four young men thought it could be acceptable to hit a woman if she had "slept with someone else"; one in five young men considered it acceptable to force a woman to have sex if she was his wife. A 2000 survey by the same Trust of 1,300 school children found that one in three boys thought violence against women was okay.[1]

Society had accepted the norm that it was okay to simply 'look the other way' when a domestic violence incident ('domestic') came to light. Kürzinger (1978; 1996) found for Southern German authorities that law enforcers would simply send the victim home and 'advise' her not to press any charges against her male partner; she should simply wait and 'give it time' until 'things had calmed down at home'. German criminal justice authorities were generally of the belief that it would be better to stay any criminal proceedings which may have been commenced by the victim. Until the late 1980s it was common practice for the police or state prosecutors of the various Länder (federal states) to persuade the victim to 'think again' or to 'let some time pass', so that she could gain some 'distance' between her reporting the incident to the police and pursuing her criminal claim against her husband. With increased pressure from the wider family, she would be persuaded to reach 'an arrangement' and to arrange herself with her partner, especially when children were involved – so that the criminal court would not be necessary. After all, this was not the place in German society to solve family conflicts.

Kury et al. (2000) undertook an international study comparing victims' reasons for not reporting domestic violence incidents, most commonly that the violence had not been 'that bad' and that even at late stages in criminal proceedings, charges were usually withdrawn or the victim became an unwilling witness at trial. The same is true of domestic violence criminal proceedings in the UK (see Kury et al., 2000: 352). The German research team came to the conclusion that domestic violence was not regarded as an actual social problem. This was founded on traditional normative beliefs where the victim was also seen as a family 'trouble maker' (usually the woman) and that she was often protecting the perpetrator. We have to see this against the background of gender stereotyping and their roles in society back to the original notion of the inherent rights and wrongs and traditional duties of family members.

From the mid-20th century onwards, we see a fundamental change in cultural reform, following the decline of formerly forbidding taboos due to a sexual liberalization originating from the United States and Canada, spreading to Western European societies. From the 1970s onwards, 'domestic violence' became an increasingly popular research topic in the US. Public opinion pollsters now touched on risqué subject matters such as 'family problems' and 'wife beating' which added enormous progress to this field of discussion and research. The French and German students' protest movements of 1968 added to the liberalization of women, making it possible to highlight certain taboos such as domestic violence. With the onset of feminism research in this context began to investigate what was happening 'behind closed doors' (see Straus, Gelles and Steinmetz, 1980). Henceforth, the idealistic notion of the family began to crumble. Increasingly, cases of domestic violence were reported to the police (either by the victims or members of the family) highlighting that weaker family members were more likely to be the victims, such as women and children. A British Home Office Study estimated that between one-third and two-thirds of children in homes where the mother was also being maltreated were at risk of being equally abused (Home Office, 1999). The 'Safe on the Streets Research Team' of the British Children's Society found that 100,000 children run away from home every year in the UK, and that four out of five children who run away from home said that they did so to escape family conflict, violence or domestic abuse (The Children's Society, 1999). The Children's Society sampled children in the northern towns of Bradford and York in 2004–05 in a follow-up study called 'Still Running Part II'.[2] Whilst in 1999, some 10 per cent had run away from home, this increased to 16 per cent in the latest cohort sample. The 2004–05 survey found that girls are more likely to run away from home than boys, and that the peak age of running away is 14–15; disabled children or those with learning disabilities, as well as those describing themselves as gay or lesbian, were more likely to running away. Those living in lone families were twice as likely to run compared with those in 'normal' families, or step families. The last survey also highlighted major issues surrounding the domestic setting (not just domestic violence) also linked to drug and alcohol abuse, as well as problems at school; of the last cohort, some 12 per cent of youngsters described themselves as 'maltreated' at home.

Further research in Britain has found that a disproportionately high percentage of children and young persons, whose mothers are beaten up at home by their male partners, have also experienced at least one violent incident themselves. In a National Children's Home (NCH) study of 104 women, 73 per cent of the mothers said their child had witnessed domestic violence at home. The same study found that 90 per cent of children had been in the same room or next door, and 99 per cent said their children had their mothers crying and upset because of the (father or partner's) violence (see NCH 'Action for Children', 1994). A study on behalf of the National Society for the Protection of Children (NSPCC) that of 111 children half had also been sexually abused and were attending an NSPCC centre for help (Hester and Pearson, 1998).

With growing research focusing on domestic violence research, public interest also increased which in turn demanded changes in law enforcement and legislation to combat domestic violence. In her groundbreaking research into the effects of domestic violence first in the US and then in Great Britain, Betsy (Elizabeth) Stanko revealed the extent and eventual cost to society of domestic violence (1988 and 1990; see also Crisp, Hale, and Stanko, 1998; Stanko, Crisp, Hale, and Lucraft, 1998). Stanko and her research team found that in the London Borough of Hackney, one in four women had experienced domestic violence in her lifetime. Her survey found – looking at a single day in the life of the marriage and relationship counselling service 'Relate' – one in five couples also mentioned issues surrounding domestic violence. Stanko's research team estimated that the London Metropolitan Police receives a call from a victim of domestic violence every minute of the day (Stanko et al., 1998).

More recent research has addressed 'risk factors' resulting from domestic violence incidences. Humphreys et al. (2005) conducted a large evaluative study of the police pilot programmes surrounding risk assessments of domestic violence cases in Cardiff, the London 'Met' and Yorkshire etc. These forces had all implemented extensive risk management strategies by

2002. One question as part of the assessment was: "What is the likelihood of becoming a victim of domestic violence?" The research team flagged up risk factors such as 'culture' (e.g., honour killings), 'alcohol', 'drugs' and 'mental health'. The Cardiff study confirmed what Robinson had already established in 2003: "Partners with drug problems inflicted significantly more violence and injuries on their partners and was therefore considered a heightened risk factor" (Robinson, 2003: vii). Such findings are now backed by extensive literature in the field; they consistently show that the presence of Class A drugs and/or alcohol heightens the severity of violence, including the level of injuries requiring hospitalization (Pernamen, 1991). Another risk factor was 'jealousy': "Analysis of the risk factors revealed that 'perpetrator is jealous or controlling' is a particularly important risk factor" (Robinson, 2004: 3). Obsessive jealousy and controlling behaviours are continuously cited in the literature as points of danger (Campbell, 1988). Similarly, 'threats to kill', either self or others, is also a significant barometer of dangerousness and high risk. Therefore, the dangers of stalking are increased when there are threats to kill oneself or others, as are the problems of isolation, separation, and attack during pregnancy (Davies et al., 1998).

Humphreys et al. (2005) established that the most controversial risk factor was 'culture'; when asked to comment, this factor had raised strong feelings and heated comments amongst several of the key informants on interview. One of the key informants with an Asian background was unequivocal that given the history of 'crimes of dishonour' (or 'honour killings'), and the known consequences for many Asian women if they were to call the police for help, would have shameful consequences, which is indicative of a heightened risk factor (see also Smartt, 2006). Generally, it was found that Asian women would call out the police in domestic violence circumstances, unless they were absolutely terrified. Their added vulnerability to isolation due to issues such as immigration status or language difficulties further compounded the risks (see below the Ahluwalia case). With a number of risk assessment programmes now in place, many police officers when questioned by Humphreys' research team (London Metropolitan and Warwick Universities, 2005) commented that the attention to risk gave a more formal framework through which they justified their decisions and actions. The research team noted that the risk assessment actually helps police officers to prioritize cases. On one hand, a number of police officers said quite categorically that the risk assessment questionnaires helped flag up high-risk cases and bring them to the fore. An equal number of interviewed officers were concerned about the opposite effect, of being prejudiced in advance hence excluding those who might be most at risk. When resourcing the force with specialist domestic violence teams, clearly, the number of 'high-risk' cases would require a high level response compared with other 'normal' incidents.

The extent and nature of domestic violence in the UK is now a substantial part of the British Crime Survey (BCS), conducted every couple of years in England and Wales via an anonymous survey of about 6,000 victims of crime. In 2000, domestic violence incidents made up nearly a quarter of all violent crime (499,000 cases of domestic violence incidences – see, 'Crime in England and Wales', Home Office, 2002). After a substantially large evaluation of face-to-face interviews and anonymous questionnaires, Mirrlees-Black found that among women, the average number of domestic abuse incidents was 20 times; with men it was seven times in 2000 (Home Office, 2002; HOSB, 18/01). Simmons et al. found that there were an estimated total number of abuse incidents against women of 12.9 million and against men 2.5 million (Home Office Research Study of 2001–02, HOSB 7/02). In 2001, the BCS representative sample of 22,463 women and men (aged 16–59) reported that over the previous period of 12 months, some 13 per cent of women and 9 per cent of men had been subject to domestic violence of one kind or other (abuse, threats or force; sexual victimization or stalking). Among the women, the average number of abuse incidents was 20 times, with men it was seven times. Approximately, 8 per cent of women and 6 per cent of men were subject to stalking in 2000 (1.2 million women and 900,000 men). The BCS 2001 further estimated that one in five women (21%) and one in ten men (10%) experienced at least one incident of non-sexual domestic violence or force since the age of 16. 24 per cent of women and 5 per cent of men had experienced some form of sexual victimization since the age of 16 (Home Office, 2004; HORS Study 276).

Taylor-Browne led the Home Office research 'Crime Reduction Programme' on the 'Violence against Women Initiative' since 1999. Her book (2001) offers a comprehensive summary on Home Office Research Studies (HORS) and evaluations on women survivors' views on domestic violence services (original study by A. Mullender and G. Hague), meeting the needs of children who live with domestic violence (by A. Mullender), the role of the health services (by L.L. Davidson, V. King, J. Garcia and S. Marchant) and monitoring costs and evaluating needs (by D. Crisp and E. Stanko). The majority of domestic violence incidents reported to the London Metropolitan Police Service (MPS) in 2000 were by female victims and their male perpetrators. Metropolitan Police figures for January to March 2001 showed that 128 of 180 victims of domestic violence in that period were unwilling to pursue the allegation. Today, the London 'Met' recognizes the fact that domestic violence occurs within same sex relationships and with male victims and female perpetrators. The MPS 'Domestic Violence Strategy' therefore seeks to identify and address the needs of all victims.

Women still make up the overwhelming majority of victims of domestic violence abuse. The BCS 2001 established that domestic violence was linked to poverty: women were at greater risk of interpersonal domestic violence than men if their annual household income was less than £10,000 per year (approx. 14,750 Euro) and that they were three and a half times more likely to suffer abuse than those with an income over £20,000 (approx. 30,000 Euro) (Home Office HORS Study 276). We must note though that approximately one in six men will also experience some form of domestic violence at least once in their lifetime (Home Office Research Study 191, 1999).

## The importance of dark figure research

### *Public opinion polls as a source of hidden criminality*

From the British Crime Survey it has become evident that victim or 'dark figure' research is vitally important to establish the true figure of crimes related to domestic violence in order to bring this to the attention of the public. From the middle to the end of the last century, there is an increase in public opinion poll research investigating the victimization and criminalization of domestic violence. Dark figure (victim) research has therefore grown in importance and public credence. Oba (1908) coined the term 'dark figure' research, and criminologists Meyer (1941) and Wehner (1957) reached initial estimated assumptions as to the possible extent of dark figure research results as vitally important in social research. Following Allport's encouraging public opinion polls "Why not ask them?" (1941, 37) we learnt more about the social variables, which would now include people's feelings and motives, beliefs and recollections. Such variables were then used as methods of inquiry in relation to criminality and domestic violence. Attitudinal research included "attitude and outlook regarding the dark (or hidden) figure would only encourage the thinking that there weren't really many other alternatives in this field" (Amelang, 1986: 142). It was assumed that the dark figure of domestic violence was probably rather high, similar to crimes of a sexual nature which were habitually under-reported. Porterfield (1943; 1949) undertook one of the first 'self-report' studies amongst college students on their own criminality (see also Amelang, 1986 101). At the same time, it is worth noting that there were male and female self-report studies, relating to their sexual behaviours. Kinsey's work is possibly the most famous in this field.

The Kinsey studies are now renowned. He used in-depth, face-to-face interviews by highly trained interviewers who established a history of covered social and economic data (e.g., physical and physiologic, marital, sexual outlets, heterosexuality etc.). Each subject was questioned on up to 521 items, depending on his specific experience (the average in each case being near 300) (see Kinsey et al., 1948). What Kinsey was most famous for is his accumulative study on "facts about sex," so that readers of his reports could make interpretations that fit with their understanding of "moral values and social significances" (p. 5, *Male*). He looked at quantifiable male sexual 'outlets' and at what factors might account for variations in sexual behaviour, including marital status, age, educational level, occupational class, rural-urban background, religious group, geographic origin, and age at adolescence. He then compiled equivalent data for the female (1953). Data was gathered from 1938 to 1963, when the project was closed. Kinsey and his fellow researchers became famous over night with their studies – though they were not without criticism regarding their research methodologies. It was particularly the Kinsey research into female sexuality which was controversial because he had touched on a taboo which had simply destroyed the common beliefs (by men) regarding the normative behaviour expected of women. Kinsey found, for instance, that 24 per cent of the females sample had had a sexual 'experience' (not necessarily intercourse) with older men prior to puberty; two-thirds were named as 'verbal propositions' or cited as 'exhibitionism' (Kinsey et al., 1953: 117ff.). Three per cent of women said they had been raped. There is no doubt that Kinsey's reports made an enormous contribution to the subject of sexuality – later linked to sexual offences, particularly in the family setting. Kinsey highlighted the complexities of a modern family, domestic violence and sexual abuse.

After Kinsey came a deluge of similar research studies emanating from the Institute for Sex Research at Indiana University, and followed by extensive publications on topics such as 'sexual deviance' and 'perversions' (for the German coverage, see Gebhard et al., 1965; Reinhardt 1957; Oliver 1967; see also Masters, 1969; Stoller, 1975; Masters and Johnson 1988). Like Kinsey's book, other similar 'sexuality' texts were translated into German and devoured by the 1960s generation of parents. There is no doubt that 'The Hite Report' was such a hit in 1976 by sex-psychologist Shere Hite (short for Shirley). The Hite Report became popular in more than 45 countries including China where it was published in full in 2006. At the same time, the increasingly progressive Chinese government produced a sex education booklet for schools, using drawings of anatomy from the Hite Report. The German equivalent was the RALF Report by Eichner und Habermehl (1978), a testament of the 'sexual behaviour of the Germans'.

This was followed by research into sexual crimes and crime prevention (see Shultz, 1965), funded by the President's Commission on Law Enforcement and Administration of Justice. After some initial pilot projects testing the viability methods of opinion poll research, two localized studies were conducted in Washington DC (see Biderman et al., 1967), Boston and Chicago

(Reiss, 1967), followed by a national study by Ennis (1967); this latter had a representative sample of 9,644 adult male US-Americans who were asked about their own victimization, or that of family members during the past year. They were also asked whether they had reported the incident to the police; and if not – why not. Gelles (1998: 178) concluded: "Over the last three decades, family and intimate violence have been transformed from an issue obscured by selective inattention to a problem that receives increasing professional, public, and policy attention". Alongside victimization 'dark figure' research in general, we can see the development regarding domestic violence and sexual abuse research (see Hentig, 1954; Mendelsohn, 1956; see also Kury, 1994; Kury et al., 2002). Sparks (1981: 4) noted that with this new form of victim inquiry also came problems in using certain methods in criminological research.

Noteworthy with all these dark figure studies was that they only measured selected crimes and not the total number of all possible crimes, which, in turn, led to the some misunderstood or misquoted conclusions of the possible dark figure of certain crimes (see a critique on this subject by Kürzinger, 1996; Kury, 2001). Social scientists now know that the size of the dark figure of victims of crime largely depends on the type of crime and offence. Some crimes (e.g., property crimes) are more reported to the police than, say, sexual offences (such as rape). Criminological research studies in victimology soon discovered that "the closer the personal relationship between offender and victim, the less likely the probability that there would be any available statistics regarding victimization in the official crime statistics, the dark figure research or mass media information (see Schneider, 2001: 12). Schneider (1987: 211) found from his domestic violence research that "more than double the offences committed are being reported to the police ... the dark figure varies from one offence to another and from one country or state to another; reporting behaviour changes its structure and nature over time (i.e., in line with changing public attitudes to report – willingness, the type of criminal offence and the seriousness of the offence). Official recorded crime statistics usually show traditional offences, i.e., the most serious crimes and the most commonly committed." Schneider found that dark figure is particularly high in crimes related to drugs, white-collar (economic) offences, violent and sexual crimes in the family (against women and children including paedophilia; rape within marriage and incest) and vandalism.

The first most reliable and therefore representative studies regarding the extent of domestic violence were found in the US studies (Straus et al., 1980; Straus, 1990; Straus and Gelles, 1990). Their research demonstrated that there was not only considerable domestic violence amongst partners but also against the children in that violent relationship; some of the highest scores of domestic violence were found amongst siblings. From the above research and publication of the 1980s onwards, there has been a notable decline in domestic violence against children; some of the most serious violations against children dropped by about 47 per cent, and the most serious abuses against women fell by 27 per cent. "The decline in domestic violence dating back to the first dark figure victimization studies in 1976 can be attributed to the fact that the publications of such results in the mass media sent such shock waves through the North American public opinion that the North American society actually grasped the problem and began to work on its first social rehabilitation of this problem area. In 1976, only ten per cent of North Americans saw violence against children as an acute problem. The problem consciousness changed after the much-publicized dark figure research results in the US mass media. In 1982, some 90 per cent of North Americans saw violence against children as a serious problem" (Schneider, 2001: 206; see also Straus and Gelles, 1990b). Straus also commented that women were treated differently in the home as a result of published research between 1968 and 1994 (Straus et al., 1997). Schneider (2001: 400) concludes: "According to modern international criminological research, sexual offences remain largely underreported coupled with badly controlled law infringements and enforcements. This is equally true for Germany."

We now know from international dark figure research that most sexual abuse occurs in the family setting or is committed by perpetrators who move in the same familial proximity as the victim. Only in very rare cases does total stranger abuse occur.

### Dark figure research into sexual abuse and domestic violence

One logical consequence of developmental research into domestic violence was the measuring of 'social' as opposed to the 'criminally' deviant sexual behaviour of perpetrators towards their victims. Until the 1960s, it was commonly believed that sexual offences centred purely on the rape of a female and on the sexual abuse and misuse of children (paedophilia). Much of this research in this field is sourced from the United States and Britain (see Stanko et al., 1970), only to be reflected later in European literature (Finkelhor, 1997: 72). It is thanks to feminist research and the human rights movement from the 1960s onwards that the sexual victimization of women and children came to the fore; not only in terms of stranger rape, but more in respect of close proximity and familial rape within the domestic social environment (see Stanko et al. 1970 see also Brownmiller, 1975; Sepler, 1990: 73). Research soon established that the majority of sexual offenders came from the social and familial proximity of the victim.

Some research findings have been disputed, especially ways in which domestic violence and abuse in the family are measures. Kelly (2003; 2005) found that the feminist movement may have had a negative side-effect on US legislation at the time, specifically where the criminal process was concerned. Legislation and the legal definition of 'rape' changed from 'sexual' to a 'violent' offence in the USA. In England, the notion of 'mistaken belief' still rests on a common law defence,[3] though the Sexual Offences Act 2003 has made this slightly more difficult for the defendant. Furthermore, there is a new focus on 'violence against women' such as under section 2 of the Sexual Offences Act, 2003 'assault by penetration'.[4] As Hillenkamp states for Germany: "With the onset of the feminist movement, we can detect a certain virulent desire whereby rape is only seen in the through the eyes of the victim" (1988: 89). In 1933, Sauer still defined 'rape' in his sociological criminological study "Kriminalsoziologie" as a "healthy expression of human life" and "as an illumination for a healthy future" ('Criminal Sociology', 1933: 614). He further argued that rape victimization is minimal and that such sexual act often produces the healthiest and strongest children. It would be inconceivable to make such a statement in today's society (Kaiser, 1996: 770). We therefore notice a change in focus regarding sexual offences, and increased research in this field. There now exists a differentiation between women and children as victims of ex-crimes. But, the outcome is still more or less the same: men are still seen as the main perpetrator and commit the majority of all sexual offences (police recorded crime statistics). Only very recently has limited research focused on sexual abuse amongst homosexual males (such as male-on male rape) (see Kury and Smartt, 2002: 417ff.).

From the 1970s onwards, research into sexual abuse increased, particularly with regard to domestic violence, including some interesting results from Germany from the 1980s onwards (Sepler, 1990: 75). From the early 1970s onwards, Villmow (1977: 114) established in his research that male tolerance levels of those surveyed was as low as with child abuse (including paedophilia). The upshot of this was an increasing demand for the changes in victim-oriented criminal justice and victim research which in turn influenced criminal justice policy (e.g., 'Weißer Ring' – German Foundation for Victims of Crime since 1996 – is now the largest private victim organization for German-speaking countries: www.weisser-ring.de/bundesgeschaeftsstelle/index.php; see also 'Victim Support' UK – Victim Support is the largest UK independent charity which helps people cope with the effects of crime: www.victimsupport.org). Central to all such organizations to alert the public to the concept of victimology, but also to take care of witnesses in the criminal courts (the Witness Service). The "Weißer Ring" Foundation was, for instance, instrumental in bringing about legislative changes regarding the relatively new offence of 'stalking' (see also Smartt, 2001–02).

There have been some rather spectacular sex crimes; though fairly unique, they have intensified the media focus on such crimes, particularly, regarding child abuse (paedophilia) (see Rüther, 1998). Jesionek points out that dark figure research focusing on domestic violence is virtually omnipresent in the current literature: "You could get the impression that violence within the family was only marginal in the past, and that there was a sudden increase in domestic violence and misuse which came about with criminological research" (1998: 897). Obviously, there are no more domestic violence incidences today compared with in the past; it is just that research and publications have increased, and therefore, the topic is very much in the public domain. One could even say that the media has overexposed the problem. 'Sex and Crime' has virtually become a bestseller for lust-hungry recipients (see also Beckett and Sasson, 2004).

### *Underreporting of domestic violence and sexual abuse*

The high dark figure of domestic violence and sexual crimes are largely attributable to the underreporting of these types of offences. Leuze-Mohr stresses that the reporting of domestic violence incidences is significantly lower than with other (e.g., property) offences; in 90 per cent of all domestic violence and sexual abuse cases women do not report the incident or the perpetrator to the police (2005: 159ff.). More than 80 per cent of abused women will not (continue) to press charges against their perpetrator; reasons for this are varied (Leuze-Mohr, 2001: 257; see also Kury, 2001). We therefore cannot grasp the true extent of domestic violence; hence, how can society possibly expect law-enforcement agencies to act and react positively and preventatively? The low or underreporting of such offences further highlights the complexity of criminality in the domestic social setting. One of the reasons for under- or non-reporting domestic violence incidents is that the victim merely wants the perpetrator to stop using violence in the home; victims often do not really seek true intervention by state authorities. Only when there is sufficiently differentiated information and knowledge about domestic violence can effective preventive measures be developed and applied; though this has already been successfully achieved by some British police forces (see above). The underreporting of such incidences is closely linked to the victim's close social proximity to the perpetrator (Kilchling, 1995; Kury et al., 1992: 133ff.).

As Leuze-Mohr (2002: 255ff.) demonstrated in an empirical study of abused women, the willingness to report domestic violence was markedly lower compared with victims of ordinary 'stranger' violence outside. She questioned female victims of domestic violence, employees in safe houses, members of the police and the criminal justice system. About 41 per cent of victims only called the police in very acutely violent situations. Every second woman pressed charges in serious cases with the police, yet three out of ten women later withdrew the charges against the perpetrator. More than two-thirds of the women would never press charges again in future in similar situations. A total of 45 per cent of the questioned women stated that they had already pressed charges against their partner one or several times. Similarly, 55 per cent of the women who had experienced serious violence had not gone to the police at all. It therefore does not seem to matter when pressing charges, whether the offence is serious or not. If and when the women report the incident to the police their main hope rests on the fact that the violence should stop, and that the offender may eventually see sense. It is then the hope and belief that the woman will be protected in the future which is her main reason for going to the police.

It is not surprising that the percentage of women who eventually withdraw the charge/s against their perpetrator is extremely high; moreover, the victims will not press charges in the future even if the violence continues. More than 80 per cent of (female) victims will not go through with the eventual criminal procedure, and will withdraw the charges, so that the prosecution will collapse against the perpetrator. Leuze-Mohr (2005: 162ff.) cites the following as the main reasons:

- Historically rooted domestic violence lies in the inequality between men and women, and their continued power struggle. It is believed (rightly or wrongly) that the male perpetrator will 'get off' during criminal proceedings. (Female) victims genuinely believe that the law is not on their side, and that the court will believe the man's side of the story; furthermore, that she will be stigmatized during the criminal process (see Kury et al., 2002; Kury and Yoshida, 2004). Victims are also afraid that their 'case' will become public as it progresses through the criminal justice system. There is always the fear that she may be told that she contributed to the 'domestic' violence.

- The (un)willingness to go to the police is considerably influenced by the proximity of victim and offender; if their relationship is 'close', it is highly likely that the victim will not report the incident. The victim tends then to be indecisive as to whether to call the police or not; mostly she just accepts the assault silently or decides to leave her partner, in order to protect the children and/or the home. Generally, female victims tend to keep domestic violence a secret – especially from children. "It is important when we talk about reducing the taboo and scandal surrounding domestic violence that victims have to be given the assurance that they can be trusted when reporting their degrading- and mal-treatment and that their feelings will be safeguarded" (Leuze-Mohr, 2005: 164).
- One of the most important factors (in non-/under reporting) are the victim's own experiences with the police and the criminal justice system in general. More than three-quarters of women reported bad experiences with the police; similarly, with the courts. Perhaps, it has been the experience that the system is pro-offender in domestic violence cases? It is therefore of utmost importance that the police gathers experience from victims of domestic violence so that they can be more effective in future when it comes to risk assessment. Very often, the victim just does not receive information as to the (future) criminal procedure in their case. Women often feel that they are just being categorized as yet another 'case' by law enforcement agencies. That they are just being stored as a crime reference number. The victims then remain alone in the system, devoid of any humane care.

## Domestic violence: Results from German, British and other international studies

In 2004, a significant study into 'Life-situations, Safety and the Health of Women in Germany' took place, which was the first study in the field of women and domestic violence in united federal Germany (Müller and Schröttle, 2004; 2004a). The research was commissioned and funded by the

'Bundesministerium für Familie, Senioren, Frauen und Jugend', the Federal Ministry for Family, Senior Citizens, Women and Young People in Germany and was conducted in both East and West German states, by the interdisciplinary Centre for Women's Studies at the University of Bielefeld. The central aim of the study was to obtain quantitative data regarding the "extent, causes and types of violence against women in the domestic setting in Germany, compatible with other pan-European studies of this kind" (Müller and Schröttle, 2004: 2). The research study was also the basis for the 1999 'White Paper' on tackling domestic violence (Bundesministerium für Familie, Senioren, Frauen und Jugend, 1999; 2003; 2004).

As part of the Bielefeld study, different types and the extent of domestic violence were measured, i.e., within families and partnerships, as well as the extended environment of the family (i.e., school, work, neighbourhood, and friends' circles). Not only physical and sexual abuse was measured, but also psychological and sexual violations (including stalking). Most of those questioned were over the age of 16, with a small sample of under 16s. Smartt (2001–02: 210) found that 'stalking' was a relatively new phenomenon at the time with the term 'stalking' not actually existent in the German language at the start of the new millennium. Since her research, the term has been transposed in its untranslated from into the German language, and now subsists as part of the 'Gewaltschutzgezetz' – the German Protection from Violence Act, 2000. Following the introduction of the English Protection from Harassment Act 1997, the Home Office included 'stalking' as a new socio-legal term in the British Crime Survey from 1998 onwards; though there is to date no legal definition in English common law (Smartt, 2001–02: 228). Similarly, in the German Criminal Code (*Strafgesetzbuch*), 'stalking' is not defined or codified in law, and remains a federal state matter for the police and law enforcement agencies (so-called 'Ländersache').

The German domestic violence study is divided into a number of sections. One major section deals with the opinion poll sweep from February to October 2003; the representative sample of 10,264 women in Germany was questioned as to their own experience of victimizations, also domestic violence, their feelings of safety in the home, their psycho-social and general health in the domestic setting. The 60–90 minute face-to-face interviews were conducted by means of standard questionnaire on domestic violence and the women's relationships to their partners (married/unmarried/cohabitees). Women were strong anonymity assurance to enhance the 'honesty' response factor. Additional smaller polls were conducted with Turkish and Eastern European women, immigrants to Germany (250 interviews conducted with interpreters). Another small sample concerned interviews with prostitutes, asylum seekers, and women in prison. Additionally, some qualitative focus groups interviews with women who had directly experienced some form of domestic violence and had sought help and support from public authorities. The response rate was 52 per cent, which was seen as very positive, considering the sensitive nature of these opinion polls.

Some of the German research findings included 13 per cent of the women who had been sexually abused at least once since the age of 16; and 40 per cent who had been physically or sexually violated. From the oral (not the written) questionnaire results, this prevalence was reduced to 12 and 35 per cent respectively. About 58 per cent in total had been abused in one form or other. In respect of violence amongst co-habitees, 7 per cent of women gave oral evidence that they had been subjected to sexual abuse; 25 per cent had been both physically and/or sexually abused (oral evidence: 5% and 17% respectively; written evidence was 5% and 23%) Müller and Schröttle, 2004: 10). This revealed a rather high victimization rate of married women in the domestic (home) setting as well as amongst co-habitees. Again, the German results showed (similar to the British Crime Survey) that the dark figure is considerably higher than the officially recorded (police) statistics. We must note the differences in the recorded and victim survey, with regards to differences methodological research approaches.

The German (Bielefeld) study on domestic violence against women was then compared and contrasted with international research results, such as a Dutch study (Römkens, 1997), another in Switzerland, Portugal and Finland (Heiskanen u. Piispa, 1998), and others in Denmark, Sweden, Iceland, Spain, Ireland,

England, Scotland and Wales (Home Office – Mirrlees-Black, 1999; see also Müller and Schröttle, 2004: 2). Then, there are extensive results from the well-publicized Canadian ('Violence Against Women Survey' – Statistics Canada, 1993), US surveys ('National Violence against Women Survey' – published in Tjaden and Thoennes, 1998), and Australia ('Women's Safety Survey', McLennan, 1996). There is now the extensive EU Action Research data bank on domestic violence research at the Northern German University of Osnabrück that continues to coliate international and EU research studies and evaluations on domestic violence against women and children ('Coordination Action on Human Rights Violations' – CAHRV).

Some of the German findings compared with international empirical results showed that the frequency of sexual-related violence occurs between 5 and 34 per cent, depending on the type and definition of research methodology. The same can be said of the Stanko et al.'s US-research compared with that of the British Crime Survey (BCS); Stanko was later criticized by a few British social scientists for her dramatic findings that "one in four women will experience domestic violence during their lifetime" (Stanko et al., 1998), but only slightly modified by the BCS 2001 which stated that one-third of victims of *any* violence are victimized twice or more within a year. Nearly three-fifths (57%) of those, who had been a victim of domestic violence, were then a victim of domestic violence again (not necessarily by the same perpetrator). In contrast to domestic violence, one in every five victims of stranger violence in England and Wales in 2000–01 was victimized on more than one occasion within a year. The BCS showed that 57 per cent of victims of domestic violence were involved in more than one incident. No other type of crime has a rate of repeat victimization as high (Crime in England and Wales, Home Office, 2002).

With regards to sexual violence amongst couples, the German study showed results of 7 per cent of physical and 25 per cent of physical and/or sexual violence, compared with other countries, where the results vary from 1 per cent to 19 per cent (sexual violence) and 10 to 35 per cent (physical and/or sexual violence) (see Table 1; Bundesministerium für Familie, Senioren, Frauen und Jugend, 2004; 2004a; 40; Müller and Schröttle, 2004:

12). The results from the domestic violence poll of German women by Müller und Schröttle (2004: 41) revealed that 52 per cent of the women cited rape, 41 per cent attempted rape, 51 per cent forced indecent assault, 29 per cent forced or coerced other sexual practices and 10 per cent unwilling coercion to practice pornographic encounters (multiple answers). Similarly, 9 per cent of the questioned women stated that they experienced various forms of sexual abuse and misuse before the age of 16 and 45 per cent in the domestic setting. This shows a tendency regarding those women who experienced sexual abuse in the family before the age of 16, and the prevalence linked to adult abuse. Of those 41 per cent of women who experienced sexual abuse before their 16th birthday, the majority also experienced sexual domestic abuse in adulthood, compared with 10 per cent of women who had no such abuse experiences prior to their 16th birthday. Müller and Schröttle established the likely link between the likelihood of adult domestic violent and sexual abuse and being abused as an adolescent or even as a child (2004: 48f.). The perpetrators were in 49 per cent of the victimized women usually the husband, partner or lover, in 22 per cent mere acquaintances, in 20 per cent friends, acquaintances or neighbours, in 15 per cent strangers, in 12 per cent work or school colleagues, and in 10 per cent members of the victim's own family (Müller and Schröttle, 2004: 50). About 69 per cent of victimizations took place at the victim's own home, 30 per cent at another home, 20 per cent in public, and 17 per cent in a car. Then, 34 per cent of the female victims reported that the perpetrator had been under the influence of alcohol, 1.3 per cent under the influence of drugs and 3.4 per cent both. Nine per cent of the women stated that they too had been under the influence of alcohol, 1.8 per cent under drugs and/or alcohol influence. Further, 58 per cent of the women reported being sexually abused. Worth mentioning is the comparison between East and West Germany: 20 per cent of the West German women and 16 per cent of the East Germans reported being a victim of sexual domestic violence over a period of twelve months.

Worth noting is that at least 48 per cent of female victims stated that they were initially partly to blame for the ensuing violent or sexual abuse; 58 per cent, however, believed that the sole responsibility lay with the perpetrator. Regarding their former partners, the victims attributed 35 per cent to their own part-responsibility, and 68 per cent stated that it was solely the partner's fault (Müller and Schröttle, 2004: 130).

**Table 1** Occurrence (prevalence) of sexual abuse in a number of European countries

| *Country* | *Occurrence of violence not dependent on victim-offender – context* | | | *Violence in partnership relationships* | | |
|---|---|---|---|---|---|---|
| | *Physical violence* | *Sexual violence* | *Physical and/or sexual violence* | *Physical violence* | *Sexual violence* | *Physical and/or sexual violence* |
| Germany, 2004 | 37% | 13% | 40% | 23% | 7% | 25% |
| The Netherlands, 1986 | | | | 26% | 7% | |
| Iceland, 1996 | 25% | 5% | | | | 14% |
| Portugal, 1995 | 14% | 25% | | 14–18% | ca. 1% | ca. 18% |
| British Crime Survey, 1996 | | | | 23–26% | 2% | |
| British Crime Survey, 2004 | | | | 21% | | |
| Finland, 1997 | 30% | 17% (4% rape) | 40% | 20% (current partner) 45% (former partner) | 6% (current partner) 19% (former partner) | 32% |
| Switzerland, 1997 | | 29% | | 13% | 12% | 21% |
| Ireland, 1996 | | | | | 4% | 10% |
| Belgium, 1998 | | | | | 17% | |
| France, 2003 | 17% | 5% from age 18 | | | | |
| Sweden, 2001 | 25% | 5% (coercion) 34% (wider definition) | 46% | 7% (current partner) 28% (former partner) | 3% (current partner) 16% (former partner) | 11% (current partner) 35% (former partner) |
| Denmark, 1991 | 19% | | | | | 13–14% |

Only 7 per cent of sexually abused women interviewed in Germany contacted the police; in 4 per cent of the cases, it was the woman's friend or relative who reported the incident to the public authorities. Reasons for non-reporting were: "the abuse wasn't that bad" (42%); "I wanted to be left in peace" (35%); "the incident was too intimate to report" (33%); "I feel ashamed" (25%) and 14 per cent of the victims felt that "the police isn't going to do anything anyway" (Müller and Schröttle, 2004: 153). Once the incident had been reported, in 11.1 per cent of the cases, the police responded; in 6.6 per cent the perpetrator was charged, of which 5.1 per cent went ahead with the prosecution; 4.2 per cent went to trial, and 2.2 per cent were found guilty. In total, 52 per cent went through the full criminal procedure (from first arrest and charge to trial) (Müller and Schröttle, 2004: 159).

We therefore note that public satisfaction regarding police responses to domestic violence cases has increased; police clear-up rates are reported to be higher, possibly attributable to increased training and information available in form of government legislation and resources, and has led to a better treatment and understanding of victims (Müller and Schröttle, 2004: 139). A recent study in the Southern German town of Freiburg revealed that public opinion regarding police and local authority dealings with victims of domestic violence is generally positive (Abbatepaolo and Sattmann, 2006). It can be noted that Western European courts are dealing with victims of sexual and violent domestic violence in a much better and improved way, due to new and improved relevant legislation and criminal procedure involving extensive victim support in the criminal courts.

In England and Wales, victims of a domestic violence now have special status in the criminal courts. Courts (including Magistrates' Courts) endeavour to provide safe entrances within their buildings, facilitating escorts via a separate entrance. Each courthouse now has a safe waiting facility for victims of domestic violence and the victim has the choice to give evidence from behind a screens or on video link (this is particularly practised with children and vulnerable witnesses). The latter practice is known as 'Special Measures'). However, the prevalence of domestic violence not wanting to give evidence in court is high;

and an unwilling witness (victim) who has to be witness summoned to court, will usually result in the acquittal of the offender. The Crown Prosecution Service for England and Wales (CPS) now appoints a dedicated 'Domestic Violence Lawyer' to oversee the day-to-day running of all case files within the service area (e.g., Gwent, Wales) and provides information and training to other organizations (e.g., Victim Support). Special consideration is given to the following (CPS Code of Practice, 2005): whether a face-to-face meeting with the victim is necessary; whether victim support is needed (e.g., a special advocate); if there is sufficient evidence to proceed *without* a victim; whether the procedure in section 23 of the Criminal Justice Act 1988 (as amended by the Criminal Justice Act 2003) is appropriate to make an application to read the witness' statement in her absence; whether a witness summons is appropriate and the consequences of failure to comply with a summons; in certain circumstances, after careful consideration, applying for a witness warrant.

In England and Wales, the courts also give a child who has been abused by a parent or family member (e.g., sibling) special measures protection. In *R v D* (sexual offences prevention order) 2006, it was necessary to make a sexual offences prevention order (SOPO) to protect the defendant's children from the (male) perpetrator who had sexually abused his daughter. But, the SOPO also included his son, to protect him from serious psychological harm likely to be caused by such further offending. The Court of Appeal in this case advised that where an SOPO is made, following sexual abuse within the family, it may be appropriate to order "the defendant to have no contact with [children's names] without an order of the court made under the Children Act 1989". An SOPO cannot be discharged within five years, unless the Chief Constable of a police force consents, but with that wording, a contact application could be made to the family proceedings in the Family [Magistrates'] Court if the situation changes. The court must conduct a risk assessment: is the defendant likely to commit another sexual offence? If so, is that likely to cause serious physical or psychological harm to someone? That could be the victim or, as in *R v D*, someone else likely to be affected by it. In cases where domestic violence is alleged, bail conditions of "no contact except to arrange contact with the children" (Children Act, 1989) are sometimes used to put pressure on the complainant.

The following time guidelines for directing the preparation of cases for trial are usually adopted (see Table 2):

**Table 2** Progression of domestic violence cases by the Crown Prosecution Service: the Gwent Domestic Violence Project, 2006

| *Process* | *Time* |
|---|---|
| Full file from police to the CPS | 21 days |
| Witness warned by witness support unit in liaison with DVU | within 7 days of pre-trial review (PTR) |
| CPS to review the file and serve primary disclosure and unused material | By 1st PTR |
| Pre-trial review hearing (defendant will not be excused attendance unless the court informs otherwise) | 4 weeks prior to trial date |

*Source:* http://www.cps.gov.uk/publications/agencies/dv/gwent_protocol.html#04

A British study into special domestic violence courts in the Midlands region examined the prevalence of criminal prosecutions' (CPS) retractions in domestic violence cases. Angela Morgan and her team (2005) from the Policy Research Institute at the University of Wolverhampton found that there were no significant changes in the rate of retraction at these specialist courts, mainly due to fear of the perpetrator and his family. "In Wolverhampton we do try and communicate in different languages and tell people what help is out there for them ...but I think that fear will always be there ... this study is focused on the Asian community and this is where most retractions take place – we need more dedicated work on this".

One Asian victim stated: "I can't see how anything can remove [my] fear...no measures can eradicate the fear completely."

German studies revealed the importance of such victim research, and the *how* victims are being questioned and interviewed. Face-to-face interviews with guided questionnaires assuring the victims of their anonymity were of utmost importance. Results from the 'orally interviewed' Bielefeld study revealed that 17 per cent experienced sexual *and* physical violence from current partners. A total number of 9,549 (i.e., 93%) of the sampled women completed the written questionnaire on domestic violence in their partnership setting. Of those who had lived in a domestic partnership, 25 per cent stated that they had been victims of physical or sexual violence by current or former partners. 39 per cent of women, who had experienced violence from a former partner, also stated that they were also experiencing abuse from a current partner; additionally, some 72 per cent had experienced both, abuse from the current and the former partner; and 11 per cent had experienced present and past partner abuse (Müller and Schröttle, 2004: 166). Of the present sample, 6 per cent reported domestic violence from the current partner at least once. The researchers itemized types of violence, including "pushing me hard"; "light slap around the head"; "twisting my arm so that it hurt"; "beating me up … to the point of unconsciousness"; "strangling me"; "burning me with hot liquid"; and "using a weapon". In all, 20.8 per cent sought medical help, 13.1 per cent reported the incident to the police and 8 per cent actually pressed charges. Of those women who reported the above recent violent abuses, some 10 per cent were also victims of sexual assault: "This shows that women who are victims of physical assault are also controlled by their partners by way of sexual violence." (Müller and Schröttle, 2004: 186)

Results from written questionnaires showed that 22–23 per cent had been sexually and physically abused (Müller and Schröttle, 2004: 164). The highest 'honesty' rate resulted from those victims who were interviewed both orally and in writing as 24 per cent of women stated that they had been victims of domestic violence. "Our research shows that every fourth woman living in Germany has been subject to domestic physical or sexual violence at least once in her life by her partner. We had assumed that it would be every fifth or seventh woman in Germany" (see also Müller and Schröttle, 2004: 164; Schröttle, 1999). This correlates with Stanko's research (1990, 1998).

Of those female victims surveyed who experienced domestic violence in their own family background (e.g., parental verbal or physical abuse) also experienced physical, mental or sexual abuse from their current (or former) partners, compared with those who came from a 'safe' family background (47% versus 21%). "Those women who experienced abuse from their own parents or guardians, were three times more likely to be victims of domestic violence in their present relationship, compared with women who did not experience any violence in their upbringing (13% versus 38%). Women, who had experienced sexual abuse before their 16th birthday, were twice as likely to being abused by their current/former partner (23% versus 54%)" (Müller and Schröttle, 2004: 204). Of the children who lived in a violent domestic setting, 57 per cent were victimized as well, by hearing parental violence, and in half (50%) of the cases, the children actually witnessed violence or abuse. Of the surveyed female victims, 21–25 per cent reported that their children had also been involved in domestic violence which makes the problem even more acute.

## The expense of domestic violence: Not only women are the victims

### *What are the costs?*

Actual costs (financial and otherwise) of domestic violence are immense. Heiskanen and Piispa (2002) conducted a study in Finland, whereby they measured the social cost of domestic violence for the state (estimated at about 91,000,000 Euro per annum). An earlier study resulted in just 48,000,000 Euro. About one-fifth of the costs amounts to health and medical care, about half in social services care, and more than a quarter in criminal procedures (see Piispa u. Heiskanen, 2000). In England, a costing study was undertaken by Walby (2004) for the UK Women's Equality Unit. She estimated annual costs resulting from domestic violence of around 23 billion Pound Sterling in 2001 (about 34 billion Euro). About £ 1 billion is spent on criminal investigations and law enforcement, £ 1.3 billion on healthcare, £ 0.2 billion on social services and £ 17 billion on human and emotional damage. These costs are attributed to the state; but there are also hidden costs, involving individual victims, such as costs to employers by way of employee's absences from work and a higher staff sickness absence rate. Though these are rough 'guesstimates' as to the nature and extent of human and social costs involved in and directly attributable to the effects of domestic violence. The more we see these escalating costs over generations, the more there is an increased public demand for preventive measures in the domestic violence setting in form of prevention and risk assessment.

### *Not only women are victims of domestic violence*

Over the past few years, research (e.g., the British Crime Survey) has shown that not only women and children are victims of domestic violence, but also men. We learnt that primarily feminist research concentrated on domestic violence against women by men. More recently, male pressure groups have pointed out that men are also subjected to domestic violence and abuse (see Kelly's US research in 2003; 2005). Approximately, one in six men will experience domestic violence during their lifetime, particularly in respect of assaults (occasioning actual bodily harm – ABH) or serious assaults (grievous bodily harm – GBH); though quantitatively these statistics are far lower than physical abuse against women or children by men (Home Office Research Study 191, 1999). Lamnek and Luedtke (2005) found in their Southern German Bavarian study that two-thirds of the surveyed households reported no domestic violence (65.7%), more than a quarter reported some parental violence towards children (28.4%), some 3.5 per cent indicated partner and/or parent-child abuse, and 2.4 per cent gave details regarding adult-on-adult partner abuse; the latter accounted for 73 per cent of "hitting with a flat hand", 33 per cent reported "being kicked", 15 per cent battery or "being struck with an object", and 10 per cent "being struck with the fist".

An equal number of men (3.2%), compared with women (3.0%), reported that they had been victims of domestic violence; but women still remain in the majority (58.3%) compared with men (41.7%) (Lamnek and Luedtke, 2005: 49; see also comparative USA data by Straus, 1997; 2001; Straus et al., 1980). We can also notice an equal correlation between the man's original home background and his domestic family setting in relation to present violence in his family: "If you grew up in a peaceful and loving family, you are more likely to live in an adult non-violent domestic set-up later in life" (Lamnek and Luedtke, 2005: 53).

The German Federal Ministry for Family, Senior Citizens, Women and Young People has planned future studies regarding violence against men (not necessarily in the domestic setting). One such pilot study was started in 2004, involving qualitative interviews with counsellors from self-help groups on domestic violence against males, and a sample of 266 selected male adult victims (see Jungnitz et al., 2004). Of these, 23 per cent of the male victim sample reported that they had experienced some form of physical or sexual violence in their relationships, of these seven per cent in 2003–04 (Jungnitz et al., 2004: 12). Early results showed that a large percentage experienced some form of abuse *outside* the domestic setting or home. It has also emerged that this type of research is proving methodologically difficult, because the topic of male abuse is still a taboo subject, and that men just do not like to discuss topics of this kind. This shows that more research is needed in the area of violence against men, including domestic violence.

## Fighting domestic violence

Most Western industrialized states have now either amended existing (criminal and civil) legislation or introduced new legislation to combat domestic violence against women and children; this resulted from extensive research in most countries. In 1993, the United Nations (UN) included 'domestic violence against women' in their Declaration on the Elimination of Violence against Women (see Report of the General Assembly Resolution of 1993). In 1997, the UN called on all member-states to ratify international agreements regarding the human rights of women. However, we can see how diverse the rights of the woman are in the different legislations around the world mainly influenced by religion and religious practices (e.g., Sharia Law).[5]

### *Changes in German legislation*

In Germany, there were a number of legislative changes over the past few years, following victim research studies in domestic violence (see conclusions by Schwind, 2006):

- In 1976, the Victim Compensation Act came into force (Opferentschädigungsgesetz – OEG)' or "Gesetz über die

Entschädigung für Opfer von Gewalttaten" of 11 May 1976). With this statute, the Federal German Government had simply copied legislative measures from other foreign countries. According to § 1 (1) OEG only those victims are compensated by the state (1) who suffered damage to their health as applied by this Act or on a German ship or aircraft resulting from a deliberate, illegal violent attack against him/her or in self-defence, when suffering damages to one's health.

- On 1 April 1987 the OEG – Victim Compensation Act, 1976 was complemented and amended by further statutory legislation, the Victims of Criminal Acts, 1987 (*Opferschutzgesetz* – OSG) "for the improvement and support of victims in criminal proceedings"). The 1976 Act is specifically aimed at the protection of the private life of victims involved in criminal proceedings; here the victim is granted increased protection from personal questions during trial proceedings; furthermore, it is the victim's right to ask for the removal of the defendant from trial proceedings whilst the victim is giving evidence, in case of victim-intimidation. Additionally, the public can be excluded from the proceedings, on application of an 'in camera' anonymity order by the victim to the presiding judge, particularly when the victim is ordered to give evidence about his/her personal or private information. The Act grants the victim an improved 'freedom of information' right, such as insight into personal data files and disclosure, and is entitled to an advocate. Victims of serious criminal offences are entitled to avail themselves of criminal procedure of a separate private prosecution against the defendant.
- On 1 December 1998, the Victim Protection Act, 1998 came into force (*Zeugenschutzgesetz* – ZSchG). This introduces statutory protection of victims and vulnerable persons and witnesses of persons under the age of 16 in criminal proceedings; these include, inter alia, taped and video evidence by such victims/witnesses, and thus avoids duplicate witness statements at the police interview stage and at court. Young witnesses are entitled to an advocate

(legal aid), whilst their evidence is being broadcast in sound and vision.

- On 1 January 2002, the Protection from Violence Act, 2000 came into force (*Gewaltschutzgesetz –GewSchG*) this civil legislation acts as a "protection for victims of violence, persecution, and other unreasonable acts (such as stalking) and for the easement of legislation regarding the allocation of the domestic and marital home during divorce proceedings." The Act provides for an exclusion order to remove or ban one (married) partner from the marital home in cases of domestic violence (see: Rössner et al. 1999). Smartt (2001: 230ff.) points out that this Act only protects those who are actually married and where the domestic violence offence occurs in the 'marital home'. Therefore, cohabitees who fight in the pub are not covered.
- On 1 September 2004, the Improvement of the Rights of Victims Act (in criminal proceedings) came into force (*Opferrechtsreformgesetz* – OpferRRG) of 24 June 2004, announced in BGBl I 2004 No. 31 of 30 June 2004). The Act states that, inter alia, victims of crime have a statutory right to legal aid and the assistance of an advocate; victims have a right to victim protection schemes and victim support in court proceedings; furthermore, that victim compensation is paid as part of the sentence – if the victim so wishes. This is similar to the 'victim compensation order' in the British Crime and Disorder Act, 1998. The victim has the right in the German 2004 Act to be accompanied at every stage of the criminal proceedings by a confidant/e or victim support person (see in detail Schwind, 2006: 425–429).
- The German Criminal Code was amended in 1997 by means of the 33rd Amendment Act (*Strafrechtsänderungsgesetz*). The Criminal Code (*Strafgesetzbuch* – StGB) now includes offences such as "sexual assault causing a person to engage in sexual activity without consent" ('sexuelle Nötigung') and 'rape' ('Vergewaltigung'); both offences are now possible offences within marriage (similarly to English law where rape within marriage can be a criminal offence since the House of Lords ruling in *R v R* in 1991).[6]

- The statutory provision that parents may no longer use 'force' against their children (*Züchtigungsrecht der Eltern gegen Kinder*) was only recently abolished and substituted by an amendment to the Child Support Act of 7 November 2000. Only since then children have the right to a violence-free education in the home, making psychological and corporal punishment and other degrading treatments of children in the domestic setting a criminal offence (Leuze-Mohr, 2005: 143ff.). We can see that – following the introduction of this legislation – more and more families have moved towards a 'violence-free' education of their children; though there are still notable exceptions.
- The First Right to Marriage Reform Act of 14 June 1976 which came into force on 18 July 1977, allows a (German) wife the right to decide freely on legal, employment and social areas of her own interest according to her own free will. Legislative discussions centring on measures to tackle domestic violence have been in existence for about ten years, but they are progressing slowly in terms of adjusting to traditional social norms and the legal standing of the (German) woman within the domestic setting, social and employment setting. The woman is still by no means equal in professional or indeed religious social life. The emancipation of women in Germany has been slow, and there is a great deal of scope in employment law and relations as well as the legislative field for female pressure groups and spokeswomen in business and political life.

Apart from the Protection from Violence Act, 2000 (*Gewaltschutzgesetz*), there are a number of regulations which have been in place over the past decade and protect women against domestic violence. However, it is up to the 16 'local' federal states (*Länder*) to use and implement such legislations at local level (e.g., police and other law enforcement agencies). They will differ from federal state to federal state (e.g., Bavaria vs. Lower Saxony). How such regulations are applied depends on the societal attitudes of the German citizens in each *Land*. Criminal legislation can only be applied if the majority of the (German) population and its local society take a fair share of such laws in a collective way. Therefore, we note a dramatic change towards public attitudes to domestic violence from the end of the 1990s onwards. The statutory right regarding the state's "protection of the marriage" (see above) which included the right to the "protection of privacy in the marital home and therefore also included domestic violence as a privacy right" (Leuze-Mohr, 2005, 144): If the police attended a 'domestic violence' at all, they were merely there to 'mediate' between the couple. In most such cases, the police ignored any police laws or the legality principle (rule of law). "The deligitimization in domestic violence cases by society, as a whole, resulted in simply ignoring violence in the family, and further resulted in social injustice and public ignorance" (Leuze-Mohr, 2005: 145). Any incidents of domestic violence were simply ignored, apart from may be the most serious cases.

Some domestic violence victims have been supported in the community over time by means of introduction of safe houses for women and children, increased social services support for children and young persons in danger of domestic violence, and the creation of family advice centres. But domestic violence is still largely seen as a family and 'psychological' problem in Germanic societies (including Switzerland and Austria) rather than a 'criminal legal' problem with state intervention by criminal justice authorities.

### *A Germanic re-think by law enforcement agencies*

With some legislative changes in Germany, a large police training programme in respect of domestic violence had to be conducted in the various 16 German states (*Länder*), in order to sensitize each force to the risks and dangers of domestic violence. Some forces have done better than others – this may have something to do with some rather traditional (Roman Catholic) states, such as the southern states of Bavaria and Baden-Württemberg, compared with the more liberal (Protestant) northern states of Lower Saxony, Hamburg or Berlin. Hagemann-White (1981) reported that a German police officer some 25 years ago would simply stand by, rather than assisting in a case of domestic violence; this was seen as 'soft policing' and rather unpopular with the force:

"We were just not able to help the woman in distress when she alleged that she had been beaten up by her husband – though police officers were forced to respond to 110-calls (similar to a 999 call in the UK); most officers said that they were not 'competent' enough to deal with 'domestics'; they felt they had no relevant police sanctions available to them at that time as part of their (*Land*) police legislation" (at p. 119).

From the middle to late 1980s, one can detect a slight re-think by some German police forces. Bergdoll and Namgalies-Treichler reported that the sampled police officers' "main aim – when dealing with domestic violence or family arguments – was the establishing of peace and quiet, i.e., mediation and a tendency to offer helpful advice and possibilities to calm things down" (1987: 62). Steffen and Czogolla even noted in 1987: "abused wives and women cannot presently rely on the help and support of the police, neither can they rely on the help from other formal authorities – something which they ought to be able to hope for and rely on since domestic call-outs are rather unpopular with the police and yet such emergency call-outs are increasing in frequency" (1987: 158). Stümper et al. noted that even 15 years ago, that calling out specialist police forces in case of a domestic violence would only "make matters worse, especially when pressing charges; police interference would therefore not be regarded as a secondary preventive measure, but rather as secondary grounds for more violence" (1990: 704). Some researchers noted a change in police opinions towards 'domestics' (see Steffen, 2005: 17ff.). For example, Grieger et al. noted: "In respect of police attitudes towards domestic violence, we can see a vast change of opinion in recent times. A few years ago, the notion of domestic violence was surrounded by myths and clichés as possible causes and victims involved. Support services for women would criticize the police for not doing their statutory duty, moreover, for leaving the initiative for a violence-free situation totally to the victims of violence. Today, every police conference and team-building exercise, the police forces are being praised for their interventionist methods and preventive measures. The police has truly turned the corner and has gained a new image, where understanding and dealing with domestic violence is concerned" (2005: 121).

But this sea change has been a slow one: changes in police perception of the domestic violence problem have been slow in forthcoming; initial taboos had to be removed regarding domestic violence and officers had to learn new approaches to helping victims, how to intervene in such situations, and how to become more effective when dealing with 'domestics'. In 1999, the Federal German Government proposed an action plan to combat violence against women in form of totally new policies and ways to act in such situations. The main aim of the White Paper was to reduce harm and violence towards women. Today, Germany has taken various comprehensive measures to tackle and deal with domestic violence, whereby political, legal and social measures are linked. A focal point centres on law enforcement, criminal and civil legislation. The state not only has the possibility but rather the duty to make sure that victims of violence are protected. There is no doubt today that domestic violence in Germany is a violation of the law. Hence, we have seen a fundamental change in public opinion.

### *'Platzverweis' (displacement, banning or exclusion order) as a new measure*

Central to the new measures are the exclusion or banning orders (*Platzverweis*) and the Protection from Violence Act (*Gewaltschutzgesetz*). Both have one motto: "he who hits, goes!" The aforementioned government action plan has the following objectives: cooperation between the authorities dealing with various anti-violence projects; a joined-up assistance approach; anti-violence programmes for the perpetrators; training and educational programmes for specialist practitioners; and an education of the public, particularly where the 'Platzverweis' and the Protection from Violence Act are concerned. The 'Gewaltschutzgesetz' offers a number of special civil measures such as non-contact orders; non-molestation orders and non-approach orders; and in 2005, stalking was actually captured by special criminal legislation.

In the Southern Federal State of Baden-Württemberg, there has been a pilot programme running since 1 June 2000, called 'operation red card' for violent offenders, whereby the 'Platzverweis' part of the anti-violence legislation has been actively applied. Eventually, some 86 towns and communities participated in the pilot project, and the police had to be involved in 2,608 cases of domestic violence, 769 of those perpetrators were given a 'red card' and were given an exclusion order (Stürmer, 2005: 173). The German 'Platzverweis' order is based on the Austrian forerunner of the 'Go-Order', which was introduced to combat domestic violence in 1997 (see Logar, 2005). The Austrian 'Go-Order' entitles the police to order the perpetrator to stay away from his home, and to not interfere or molest the victim (see Logar, 1998). The exclusion or banning order model (Platzverweis) was so successful in Baden-Württemberg, that it became law from 2001 onwards (Stürmer, 2005: 173). The number of 'Platzverweis' orders have steadily increased. Incidentally, the German anti-violence legislation was also based on the Austrian example, and Luxembourg followed suit (see, Klein, 2005; Wagner-Wies et al., 2005).

First research results show that the 'Platzverweis' exclusion order is largely being accepted as a warning (or 'red card') by the perpetrators (with a few exceptions). Since the 'Platzverweis' is a police measure, it has been administratively supported and the order is being used ever more frequently. Latest police statistics from 2005 have revealed that the 'red card' measure has been very successful with violent husbands or partners in the third largest German federal state with about 10.7 million inhabitants: there were 8,966 domestic call-outs, and in 2,968 of the cases the police made an exclusion order (2,559 in 2004). There were 927 victims who pressed charges in connection with molestation, harassment or stalking. The pilot project 'Platzverweis' and the various banning and exclusion orders have been seen as a success combating domestic violence behind closed doors. The length and type of banning 'Platzverweis' order depends on each federal state (*Land*) and can last from seven to fourteen days. The suspected perpetrator cannot return to his own home within that time. Stalking offences are being treated separately since October 2004, and are being recorded separately on the national police computer system. The Southern German regional newspaper '*Badische Zeitung*' reports that there have been almost 1,300 separate recorded offences of stalking (Badische Zeitung, 2006: 6).

Looking at press reports from 2006 in the population-wise largest German state, North Rhine-Westphalia, with 18.1 million inhabitants, police figures recorded that there were 17,991 'domestic' call-outs in 2005. The Northrhine-Westphalian Ministry of the Interior stressed that the police was to make clear to the offender that he had done harm and that the police and state authorities would not abandon the victim. Victims (women and young girls) stressed that it was very important to them that the police was taking them seriously.

The actual practicalities of a 'Platzverweis' order look such that the house keys are taken off the perpetrator, and there are regular police checks that he has not returned to the (marital) home. If he breaches the order, he will be ordered to pay a fine. During the ten-day exclusion or banning order, the victim can apply for an extension of the exclusion order with at the civil court. Should the court agree, the extension given is normally another ten days and so on.

Statistically, most police call outs have to deal with actual bodily harm or assault by beating (14,998 cases = 83% of all cases), threats (2,435 cases=14%), sexual assault and rape (175 cases=1%). With the low-recorded sexual offences rate, it is to be assumed that reporting of such offences by the victims remains very low indeed. Once at the police station, the victim will be informed of her rights and will be given victim support, legal advice and refuge facilities by the police. If the victim so wishes, the police will contact the victim support and rescue services. The state of North Rhine-Westphalia currently supports 62 female refuge hostels, 55 female victim advice centres and 48 establishments that deal with sexual assaults and rapes and offers these female victims advice and refuge centres. About 70 per cent of victims make use of these facilities.

There are clearly more police call-outs to 'domestics' for the North Rhine-Westphalian police compared with Baden-Württemberg. If we look at the figures in Baden-Württemberg more closely, there are 83 call-outs per 100,000 population, compared with 99 in North Rhine-Westphalia. The 'Platzverweis' order for police call-outs is 50 per cent in North Rhine-Westphalia, and 33 per cent in Baden-Württemberg. One reason is the difference in population structure, and the differences in lifestyle between the Southern and the middle-German states. The Southern Baden-Württemberg has a slightly higher rate of foreigners (12% v. 10.8%), but a much lower unemployment rate (average 7% in 2005 compared with 12% in the middle-German Land). This puts much more pressure on North Rhine-Westphalia which is then reflected in its domestic violence and police call-out rates.

### *Legal basis for the 'Platzverweis'*

The Protection from Violence Act is essentially a civil-legal remedy and the exclusion or banning order is being used with increased frequency as a first-time measure. Criminal measures in form of the victim's pressing charges are also increasing in domestic violence cases (see Leuze-Mohr 2001: 203ff.; 312ff.). However, as is the case in England, Wales and Scotland, most cases collapse or end up in a cracked trial. The state prosecution service now insists that once the police has gone ahead with the charge, the prosecution will go ahead regardless. This is similar policy in England with the Crown Prosecution Service (CPS) and the Procurator Fiscals' Office in Scotland. Leuze-Mohr stresses that only "this way we can tackle domestic violence, and the law enforcement authorities will continue to take domestic violence seriously. We have to protect the victim and realize that these are criminal offences" (2005: 148; see also Schweikert and Baer, 2002). Most importantly, the perpetrator has to realize that he has done wrong, and that he begins to empathize with the victim. According to the new legislative regulations, "domestic violence is regarded by the state prosecution authorities as a violent offence and will be prosecuted by all criminal courts in each [of the 16 federal] states" (Leuze-Mohr, 2005: 149; see also Schweikert and Baer, 2002: 92; Winterer, 2005).

Leuze-Mohr gives us a good overview of German legislation and regulations regarding domestic violence (2005: 149ff.). It is specifically the police that deals with crime prevention and official sanctions in domestic violence. Additionally, the victim of domestic violence can take civil-legal steps as well as make a victim compensation claim in the local court. The 'Platzverweis' order gives the state of Baden-Württemberg additional police powers and is therefore much respected in the *Land*. The police can also avail itself of sections 1 and 3 of the Police Act of Baden-Württemberg[7] in order to remove the perpetrator from his home, to place an exclusion order on him or to take special measures. One such measure is the 'Platzverweis' order, similar to an English exclusion order, which curtails or limits the perpetrator's movements, and usually bans him from his own home.

The German injunction of 'Platzverweis' is "usually applied in conjunction with an order relating to breach of the peace and to maintain public law and order" (Leuze-Mohr, 2005: 151). One of the central aims is to safeguard the health and well-being of the victim, and to protect the individual human rights and the privacy of the victim (life, health, physical safety, freedom, honour and personal assets). It is strictly the police duty to prevent crime and danger to the victim of domestic violence. The new Act and secondary police legislation in this respect give the police enhanced powers to avert and prevent possible danger to the victims by applying the above measures granted to them by law.

The police now has extensive powers to make a 'Platzverweis' order *in situ,* i.e., can act immediately when dealing with a case of domestic violence. Once the exclusion or restriction order is made, the local police authority has to investigate how long the order can be made for "just like with any injunction, a Platzverweis – order needs to be realistically applied in terms of length of time and reasonable measures in the interests of both the offender and the victims in each case". Research experience in the state of Baden-Württemberg has shown that such orders usually last about one week in nearly half of the cases (47.3%). About a quarter (24.4%) of the orders are made for about two weeks to three months. Leuze-Mohr states that Platzverweis orders are now generally between one and two weeks long (2005: 152). Door keys are usually confiscated as part of the order, and in extreme cases of violence, the perpetrator may be taken into police custody. "A Platzverweis order usually diffuses the situation in the first place, and initially seeks to calm the violent situation down. Once the order has stopped, the victim needs further and longer lasting protective measures."

These are then sought with criminal and civil legislation and further legal action.

German Criminal Law in form of the Penal Code (*Strafgesetz*) is still the most important legislation to deal with domestic violence and its perpetrators, since there are usually a number of offences; mostly the police will be dealing with repeat offending and considerable criminal damage. Most commonly, the courts will deal with charges of assault and battery to grievous bodily harm; sexual type offences to rape; and hostage-taking with sometimes the most serious consequences such as the death of the victim. The ensuing public interest in bringing such perpetrators to justice has only come to light in recent times. The media has contributed 'positively' in this respect (such as the '*Badische Zeitung*') for openly discussing this former taboo subject and demanding harsh sanctions for the offenders.

Apart from the usual sanctions of a fine, imprisonment or unpaid community work, the courts and the police usually involve victim and mediation services so that the family can continue to function and does not leave children and vulnerable members of the family permanently damaged. Furthermore, one form of punishment can be a programmed (probation service) activity as part of the community sentence, such as alcohol or drug treatment orders, anger management and anti-aggression therapy orders, as well as victim-offender-mediation and compensation to the victim/s. The fine can be ordered to go towards 'domestic violence victim funds' set up all over Germany. Leuze-Mohr stresses, however, that the offender must realize that only he is responsible for his crime and actions of physical and psychological violence he has inflicted on his wife and/or family (2005: 154; see also Rabe, 2002: 111ff.). Naturally, if there is to be any victim-offender-mediation, the victim has to be consulted; this has resulted from the much improved 'victims of domestic violence agenda' and victim protection scheme, published by the German Government (*Bundesregierung*) over recent years. The Victim Protection Reform Act has also increased the victim's rights and future protection; this includes the victim's input and opinion during trial and at sentencing stage, and has reduced future damage and harm (Ferber, 2004:

2562ff.). Therefore, Leuze-Mohr (2005: 166ff.) concludes her thesis regarding the 'Platzverweis' order:

- Its immediate applicability and the 'teaching the perpetrator a lesson' facility. This creates room for a rethink regarding the law enforcement and policy domestic violence. By its new legislation the state has sent a message to all perpetrators that it will not tolerate any violent behaviour in the family, that no form of violence is to be treated lightly, since ultimate damage is always high.
- A 'Platzverweis' order cannot give the victim/s ever-lasting protection; if there are no follow up (civil and/or criminal) measures, the order will have no lasting effect.
- The order has to be coupled with other [legal] measures in order to effective in the long run. "The 'Platzverweis' alone is too short-lived. It will only make sense if the perpetrator is given adequate support from all criminal justice and social services agencies" (Leuze-Mohr, 2005: 166).
- The 'Platzverweis' order has to be seen as part of a total domestic violence criminal – and civil justice package, only then will the order be effective.
- Society must not avert its eyes and must view domestic violence as a serious offence.

### *Empirical research on the 'Platzverweis' (exclusion order and injunction)*

Grieger et al. (2005) report on the first empirical research results regarding the effect of the 'Platzverweis' (exclusion or restraining) order in pilot projects in the German federal states (*Länder*) of Berlin, Mecklenburg-Vorpommern and Baden-Württemberg (Stuttgart). The results vary from *Land* to *Land*. Results from Stuttgart Police show that 91 per cent of perpetrators and victims co-habited in the same household at the time of the reported and recorded offence; 58 per cent were married, and in 90 per cent of the reported cases the police were called. Of the 90 per cent call-outs, there were some serious offences; with 42 per cent including verbal assaults not usually in themselves the major reason for calling out the police.

One main factor for the police issuing a 'Platzverweis' order was in about 70 per cent of the cases the fact that there had been a physical assault to the victim; 29 per cent were slight injuries, 33 per cent bore medium and 8 per cent serious physical injuries. Some 46 per cent of male or female perpetrators had already appeared in police statistics, and there had been – in parts – more than one 'Platzverweis' order. The authors note that such orders vary considerably from one region to another (Grieger et al., 2005: 133). Because of regional differences in quotas, documentation, the measuring and defining of 'Platzverweis' orders, as different in each German *Land*, this research data was not seen as a satisfactory measure to evaluate the measure of the 'Platzverweis' to combat domestic violence.

The south-western German city of Freiburg has also made use of the 'Platzverweis' order as a measure to tackle and reduce domestic violence. The year 1998 saw a new initiative, namely, the 'Freiburger Interventionsprojekt gegen häusliche Gewalt' (FRIG) (Freiburg Intervention Project Against Domestic Violence) (see Weiß, 2005; Winterer, 2005; Drumm, 2005). In 2003, some 305 cases of domestic violence were recorded (of about 200,000 inhabitants); there were 169 cases in the wider region of the Black Forest (Breisgau-Hochschwarzwald) – once again, we have to note differences in the way that the local police record such cases, and whether individuals report the incidents. Kury et al. (2005) conducted a research study into police investigations of domestic violence cases in the Freiburg area. The researchers investigated and analyzed all reported and recorded incidences during the first half of 2002, and 35.5 per cent of all domestic violence cases were recorded by the police at that time. A total of 38.5 per cent were recorded as simply a 'quarrel', without using the word 'domestic violence', and 22.1 per cent were recorded as 'assault' without referring to the notion of 'domestic' at all. Therefore, it was difficult to record exact 'domestic violence' data at all. This has changed now. The Freiburg Police now records 'domestics' separately.

There were 342 police call-outs to 'domestics' during the first half of 2002, and 358 in the second half. While analyzing the call-out data, Kury et al. noted that 'domestics' largely took place in problem areas of the city. This may also be connected to the fact that this concerned families from lower strata of society as well as their different attitudes to relationships. A quarter of the incidents took place between 9 p.m. and midnight; in 43.8 per cent of the cases it was the female victim who had informed the police; and in 21.8 per cent of the call-outs, there was also a child present during the couple's conflict. In 75.2 per cent of the cases, it was a relationship and in 20.5 of the cases a family conflict situation. In 78.2 per cent of the 'domestics', police found two-sided verbal abuse and in 3.3 per cent one-sided verbal abuse. There were 13.6 per cent of actual verbal assaults, 29 per cent of battery, and 28.7 assaults in the domestic aggressive conflict. Of these, some 27.8 per cent were previously known to the police for similar domestic conflicts and were known as 'problem families'. The police ordered a verbal 'Platzverweis' (non-contact order) in 7.6 per cent of the cases for the male perpetrator, and in 0.3 per cent of the cases, such an order was given to the female. Of all the recorded cases during the time, 'Platzverweis' orders were given in 10.6 per cent of the recorded cases, i.e., every tenth 'domestic' receives a non-contact order from the police in Freiburg.

We noted that women are largely the victims of domestic violence – yet it is they who are also partly to blame in the majority of all cases (Obergfell-Fuchs and Kury, 2005: 289). It might be obvious, but the number of female perpetrators lessens, the more severe the criminal assault. But it is usually women who originate from a violent domestic background who also find themselves in a violence relationship – those who are 'used to violence' seem to seek out violent partners. Once in such a violent domestic set-up, women cannot seem to find the strength to give themselves (and their children) a chance to start a new life, away from their violent partner/s (see Helfferich, 2005).

## Discussion and conclusion

We have come a long way since feminists such as Shere Hite alerted us by way of her now 30-year old 'Hite Report' that family life and relationships can be terrifying. Domestic violence has been brought to the fore, and Western feminists have moved on. In her recent lecture in London, Shere Hite addressed a large audience on "Sexual Purity and the New Global Terrorism" in which she linked sex to human rights, and "the issue of sexuality is central to the global conflict and bemoans the fact that some women have to cover the bodies and faces up with black garments. Hite has moved on, now touching on topics such as Afghanistan and the 9/11 terrorism attacks on New York. She and other feminist writers of the 60s and 70s have achieved one aim though, that domestic violence is with us and has to be addressed by society at large.[8]

Whatever form it takes, domestic violence is rarely a one-off incident. More usually, it is a pattern of abusive and controlling behaviour through which the abuser seeks power over their victim. Domestic violence occurs across society, regardless of age, gender, race, sexuality, wealth and geography. The figures show, however, that it consists mainly of violence by men against women. Victims of domestic violence suffer on many levels – health, housing, education – and lose the freedom to live their lives how they want, and without fear. We aim to support victims of domestic violence with a range of new measures. The British Government has invested £ 14 million (about 21 million Euro) into tackling the problem of domestic violence, this is being put into action by the 'Domestic Violence National Action Plan' (see Home Office 2005). The Domestic Violence National Action Plan (2005) sets out the progress so far in tackling this particular form of crime and contains substantial proposals to further improve support for victims and bring more perpetrators to justice. Britain has introduced new legislation with the Domestic Violence, Crime and Victims Act, 2004 to increase the protection, support and rights of victims and witnesses. The 2004 Act also gives the police and other agencies the tools to get to the heart of domestic violence crimes. The Act, which came into force on 15 November 2005, tackles domestic violence and involves all agencies within the British criminal justice system. In practice, this means that any victim of domestic violence, or a concerned friend or relative, can get the help and support they need. This includes the police, but also other agencies such as social services who can give women and children help and practical advice including: emergency refuge accommodation in safe houses, safety planning and advice as well as translation facilities. Furthermore, the Government has addressed children's needs specifically with its White Paper 'Every Child Matters' of 2003 (this includes the protection of the unborn child).

We learnt that domestic violence accounts for around 16 per cent all violent crimes in Britain at a cost in excess of £ 23 billion a year (about 34 billion Euro; Home Office 2004–05 Report). The German and British studies revealed that domestic violence is the largest cause of morbidity worldwide in women aged 19–44, which greater than war, cancer or motor vehicle accidents. Stanko et al. (1998) noted that domestic violence affects one in four women, and one in six men, in their lifetime. Legislative measures in civil law set up by the Department of Constitutional Affairs (DCA) for England and Wales now include the making of a non-molestation order (the breach of which is a criminal offence, punishable by up to five years' imprisonment on indictment). Giving co-habiting same-sex couples the same access to non-molestation and occupation orders as heterosexual couples and making couples who have never co habited or been married eligible for non-molestation and occupation orders. In criminal legislation, common assault (as part of domestic violence) is now an arrestable offence, and a police officer may arrest without a warrant. All courts (including Magistrates' Courts) can now impose a 'Restraining Order' when sentencing for any offence linked to domestic violence. Additionally, the British Government set up a 'Domestic Violence Advisory Group' in 2005 made up of police officers, lawyers, judges, social workers and other agencies to ensure a joined-up approach to tackling domestic violence. The Adoption and Children Act, 2005 now makes clear that when a Family Court (part of the Magistrates' Court in civil matters) is considering whether a child has suffered, or is likely to suffer harm, it must consider harm that a child may suffer not just from domestic violence, but from witnessing it.

The German studies have shown similar results. A recent comparative victim study into sexual violence between Germany and Japan revealed that though Japan has a generally low crime rate, the victimization in relation to sexual and/or physical violence in the family was about the same as in Germany (see Kury and Yoshida, 2004). One reason for this might be that the control mechanisms and law enforcement for domestic violence [in Japan] are not as intrusive and prevalent as for other 'outside' crimes. Generally, the family is regarded as sacrosanct in Japan, and that the state does not like to interfere in family and domestic matters (see Kühne and Miyazawa, 1991).

Throughout Europe, we have seen changing legislation in favour of curtailing domestic violence, and to protect the victim. Battered women use to have to leave the family home; some found refuge in safe-houses or hostels. Today, certainly in the UK and Germany, "he who batters – goes!" – it is usually the perpetrator who has to leave the domestic home by means of civil injunctions under the English Harassment Act, 1997 or a number of court orders (e.g., in the Magistrates' Court: exclusion orders, non-contact orders, curfew orders etc.) and the German 'Platzverweis' (exclusion) order. German experts warn that the 'Platzverweis' order is only temporary and not a solution in its own right; the order (similarly to the temporary orders by the English courts) does not solve domestic violence and the root causes for such conflict. Such police or court orders are effective immediate measures, which prevent any further aggression and harm against the victims, but they are not a permanent solution to complex family problems. Sometimes, as was the case of Kiranjit Ahluwalia, the battered woman is driven to extreme measures, whereby she kills her husband or partner after years of physical and mental abuse.[9] A young Asian woman, living in Southall, West London, had been subjected to ten years of spousal violence and psychological degradation; she doused her husband in petrol whilst he was asleep, set him alight, and he died of his fatal injuries. She was convicted of murder since the prosecution (rightly) proved her intent to kill. On retrial, Lord Chief Justice Taylor commented on the fact that (until that time) women found it difficult to avail themselves of 'self-defence' in court when accused of murder. After a long campaign by the 'Black Sisters of Southall' new evidence was permitted to allow the 'slow burn' effect (to long-term spousal abuse) was permitted as a form of defence. At the Court of Appeal, the 'battered woman syndrome' defence was allowed, quashing Ahluwalia's murder conviction on the basis of her depressed condition at the time. She was freed in 1992. Now, the battered woman's syndrome – defence is slowly being accepted by the British courts was successfully used in the case of Sara Thornton.[10] Her case was similar in that she killed her husband by stabbing him with a knife, after they had had years of arguments; her killing was equally planned and the *mens rea* element was equally present as was the *actus reus*: she sharpened a knife and stabbed him in the stomach. In both cases, the reasoning behind the original convictions was that the time lapse between the violence or threats of violence and the murder removed the option of a defence of provocation ('sudden and temporary loss of self-control'). A 'crime of passion' defence (as in France) does not exist in England.

But, the above cases are extreme, and the police forces – both in England and Germany – now seek to prevent violent acts, by protecting the victims well in advance. The London Metropolitan Police ('The Met') developed a risk assessment process (also known as SPECSS), as the result of findings from a project on 'Domestic Violence Murder' Reviews for London in 2003 and evaluated by Laura Richards. The highest six risk factors in respect of domestic violence are: separation (child contact); pregnancy/new birth; escalation (attacks worsen/happen more often); cultural issues; stalking; and sexual assault (make up the acronym SPECSS). Richards found that the SPECSS risk assessment model helped in the training of police officers when attending 'domestics' as well as developing systems to support the risk assessment process in respect of (future) victims of domestic violence.[11] The Association of Chief Police Officers (ACPO[12]) 'Guidance on Domestic Violence' model now makes it clear that risk assessment in domestic violence cases is a complex process requiring training, which should be used to enhance victim safety and improve the standard of investigation. The SPECSS risk assessment was then implemented in pilot programmes in London, West Yorkshire, Cardiff and Thames Valley, aimed to independently evaluate the effects of the risk assessment by assessing whether the model addressed victims needs in terms of risk, addressed future safety planning and could easily be managed with police forces' resources and limitations (especially in respect of recent terrorist attacks on London, especially 7th July, 2005). More research is needed in respect of the SPECSS factors and whether they are of equal or more importance in cases of serious domestic violence offences (e.g., the Pemberton murders in 2003[13]). Richards' research also recommended that police forces use 'culture' as a category, as it is generally underutilized except in relation to black and minority ethnic communities and families (e.g., London, the Midlands or West Yorkshire). ACPO Risk Assessment Evaluation Risk Assessment has become an increasingly significant aspect of police work in relation to domestic violence.

In Germany, there are a number of risk models and pilot projects, such as the one in Freiburg. But more risk assessment and anti-violence training (of violent perpetrators) are needed in order to prevent future harm to potential victims (see Stürmer 2005: 179; Arnold, 2005). The new German government action plan to combat and prevent domestic violence looks at the complexities involved, and needs the cooperation of a number of agencies in order to assist with measures (such as the 'Platzverweis' order), aggression training programmes, the training of police and prosecution staff, and victim support agencies. It is important to strengthen the (German) criminal laws in order to support civil measures and victim-support programmes (i.e., that breached civil orders as the non-contact or exclusion orders are punished properly in the criminal courts). The 'Platzverweis' order, as a temporary short-term measure alone, is not sufficient, there need to be interventions such as victim support, and restorative justice type programmes, such as mediation between the domestic violence perpetrator and the victim, as well as family liaison programmes to combat and prevent conflicts.

And finally, we need to realize that domestic violence is part of a societal problem and cannot be ignored, least of all by the legislators and those who have to deal with the consequences, namely, the law-enforcement agencies. Domestic violence is now a recognized social problem in most Western civilizations, often closely linked to poverty, unemployment, poor standards of living and economic deprivation. Therefore, it is not just the criminal justice, but also social policy legislation that needs to address this issue.

## Notes

1. See: Hitting Home Factfile: http://www.bbc.co.uk/pressoffice/pressreleases/stories/2003/01_january/17/hitting_home_facts.pdf
2. A total of 10,772 schoolchildren aged 11–16 were sampled in 70 mainstream schools by way of face-to-face oral interviews backed up by standard anonymous questionnaires with tick boxes. The return rate was 73 per cent in the 2004-05 survey.
3. *DPP v Morgan* [1976] A.C. 182: "If D honestly believes any element of the *actus reus* is missing, s/he is entitled to be acquitted. The burden is on the prosecution to show that there was no such belief [of consenting to sexual intercourse by the victim]. So, according to this argument, on the facts... D is entitled to an acquittal if the jury things he might have honestly believed, whether reasonably or not, that the victims was 14 or more and... [consented to sexual intercourse]."
4. "(1) A person (A) commits an offence if – (a) he intentionally penetrates the vagina or anus of another person (B) with a part of his body or anything else, (b) the penetration is sexual, (c) B does not consent to the penetration, and (d) A does to reasonably believe that B consents."
5. Sharia Law, which derives from the teachings of the Koran and from Sunna (the practice of the prophet Mohammed), is implemented to varying degrees in different Islamic countries – from the beheadings of Saudi Arabia, to the relatively liberal social mores of Malaysia. On 20 August 2002, an Islamic court in Nigeria upheld a sentence of death by stoning for a woman accused of adultery. The case is the latest in a series of sentences passed under Sharia Law – a set of religious laws adopted over the past two years in northern regions of Nigeria, which have predominantly Muslim inhabitants.
6. *R v R* [1992] 1 A.C. 599, House of Lords. The defendant married his wife in 1984. As a result of matrimonial difficulties the wife left the matrimonial home in 1989 and returned to live with her parents, informing the defendant of her intention to petition for divorce. The defendant also communicated to the wife his intention to "see about a divorce". While the wife was staying at her parents' house, the defendant forced his way in and attempted to have sexual intercourse with her, in the course of which attempt he assaulted her. He was charged on indictment with 'rape' and 'assault occasioning actual bodily harm' (ABH). The judge rejected his submission that by virtue of section 1(1) of the Sexual Offences (Amendment) Act 1976 the offence of rape was one which was not known to the law where the defendant was the husband of the alleged victim. He thereupon

pleaded guilty to attempted rape and assault occasioning actual bodily harm and was convicted. On the defendant's appeal against his conviction of attempted rape, the Court of Appeal (Criminal Division) dismissed the appeal.

7. *Polizeigesetz von Baden-Württemberg*: Rechtsvorschriften (vom 13 January 1992 (GBl. S. 1, ber. S. 596, 1993 S. 155) Zuletzt geändert durch Gesetz vom 1.7.2004 (GBl. S. 469) m.W.v. 1 January 2005
8. Ref. Interview with Clive Anderson on Channel 4 TV, UK. 27 April 2006.
9. *R v Ahluwalia* [1994] 3 WLR 288.
10. *R v Thornton* [1992] 1 All ER 306.
11. http://www.met.police.uk/csu/pdfs/AppendixIII.pdf
12. The *Association of Chief Police Officers* (ACPO) is an independent, professionally led strategic body. In the public interest and, in equal and active partnership with Government and the Association of Police Authorities, ACPO leads and coordinates the direction and development of the police service in England, Wales and Northern Ireland. In times of national need ACPO, on behalf of all chief officers, coordinates the strategic policing response: http://www.acpo.police.uk
13. Julia (48) and her son William Pemberton (16) were shot and killed at their family home in Hermitage, near Newbury, Berkshire, Southern England in 2003. The murders, at the hands of William's father, Alan, came after a series of incidents which family members believe should have been recognized as clear alarm bells. At the time of the tragedy, Mr Pemberton was already the subject of a court order banning him from going anywhere near the family home. At an inquest in 2004, Thames Valley Police was severely criticized by the coroner for taking six hours to get to the scene of the crime, after repeated distress calls from Mrs Pemberton. The inquest heard on 27 September 2004 how Mrs Pemberton had pleaded with a police operator that she had "about one minute before I die", as she hid in a downstairs cupboard while her husband rampaged through their home in Hermitage. The case is now about to become the subject of a formal review (Thames Valley Police) which will be the first to be examined under the homicide review procedure introduced under the Domestic Violence Crime and Victims Act, 2004.

## References

Abbatepaolo, M., and Sattmann, M. (2006). Ein Vergleich von polizeilichen Interventionen bei häuslicher Gewalt mit und ohne Platzverweis – Die Effektivität aus Sicht der Opfer – Freiburg: Psychologisches Institut der Universität, unveröffentlichte Diplomarbeit.

Allport, G.W. (1941). *The Use of Personal Documents in Psychological Science.* New York: Social Science Research Council.

Amelang, M. (1986). Sozial abweichendes Verhalten. Entstehung – Verbreitung – Verhinderung. Berlin: Springer.

Arnold, H. (2005). Psychosoziale Intervention infolge von Platzverweis bei häuslicher Gewalt. In: Kury, H., Obergfell-Fuchs, J. (Hrsg.), Gewalt in der Familie. Für und Wider den Platzverweis. Freiburg: Lambertus, pp. 330–358.

Badische Zeitung. (2006). Mehr Platzverweise. Gegen prügelnde Ehemänner. Badische Zeitung vom 4. April 2006, S. 6.

Beckett, K., and Sasson, T. (2004). *The Politics of Injustice. Crime and Punishment in America.* Thousand Oaks/California. Sage.

Bergdoll, K., and Namgalies-Treichler, C. (1987). Frauenhaus im ländlichen Raum. Stuttgart: Schriftenreihe des Bundesministeriums für Jugend, Frauen, Familie und Gesundheit, Bd. 198.

Biderman, A.D., Johnson, L.A., McIntyre, J., and Weir, A.W. (1967). Report on a pilot study in the district of Columbia on Victimization and attitudes toward law enforcement. Washington, D.C.

Brownmiller, S. (1975). *Against Our Will: Men, Women, and Rape.* New York.

*Bundesministeirum für Familie, Senioren, Frauen und Jugend* (1999). Aktionsplan der Bundesregierung zur Bekämpfung von Gewalt gegen Frauen. Bonn.

—— (2003). Mehr Schutz bei häuslicher Gewalt. Informationen zum Gewaltschutzgesetz. Berlin.

—— (2004). Gemeinsam gegen häusliche Gewalt. Kooperation, Intervention, Begleitforschung. Berlin.

—— (2004a). Lebenssituation, Sicherheit und Gesundheit von Frauen in Deutschland. Eine repräsentative Untersuchung zu Gewalt gegen Frauen in Deutschland. Zusammenfassung zentraler Studienergebnisse – Berlin.

Campbell, J. (1995) *Assessing Dangerousness: Violence by Sexual Offenders, Batterers and Child Abusers.* Thousand Oaks, CA, Sage.

*Children Society, The* (1999 and 2005) 'Safe and sound. Making England safe for young runaways'. First and second national survey of young runaways. 'Still running'. Parts I and II. London. http://www.the-childrens-society.org.uk/media/pdf/Campaigns/StillRunning2Final.pdf

Crisp, D., Hale, C. and Stanko, E. (1998) *A Measure of Pain: The Social and Economic Cost of Domestic Violence.* The Children's Report. The Children's Society. London.

Davies, J., Lyon, E. and Monti-Catania, D. (1998) *Safety Planning with Battered Women. London, Sage.*

*Deutsche Bischofskonferenz* (Hrsg.)(2006). Enzyklika Deus Caritas Est von Papst Benedikt XVI. Verlautbarungen des Apostolischen Stuhls Nr. 171. Bonn (English version: Pope Benedict XVI's First Encyclical Letter: Deus caritas est: of The Supreme Pontiff Benedict XVI to the Bishops, Priests and Deacons, Men and Women Religious and all the lay Faithful on Christian Love. German Bishops' Conference (ed.), 2006.

Drumm, M. (2005). Platzverweis in Fällen häuslicher Gewalt am Beispiel der Polizeidirektion Freiburg. In: Kury, H., Obergfell-Fuchs, J. (Hrsg.), Gewalt in der Familie. Für und Wider den Platzveweis. Freiburg: Lambertus, pp. 242–260.

Eichner, K., and Habermehl, W. (1978). Der RALF-Report. Das Sexualverhalten der Deutschen. Hamburg: Hoffmann and Campe.

Ennis, P.H. (1967). *Criminal Victimization in the United States.* Washington, D.C.

Ferber, S. (2004). Das Opferrechtsreformgesetz. Neue Juristische Wochenschrift, pp. 2562–2565.

Finkelhor, D. (1997). Zur internationalen Epidemiologie von sexuellem Missbrauch an Kindern. In: G. Amann and R. Wipplinger (Hrsg.), Sexueller Missbrauch. Überblick zu Forschung, Beratung und Therapie. Ein Handbuch (S. 72–85). Tübingen: Deutsche Gesellschaft für Verhaltenstherapie.

Gebhard, P.H., Gagnon, J.H., Pomeroy, W.B., and Christenson, C.V. (1965). *Sex Offenders. An Analysis of Types.* New York: Harper and Row.

Gelles, R.J. (1998). Family Violence. In: M. Tonry (Ed.), *The Handbook of Crime and Punishment* (S. 178–206). New York, Oxford: Oxford University Press.

Grieger, K., Kavemann, B., and Rabe, H. (2005). Täterorientierter Opferschutz durch Platzverweis – erste Erfahrungen aus Deutschland. In: Kury, H., Obergfell-Fuchs, J. (Hrsg.), Gewalt in der

Familie. Für und Wider den Platzverweis. Freiburg: Lambertus, pp. 121–142.

Hagemann-White, C. (1981). Hilfen für misshandelte Frauen. Schriftenreihe des BMJFFG, Band 124, Stuttgart.

Heiskanen, M., Piispa, M., and Hope, F. (1998). *Battering. A National Victim Survey on Men's Violence Against Women in Finland.* Helsinki.

Heiskanen, M., and Piispa, M. (2002). *The Costs of Violence in a Municipality: A Case Study of Violence Against Women and its Costs in the City of Hämeenlinna 2001,* based on estimates provided by authority representatives. Helsinki: Ministry of Social Affairs and Health.

Helfferich, C. (2005). Die Wahrnehmung der eigenen Handlungsmacht und die Konstellation Opfer – Polizei – Täter bei häusliche Gewalt. In: Kury, H., Obergfell-Fuchs, J. (Hrsg.), Gewalt in der Familie. Für und Wider den Platzverweis. Freiburg: Lambertus, pp. 309–329.

Hentig, H.V. (1954). Zur Psychologie der Einzeldelikte. Bd. 1: Diebstahl, Einbruch. Raub. Tübingen: Mohr.

Hillenkamp, T. (1988). Hausarbeit Nr. 2: Viktimologische Grundfragen am Beispiel eines Vergewaltigungsfalles. In: H. Jung (Hrsg.), Fälle zum Wahlfach Kriminologie, Jugendstrafrecht, Strafvollzug (S. 85–108). München: Beck.

Hite, S. (1976). *The Hite Report on Female Sexuality.* New York.

*Home Office* (1999). Domestic Violence: Findings from a new British Crime Survey self completion questionnaire. Mirrlees-Black, C. London: HORS Study 191.

— (2002) *Crime in England and Wales.* British Crime Survey 2001/02. Simmons, J. et al. HOSB 7/02.

— (2002) *The 2001 British Crime Survey.* HOSB 18/01.

— (2004) Domestic Violence, Sexual Assault and Stalking: Findings From the British Crime Survey. Walby, S. and Allen, T. HORS Study 276.

— (2005) *Crime in England and Wales,* 2004–2005.

— (2005) Domestic Violence: A National Report. http://www.crimereduction.gov.uk/domesticviolence51.pdf

— (2006) Domestic Violence – Crime Reduction. http://www.crimereduction.gov.uk/dv01.htm

Humphreys, C., Thiara, R., Gibson, A., Regan, L., Lovett, J. and Kennedy, L. (2005). 'Prevention not prediction? A preliminary evaluation of the Metropolitan Police Domestic Violence Risk Assessment Model. Commissioned by the Association of Chief Police Officers (ACPO). Final Report. July 2005 (unpublished).

*Innenministerium Nordrhein-Westfalen* (2006). Jahresbilanz 2005 häusliche Gewalt: Über 8.000 Wohnungsverweise und Rückkehrverbote in NRW. Pressemitteilung vom 19. April 2006.

Jesionek, U. (1998). Die Entdeckung des Opfers häuslicher Gewalt. In: H.D. Schwind, E. Kube, and H.H. Kühne (Hrsg.), Festschrift für Hans Joachim Schneider zum 70. Geburtstag am 14. November 1998. Kriminologie an der Schwelle zum 21. Jahrhundert (S. 897–911). Berlin: de Gruyter.

Jungnitz, L., Lenz, H.J., Puchert, R., Puhe, H., and Walter, W. (2004). Gewalt gegen Männer. Personale Gewaltwiderfahrnisse von Männern in Deutschland – Ergebnisse der Pilotstudie – Berlin: Bundesministerium für Familie, Senioren, Frauen und Jugend.

Kaiser, G. (1996). Kriminologie. Ein Lehrbuch. Heidelberg: C.F. Müller.

Kelly, L. (2003). Disabusing the definition of domestic abuse: How women batter men and the role of the feminist state. *Florida State University Law Review* 30, pp. 791–855.

— (2005). Die feministische Verzerrung von Gesetzen und Theorien zur häuslichen Gewalt in Amerika. In: H. Kury, and J. Obergfell-Fuchs, J. (Hrsg.), Gewalt in der Familie. Für und wider den Platzverweis (S. 73–86). Freiburg: Lambertus.

Kilchling, M. (1995). Opferinteressen und Strafverfolgung. Freiburg: iuscrim.

Kinsey, Alfred C., Pomeroy, W.B., and Martin, C.E. (1948/1998). *Sexual Behaviour in the Human Male. Philadelphia: W.B. Saunders; Bloomington, Indiana*: Indiana University Press.

Kinsey, Alfred C., Pomeroy, W.B., Martin, C.E., and Gebhard, P.H. (1953–1998). Sexual Behaviour of the Human Female. Philadelphia: W.B. Saunders; Bloomington, Indiana: Indiana University Press.

Klein, I. (2005). Das Gesetz gegen häusliche Gewalt: Luxemburg. In: Kury, H., Obergfell-Fuchs, J. (Hrsg.), Gewalt in der Familie. Für und Wider den Platzverweis. Freiburg: Lambertus, pp. 111–114.

Kühne, H.H., and Miyazawa, K. (1991). Kriminalität und Kriminalitätsbekämpfung in Japan. Versuch einer soziokulturell-kriminologischen Analyse mit Daten und Anmerkungen zum internationalen Kriminalitätsvergleich. Wiesbaden: Bundeskriminalamt.

Kürzinger, J. (1978). Private Strafanzeige und polizeiliche Reaktion. Berlin: Duncker und Humblodt.

— (1996). Kriminologie. Eine Einführung in die Lehre vom Verbrechen. Stuttgart: Boorberg, 2. Aufl.

Kury, H. (1994). Zum Einfluss der Art der Datenerhebung auf die Ergebnisse von Umfragen. Monatsschrift für Kriminologie und Strafrechtsreform 77, pp. 22–33.

— (2001). Das Dunkelfeld der Kriminalität. Oder: Selektionsmechanismen und andere Verfälschungsstrukturen. Kriminalistik 55, pp. 74–84.

Kury, H., and Yoshida, T. (2004). Zur Frage, wie Opfer von Straftaten gesehen werden. *Journal für Strafrecht,* H. 1, pp. 10–15.

Kury, H., Dörmann, U., Richter, H., and Würger, M. (1992). Opfererfahrungen und Meinungen zur Inneren Sicherheit in Deutschland. Wiesbaden: Bundeskriminalamt.

Kury, H., Obergfell-Fuchs, J., and Würger, M. (2000). Gemeinde und Kriminalität. Eine Untersuchung in Ost und Westdeutschland. Freiburg: iuscrim.

Kury, H., Obergfell-Fuchs, J., Smartt, U., and Würger, M. (2002). Attitudes to punishment: How reliable are international crime victim surveys? *International Journal of Comparative Criminology* 2, pp. 133–150.

Kury, H., Pagon, M., and Lobnikar, B. (2002a). Wie werden Opfer von (Sexual)-Straftaten von der Polizei gesehen? Zum Problem der Stigmatisierung. *Kriminalistik* 56, pp. 735–744.

Kury, H., and Obergfell-Fuchs, J. (2005). Gewalt in der Familie. Für und Wider den Platzverweis. Freiburg: Lambertus.

— (2005). Polizei und Platzverweis – Ergebnisse einer empirischen Untersuchung in Freiburg. In: Kury, H. Obergfell-Fuchs, J. (Hrsg.), Gewalt in der Familie. Für und Wider den Platzverweis. Freiburg: Lambertus, pp. 261–284.

Kury, H. and Smartt, U. (2002) 'Prisoner-on-prisoner violence: victimization of young offenders in prison. Some German findings'. In: *Criminal Justice,* Vol. 2, No. 4, November 2002, pp. 411–439.

Lamnek, S., and Luedtke, J. (2005). Gewalt in der Partnerschaft: Wer ist Täter, wer ist Opfer? In: Kury, H., Obergfell-Fuchs, J. (Hrsg.), Gewalt in der Familie. Für und Wider den Platzverweis. Freiburg: Lambertus, pp. 37–69.

Leuze-Mohr, M. (2001). Häusliche Gewalt gegen Frauen – eine straffreie Zone? Warum Frauen als Opfer männlicher Gewalt in der Partnerschaft auf Strafverfolgung verzichten – Ursachen, Motivationen, Auswirkungen. Baden-Baden.

— (2005). Das rechtliche Maßnahmensystem bei häuslicher Gewalt und die Berücksichtigung des Anzeigeverhaltens der Opfer als wirksames Opferschutzsystem. In: Kury, H., Obergfell-Fuchs, J.

(Hrsg.), Gewalt in der Familie. Für und Wider den Platzverweis. Freiburg: Lambertus, pp. 143–168.

Logar, R. (1998). Der Herr im Haus darf nicht mehr tun was ihm beliebt. Das neue Gesetz zum Schutz vor Gewalt in Österreich. In: Heiliger, A., Hoffmann, S. (Hrsg.), Aktiv gegen Männergewalt. Kampagnen und Maßnahmen gegen Gewalt an Frauen international. München, pp. 90–104.

— (2005). Nicht nur wegweisen, sondern auch den Weg weisen – Erfahrungen mit dem Geweltschutzgesetz in Österreich. In: Kury, H., Obergfell-Fuchs, J. (Hrsg.). Gewalt in der Familie. Für und Wider den Platzverweis. Freiburg: Lambertus, pp. 89–110.

Masters, R.E.L. (1969). Abnorme Triebhaftigkeit. Fallstudien zur Sexualpathologie. München: Lichtenberg.

Master, M. and Johnson, V. (1988) *Masters and Johnson on Sex and Human Loving*. Little, Brown and Company. NY, USA.

McLennan, J. (1996). *Women safety*. Australian Bureau of Statistics. Canberra.

Mendelsohn, B. (1956). La victimologie. Revue Internationale de Criminologie et de PoliceTechnique 10, 95–109. Meyer, K. (1941). Die unbestraften Verbrecher. Leipzig.

*Metropolitan Police Service (MPS)* (2001) *Understanding and Responding to Hate Crime*. MPS Domestic Violence Strategy.

Möbius, P.J. (1900). Über den physiologischen Schwachsinn des Weibes. Halle (12. Auflage 1922).

Morgan, A., Roche, M., Thandi, K and Bunce, D. (2005) Evaluation of the Wolverhampton Specialist Domestic Violence Court: A Baseline Study to inform LPSA DV targets. Final Report. 2 August 2005.

Müller, U., and Schröttle, M. (2004). Lebenssituation, Sicherheit und Gesundheit von Frauen in Deutschland. Enddokumentation Hauptuntersuchung. Bielefeld: Interdisziplinäres Frauenforschungs-Zentrum der Universität Bielefeld.

— (2004a). Lebenssituation, Sicherheit und Gesundheit von Frauen in Deutschland. Eine repräsentative Untersuchung zu Gewalt gegen Frauen in Deutschland – Zusammenfassung zentraler Studienergebnisse – Berlin: Bundesministerium für Familie, Senioren, Frauen und Jugend.

Oba, S. (1908). Unverbesserliche Verbrecher und ihre Behandlung. Berlin.

Obergfell-Fuchs, J., and Kury, H. (2005). Umgang mit häuslicher Gewalt – eine Gruppendiskussion mit PolizeibeamtInnen. In: Kury,

H., Obergfell-Fuchs, J. (Hrsg.), Gewalt in der Familie. Für und Wider den Platzverweis. Freiburg: Lambertus, pp. 285–306.

Oliver, B.J. (1967). *Sexual Deviation in American Society: A Social-psychological Study of Sexual Non-conformity*. New Haven, CN: College and University Press.

Pernamen, K. (1991) *Alcohol in Human Violence*, New York, Guilford.

Piispa, M., and Heiskanen, M. (2000). *The Price of Violence: The Costs of Violence against Women in Finland, Helsinki:* Tilastokeskus SVT Oikeus.

Porterfield, A.L. (1943). Delinquency and its outcome in court and college. *American Journal of Sociology* 48, pp. 199–208.

— (1949). *Youth in Trouble*. Fort Worth.

Rabe, H. (2002). Der Täter-Opfer-Ausgleich bei häuslicher Gewalt. STREIT, pp. 111–119.

Reinhardt, J.M. (1957). *Sex Perversions and Sex Crimes*. Springfield, IL: Charles C. Thomas Publisher.

Reiss, A.J. (1967). *Public Perceptions and Recollections about Crime, Law Enforcement, and Criminal Justice*. Washington, D.C.

Robinson, A. (2004) Domestic violence MARACS (Multi-Agency Risk Assessment Conferences) for very high-risk victims in Cardiff, Wales: A process and outcome evaluation.Cardiff, Cardiff University: http://www.cf.ac.uk/socsi/whoswho/robinson.htm.

— (2003) *The Cardiff Women's Safety Unit: A Multi-agency Approach to Domestic Violence. Cardiff,* Cardiff University.

Römkens, R. (1997). Prevalence of wife abuse in the Netherlands: Combining quantitative and qualitative methods in survey research. *Journal of Interpersonal Violence*, pp. 99–125.

Rössner, D., Bannenberg, B., Kerner, H.-J., Weitekamp, E. (1999). Mediation und Täter-Opfer-Ausgleich bei Gewaltstraftaten in Paarbeziehungen. Baden-Baden.

Rüther, W. (1998). Internationale Erfahrungen bei der Behandlung von Sexualstraftätern. Monatsschrift für Kriminologie und Strafrechtsreform 81, pp. 246–262.

Sauer, W. (1933). Kriminalsoziologie. Berlin.

Schneider, H.J. (1987). Kriminologie. Berlin, New York: de Gruyter.

— (2001). Kriminologie für das 21. Jahrhundert. Schwerpunkte und Fortschritte der internationalen Kriminologie. Überblick und Diskussion. Münster: LIT Verlag.

Schröttle, M. (1999). Politik und Gewalt im Geschlechterverhältnis. Eine empirische Untersuchung über Ausmaß, Ursachen und

Hintergründe von Gewalt gegen Frauen in ostdeutschen Paarbeziehungen vor und nach der deutsch-deutschen Vereinigung. Bielefeld: Kleine Verlag.

Schweikert, B., Baer, S. (2002). Das neue Gewaltschutzrecht. Baden-Baden.

Schwind, H.D. (2006). Kriminologie. Eine praxisorientierte Einführung mit Beispielen. Heidelberg: Kriminalistik Verlag.

Sepler, F. (1990). Victim advocacy and young male victims of sexual abuse: An evolutionary model. In: M. Hunter (Ed.), *The Sexually Abused Male: Prevalence, Impact, and Treatment*. Vol. 1 (S. 73–85). New York: Lexington.

Shultz, G.D. (1965). *How Many More Victims? Society and the Sex Criminal.* Philadelphia, New York: Lippincott Company.

Smartt, U. (2001/02). 'The stalking phenomenon: trends in European and international stalking and harassment legislation. In: European Journal of Crime, Criminal Law and Criminal Justice. Vol. 9/3, 2001–02: 209–232. The Hague: Kluwer Law International, The Netherlands.

Smartt, U. (2006). 'Honour Killings'. In: *Justice of the Peace Journal.* Butterworths/Lexis. Vol. 170, pp. 4–7.

Sparks, R.F. (1981). Surveys on victimization. In: Morris, N., Tonry, M. (Eds.), *Crime and Justice*. Yearbook I, Band 3, Chicago, London, 1–60.

Stanko, E. A. (1988). 'Hidden violence against women'. In: M. Mauire and J. Pointing (Eds.), *Victims of Crime: A New Deal*. Milton Keynes: Open University.

— (1990). *Everyday Violence: How Women and Men Experience Sexual and Physical Danger*. Rivers Oram Press. London.

Stanko, E.A., Crisp, D., Hale, C. and Lucraft, H. (1998). Counting the costs: estimating the impact of domestic violence in the London Borough of Hackney: Swindon: Crime Concern.

*Statistics Canada* (1999). *Family Violence: A Statistical Profile*. Ontario.

Steffen, W. (2005). Gesetze bestimmen die Taktik: Von der Reaktion auf Familienstreitigkeiten zur Umsetzung des Gewaltschutzgesetzes. Veränderungen im polizeilichen Umgang mit häuslicher Gewalt – zugleich ein Beispiel für die Praxisrelevanz kriminologischer Forschung. In: Kury, H., Obergfell-Fuchs, J. (Hrsg.), Gewalt in der Familie. Für und Wider den Platzverweis. Freiburg: Lambertus, pp. 17–36.

Steffen, W., and Czgolla, P. (1987). Gewalt von Männern gegenüber Frauen. München.

Stoller, R.J. (1975). *Perversion. The Erotic Form of Hatred.* New York: Pantheon Books.

Straus, M.A. (1997). Physical assaults by women partners: A major social problem. In: Walsh, M.R. (Ed.), *Women, Men and Gender: Ongoing Debates.* New Haven, pp. 210–221.

— (2001). Physical aggression in the family. In: Martinez, M. (Ed.), *Prevention and Control of Aggression and the Impact of its Victims.* New York, pp. 1–20.

Straus, M.A., Gelles, R.J., and Steinmetz, S.K. (1980). *Behind Closed Doors: Violence in the American Family.* Garden City/N.Y.: Anchor Pr./Doubleday.

Stumper, A., Gemmer, K., Hamacher, H.W., and Salewski, W. (1990). Verhinderung und Bekämpfung von Gewalt aus der Sicht der Polizeipraxis. Gutachten der Unterkommission V. In: Schwind, H.-D., Baumann, B. u.a. (Hrsg.), Ursache, Prävention und Kontrolle von Gewalt. Analysen und Vorschläge der Unabhängigen Regierungskommission zur Verhinderung und Bekämpfung von Gewalt (Gewaltkommission). Band II, Berlin, pp. 607–753.

Stürmer, U. (2005). Das Platzverweisverfahren als Paradigmenwechsel im Umgang mit Gewalt im sozialen Nahraum: Erfahrungen und Perspektiven zur Fortentwicklung der Intervention in Baden-Württemberg. In: Kury, H., Obergfell-Fuchs, J. (Hrsg.), Gewalt in der Familie. Für und Wider den Platzverweis. Freiburg: Lambertus, pp. 169–191.

Taylor–Browne, J. (Ed.) (2001). *What Works in Reducing Domestic Violence? A Comprehensive Guide for Professionals.* Whiting and Birch Ltd., London.

Tjaden, F., Thoennes, T.H. (1998). *Prevalence, Incidence and Consequences of Violence Against Women:* Findings from the National Violence against Women Survey. Washington, D.C.

United Nations (2000) *Domestic Violence Against Women and Girls.* Report of June 2000. No. 6.

Villmow, B. (1977). Schwereeinschätzung von Delikten. Berlin: Duncker & Humblot.

Wagner-Wies, V., Ronkar, C., Strasser, O., and Blitgen, M. (2005). Service d'Assistance aux victimes de Violence Domestique in Luxemburg: Konzeption und erste Erfahrungen. In: Kury, H., Obergfell-Fuchs, J. (Hrsg.), Gewalt in der Familie. Für und Wider den Platzverweis. Freiburg: Lambertus, pp. 115–120.

Walby, S. (2004). *The Cost of Domestic Violence.* London: National Statistics, Women Equality Unit.

*Webster's Dictionary* (1913; 2005). Merriam-Webster's Collegiate Dictionary. 11th (ed.) London.

Wehner, B. (1957). Die Latenz der Straftaten. Wiesbaden.

Weiß, A. (2005). Platzverweis als Heausforderung an kommunale Behörden und Einrichtungen. Erfahrungen aus dem Freiburger Interventionsprojekt gegen häusliche Gewalt. In: Kury, H., Obergfell-Fuchs, J. (Hrsg.), Gewalt in der Familie. Für und Wider den Platzverweis. Freiburg: Lambertus, pp. 217–241.

Weisser Ring (Hrsg.) (1996). Täterrechte – Opferrechte: Neue Gewichtung im Strafprozess. Mainz: Weisser Ring: http://www.weisser-ring.de/bundesgeschaeftsstelle

Winterer, H. (2005). Strafverfolgung bei Gewalt im sozialen Nahbereich: das Freiburger Modell. Entwicklungen und Tendenzen am Beispiel der Staatsanwaltschaft Freiburg. In: Kury, H., Obergfell-Fuchs, J. (Hrsg.), Gewalt in der Familie. Für und Wider den Platzverweis. Freiburg: Lambertus, pp. 192–216.

CHAPTER TWENTY

# Violence against women in France, in light of the Indian debate

*Hugues Lagrange*

Violence has to be specified: physical violence is not cruelty,[1] psychological pressure and restriction on freedom are different forms of violence to be considered. I will neither deal with the violence against women in the public space, nor with violence in workplace, possibly associated to frustrations in regard to social and economic achievements. I am concerned here with domestic violence in ordinary life. These forms of violence are often a consequence of power struggle, linked to autonomy between husband and wife – autonomy not conceived as a stable situation but as an ongoing process. Interpersonal physical and psychological violence are much more present in the private sphere, which is the domain of strong affective ties than anywhere else. The emphasis will be focused on the consequences of multicultural settings, where violence may also be linked to the alteration of norms and balance of power which arises when traditional norms are challenged and new ones not yet established.

What are the possible parallels between debates about family violence against women and human rights in India and France? I have to confess that for a French reader, dealing with law, gender inequality and violence, the Indian debate about a Uniform Civil Code is fascinating. A plurality of civil laws exists in India, as you know, a long time ago. By observing the evolution of these dispositions, it is as if we had the possibility to experiment a very different legal arrangement and to discuss its merits and consequences in light of experience. I did not dare to argue that examining violence in France from India is sufficient to provide an Indian perspective and to give clues to a better understanding of violence against women. But I defend the idea that Indian debates, past and present, could enlighten our reflection.

An Indian researcher, Flavia Agnes, wrote in a recent book: "Within a complex social, political and economic structure, the demand of gender equality cannot be confined within a linear mould of granting uniforms rights to woman of all communities. An all-encompassing Uniform Civil Code cannot be viewed as a magic wand which will eliminate the woes and sufferings of Indian women in general and minority women in particular."[2] This position is interesting coming from someone who is also an activist in the feminist movement, because she defends civil differences but at the same time reasserts her attachment to the maintenance of a uniform (Indian) Penal Code. It raises the question: Will a plurality of civil laws allows for a better understanding and treatment of differences of values, mores and norms?

As European history, Indian history teaches us that the decline of collective property of land has reduced the autonomy of women during the 19th century. But also, that through the development of an industrial or post-industrial society, new provisions have been taken in order to secure protection for women in case of divorce. There has been in India a convergence between the personnel laws, driven by mutual influences of Muslim and Hindu personal laws, under the large influence of British laws. The plurality of civil laws is part of the legacy of colonial India. "It is interesting to note that at the time of independence, woman's rights under the Muslim law where far superior to both the Hindu as well as the Christian laws."[3] Up to 1986, the Shah Bano case, the plurality of civil laws – under the name of personal laws – did not prevent a progressive evolution toward the autonomy of women in India.[4] This convergence allows one to think that a Uniform Civil Code was not necessary to foster an evolution in favour of gender equality. In spite of the decision of the apex court in the Shah Bano case, there has been a backlash, the subsequent Muslim Women's Bill, exclude, in case of divorce, Muslim women from the right to alimony from her husband. And it has strengthened the positions of those who are in favour of a Uniform Civil Code.

In 1980, the Backward Classes Commission from the Government of India established a caste-wise composition of the population,[5] revealing a double division along religious lines and along caste lines, and this division seems to be central to the portrait of the society.[6] This double division, obviously, does not exist in France. In the recent past, during the sixties, religious diversity in France was not an important matter and, as the religious practices were falling, one could say that the religious question has reached a historical minimum, sometimes during the seventies. Since two or three decades, we are facing, besides a diluted Catholicism and a renewed Judaism, an ongoing process of Islamization among members of the young generation. Coming from North Africa and the Sahel region, the Muslims are approximately four millions; this is the second religious affiliation in France. During the last quarter of the 20th century, the migrant population has not increased but, mainly, European migrants have been substituted by African migrants. This new situation in terms of ethnic and religious diversity, in a context of economic recession, has raised xenophobic attitudes among French people, which gained visibility through vote in favour of the National Front (extreme right). This wave of xenophobic attitudes is not limited to France: the Netherlands, Austria and Italy have witnessed similar reactions. But, the ways to cope with this new stakes are specific to each country. In this respect, the main point to be address, in my view, is a strong French denial of its pluralism, which is linked to the claim of universalism.

We inherited from the French Revolution the assertion that our society should be blind to race, culture and religion.[7] The differences of status – not wealth – have been combated with the most extreme severity (see Le Chapelier Act 1794). Many ascriptives differences, as opposed to acquired differences, are unthinkable in the French legal framework. We know that the span of this universalism was restricted to a small fraction of financially capable men long after the Revolution and that, up to

1975, women's rights were restricted in many respects, but we maintain the view that ascriptive differences must not be taken in account.

Now, our universalism turns to French exceptionalism, as could be seen in many areas. In the very recent past, to give only few examples of our particularism, I would mention the law about woman's veil, the 'no' to the European constitution, our incapacity to adapt our welfare state which give the image of an immobile society. Those are not minor problems, they reveal an entrenched society. The difficulties that we have to deal with, concerning some of the most important social questions, are strongly linked, in my view, to the denial of our ethno-cultural pluralism, and to a lack of self-confidence. I consider that our universalism has to be 'upgraded' because, as such, it inhibits our ability to take in account the situation we are facing and that the French society needs to scrutinize its conceptions and practices, bearing in mind that the US model is not the only alternative.

We could draw tentatively a table as under showing which category of women is concerned by dependence, protection and autonomy in the two contexts:

**Table 1**

| | | *India* | *France* |
|---|---|---|---|
| Dependence | From the husband or the family | Divorce difficult or impossible, without rights when women remarry: Hindu after 1856, Muslim after 1986 | Divorce difficult: No social benefits or competition for the access to social benefits: African migrants in France |
| Protection | Coming from community/society | Divorce easier and maintenance/ inheritance rights: Hindu after 1956, Muslim before 1986 | Divorce easier, social benefits granted for the mother with dependant children: French upper class women |
| Autonomy | | ? | Divorce easier women working and protected by social insurances: mainstream middle class women |

By mentioning these debates, my point is only to emphasize that the plurality of norms in the society must at least be taken in account, whatever be the legal framework, to enforce human rights and protect women from domestic violence. This consideration of a plurality of norms is especially lacking in France.

Besides that, there is a simple reason to look at violence against women in France from abroad, which is linked to our emphasis on violence in multicultural contexts.[8] This perspective is important when dealing with family violence in deprived areas where this ethnic plurality takes place. Many African families, from North or Sub-Saharan African origins, whose culture and habits are very different from the "mainstream French family," live in poor districts scattered around Paris and other big cities.

### *The recent evolution of violence against women in France*

Violence against women in contemporary France seems to have risen during the last decades. This escalation followed a process of intense legislative change regarding mainly women's rights and children's rights, engaged during the late sixties and pursued up to the nineties. To mention only a few aspects of the legal evolution: divorce on mutual consent (1960), access to contraceptive pill (1967), suppression of the father pre-eminence (1970) equal sharing of parental authority between husband and wife (1970), law according right to abortion to women within ten weeks of pregnancy (1974), sexual aggression is no longer a trouble to public order but an offence against a person, and rape is considered as crime punished by a prison of at least ten years (1978), and new penal code defines rape as any act of penetration without consent (1992). These provisions have given women much more rights and consideration. This legislative evolution, concerning women's rights and recent children's rights, seems to be the continuation and, may be the last step, in a process of building a full universalism.[9]

Most of the progress concerning the freedom of women and equality of rights took place during the period when the French society was 'integrative' and where inequalities of wealth were receding. During the sixties and seventies, the migration from Africa acquired its maximum pace. But, up to the early eighties, the migrants were perceived as migrant workers and not as migrant families desiring to stay. The process or family gathering was slowly ongoing but it was not so visible. By this time, there was no interference between these two questions, and a great tolerance. The success of the woman's rights movement has been one of the main social transformations of the society during the seventies, violence against the women and child abuse remained at a relatively low level. To take one of the best indicators, the number of registered rapes was located around 2,000 a year for a country of 60 million people.

During the nineties, the figures for rape in the police records have increased five-fold, which is considerable, and the figures for sexual violence have been multiplying in the same proportions. Often, it is very difficult to distinguish an increase in reporting from an increase in acts and behaviour that could, under the provision of the 1980's laws, be considered as rape. Since 1992, with the ACSF, the *Baromètre-Santé,* the ENVEFF, three surveys, unfortunately only partially comparable, have been made in France, which enable us to take a much more accurate measure of rape and sexual harassment, and could be confronted to police data.

### *Comparative results on sexual violence against women in different recent surveys*

Between 3 and 4.5 per cent of women in France claimed that they have been, once in their lifetime, victim of rape or forced intercourse. It is not possible, from the surveys, to decide if there was an increase or a decrease of these violences, because the words used and the order of the questions about sexual violence has been built are not the same in each survey. Meanwhile, they give a coherent estimation of the life prevalence of rape.

**Table 2** Prevalence of rape or forced sexual intercourse in France, 1992 and 2000

| *Population* | *ACSF, 1992* | *Baromètre-santé, 2000* | *ENVEFF, 2000* |
|---|---|---|---|
| Surveyed | Women 18–59 years old | Women 20–54 years old | Women 20–59 years old |
| prevalence | 4.5% | 3.2% | 2.9% |

The word 'rape' was not used, except in the ENVEFF.

I will mainly use figures drawn from the ENVEFF, which is the only survey dealing fully with violence against women, to introduce my comparative considerations on the situations of women coming from different ethnic and cultural backgrounds. The ENVEFF survey leads us to an estimation of 0.3 per cent of women victim of rape during the last twelve months (in 2000).

ENVEFF: 6970 women aged 20 to 59 years, surveyed in 2000 in France, from which

— 61 per cent are married
— 14.5 per cent 'bachelor' in couple
— 7.5 per cent divorced (1% are leaving in couple)
— 5.5 per cent living with parents
— 11.5 per cent living alone

The meaning of forming a couple, in the ENVEFF survey, is completely subjective: "Would you say you are a couple, either you live with your partner or not?". The following results concern women who, at a moment of their life, have been in couple, in this sense:

**Table 3** France, 2000: Insults and psychological pressures against women living in couple

| *During the last twelve months* | *At least once (%)* |
|---|---|
| Have you been insulted? | 4.2 |
| *(Did your partner)* prohibit you to meet friends or to speak with? | 3.2 |
| to speak with other men? | 4.4 |
| oblige you to tell with whom you were? | 15.5 |
| impose you way of dressing? | 7.1 |
| deprive you to access to the joint banking account ? | 1.2 |
| threaten you to separate you from the kids? | 1.1 |
| threaten you to suicide himself? | 1.0 |

**Table 4** France, 2000: Physical aggressions against women living in couple

| *During the last twelve months....* | *At least once (%)* |
|---|---|
| *Did your partner* Hurts the kids or separate you from them? | 0.3 |
| Throw an object against you | 2.0 |
| Slap on you or has done other physical arms | 1.1 |
| Deprived you to enter your apartment | 0.5 |
| Threat you with a knife or a gun | 0.1 |
| Threat to kill you | 0.2 |
| Use force to have sexual intercourse | 0.2 |
| Oblige you to perform sexual acts you do not wanted | 0.8 |

The rape rate given by the ENVEFF, for women living in couple, is 0.2 per cent for the year 2000 and 0.3 per cent for all categories of women; the police data for the same year give a rate of 0.05 per cent, which means that the survey rate is six times the police rate.

But, the ENVEFF survey, in agreement with most other recent surveys, and, as we have seen in a Bangladeshi survey, shows that the victim knows usually the rape perpetrator. This could lead to a high level of underreporting. Let us do a simple calculus: if, let say, half of the cases where the perpetrator if known to the victim are reported against a hundred per cent when the perpetrator is not known, we have the following result with the rate of rape found in the survey (0.3%):

Hypothetical rate of registered rape

$$= 0.3 \times 0.125) + (0.3 \times 0.5 \times 0.875) = 0.17 \text{ per cent}$$

This last figure is closer to the police one, but still higher. This computation also suggests that the police figures for 1992 – one-fifth of this level – were very much underestimating violence against women, as it is very unlikely that the rate of rape has increased more than 100 per cent during these last eight years of the nineties; most of the increase should be a consequence of a higher reporting. Therefore, we must conclude that the nineties have been in France a period where disclosure of sexual harassment and sexual violence became much more accessible to women. A fact that is plausible when you consider the embarrassment about these questions twenty years ago. Up to the early eighties, domestic violence did not end up frequently in police records: sexual violence was for the most part a private behaviour that remains behind the walls. I would suggest that the development of a new sensitivity to women's rights has made this disclosure of intimate suffering easier for women belonging to many social strata. And, hopefully, we could expect it to reduce the incidence of criminal acts in the future.

However, there is a less positive evolution. As shown by many surveys, the public opinion continues to consider that the most likely perpetrator of rape is an unknown person. This inaccurate perception fuels a feeling of insecurity turned toward the usual scapegoat: the stranger in a broad meaning. In this domain of intimate violence, no less than with non-sexual crime, the perceptions are not based on experience but on a mix of experience and prejudice.

When reading the ENVEFF report, one finds other results concerning the frequency of violence on women which goes against the common knowledge: the fact that psychological as well as physical violence occurs with the same frequency in all strata of the population. But, when looking more closely to the results, you can see that unemployed women, particularly those who are deprived of social benefits, for whatever reason, are much more often the victims of violence than any other category. Intimate violence does not seem so much a question of professional content or of position on the social ladder than a phenomenon directly linked to precariousness. The sad side of this story is that violence strikes more the women who are already fragile and disaffiliated.

The survey also shows that the prevalence of violence is two times higher among women reared in Jewish or Muslim confession than among Christians and atheists. The level of violence suffered is also three times higher among migrant women under 35 years of age living in families coming from Africa (8.9% against 2.3% on average). The ENVEFF survey does not allow us to go beyond this general statement about migrant from Africa because there are only 150 women of African ascendancy surveyed.[10] Concerning the accuracy of this fact, we have very few reasons to think that women from African background have been more inclined to disclose these violence than women of another origin. On the contrary, the feeling of solidarity with their community – usually stronger among minority group's members – should have led to a higher level of understatement of violence. These considerations oblige us to ask why is it a problem link to other factors? Aren't these women of African ascendancy also more precarious and illiterate? If this is true, a multivariate analysis, controlling for unemployment and social benefits, should give interesting results.

**Table 5** Indicator of level of violence broken down by religious rearing of women

| | |
|---|---|
| No religious affiliation and rearing practices | 7.8% |
| Christian families and rearing | 9.1% |
| Jewish and Muslim families and rearing | 17.0% |

*Source:* ENVEFF.

The level of importance accorded to religion is correlated with violence against women; using alcohol, either husband or wife, make violence more likely; extra-marital relations or other partners raised also occurrences of violence.

My hypothesis to explain violence against women in these categories is as follows: In the context of migration, the equilibrium of power inside the family between men and women has been jeopardized. Specifically, the poor African families in the context of migration are dismembered families: there are no uncles, no aunts to counterweight the power of the husband. In addition, violence is much more likely to occur when there is an aspiration to autonomy that is thwarted or limited by economic constraints, which is often the case in those poor districts. In general, violence is less likely when autonomy is guaranteed by material resources and legal provisions. The survey made on Bangladeshi women suggests that violence became more frequent when, through involvement in small textile business, women acquired some autonomy, earned their own money. One can imagine that in the new context, women were less submissive and challenged the husband power. And, those men unable to face this shift of power react violently.

A contrary argument seems to emerge from the analysis of the recent decline of the murder rate in poor areas of the United States. Alfred Blumstein shows that, with the elevation of the divorce rate in the nineties, especially among black people living in poor areas of the centre cities, a decline in the intimate murder rate has been witnessed.[11] In fact, this is not a counter-argument: violence in the couple exists as long as women and men remain intimate and continue to form a binding entity. In the case of the black families, the frame was partly destroyed and thus, during the eighties, violence linked to this shared frame of living declined.

### *Domestic violence against women in Paris' suburbs*

This interpretation of the relatively high level of violence against women, in the recent years, is also supported by our research on Paris' suburbs. We made in-depth interviews in a medium city with an important population of African families, 50 kilometres west from Paris. If polygamy is not frequent among most of African families, in certain groups like families coming from the rural areas of Mali, one-third of the families are polygamous.[12]

The aspiration of women toward personal autonomy is supposed to be high from the late fifties up to the end of the 20th century in France, and this aspiration to autonomy percolates in the society through mass media and interactions between migrant and non-migrant women.

On the woman side, there has been a discrepancy between their expectation and their situation in France, which deprived them of the ancient protection and jeopardize the fragile equilibrium that they had reached in Africa through various mechanisms. The extended family no longer exists in France, and therefore women are often isolated, especially when they do not speak French. This isolation, the ignorance of the provisions of law, the very weak level of literacy and, for a wide fraction of them, the lack of professional qualification deprived them of the economic and cultural abilities necessary to make the new rights actual.

For men coming from patriarchal societies, namely, societies of the Maghreb and the Sahel, woman aspiration to autonomy is supposed to be less acceptable. As husbands, these men rely on their ancient prerogatives. In many cases, these men were employed as manual workers in automobile plants; during their professional life they have not received the gratification they think they deserve. Violence inside the family, and between men and women, is linked to the tensions aroused by the fact that these men lost their prestige. Older than their wives, they are often retired – some of them have lost their jobs. Most of them, during the years when they make money, sent part of their money to kins in the villages but, here, they are still poor. To maintain their self-esteem, these men feel the necessity to strengthen their power upon their spouses and children. Partly because they are deprived in France of the dignity they had in Africa, in a patriarchal context. Precisely those men who were the least successful in France turned their eyes and their mind toward Africa. They took a second wife, and they did not pay attention to the kids' achievement in school. Often, when their spouses tried to learn French, they were reluctant and sometimes forbid them to go out. This way of doing was quite easy with spouses younger than them and children, on which family pressures were heavy and who did not come with official Id. But, later on, men got problems with the boys in school and outside school: the boys began to steal and to hang out in the street. During the early nineties, there were only few "African NGOs" able to provide learning supports. Boys escaped mother's guardianship and father's authority, they were encouraged to do so because their mothers do not master French, were submissive and secluded at home. At the same time, boys despised their fathers, not in public but in their mind, and considered them as losers. This has created a very bad climate in black families, even in those who were doing better.

### *Formal rights and procedures and the reduction of the violence*

For a part, among immigrants from Africa, violence against the women results from the displacement of conflicts and frustrations experienced by men in their professional life. We have been facing a destabilization of these communities: the boys were more and more the clients of the penal system and often serve prison terms. The women were hesitating to launch civil procedure against their husbands in order to divorce. The husbands send boys and girls to Africa without the consent of their wives, and obliged them to recourse to the judicial system to recover guardianship on their children. Was the answer a greater severity of law against youngsters and fathers?

In most cases, in a traditional society, these tensions should have been settled down by mediation or conciliation between the spouses. As far as minor domestic violence was concerned, we have begun in France in the late nineties, very reluctantly, to set in motion conciliatory and mediation procedures. These procedures could work in the civil as well as the penal domain. But, the idea of a mediator to regulate minor conflicts has been quickly criticized by supporters of formal procedures. Instead of giving these procedures the publicity they deserve, we have continued to consider them as marginal derogative ways. These practices were not generally implemented and their application relied mainly dependent on the charisma of NGO leaders. Even under the left governments, they were not widely used. Once more, because of the lack of guarantees and of publicity of these procedures, many situations of conflict have not been dealt with in the early phases. This lack of prevention of conflicts resulted in an escalation of violence against women or children and often on both.

I would like to raise a parallel between the debate on personal laws and the alternative found to formal procedures to cope with situations of minor domestic violence, especially among migrants. This question is linked, in my view, to the debate on the plurality of civil laws in a multicultural society. I am convinced that sometimes we are criminalizing conflicts arising in the family because of our inability to treat them with the appropriate means. I argue that the recognition of the plurality of norms and values is a strong necessity in France, and that this recognition could facilitate an inclusive process. The level of protection of women is certainly linked to women's rights in the society, but a society who ignores its own diversity and applies uniformly judicial procedures, does not always reduce violence and constraints against women, because it encourages silence about the violence perpetrated among migrants' communities. Women to a certain extent prefer to sacrifice themselves in order to avoid the breaking of strong ties.

## Notes

1. It seems that the use of the word 'cruelty' is different in India from what it is in France.
2. Flavia Agnes, *Women and Law in India*, op. cit., p. X.
3. Flavia Agnes, op. cit., p. 35.
4. The Hindu Succession Act of 1956 bestows women paternal inheritance rights in joint property and this was a crucial step towards a convergence of laws.

5. See Flavia Agnes, Sudhir Chandra, Monmayee Basu, *Women and Law in India*, Oxford University Press, New Delhi, 2004, p. 243.
6. Textbooks like Sociology of Indian Society, by C.N. Shankar Rao (S. Chand & Company Ltd.), published in 2004, devote half the pages to religious and caste divisions.
7. The effects of colonialism, in France, have caused difficulty for contemporary society to see itself properly.
8. One could wonder if my hypothesis of France as a pluralistic society is valid. But, at least, things are evolving in this direction.
9. The French welfare state, as shown by G. Esping-Andersen, is mostly familistic and paternalistic and, in this respect, very different from the northern welfare states in Europe.
10. Four hundred women of this survey were immigrants, a smaller amount than in the real population and few from black Africa to give an idea of the situation between different cultures of black Africa.
11. Alfred Blumstein and Joel Wallman, *The Crime Drop in America*, Cambridge University Press, 2000.
12. Usually, in these cases, the second wife came either before 93 on a legal basis, or after 93 under the guise of a cousin or a sister. Among these families, age differences between the spouses are usually important, more than 10 years on average.

## References

### *(surveys on sexual behaviour and violence against women in France)*

Bajos, N. and Spira, A. (1993). *Les Comportements Sexuels en France*, Paris La Documentation Française (ACSF).

Guilbert, Ph. et al. (2000). *Baromètre Santé*, Paris, CFES.

Jaspard, M. et al. (2003). *Les violences en vers les femmes*, Paris, La Documentation française (ENVEFF).

Lagrange, H. and Lhomond, B. (1999). "Les comportements de précaution des adolescents face au risque du VIH" in Moatti J-P et al. dir. *Aids in Europe*, Londres, New York, Los Angeles, Taylor & Francis (ACSJ).

CHAPTER TWENTY ONE

# Local solutions for global problems

## The challenges encountered by the anti-domestic violence campaign in Armenia

*Armine Ishkanian*

Since any form of civic organizing and activism does not occur in a vacuum it is important to examine the international, national and local political environments, which have an important bearing on how people organize, the issues they articulate and the discourses they use (Howell, 2005: 242–243). In this paper, based on ten years of research on Armenia, I examine how the domestic violence became an issue addressed by women's rights and human rights NGOs in Armenia in the early 2000s and how and why the 2002–04 USAID funded anti-domestic violence campaign met with widespread resistance and criticism from civil society. I argue that domestic violence was not an issue that was readily identified by local women or NGOs in the mid–1990s. Indeed, it was not an issue in Armenia before the arrival of feminist and NGO activists and Western consultants who introduced the idea that domestic violence is a social/public problem which must be addressed with the cooperation of law enforcement and judicial bodies. To be clear, I am not arguing that domestic violence does not occur in Armenia. It does, as in every other country in the world. Nor am I saying that individual Armenian women and men are not concerned or that they should not be deeply concerned about it; it is a serious problem after all. Rather, I mean that it was not locally recognized as a public issue that could be addressed (solved?) with the creation of crisis shelters and hotlines and the intervention of law-enforcement officials, until it was identified as such by Western donors and experts. By examining how domestic violence became an issue and why it sparked such widespread resistance and criticism, I will show how NGO-donor relationships shape knowledge production, decision-making and project design, and how this in turn influences the perceptions, acceptance and effectiveness of programmes locally.

I begin by discussing the post-Soviet support for women's organizations and gender issues in order to contextualize my discussion of the anti-domestic violence campaign in Armenia.

## Support for women's organizations and gender issues

Throughout the world, including in Africa, Latin America, Asia and Eastern Europe, international donor agencies have played a key role in fostering the development of local NGOs and promoting gender agendas (Howell, 2005: 243). This focus by donors on women began in the 1970s when international development agencies began to make "women" visible as a category in development and research policy (Kabeer, 1994: xi). This came to be known as the Women in Development (WID) approach. The thinking went thus: if policy makers, donors and planners could be made to see women's concrete and valuable contributions to their economies, then women would no longer be marginalized in the development process. Donors and policy makers began to say that women were more "cost-effective" as beneficiaries of development and civil society aid than men (Buvinic et al., 1996: 13). This trend became more marked in the 1990s and continues today, as many of the largest donors, including the World Bank, US Agency for International Development (USAID) and various United Nations agencies, all have departments focused on gender issues intended to promote gender equality in development.

Following the collapse of communism, support for women's organizations in the post-socialist states in Eastern Europe and the former Soviet Union became a significant component of democracy promotion and civil society development aid programmes. Once women's NGOs and NGOs working on women's rights were identified as important to democracy promotion and civil society development in the former Soviet states, donors began providing support for women's empowerment and leadership training, women's rights education, skills development, electronic networking and health related projects (Hemment, 2004: 219). Women's NGOs currently represent a significant proportion of NGO activism in these countries (Berg, 2004; Hemment, 2004; Henderson, 2003; Ishkanian, 2004; Olson, 2003; Richter, 2002; Tohidi, 2004).

As in the other states of the former Soviet Union, the majority of NGOs in Armenia are run by women. According to the NGO Resource and Training Centre in Yerevan, 80 per cent of NGO leaders are women and over 80 per cent of members are women (Democracy Today, 2004: 19). There are several factors that have contributed to the feminization of the NGO sector in Armenia. First, the removal of the Soviet era quota system led to a sharp decline in the number of women in official positions and although women had been crucial in the independence movement by participating in the demonstrations, work and hunger strikes, making speeches and collecting money for the effort, once independence was achieved, they found themselves tacitly excluded from the new government. NGOs became a popular path for public participation for the women who were excluded from the political parties and government positions. Second, men initially demonstrated little interest in the "non-governmental" sector, since any man who wished to be active in political or public life could do so through the government or political parties. In addition, men generally regarded the rewards of NGO participation, in terms of grants and micro-credit programmes, as too small and the bureaucratic details of operating an NGO as too numerous. Men preferred the business sector where they felt they could make more money. Third, because NGOs are non-governmental and non-political (to some extent), most women view them as a better alternative for public participation than political parties that are seen as inherently dirty and corrupt (Ishkanian, 2004). Finally, as argued earlier with reference to support for women's organizations and issues in Eastern Europe and the former Soviet states more broadly, donors' support for and preference in supporting women's initiatives (e.g., gender equality) and women's organizations also played an instrumental role in Armenia.

Armenian women's NGOs recognize the donor focus on gender issues and many have become quite adept at employing the appropriate discourses needed for winning grants. As one of my respondents explained, in the 1990s "talking gender" became an important factor in winning grants. She said:

> You learn what the donors fund and then you talk about that in your grant proposal. They all like gender issues (*genderi hartser*) so women have a better chance at getting grants, as do women's organizations. (*Gohar*, 15 May 1996)[1]

In addition to the donor support, the rise of the international women's movement and associated global civil society activism on women's issues also influenced the growing focus on women's issues in Armenia and affected local agenda setting and the framing of issues.

## Global campaign on violence against women: Beijing and beyond

Of the various global events and initiatives focusing on women, the event which had the greatest impact on the development of women's NGOs in Armenia was the 1995 United Nations Fourth World Conference on Women in Beijing. The women who attended it – either as members of the government delegation or as NGO members – returned to Armenia informed and educated about global gender discourses, issues and concerns, which they proceeded to translate into the local Armenian context. Beijing subsequently led to a sharp rise in the number of women's NGOs and NGOs led by women in Armenia because it stimulated greater funding and interest in the role of women in developing and transition countries. This rise in the number of women's NGOs is not unique to Armenia; scholars working in Asia and Latin America have also documented the impact of the various UN conferences (including Beijing) on local women's organizing and discourses. For instance, according to Mary Fainsod Katzenstein, anticipation of the 1975 UN conference on women in Mexico City played an important role in the emergence of the contemporary women's movement in India (1989). Sonia E. Alvarez meanwhile describes the Beijing conference as an effusive celebration of "global sisterhood", adding that it was the site where professionalized, thematically specialized and transnationalized feminist NGOs focused their energies on influencing the International Platform for Action and in helping articulate the "global women's lobby". Alvarez explains how this professionalization and specialization of women's groups as the "NGOization" of the Latin American women's movements led to a growth the number of women's NGOs throughout Latin America (1998: 293–296)

In addition to sparking a growth in the number of women's organizations globally, the Beijing conference also put the campaign combating violence against women on a global platform. In examining the rise of the global women's network, Margaret Keck and Kathyrn Sikkink discuss the violence against women as the issue, which unified all women's groups. They argue that by the 1990s the violence against women was the most important international women's issue that became the centrepiece of the platform at the 1995 Beijing conference and a common advocacy position. They describe how violence against women differed from other issues being addressed by women's groups transnationally in that it was the only issue that resonated with women from the global North and South and led to local organizing in many parts of the world.

In discussing the development of women's NGOs in Russia, Julie Hemment examines the influence of Beijing and local developments. She describes the 1995 conference as "a pivotal moment" in the global campaign addressing violence against women and on Russian women's organizing. She writes:

> Combating violence against women emerged as a central policy agenda both of the international women's movement and of international development. The campaigns have galvanized support across diverse constituencies, among politicians and donors. In the late eighties major US foundations decided to make violence against women a funding priority, channelling funds to NGOs that address the issue (Hemment, 2004: 819).

Hemment links this discussion of how US foundations turned their focus on violence against women and made it a funding priority to the introduction and popularity of the issue among Russian women's NGOs (2004). This was true in Armenia as well and as one women's NGO leader who attended the Beijing conference explained:

> Even though back then my English was not as good as it is now, I spent my time going from one session to another just to be able to get as much information at the NGO forum in Beijing. I came back to Armenia more informed because I had learned a lot about the issues facing women in Beijing. I only came to think about this issue of domestic violence after attending that conference and it was not something I had considered as a serious problem facing Armenian women until that time. (*Satenik*, 12 March 2003)

Although the issue was being discussed in global forums and funding was becoming more readily available in the mid-1990s, there were only two local Armenian NGOs working on domestic violence (*undanegan prnootyun*), as the issue of violence against women is locally referred, at the time. Both NGOs encountered difficulties introducing the issue in Armenia and were criticized by other NGOs for their work in this area. According to the leader of one of the two NGOs working on domestic violence at that time:

> Many people, NGO leaders, and among them many women, were resistant to our efforts in this direction. They did not understand what domestic violence is and how widespread it is in Armenia. These people accused us of wanting to destroy Armenian families and Armenian society. But when World Learning announced a domestic violence grant programme at the end of 2001, the number of NGOs working on the issue mushroomed. To my surprise over 120 NGOs applied for this grant. I couldn't believe it! When did all these NGOs that had not been working on domestic violence become so interested in this issue all of the sudden? After all, only a few years before that they had accused us of all sorts of terrible things (*Satenik*, 12 March 2003).

Since the issue of domestic violence in the 1990s was not locally recognized in Armenia as a public or social issue that could be addressed (solved?) with the intervention of law enforcement and judicial bodies and crisis shelters, until it was identified as such by Western donors, consultants and experts, the problem itself as well as the proposed solutions were perceived as being artificially imported and imposed by donors. This led to widespread criticism and critique of the efforts of the NGOs involved in the 2002–2004 anti-domestic violence campaign. Although much of the criticism was directed at specific policy solutions (e.g., shelters, hotlines, law enforcement trainings), the metanarrative of the critique was much larger and directed at the influence of donors on the work of NGOs and post-Soviet political and social processes more generally. As the campaign unfolded, the greatest challenge for the six NGOs involved became countering the persistent civil society resistance to and critique of the campaign which alleged that the issue was being imposed by donors and that the six NGOs' involvement in the campaign was motivated by greed and grant-seeking. This led the six NGOs involved to spend a great deal of their time demonstrating that the problem existed in Armenia, arguing that they were not working on the issue because of the grant money, and explaining that they considered local cultural practices and beliefs while designing their programmes. In addition, the six NGOs defined violence against women as a human rights issue and maintained that addressing the problem was in fact a critical component for democracy building.

## Anti-domestic violence campaign of 2002–04

### *From taboo to public issue*

The Armenian authors of the August 1995 United Nations Department of Public Information Review dedicated to the 1995 Fourth World Conference on Women in Beijing wrote:

> Violence against women, although there are no records kept in Armenia, is a universal phenomenon. Therefore, Armenian women must have experienced some form of violence against them. Reporting of violence is not customary. The definition of violence is not clear. Psychological violence, violence of sexual nature and physical violence are not clearly understood or identified or distinguished. (UN DPI Review, 1995)

In the mid-1990s domestic violence was still a new topic in Armenia's NGO sector and to some extent a taboo subject. This was also the case in Georgia (Olson, 2003), the five Central Asian states (Akiner, 1997: 284) and Russia (Attwood, 1994). Women's NGOs in Armenia opposed public discussion of what they deemed a private, family issue. In 1996 members of a transnational feminist NGO called the Young Women and Democracy Programme (YWDP), which had funding from the European Union's PHARE–TACIS programme, began work in Armenia. They set out to assist in creating a coalition of local women's NGOs to address the issue of violence against women, together with other women's empowerment programmes. This group had funding to help local NGOs create crisis centres and hotlines, but local groups resisted working with the YWDP. They argued that domestic violence was not the most critical issue facing Armenian women and added, "We don't air our dirty laundry in public" (12 April 1996). Also, in 1996, Azniv, an American-Armenian expatriate, created a study group to examine the problems of battered women. Azniv organized several meetings during the spring and summer of 1996 to discuss the issue of domestic violence in Armenia. These meetings were attended by American expatriates working in Armenia and by a few local Armenian scholars. At one meeting, which was held in the cafeteria at the American University of Armenia, one of the American participants suggested that women's NGOs should be involved, and in fact take the lead, in addressing the issue of domestic violence in Armenia. In response to this suggestion, an American training coordinator at the Armenian Assembly of America's NGO Centre expressed her concern that many women's NGOs did not want to address this issue and added, "Many of the women's NGOs do not necessarily address women's problems and the issue of domestic violence will not be well received by such groups" (4 April 1996). Members of various women's NGOs had been invited to attend, but none were present at any of the meetings I attended. When I asked one of these women's NGO members why she did not attend, she replied, "That is not a problem we wish to discuss in public. If she [Azniv] wants to do so, it is her choice, but she will not receive any support from us" (Anahit, 14 May 1996). While Azniv's efforts were well met by the American expatriates and a few local women, nearly all of the women's NGOs continued to avoid addressing the issue of domestic violence in 1996–97. According to the UNDP Women's Status in Armenia Report, "Public opinion is what matters most [and] unfortunately, the opinion prevails that the family is an entirely private sphere and is not open to public intervention." (1999: 47).

This situation in Armenia and the other Soviet states began to change in 1999 when increased funding was made available by international donors for local NGOs to address the problem of domestic violence throughout the former Soviet Union. In Russia, for example, the campaign against violence against women became one of the most prominent among Russian women's organizations in that it was an issue addressed by almost all the main women's NGOs in some form or another at that time (Hemment, 2004: 816). Support for the campaign in various post-Soviet countries came from a number of sources, including the 1999 US State Department grants to the US based NGOs Sister Cities International, Project Harmony, and Winrock International to conduct anti-domestic violence programmes in Russia, Ukraine, Moldova, Uzbekistan, Armenia and Georgia (US State Department website). Winrock International received a grant of $1,558,656 (during 1999–2001), Project Harmony received a total of $1,518,442 ($ 499,548 for 1998–2000 and $ 1,018,894 for 2000 to 2002), and Sister Cities International, which received two grants to conduct domestic violence prevention programme from 1998 to 2001, did not have any projects in Armenia (US State Department website).[2] In addition to the State Department's domestic violence prevention grants, in 1999, the International Research and Exchanges Board (IREX) was selected by USAID-Russia to administer the USAID Programe to Support Crisis Centers for Women in Russia. This three-year $600,000 programe that was aimed at "strengthening and supporting Russian institutions that provide crisis counseling and other services to victims of domestic violence, that raise awareness of domestic violence issues among specialists and the general public, and that promote alternatives to violence"(IREX website). Grants ranging from one thousand to ten thousand dollars were awarded to Russian NGOs. While IREX did not provide any grants to Armenian NGOs, its programme initiatives are similar to those of other organizations, including the Open Society Institute, the Global Fund for Women, and World Learning, among others, that have awarded grants to local NGOs in Armenia for addressing domestic violence. The largest grant programme in Armenia on this issue was funded by USAID.

In September 2002, USAID awarded a total of US $ 476,367 to six local NGOs in Armenia to address domestic violence. This grant supported the 2002–2004 anti-domestic violence campaign, which is discussed in this paper. The grants given under this programme were the first direct USAID grants to local Armenian organizations for activities in Armenia (USAID, 18 October 2002). The six local groups that received grants from USAID were the Helsinki Association, Maternity Fund, Women's Rights Center, Ajakits, Martuni Women's Community Council, and Armenian Caritas NGOs. The grants, according to USAID, would allow the six NGOs involved to:

> ...expand and enhance services that they already provide, and in some cases allow them to organize shelters for victims of domestic violence and their minor-age family members. Other services include court monitoring and training for lawyers and judges, public awareness campaigns and the promotion of alternatives to violence. (USAID Domestic Violence Press Release)

According to an official USAID report on its assistance to Armenia, the grants to the six NGOs for fighting violence against women were part of the USAID Democracy Program (USAID 2002: 32–34). Activities under the Democracy Programme are aimed at increasing citizen participation with government at the local and national levels, developing NGOs and independent media, promoting civic education in secondary schools, strengthening local government and the legislature, and supporting legal reform. According to the report, USAID planned to achieve these goals by supporting programmes that increased citizen participation in policy development and oversight of government; increased the quantity and improved quality of sources of information and analysis; supported more responsive and effective local government; *assisted victims of domestic violence*; encouraged

Parliament to be more effective and responsive; and developed a transparent, dependable and effective legal system (2002: 33, emphasis added). Many local NGO leaders were shocked that the USAID had provided direct funding to local NGOs and for such a large amount. This was an unprecedented event and many felt was clear evidence of the imported nature of this issue. It is worth noting how in the aforementioned report the assisting victims of domestic violence is listed as an important component of democracy building whereas assistance to victims of other forms of violence (e.g., victims of police torture, army conscripts) are omitted. Many of the civil society activists I interviewed discussed the overall increase of violence in Armenia over the past few years and argued that focusing on domestic violence in isolation and as a "women's issue" meant that the larger structural and economic factors leading to violence as well as public manifestations of violence were ignored. As one women's NGO leader said:

> Why are we always talking of domestic violence? It is true that women are the majority of victims of domestic violence, but there is also violence against men, against children, and against the elderly both in the home and outside of it. When there are different forms of public and private violence, the narrow focus on women and domestic violence does not resonate with society. On the contrary, it is seen by many people as a 'grant problem' that is created by donors and for donors. (Rosa, 3 April 2003)

As I have already discussed, donor funding affects the type of organizations that are supported (i.e., women's organizations or organizations working on gender issues) and the issues that receive funding (i.e., anti-domestic violence programmes). The processes by which donors determine funding priorities and policy initiatives is influenced by their own sources of funding as well as by global trends.

## The 2002–2004 campaign

The six NGOs that were awarded the USAID grant in 2002 engaged in a variety of programmes, including women's rights education trainings, court representations, crisis centres, shelters, hotlines and publishing projects. Although funded under the same programme, there was very little cooperation between the groups over the two-year period of the grant.[3] Once the grant ended in 2004, the projects or components of the projects organized by these NGOs also ended. In a follow-up research project[4] conducted in 2005, I found all the shelters opened with funding from the USAID save one had closed down because the NGOs responsible for operating them could no longer cover the rent and maintenance costs. The single shelter that remained open was because the NGO owned the shelter building and had some funds to continue running it for a few more months.

Skills and human rights training and civic awareness programmes were identified as being the most successful components of the programme. Many of the NGO leaders shared the belief that it was important to increase awareness of the issue and also to provide women with the skills necessary to make them economically self-sufficient because economic problems were seen as one of primary causes of violence. The leader of NGO 'G' argued that skills training and women's economic independence were important factors in combating domestic violence. She said:

> Women need to acquire new skills and to find jobs through which they can provide for themselves and their families. Subsequently our programmes in this area were very well received by the community. Since the major cause of violence tends to be the difficult economic situation in Armenia, I believe that incidences of domestic violence will decrease as the economic situation in the country improves. I am not saying that the problem will disappear entirely, but I believe that those cases of violence which are brought on by the harsh socio-economic difficulties will be eliminated. What will remain are those rarer cases of violence that are perpetrated by barbaric (*vayreni*) people who have violence flowing in their veins. (18 April 2005)

There was also broad consensus that even though the anti-violence campaign had not fully overcome the resistance and criticisms encountered from the outset, at least it had accomplished the difficult task of introducing the topic to the public. The NGO leaders argued that those segments of the population that had participated in the trainings had come to accept the problem, but that much remained to be done. Most agreed that there should be a more systematic approach to resolving the problem in the future which might include government participation and support for the programmes so that it would not be seen as a foreign supported programme.

There was disagreement however over the impact of the shelters and law enforcement trainings. Regarding the law enforcement trainings, the majority of the NGOs expressed deep consternation regarding police attitudes toward the women who sought their assistance. As one of NGO leaders whose NGO had conducted trainings with law enforcement officials, said:

> The police don't have good approaches to women who have been battered. They can be very rude to these women. Often the police will send a woman back to her husband if she seeks assistance blaming her for overreacting. Also people fear bringing the police into a dispute because it becomes a source for extorting bribes (*kasharki aghpiur*). The trainings haven't done much to change police attitudes (NGO 'E', 6 May 2003)

The leader of NGO 'F' meanwhile felt that while police were resistant to involving themselves in domestic disputes, the law enforcement trainings had made police officers more understanding of the plight of women. She said:

> We had very good cooperation with law enforcement officials. Our agreement with them was such that whenever they received a call from our NGO they would immediately come without asking any questions because sometimes there were situations in which the angry husband would turn up at the office and begin creating a disturbance. In such situations I could not explain to the police what was going on over the phone since I had to deal with the situation in my office. (21 April 2005)

In addition to disagreements over the efficacy of law enforcement trainings, there were also different opinions regarding the impact of shelters, which were the most contentious component of the campaign. While some of the NGOs, which sponsored shelters, felt that they were successful initiatives, others did not agree. The leader of NGO 'E', whose NGO had sponsored a shelter, explained that the lack of interest in the shelter was influenced by structural, socio-economic and cultural factors. She said:

> The women weren't coming to the shelter because the people in this city are very conservative and traditional. If the wife left the home the husband would not take her back and her parents would be upset that she had gone to a shelter instead of them for help. For this reason many women would not come to the shelter because they were afraid of what would happen to them after leaving the shelter. They would ask us, "Where will we go after the shelter?" We often didn't have a very good response to this question given the shortage of housing and the lack of funds to provide women with alternative housing choices. There was also the fear of public opinion and what their neighbours or family would think. Here people live for the opinion of others, so the fear of what their neighbours or friends would say about them meant that very few women came to the shelter and the shelter, even after two years of operation, remained too artificial and foreign to the majority of people. (NGO 'E', 11 April 2005)

The leader of the NGO that still had the functioning shelter however disagreed, saying:

> 'We had so many people coming to the shelter that we had a problem deciding who to accept and who to turn away. (NGO 'G', 18 April 2005)

Her statement regarding the shelter being overrun by women contradicted the statements of the other NGOs that had run shelters in other locations. Furthermore, her statement seems particularly strange given the location of the shelter and her statements in a 2003 interview in which she told me that people in the location where her NGO worked were 'very traditional' (*avantabashd*) and 'conservative' (*pahpanoghakan*).

Aside from this variance over the utility of shelters, the six NGOs involved in the campaign unanimously agreed that unless public opinion on the matter changed, the resistance would continue and the problem could not be sufficiently addressed. They argued that two years were hardly enough to overcome the resistance and criticism and that if the programme had been longer, they would have made greater progress in changing public opinion regarding the issue.

## Civil society resistance to the campaign

Unlike in the US or Europe, where the issue of domestic violence was first raised and addressed by local women's organizations and groups of battered women (Keck and Sikkink, 1998: 174), in Armenia, there was no broad-based grassroots movement pushing for recognition of the problem. Most of the women's or human rights NGOs that worked on the issue did not begin doing so until the announcement of large grant programmes. Therefore, in spite of the amount of Western support and more likely because of it, there was a great deal of local resistance toward and criticism of the anti-domestic violence campaign. The resistance and criticism came from the public, journalists, intellectuals, and other NGOs. The main criticism was that the issue was being imported by donors and that domestic violence in Armenia was not as acute (i.e., one in three women is battered) as claimed by some of the NGOs involved in the campaign. Even some of the six NGO leaders of the campaign admitted that they too had initially not believed that domestic violence was a big problem in Armenia. As one NGO leader, who was involved in the USAID grant, said:

> In 2001 domestic violence was a new problem in Armenia except that *Satenik* was more active in it. None of us could comprehend the problem. I too did not accept it. When World Learning announced the grant programme, we did some research to see whether the problem existed and sadly we found out that domestic violence does exist in Armenia. So, we decided to work on it by taking into account our national *mentalitet* (mentality) and traditions. Our goal was to prevent family conflict. (NGO 'B', 23 April 2003)

The leader of NGO 'E' said that while her NGO decided to work on the issue, she believed that attention to issue had emerged more from the urging of donors rather than from a locally perceived need. She explained:

> When I first became involved in this programme I thought that the issue of domestic violence, while existing in Armenia, was not an issue that was raised from below; it was suggested from above. The donors announced the funding proposal and everyone thought, "Why not, we can work on this." It wasn't as

> if we said, "We do not have water to drink, let's find some water." On the contrary, the situation was that they were giving us water and we thought, "Why shouldn't we drink some water since it is available?" (NGO 'E', 11 April 2005)

The primary donor, USAID, recognized the resistance and criticism directed at the campaign but felt there was a local need for such programmes. As a USAID representative said:

> The domestic violence programme was the first time in ten years that local NGOs were given a direct grant by USAID. The direct grant was prompted when we started a special initiative grant with World Learning and recognised the need for addressing this problem...We wanted the approaches to be adapted to local contexts. But we have received a great deal of criticism from the local press and there has been public resistance to the project given that they see it as coming from the outside. (25 April 2003)

These arguments that the issue was not imported and that the campaign was not donor-led or driven were largely ignored by the critics of the campaign. Many journalists, academics, and women's and human rights NGO leaders I interviewed argued that the problem with the campaign was not that domestic violence did not occur in Armenia, but rather that the issue was defined by Western donors and their consultants and that the solutions (e.g., shelters, hotlines and law enforcement trainings) proposed were incompatible to Armenia.

The definitive local study of domestic violence, *Domestic Violence in the Republic of Armenia: A Sociological Survey* (*Undanekan Brrnutuiuneruh Hayastanoom: sociologiakan hedazotootyoon*) was written by the Akunk Center for Ethnosociological Studies NGO and funded by a grant from the US-based World Learning NGO. The report was based on field research conducted from September 2001 to March 2002 by a ten-member team from the Akunk Center who interviewed 2,715 respondents in the ten regions of Armenia using a mix of qualitative and quantitative methodologies. Many of the respondents in the Akunk study said that the primary causes of violence were the difficult socio-economic conditions (57.3%) and the cramped living conditions (25.6%) in Armenia (Galstyan et al., 2002: 43). The overwhelming majority of respondents identified the improvement of socio-economic conditions in Armenia as the best method (86.8%) of addressing domestic violence as compared to the 3.1 per cent of respondents who identified shelters as an appropriate approach (2002: 84), According to the report:

> We should note that shelters in several European countries and in the US are considered an important mechanism in the prevention (*kankhargelman*) of domestic violence. Based on our surveys with both the public and specialists, shelters received the lowest percentage as a prevention method – 3.1 per cent [public] and 11.1 per cent [specialists]. In the opinion of survey participants, shelters will not only not work in Armenia, but that they will have the opposite effect of weakening families. Such an approach according to respondents was explained by ethno-psychological peculiarities, as well as by national traditions and practices. According to the respondents, the structure of the Armenian family and the strongly maintained kin ties provide an opportunity to prevent such occurrences, and particularly at the level of communities, social opinion does not support the creation of such shelters (2002: 86) [my translation].

While the USAID representative quoted earlier acknowledged the importance of this report in demonstrating that domestic violence exists in Armenia, her comments are based on the brief English language executive summary. It is highly unlikely that the representative had read the entire report given that it was only published in Armenian. Some of the local scholars who had worked on the report said they had expected that their report would be ignored given that their findings were highly critical of the proposed approaches (e.g., hotlines and shelters) which later received funding from USAID (12 May 2003). An academic, whose research is focused on the family life in Armenia and who had worked on the Akunk study, told me:

> When we interviewed people across Armenia about their opinions regarding shelters, some people thought shelters would be like dormitories while others called them 'brothels.' There is the common belief, even among women who have been subjected to violence, that shelters won't work unless the woman has decided to leave her husband for good because if

> she is unsure, taking the step to go to the shelter will mean that she can never go back home. Yet USAID and the NGOs who received the USAID grant ignored our findings and went ahead with the shelters. I am certain the shelters will fail based on my knowledge of Armenian families. (Sarkis, 8 June 2003)

Given that the report was published in September 2002 and the shelters were opened a month later, this lent further weight to the argument that the campaign was being driven by donors since the authors of the report had unequivocally argued that shelters would not work in Armenia. They had suggested alternative approaches to addressing the problem of domestic violence which were subsequently ignored as the NGOs instead chose to implement the shelters, hotlines and trainings by the international experts.

The critique of and resistance to the anti-domestic violence programme emanated solely from civil society. Government officials working in the Ministries of Health and Social Welfare adopted an attitude of condescending indifference regarding the issue. The National Assembly meanwhile seemed prepared to accede to any international convention put before them addressing the rights of women including the UN Convention on the Elimination of All Forms of Discrimination Against Women (CEDAW), the UN Convention on Equal Pay for Women and Men, the UN Convention on the Political Rights of Women, and the UN Convention on the Citizenship of Married Women (Democracy Today, 2002: 7). Most of these conventions were adopted without much debate or resistance from MPs. The fact that most of these conventions are not enforced was a matter of concern for women's NGO leaders I interviewed.

While government officials remained dispassionate regarding the campaign, journalists, intellectuals and NGO leaders were fervently critical. Journalists in particular often wrote disparagingly of the campaign and took any opportunity to question the motivations and programmes of the campaign. For instance, at a conference on gender issues in Armenia, one journalist asked a key note speaker:

> Why do you keep working on this domestic violence issue? Isn't it better to deal with the actual problems facing poor

> women and children in Armenia instead of implementing what the foreign anti-national (*odar apazgayin*) organizations want? (25 April 2003)

The speaker ignored the question saying the press should learn to accept that the problem exists in Armenia. At another conference, a journalist argued:

> All you do is talk about the results of violence, but what about the causes that have led to violence? Why are women being beaten? You ignore the economic aspects and focus on feminist arguments. You should recognize that we have our own national mentality (*azgayin mentalitet*) and that your explanations about the causes of violence and your importing of foreign institutions such as shelters is absolutely wrong. It will only sharpen negative social opinion about this issue. (29 April 2003)

In response to a three-day training seminar held for police officials at the OSCE offices in Armenia in June 2003 to "enable Armenian police officers to more efficiently combat domestic violence"(OSCE website), a journalist for the pro-government *Hayots Ashkhar* (Armenian World) daily newspaper wrote:

> These international organizations are making us angry as they widen their scope of work day by day. First they poked their noses into our bedrooms and private lives under the guise of "family planning," next they began to tell us what to do regarding "violence against women" and trafficking. And now, the matter has come down to "family violence" and the role of the police in this matter. But in truth, this is just another opportunity for some people to "snatch" grants and to enrich themselves (Matevossian, 2003)

The opposition *AybFe* newspaper, while always disagreeing with interpretations of *Hayots Ashkhar*, surprisingly had a similar response with regards to the trainings:

> In Armenia the problem [of domestic violence] needs to be solved in a specific way. Armenians will still avoid appealing to the police over the violence in families. Nothing will change in the Armenian families, as neither an Armenian woman nor other family members will ever call the police to accuse their relative. (A1+ website)

Several intellectuals who work on women's issues also agreed that the approach adopted by donors was problematic. One went so far as to argue:

> It [this campaign] is an attempt to destroy our culture. The donors have other intentions in mind when they began promoting these projects and for local NGOs, it is all about getting the grant money. They don't care about what they are doing as long as they have their grants. Even these attempts at trying to "liberate" women from their families are false. Their [donors] efforts are similar to those employed by the Soviet in the 1920s. All this talk about domestic violence is just another attempt to free and liberate us from ourselves. (Sveta, 14 May 2003)

Even the leaders of various women's NGOs criticized the campaign. For instance, the leader of one of the oldest and largest women's NGOs argued that the problem of domestic violence exists in Armenia as it does elsewhere in the world, but that addressing the issue without considering the social, cultural, economic and political context of Armenia was problematic. She explained:

> All practices and beliefs are part of a cultural context. We have to understand the cultural and social context in order to implement projects that will work and benefit society. Otherwise, what we find is a "*profanatsiya*" (imitation or charade) in that there is a pretense that the problem is being resolved, but in reality the problem is far from being addressed. (Rosa, 3 April 2003)

The argument that this campaign was a '*profanatsiya*' (imitation or charade) was shared by other women's NGO leaders who agreed that while the problem of domestic violence exists in Armenia, the solutions for dealing with the problem had to be locally generated. I interviewed a number of women's NGO leaders who disagreed with what they perceived were donor recommended solutions arguing that these solutions, particularly the shelters, did not take into account local socio-economic realities and cultural beliefs. For instance, the leader of another women's NGO argued:

> I am categorically opposed to shelters (*categorik dem em*). I believe that they do not work. They are only a temporary thing and they do not solve the problem of violence. But let's look, for arguments sake, at what the US does to solve this problem [of domestic violence] and see if it fits our situation. In the US there are shelters. If a woman is subjected to violence, she and her children go and live in the shelter for, say, 6 months. In those 6 months either the woman reconciles with her husband and moves back home or the shelter and government agencies help her find a job or they provide her with a job-training programme. The shelter staff and the government help the woman find an apartment and they enroll her children in school. There is an entire social welfare system that supports the shelter approach, but this social welfare system does not exist in Armenia. We don't have the ability to provide a woman with a job, an apartment, and financial assistance. So what are we asking her to do? All we are asking the woman to do is to leave her home, stay a few weeks or months in that shelter and then she will either have to return to her home or end up in the streets somewhere. We have an organization that gives women temporary shelter. But if all the poor, hungry, and tired people in Armenia hear about this crisis shelter, the NGO will be inundated with requests and applications. I predict that over 100,000 women will want to go there not because they are battered, but because they are tired, hungry, and living in a crisis situation. (Flora, 25 March 2003)

Some of the leaders of the six NGOs involved in the anti-domestic violence campaign were particularly defensive on this matter of being portrayed as destroyers of families or traditions. One of the NGOs, the Women's Rights Center, continued to defend itself even after the campaign had ended. For instance, in a booklet, published in 2005, it states:

> When we started working in the sphere of violence against women we often heard people saying that there was no such problem in Armenia, that it was artificially imported from foreign countries. We have even been accused of selling ourselves and by supporting the process of implementation of [an] alien life-style, participating in the destruction of traditionally strong families...according to which by destroying the families they [donors] want to destroy the country. This exquisitely developed tactics [sic] hindered the noble cause and

> defamed the activity of the organisation whose aim was to support women subjected to violence to properly evaluate and protect their rights (2005: 41) [emphasis added].

The report rails against the critics arguing that their actions mitigated the impact of the campaign.

## Conclusion

This paper examined the challenges involved in changing public opinions, values and behaviours, and the implications of foreign aid and global developments (i.e., the international movement against violence against women) on the work of NGOs addressing domestic violence in Armenia. Understanding why the anti-domestic violence campaign met with such great resistance is important as it contributes to understanding the challenges civil society organizations face in promoting changes in society and the state. In this case, the framing of the issue, the nature of the solutions being proposed, the absence of a grassroots movement supporting the campaign, and the way in which it was funded (i.e., a direct grant from USAID) generated widespread criticism that it was an "invented" or "imported" problem. Scholars studying the dominance of the issue of violence against women globally argue that the issue was strengthened in that it sparked local attention. Local manifestations of the violence against women campaign include women's activism against dowry deaths in India, protests against domestic violence and state sponsored disappearances in Latin America, and discussion about female genital mutilation in Africa. Such local organizing did not occur in Armenia as I have demonstrated. On the contrary, following the Beijing conference, only two local NGOs were addressing this issue. These two NGOs were part of the six that received funding from USAID, but the remaining four groups, had never addressed domestic violence until funding was made available by World Learning and USAID in 2001 and 2002 respectively. The fact that the majority of the NGOs that received funding from World Learning and USAID had not been working on the issue previously delegitimized the campaign as accusations of grant chasing hounded the six NGOs during the two years of the campaign. The motivations of the

NGO leaders involved in the campaign were questioned by fellow civil society activists as well as by journalists and intellectuals. This questioning of the motivations of the leaders of the NGOs involved in the campaign limited the impact they had on public opinion.

The increased poverty in Armenia has meant that few organizations are membership based and supported. This has meant that the overwhelming majority of funds for NGOs come from foreign or diaspora donors. Given that some NGOs, for reasons of economic dependency, are compelled to address issues that are deemed important by donors, to constantly keep up with the shifting demands of these donors, and to address issues in the paradigms suggested by donors, this has brought local NGOs into disrepute, because they are seen as grant-seekers who shift priorities and address issues promoted by donors instead of addressing issues that are considered important locally. This tendency has intensified the existing disillusion with democratization and civil society, and has led to accusations of grant-eating (*grantakerutiun*).[5] Accusations of NGO corruption or grant-eating harmed the anti-domestic violence campaign and more generally development of the NGO sector in Armenia. Even one of the six NGO leaders involved in the campaign argued that the behaviour of some of her colleagues had a detrimental impact on their work. She said, "I can say that certain NGOs dealing with women's issues that are part of this campaign have to some extent ruined our image through their grant-eating" (NGO 'G', 18 April 2005).

NGO activists and scholars of development, including Arturo Escobar (1991), William Fisher (1997), James Ferguson (1990), Naila Kabeer (1994) and Jonathan Crush (1995), have argued that to truly make development (in this case "transition") "work," it is necessary to allow locals to define the problems and search for local based solutions and not to compromise the agency and ability of local groups in determining their own development and political agendas. In addition to my case study of the Armenian anti-domestic violence campaign of 2002–2004, I will also draw on two studies to illustrate my point for the need for local approaches to global problems. One is from the United Kingdom and the other is from Canada. In the UK, the

Department of Health's Women's Mental Health Strategy foregrounds the issues of violence and abuse in its strategies. While this is a laudable strategy, the researchers Erica Burman, Sophie Smailes and Khatidja Chantler (2004) found that the way in which UK domestic violence services are structured produce barriers and effectively exclude women from particular ethnic and religious groups including Irish, Jewish, Muslim, African, Afro-Caribbean and South Asian women (2004: 351). They argue that this is due to the fact that domestic violence is intimately connected with broader social structures that implicate all kinds of intersections with class, race and cultural relations. The women from these groups who were interviewed expressed reluctance of seeking such services for fear of compromising confidentiality, encountering racism, or because those services fail to provide an appropriate context in which to raise the specific and controversial issue of domestic violence. The Manchester domestic violence hotline, for instance, reported a drastic reduction in calls from Muslim women since September 11 (2004: 351). The researchers urge policy makers to implement approaches that understand, accept, and are sensitive to the intersections between gender, culture, race and religious issues.

In Canada, meanwhile, which has some of the most advanced domestic violence policies in the world along with a well-articulated policy of multiculturalism, there were still problems (Shirwadkar, 2004: 861). The major policy interventions in Canada are the criminal justice and support services programmes including housing facilities or shelters for abused women. Swati Shirwadkar argues that in spite of these comprehensive laws and provisions, for women from immigrant Indian communities, access to the justice system and services is not the same as other women in Canada (2004: 868). The reasons for this lack of equal access and utilization of these services include Indian women's fear of racial discrimination from police and that a woman who does take the matter to the public domain is often criticized and loses the support of her community in effect becoming ostracized (Shirwadkar 2004: 869). Shirwadkar contends that since Indian women are suppressed by multiple layers of domination, policies need to create more awareness of domestic violence within these communities, to establish networks of culturally specific institutions and to provide social support that does not isolate the women in shelters which then leads to exclusion from the community.

Finally, precisely because the manner in which domestic violence is conceptualized and interpreted is affected by culture, race, class and religion as my case study of Armenia as well as the UK and Canadian studies demonstrate, solutions to the problem should take consider these multiple factors. Otherwise, by promoting and applying "one-size-fits-all" approaches, the problem will not be sufficiently addressed and instead, as the Armenian case demonstrates, it might even lead to a rejection of and resistance to the issue. For the sake of the victims of violence, it is imperative to start thinking beyond the standard models and to develop more nuanced approaches that take into account the social, economic and cultural complexities.

## Notes

1. Per anthropological conventions I use pseudonyms for individuals who are not public officials or prominent NGO activists.
2. Winrock International, "1999 Projects"; available from <http://www.winrock.org/general/Publications/1999_projects.pdf>; and Project Harmony, "About Us: Financial Profile"; available from <http://www. projectharmony.org/about_us/finances.html>. When I attempted to ascertain the amount of the Sister Cities International grants, I received the following message: "The requested page is either nonexistent or is unavailable at your current access level" available from – http://www.sister-cities.org/icrc/sciprogrammes/grants/US-NIS-ICRC/index. This type of information is only available through a paid membership, available from <http://www.sister-cities.org/sci/aboutsci/faqs >
3. In order to protect the anonymity of my respondents from the six NGOs involved in the anti-domestic violence campaign, I refer to them as NGO A, NGO B, NGO D, NGO E, NGO F, and NGO G. So as to avoid confusion with the NGO Centre (NGOC), there is no NGO C.
4. I was assisted in this research by post-doctoral students from Yerevan State University from March–April 2005.

5. Bribes are called kashark in Armenian, and corruption is known as "bribe consumption" or "bribe eating" (*kasharakerutiun*). *Grantakerutiun* is another form of corruption and can be seen as the continuation of the *kasharakerutiun* that began during Soviet times and continues unchecked today.

## References

A1+ http//www.a1plus.am/eng/?goto=news&id=3840

Akiner, Shirin (1997) "Between tradition and modernity: the dilemma facing contemporary Central Asian women".

Alvarez, Sonia E. (1998) "Latin American Feminisms 'Go Global': Trends of the 1990s and Challenges for the New Millennium," in *Culture of Politics/Politics of Cultures,* (eds.) Sonia E. Alvarez, Evelina Dagnino, and Arturo Escobar. Boulder, Colo.: Westview Press.

American Bar Association (2002) *CEDAW Assessment Tool Report: Armenia.* Washington, DC: American Bar Association and Central European and Eurasian Law Initiative.

Attwood, Lynne (1997) "She was asking for it: rape and domestic violence against" in *Post-Soviet Women: From the Baltic to Central Asia'* (ed.) Mary Buckley. Cambridge: Cambridge University Press.

Berg, Andrea (2004) "Two Worlds Apart: The Lack of Integration between Women's Informal Networks and Nongovernmental Organizations in Uzbekistan" in *Post-Soviet Women Encountering Transition: Nation-Building, Economic Survival, and Civic Activism.* Edited by Carol Nechemias and Kathleen Kuehnast. Baltimore: Johns Hopkins Press in-conjunction with Woodrow Wilson International Center for Scholars Press.

Buvinic, Mayra et al. (1996) *Investing in Women: Progress and Prospects for the World Bank* Washington, D.C.: Overseas Development Council in cooperation with the International Center for Research on Women.

Burman, Erica, Sophie Smailes, and Khatidja Chantler (2004) "Culture as a barrier to service provision and delivery: domestic violence services for minoritized women" in *Critical Social Policy,* Vol. 2, No. 3, pp. 332–357.

Crush, Jonathan (1995) *Power of Development*. New York: Routledge.

Democracy Today (2002) *'Kanants tem khdtakanutyan polor tzeveri veratzman masin' mitchasgayin conventsiayi irakanatsman arnchutyamp Hayastani Hanrapetutyan Krarvarutyan Yekrort parberakan hasvedvurtyan sdeverayin hasvedvutyun (Shadow Report to the Second*

*Periodic Report of the Government of the Republic of Armenia on the Implementation of the Convention on the Elimination of all forms of Discrimination Against Women)* Yerevan: El Guna Publishing House.

Escobar, Arturo (1991) "Anthropology and the Development Encounter: the Making and Marketing of Development Anthropology", in *American Ethnologist*, Vol. 18, No. 4, pp. 658–682.

Ferguson, James (1990) *The Anti-Politics Machine: 'Development', Depoliticization and Bureaucratic Power in Lesotho*. Cambridge: Cambridge University Press.

Fisher, William (1997) "Doing Good? The Politics and Anti-Politics of NGO Practices," *Annual Reviews in Anthropology* 26.

Galstyan, Mihran et al. (2002*) Undanekan Prnootyoonneruh Hayastanoom: Sociologiakan Hedazotootyoon (Domestic Violence in the Republic of Armenia: A Sociological Survey*). Yerevan: Zangak Press.

Hemment, Julie (2004) "The Riddle of the Third Sector: Civil Society, International Aid, and NGOs in Russia", *Anthropological Quarterly:* Vol. 77, No. 2, Spring, pp. 215–241.

Henderson, Sarah L. (2003) *Building Democracy in Contemporary Russia: Western Support for Grassroots Organizations*. Ithaca: Cornell University Press.

Howell, Jude (2005) Conclusion in *Gender and Civil Society: Transcending Boundaries* (eds.) Jude Howell and Diane Mulligan. London: Routledge.

International Research and Exchange Board (IREX) website, at <http://www.irex.org/programmes/completed/wcc/index.asp>.

Ishkanian, Armine (2004) "Working at the Global-Local Intersection: The Challenges Facing Women in Armenia's NGO Sector," in *Post-Soviet Women Encountering Transition: Nation-Building, Economic Survival, and Civic Activism*. Edited by Carol Nechemias and Kathleen Kuehnast. Baltimore: Johns Hopkins Press in-conjunction with Woodrow Wilson International Center for Scholars Press.

Kabeer, Naila (1994) *Reversed Realities: Gender Hierarchies in Development Thought*. London: Verso.

Katzenstein, Mary Fainsod (1989) "Organising against Violence: Strategies of the Feminist Movement in India" *Pacific Affairs* Vol. 62, No. 1, Spring.

Keck, Margaret and Kathryn Sikkink (1998) *Activists Beyond Borders: Advocacy Networks in International Politics*. Ithaca, N.Y.: Cornell University Press

Matevossian, Shushan (2003) *Hayots Ashkhar (Armenian World)*, June 24.

Olson, Lara (2001) "Women and NGOs: Views from Conflict Areas in the Caucasus." New Bridges to Peace Occasional Papers, Women in International Security, Washington, D.C, July 2001.

Organisation for Security and Cooperation in Europe news report available from <http://www.osce.org/news/show_news.php?id =3383>

Project Harmony, "About Us: Financial Profile"; available from <http://www. projectharmony.org/about_us/finances.html>.

Richter, James (2002) "Evaluating Western Assistance to Russian Women's Organisations" in *The Power and Limits of NGOs: A Critical Look at Building Democracy in Eastern Europe and Eurasia* (ed.) Sarah E. Mendelson and John K. Glenn. New York: Columbia University Press, 2002.

Shirwadkar, Swati (2004) "Canadian Domestic Violence Policy and Indian Immigrant Women" in *Violence Against Women*, Vol. 10, No. 8, August, pp. 860–879.

Tohidi, Nayereh (2004) "Women, Building Civil Society, and Democratizationin Post-Soviet Azerbaijan" in *Post-Soviet Women Encountering Transition: Nation-Building, Economic Survival, and Civic Activism*. Edited by Carol Nechemias and Kathleen Kuehnast. Baltimore: Johns Hopkins Press in-conjunction with Woodrow Wilson International Center for Scholars Press,

UNDP (1999) *Women Status Report: Impact of Transition*. UNDP, Armenia.

UN Department of Public Information Review (1995), Yerevan, Armenia, August.

USAID Mission to Armenia, Press Release on USAID Grants Programme to Help Victims of Domestic Violence October 18, 2002 Domestic Violence available from <http://www.usaid.gov/am/ pr10_02_DV.html>

USAID (2002) *United States Assistance to Armenia*, USAID Mission to Armenia.

US State Department, "Fact Sheet: State Department Programmes to Combat Trafficking in Persons," 1 February 2001; available from <http://usinfo.state.gov/topical/global/traffic/01060101.htm>

Winrock International, "1999 Projects"; available from http:// www.winrock.org/general/Publications/1999_projects.pdf

SECTION FIVE

# Conclusion

# CHAPTER TWENTY TWO

# Family violence and human rights

*Justice Sujata Manohar*

I must thank the Department of Sociology, University of Pune for inviting me to give the valedictory address of this important seminar on "Family Violence and Human Rights". I am very happy that the seminar has discussed family violence in the setting of human rights. It is not often realized that there is a direct nexus between family violence and violation of human rights as traditionally understood.

Human rights have been traditionally and historically associated with the struggle of individuals against the might of the state. Therefore initially, the emphasis was on an individual's right to freedom of speech and expression, freedom of movement, right to equality and non-discrimination, freedom from arbitrary arrest, not being tried for the same offence twice etc. Social and economic rights were slow to get acceptance as human rights. When we framed the constitution in 1950, it was the civil and political rights which were incorporated in Chapter 3 on Fundamental Rights and were made justiciable. Social and economic rights found an honourable mention in the chapter on Directive Principles of State Policy. Under the constitutional scheme, social and economic rights were to be enforced through appropriate policies framed by the executive. They were not considered as judicially enforceable rights, or enforceable in the same manner as fundamental rights.

---

Text of the valedictory address delivered by Justice Sujata Monohar at the seminar on "Family Violence and Human Rights" conducted by the Department of Sociology, University of Pune on 25th and 26th September, 2006.

There has been a tremendous change in the concept and content of enforceable human rights, and the state obligation with regard to these human rights since then. Primacy, which was traditionally given to civil and political rights, aimed at protecting men within the sphere of their public life and their relationship with the government. The same importance was not generally accorded to economic and social rights because these rights can affect not merely rights in the public domain, but essentially also rights in the private domain – in the private world of women, children, the elderly, the disabled and other vulnerable people. The violation of their human rights – the right to food, shelter, health care, the right to lead a life with dignity, the freedom to make appropriate choices, the right to education, etc., occurs at the hands of private parties as well as the state. It is necessary to overcome the private-public divide before the human rights of the vulnerable can be effectively protected.

Law has undergone major changes as a result of the growing public awareness of the need to protect the underprivileged, the discriminated and the vulnerable. It has facilitated application of human rights norms in all spheres of life – not just public life. Civil, political, social and economic rights are now perceived as interdependent. People who do not enjoy social and economic rights are not in a position to effectively enforce their civil and political rights, while social and economic rights without civil and political rights are at the mercy of the state. A full enjoyment of these rights and their enforcement require that an obligation should be legally imposed on the state as well as private parties to respect these rights, and there is an obligation on the state to ensure that there is a law enforcement machinery in place to enforce such rights. The dichotomy between the two sets of rights (which formed the subject matter of the two famous United Nations covenants in 1966) is artificial and has actually hampered the proper promotion and protection of human rights. Unlike civil and political rights, socio-economic rights do not necessarily have the state as an antagonist. At the core of a right to a life with dignity, undoubtedly, there are certain socio-economic rights, which need enforcement against the state, e.g., for environmental protection and prevention of pollution, the state is primarily responsible though there may be private violators who need to be controlled by the state. The right to shelter, the right to food, the right to health care, cast an obligation on the state as well as on other private players. Preventing discrimination and the right to equality are not just civil and political rights; they are also socio-economic rights, which are at the core of the current developmental philosophy.

Domestic or family violence is not just an offence; it is a major hurdle to enjoyment of human rights. Such violence affects the capacity and the ability of vulnerable people to access civil and political rights and is a major denial of their social and economic rights. The task of enacting appropriate laws for the protection of vulnerable, and enforcing such laws, becomes an important aspect of government programmes and policies. These also include programmes for empowerment and institutional structures that support the vulnerable. The third organ of governance, namely, the judiciary, is also required to play a role in enforcing such laws and in promoting and protecting human rights in the widest sense of the term.

The 1993 United Nations Declaration on the Elimination of Violence against Women has emphasized linkages between inequality, discrimination against women and women-specific violence, whether domestic or societal. Such violence effectively perpetuates women's inability to exercise their basic human rights. CEDAW seeks to protect women against discrimination in varied forms. CEDAW committee, in its general recommendation 19, has explained Article 2 of CEDAW by stating that the definition of discrimination includes gender-based violence. This is violence which is directed against a woman because she is woman, or violence which affects a woman disproportionately. The Protocol of 2003 to the African Charter on Human and People's Rights also includes violence against women as discrimination and denial of equality. The Beijing Platform of Action (paragraph 112) describes violence against women as nullifying women's human rights and fundamental freedoms. It is an obstacle to the achievement of equality, development and peace.

Around fifty population-based surveys from around the world have found that across the globe from 10 to 50 per cent of women are battered by an intimate male partner. In the first ever study conducted in India by the International Centre for Research on Women, 45 per cent of the women interviewed had been victims of domestic violence in some form or the other. So, we appear to be at the higher end of the scale of domestic violence. In the Asian cultural scenario, violence of this kind is often justified as a man's right to chastise his wife and children. Such violence is not often reported because of this strong cultural bias. Women prefer to suffer silently, and may even believe that men are justified in beating them. Or, a woman may feel that she has no other alternative for improving her situation and therefore she may suffer in silence in order to protect her marriage and her children. Therefore, the actual percentage of women who experience family violence may be higher than reported.

Such violence causes serious physical and emotional stress on women. Severe social discrimination based on gender is also reflected in other harmful practices and customs such as female foeticides, female infanticides, child marriages, high rates of maternal mortality and morbidity, denial of health care to women and girl children, denial of adequate nutrition to women and girl children, denial of education to the girl child, denial of reproductive rights to women and girl children, and lack of protection to women and girl children against HIV/AIDS. Domestic violence is reflected in the so-called "honour killings" of girls who choose their own marriage partners. It is reflected in the practice of a bride's parents paying a heavy dowry to the groom's family, in dowry-related crimes against women, and in dowry deaths. Violence against women resulting from demand for dowry is well documented. Trafficking of young women and girls, ill-treatment of widows who may be driven out of their homes or sent off to religious places of worships such as Brindavan or Banaras, are other horrendous forms of family violence. Violence against the children can take the serious form of sexual abuse within the family, whether by a stepfather or a relative or sometimes a neighbour, and may end up in trafficking of girl children. Children can be trafficked either for labour exploitation or for sexual exploitation. Children can be sent to tourist resorts to cater to sex tourism. Using children for begging, for organ transplant, for camel jockeying are other aspects of trafficking reflected in the definition of trafficking under the UN Protocol on Trafficking, which supplements the UN Convention on Transnational Organized Crimes.

Violence against the elderly in the family is another serious denial of their human rights. The existence of such violence was not acknowledged for a long time and was considered alien to our culture. However, a recent survey carried out by Helpage India has pointed out that the elderly in our country have been increasingly marginalized and emotionally isolated from the mainstream society. The population of older persons is estimated at present at 75 million and it is expected to go up to 177 million by the end of 2025. About 80 per cent of the elderly live in rural areas where there is very little health care available to them. Our primary health centres are in poor shape and very little geriatric care is available. The same is true even in the cities where also the medical profession is not yet trained or ready to provide such care with any sensitivity. As a result, medical needs of the elderly are not looked after. The extended family system, which earlier served the elderly and provided protection to them, is fast disintegrating. The smaller or nuclear family seems unwilling to spend the time, effort or money in looking after the elderly family members. Quite often, when in a nuclear family, both men and women are employed outside the home, there is nobody to take care of elders. The lack of concern for the elderly can, and at times, does degenerate into violence against them. There have been newspaper reports of elderly parents committing suicide because their children are subjecting them to harassment for various reasons. Cases of the elderly leaving their homes and disappearing are also frequent. The National Human Rights Commission received complaints from the elderly who had been thrown out of their own homes by their children.

The disabled also face violence at the hands of their family members. Reports from various mental homes or protective homes for the mentally challenged show that a large number of mentally challenged persons are abandoned in such homes by their family members who often give false names and addresses. At times, such disabled persons are left at the doorsteps of the mental homes by their family members, who disappear without leaving a trace. In the National Human Rights Commission we had the case of a wife of a professor who had been treated effectively at a mental home and was in a position to be managed by her family in her own house. She was looking forward to reunite with her family. But, the family declined to take her back. She has now lapsed into a state of deep depression. In another case, where an extremely wealthy family had abandoned a mentally challenged person in a mental home, that person, after medical treatment was sufficiently self-reliant to live an independent life in a small cottage provided to him. But, his family declined to take him back. Village children who are mentally challenged are recruited by agents to work in factories in urban areas promising parents that the child will be looked after and will send a regular wage home. These children, who are incapable of conveying their hardships to anybody, are then used as slave labour, made to work long hours and are ill-fed and ill-housed.

Thus family violence can take varied forms. We have recently enacted a law which has just come into operation, for protection of women against domestic violence. The Act requires appointment of protection officers who will handle complaints of violence within the family. The effectiveness of the law will depend to a large extent on the training and sensitization of these protection officers and in creating institutional framework for the protection of victims. Laws for prevention of or protection against any form of family violence require the support of programmes for sensitization of the society against prevailing domestic violence, for providing options to those who are subjected to family violence which are viable and usable, and programmes and policies which can be implemented not just by the government but also by NGOs and by the civil society.

It is important that we highlight the obligation of the state in this area. There is a growing acceptance that a state which is negligent in preventing gross violations of human rights of its citizens can be held accountable under international human rights law, e.g., under the Statute of Rome, a state is accountable for gross violation of human rights committed even by private parties. In the famous decision in *Velasquez Rodriquez* case, the Inter-American Court of Human Rights held the state to a due diligence standard to prosecute private individuals who violate human rights, and it held that the state would be held responsible for such major crimes. States are now required to give up the traditional attitude with regard to the privacy of home and are required to intervene effectively to prevent serious domestic violence. It is in this context that the new legislation against domestic violence has to be welcomed. The state must sensitize its law enforcement machinery; it should train its police, its investigators, its judicial officers and medical experts in issues relating to such violence. The state must set up support services for victims. It should collect data and research the problem of family violence. It is required to engage in educational programmes to raise awareness and prevent harmful practices. These are new ideas in human rights jurisprudence. In a sense, these are an expansion of the state's responsibility for promotion and protection of human rights, making the state liable for actions of even private individuals in areas where state assistance can lead to prevention and prosecution of gross crimes, or can bring about an effective stop to harmful attitudes and practices. The prevention of pre-natal sex determination tests through enactment of law is another recent example where the state has formulated a law to counter violence against women. However, the responsibility of the state does not cease on the enactment of laws. What is important is creating an infrastructure within the state – whether private or public – which will ensure effective implementation of laws.

Judiciary also plays an important role in protecting human rights of the vulnerable, the underprivileged or the discriminated. The judiciary has evolved a mechanisms of public interest litigation, which can be brought on behalf of such vulnerable people before the court for the purpose of enforcement of their rights. We have developed a very extensive jurisdiction under public interest litigation for protection of human rights. The Supreme Court has interpreted the constitutional provisions on fundamental rights and directive principles of state policy to compel the state to respect human rights. The court has given directions to the state and its administrators for the implementation of these rights. It has appointed monitoring and expert committees, or has taken the help of the National Human Rights Commission to make these rights a reality. I will not go into the large number of cases which have been decided by the Supreme Court dealing with the right to a life with dignity in its various aspects. Creating a socio-economic and political order that respects human rights is today the goal of development. Realizing that family violence is a major denial of human rights is the first step towards its prevention. I hope, this seminar has helped to throw up fresh ideas for protection against and prevention of family violence.

# Index